TRUMAN CAPOTE ▷

[logo to come]

EDITED BY R. Barton Palmer AND Matthew H. Bernstein

TRUMAN CAPOTE

A Literary Life at the Movies ▶ *Tison Pugh*

THE UNIVERSITY OF GEORGIA PRESS   ATHENS & LONDON

© 2014 by the University of Georgia Press
Athens, Georgia 30602
www.ugapress.org
Designed by Erin Kirk New
Set in 10 on 14.5 Warnock Pro
Printed and bound by

The paper in this book meets the guidelines for
permanence and durability of the Committee on
Production Guidelines for Book Longevity of the
Council on Library Resources.

Most University of Georgia Press titles are
available from popular e-book vendors.

Printed in the United States of America
18   17   16   15   14   P   5   4   3   2   1

Library of Congress Cataloging-in-Publication Data

British Library Cataloging-in-Publication Data available

To David Dean, who not once complained
about being parked in coffee shops and public libraries
throughout the research for this book.

Contents

Cinema Stills and Photographs

Acknowledgments

Truman Capote: A Literary Life at the Movies was born, like Capote himself, in Louisiana but, unlike Capote, in a high school classroom in Baton Rouge. I am indebted to my teacher, Mitch Billings, for his magnanimity of vision in assigning a yearlong series of reports on Capote's literature. The writing of this book was funded in part by the University of Central Florida's College of Arts and Humanities, the Office of the Provost and Executive Vice President, and the Office of Research and Commercialization through the College of Arts and Humanities Research and Development Program. I deeply appreciate the support of José Fernández, dean of UCF's College of Arts and Humanities, and Patrick Murphy, chair of the Department of English, and in particular the assistance of Nancy Stanlick, Kristin Wetherbee, Grace Nicholl, and Patricia Tierney. I would also like to thank Nicole Kristal, Shannon Salmon, Angela Jane Weisl, Bob Squillace, Nandini Sinha, Beth Techow, Jason Primm, Lilybeth Primm, and Annabelle Primm for their generous hospitality during research trips to Los Angeles and New York City, as well as Lisa Roney, for sharing food and good fellowship. Bruce Janz, director of the UCF Humanities and Digital Research Center, provided invaluable support and assistance. Warm welcomes were extended by the librarians and administrators of the Paley Media Center at both its Los Angeles and New York City branches, and in particular Richard Holbrook, senior librarian; the University of California, Los Angeles, Film and Television Archive, and in particular Mark Quigley, manager of the Research and Study Center; the Margaret Herrick Library of the Academy of Motion Picture Arts and Sciences; and the New York Public Library, Stephen A. Schwarzman Building. Finally, I thank Barton Palmer and Matthew

Bernstein, editors of the series The South on Screen, as well as the editorial, production, and administrative teams at the University of Georgia Press, including Walter Biggins, Jon Davies, Beth Snead, and Lisa Bayer, who supported this project throughout its development. Material from Truman Capote's unpublished screenplays is quoted with kind permission of the Truman Capote Literary Trust, Alan U. Schwartz, trustee.

Abbreviations

To minimize the documentary apparatus of this book, the following abbreviations of Capote's works are used for in-text citations. Also, each chapter's endnote citations are condensed; for complete documentation, consult the Works Cited section.

AP   *Answered Prayers: The Unfinished Novel*

BT   *Breakfast at Tiffany's, and Three Stories*

CB   *In Cold Blood: A True Account of a Multiple Murder and Its Consequences*

CS   *The Complete Stories of Truman Capote*

DB   *The Dogs Bark: Public People and Private Places*

GH   *The Grass Harp, and A Tree of Night and Other Stories*

LC   *Local Color*

MC   *Music for Chameleons*

O   *Observations*

OV   *Other Voices, Other Rooms*

PO   *Portraits and Observations: The Essays of Truman Capote*

SC   *Summer Crossing*

T   *Trilogy: An Experiment in Multimedia*

TRUMAN CAPOTE ▶

Capote and the Cinema ▶ An Overview

Truman Capote once remarked, "My primary thing is that I'm a prose writer. I don't think film is the greatest living thing."[1] In privileging his professional and artistic identity as an author of literary fiction, Capote diminishes the role of the cinema in his career, yet the truth of the matter is far more complex than a simple preference for his pen over film. For Capote truly lived in and through the movies. He avidly watched films throughout his life, publicly commenting on their merits and shortcomings, and the characters of his short stories and novels often see themselves and their dreams through a Hollywood lens. He wrote several screenplays, most notably *Beat the Devil* (dir. John Huston, 1953), *Indiscretion of an American Wife* (dir. Vittorio De Sica, 1953), and *The Innocents* (dir. Jack Clayton, 1961). Adaptations of his fiction, including Blake Edwards's beloved *Breakfast at Tiffany's* (1961) and Richard Brooks's riveting *In Cold Blood* (1967) among numerous others, brought him wider fame and greater acclaim among readers. Additionally, he counted many Hollywood celebrities, producers, and directors as close friends, including Marilyn Monroe, David Selznick, Charlie Chaplin, Humphrey Bogart, and John Huston. Capote may have seen himself primarily as a fiction writer, but he lived his life as a celebrity, blurring the border between these ostensibly separate spheres of his career.

Born in New Orleans on September 30, 1924, Truman Streckfus Persons spent his early years with various relatives after his parents divorced. His mother remarried in 1932, and he took his new surname from his stepfather Joe Capote on February 14, 1935. In reminiscing about his childhood, Capote described his early love for fiction, film, dance, and art: "the only four things that interested me were: reading books, going to the movies, tap dancing, and drawing pictures" (*MC* xi). Of these four pastimes, fiction and film gained preeminence, and in an 1976 interview he credited his talents as a writer to his childhood delight in playacting the movies: "I really think this explains my interest in narrative prose writing. . . . You should have seen me do *King Kong*: 'Fay Wray, why do you want to be in the movies?'" to which he would reply to himself, in Wray's persona with an appropriately squeaky voice, "Because . . . it's FAME, it's FUN, it's MONEY."[2] Capote's passion for the cinema continued in his adolescence, and when he and his friends attended films, they frequently lifted their collective spirits with marijuana: "We used to go to the movies and sit in the balcony, smoking up a storm. . . . I remember smoking all the way through a Bette Davis movie, laughing louder and louder as she got cloudier and cloudier."[3] Capote also enjoyed solitary screenings, particularly for the freedom to abandon a tiresome film and thus to escape its aesthetic dissection with any companions: "I am partial to films, too—though I leave in the middle quite a lot. But I only go to films alone, and only in the daytime when the theatre is mostly empty. That way I can concentrate on what I'm seeing, and depart when I feel like it without having to discuss the merits of the project with someone else: with me, such discussions always lead to argument and irritation" (*DB* 408). Jack Dunphy, Capote's longtime romantic partner, recalled how Capote would often see a movie and, upon returning home, pronounce it "lousy"; Dunphy adds, "They usually were, but he liked going to them all the same."[4]

Never shy to express his opinions, Capote shared with friends his assessments of movies, and these miniature reviews evince his keen critical eye. He adjured John Malcolm Brinnin to "let me warn you not to miss" *Les Enfants du Paradis* (dir. Marcel Carné, 1945), and he proclaimed *The Third Man* (dir. Carol Reed, 1949) "the most wonderful movie. . . . Orson Welles is in it—superbly so, believe it or not. And it has a marvelous musical score."[5] Capote's alter ego P. B. Jones, the protagonist of *Answered Prayers*, stated that *A Place in the Sun* (dir. George Stevens, 1951) was "not . . . all that great, but still it was very good, especially the final scene . . . Clift and

Taylor standing together, separated by the bars of a prison cell" (*AP* 102).[6] Capote declared that Charles Laughton's *Night of the Hunter* (1955) was "a fabulous movie"; praised Billy Wilder's *Love in the Afternoon* (1957) with Audrey Hepburn as "Much the best picture she's made"; and lauded David Lean's *The Bridge on the River Kwai* (1957) as an "excellent film."[7] Despite his aversion to Ernest Hemingway, he conceded that *Old Man and the Sea* (dir. John Sturges, 1958) was "*Pretty* good."[8] He found *Suddenly Last Summer* (dir. Joseph Mankiewicz, 1959), which was based on Tennessee Williams's play, "Quite good,"[9] despite the fact that his nemesis Gore Vidal collaborated with Williams on the screenplay. He extolled a documentary on sharks, *Blue Water, White Death* (dir. Peter Gimbel and James Lipscomb, 1971), as captivating—"Wasn't that a terrific movie?" (*MC* 162)—and in conversation with Andy Warhol he praised *Heat* (dir. Paul Morrissey, 1972), a parody of *Sunset Blvd.*: "I thought it was very good."[10] In a letter to Jack Dunphy, Capote insisted that he watch *The Story of Adele H.* (dir. François Truffaut, 1975): "You would love it. Be *sure* to see it."[11]

In complementary contrast, Capote divulged his equally candid opinions of movies that he disliked, dismissing the Oscar-winning *The Best Years of Our Lives* (dir. William Wyler, 1946) as a "maudlin, false, dull piece of hokum!"[12] Of Sidney Lumet's *The Fugitive Kind* (1960), he simply proclaimed, "A real stinker."[13] He condemned numerous films typically appreciated as masterworks of their acclaimed directors, ridiculing Federico Fellini's *La Dolce Vita* (1960) as "*So* pretentious, fake arty, and BORING"; complaining that, in *Psycho* (1960), "Hitchcock left too many gaps. He took advantage of the viewer"; exclaiming of Dennis Hopper's *Easy Rider* (1969), "Well, what a FAKE!"; and deriding Bernardo Bertolucci's *Last Tango in Paris* (1972) as "terrifically bad . . . vulgar beyond words."[14] Films garnering mixed reviews from Capote include John Huston's *Moby Dick* (1956; "uneven, poorly acted, but remarkable all the same") and John Cromwell's *Of Human Bondage* (1934; "I can't say exactly why, but it's the first movie I remember making a real impression on me").[15] Of William Wyler's *Wuthering Heights* (1939), he simply commented that "it wasn't a great movie but at least it had the atmosphere of the book,"[16] while his heroine Holly Golightly effuses of the film in *Breakfast at Tiffany's*, "God, I cried buckets. I saw it ten times" (*BT* 62). Assessing African American cinema in the 1970s, Capote derided *Shaft* (dir. Gordon Parks, 1971) as "a big vulgar film" and ridiculed *Sounder* (dir. Martin Ritt, 1972): "It's bad, it's so terrible it makes you *cringe!*"[17] These snippets of cinematic analysis, none of which receives Capote's sustained attention, highlight his aesthetic interest in film. Many of these insights, such as his reviews of *Moby Dick*, *Wise Blood*, and *Wuthering Heights*, also illustrate his interest in how cinematic adaptations succeed or fail in translating literature to the screen, a topic of considerable interest to Capote in regard both to the Hollywood adaptations of his literature and to his own screenwriting.

Before focusing our attention on Capote's film career and the various cinematic adaptations of his fiction, a brief review of his literary life is warranted to better contextualize his corpus and his interest in incorporating cinematic elements into his works. Capote's fiction places him among the ranks of the great authors of the Southern Renaissance, the literary revival beginning in the 1920s and extending through the following decades that brought to the public eye such writers as William Faulkner, Katherine Anne Porter, Tennessee Williams, Eudora Welty, Robert Penn Warren, Carson McCullers, and Flannery O'Connor. According to Jeffrey Folks, the writers of the Southern Renaissance brought fresh perspectives to longstanding questions of southern identity: "The Southern Literary Renascence . . . involved a critical reexamination of southern history, a new awareness of the restrictions of traditional racial and gender roles, an interest in literary experimentation, an examination of the role of the southern artist in relation to the southern community, and an increasingly realistic presentation of social conditions in the South."[18] The Civil War and its aftermath, particularly during Reconstruction, devastated the U.S. South for several generations; despite the fact that many of these wounds were self-inflicted, the resulting cultural disequilibrium and heightened sense of alienation from the United States as a whole quelled artistic and cultural creations for many years. With the revitalizing influence of this renaissance, southern authors began taking pride of place in the American literary arts. Blake Allmendinger asserts that the "themes and predicaments that attract most readers of Southern American fiction" include "the Gothic, the grotesque, the obsession with the past, the use of local color and dialect,"[19] and these tropes spurred the popularity of Southern Renaissance fictions while also coding the South as a separate realm within the American cultural imaginary.

The influence of the Southern Renaissance continues into the present, with some critics contending that the renaissance has not yet ended. Doreen Fowler defines the Southern Renaissance as "the upsurge of Southern literature which began after the First World War and which has continued, possibly somewhat abated, to the present day."[20] The duration of the Southern Renaissance invites debate, and Capote's position in this literary tradition shifts depending upon how such lines are drawn (and upon who draws them for what reasons). In contrast to scholars such as Fowler who argue that the Southern Renaissance continues into the present, Richard King posits an earlier terminal date, suggesting that its "seminal or 'growth' stage was over around 1942, the year in which Faulkner published his last great work, *Go Down, Moses*."[21] King also theorizes that "one might conveniently locate the end of the main phase of the Renaissance somewhere around 1955. After that year the South was preoccupied with 'other voices, other rooms.'"[22] Since Capote's *Other Voices, Other Rooms* was published in 1948, not 1955, King's dismissive allusion to Capote's readers—as somehow "preoccupied" with his work—is somewhat puzzling; nonetheless, the temporal parameters that he establishes exclude Capote from membership among its rarefied ranks. Indeed, King accuses Capote of the ultimate transgression for a southern writer: "Some Southern writers who went north in the 1940s and 1950s—McCullers, Truman Capote, and Tennessee Williams in particular—seemed bent on perpetuating the image of decadence that careless readers of Faulkner and Erskine Caldwell in the 1930s had taken to be typical of things south of the Mason-Dixon line."[23] It is perhaps coincidental, but no less curious, that the writers whom King disparages in these lines transgressed not merely in their journeys northward but in their sexualities, for this triad is remembered today for their frank (if coded) treatments of homosexuality in their southern fictions.

As King's assessment of the Southern Renaissance obliquely illustrates, Capote's homosexuality and homosexual themes in his literature have long complicated his place in the southern literary canon. Throughout the twentieth century the overarching homophobia of the United States kept multitudes of homosexuals closeted, but Capote openly professed his sexuality: "I always had a homosexual preference, and I never had any guilt about it. As time goes on, you finally settle down on one side or another, homosexual or heterosexual. And I was homosexual."[24] John Malcolm Brinnin, an acclaimed poet and a close friend of Capote's, recalls an instance when a man at a bar mumbled some homophobic insults, and Capote informed Brinnin that he would never camouflage his sexuality to appease the masses: "I wasn't more than fifteen years old when I decided to be so obviously who I am and what I am that anyone who so much as asked the question would look like a fool."[25]

Both professionally and privately, however, Capote was attacked for his openness concerning his sexuality. In the infancy of his career, some of the criticisms launched at *Other Voices, Other Rooms* were explicitly homophobic. The reviewer for *Time* magazine asserted that "the distasteful trappings of its homosexual theme overhang it like Spanish moss," and Diana Trilling's review, while employing a more nuanced phrasing, also vilifies Capote's fiction for its ostensible moral depravity: "I find myself deeply antipathetic to the whole artistic-moral purpose of Mr. Capote's novel."[26] Marking Capote as an outsider due to his homosexuality, some critics could see only the queer themes in his works, which, for them, obscured their artistry. Such views profoundly affected his literature's reception and his position in the culture of American arts.

Notwithstanding his southern roots, Capote's relationship to the U.S. South was characterized by ambivalence, if not antipathy. In a 1948 interview he rejected his southern identity entirely, declaring, "I have lived in many places besides the South and I don't like to be called a Southern writer."[27] In the following year he reiterated this rejection of his southern roots: "When people say Truman Capote is a southern writer, I merely find it irritating."[28] Given the southern landscapes of several of his works, including *Other Voices, Other Rooms* and many of the stories collected in *The Grass Harp*, such a stance is perhaps surprising, but Capote insisted that only his short story "A Christmas Memory," an autobiographical tale, necessitated a southern landscape: "Actually, the only thing I've written that *depended* on its southern setting was a story called 'A Christmas Memory.'... The moment I wrote that short story I knew I would never write another word about the South. I'm not going to be haunted by it any more."[29] There are multiple reasons for doubting Capote's assessment of his literature and his literary career in this statement, primarily because he returned to southern landscapes in subsequent fictions, such as "The Thanksgiving Visitor" (1967) and "One Christmas" (1982). Also, he relied heavily on southern gothic tropes—mysterious events and family secrets, the legacy of the Civil War in the decadent South, grotesque characters in nightmare worlds—in *Other Voices, Other Rooms* and other works. Robert Lee sees the gothic "as somehow always integral to Southern writing," and its influence on Capote's southern fictions is apparent in his decaying landscapes and grotesque characters.[30] Moreover, Capote's use of southern gothic elements builds upon his treatment of homosexuality, showcasing the complementarity of these interweaving themes. Louis Gross observes that the gothic, with its emphasis on repression and secrecy, serves as an apt genre for addressing homosexual themes: "the entire Southern Gothic movement of Tennessee Williams, Truman Capote, Carson McCullers, and William Inge is shaped by those qualities culturally associated with gays, and therefore defined as unhealthy. No other genre so welcomes culturally defined 'sickness' and horror as the Gothic."[31] Southern gothicism imbues several of Capote's fictions with a foreboding atmosphere in which repressed desires circulate uneasily; it is difficult to envision how these stories would have survived, if transplanted to other geographies.

It is equally true that many of Capote's works are not set in the South and do not rely on the tropes of southern gothicism, and so Capote's position as a writer of the Southern Renaissance is complicated by his sustained attention to nonsouthern landscapes and story lines. *The Muses Are Heard* records his experiences in Russia with a touring company of *Porgy and Bess*, and *Breakfast at Tiffany's*, *Answered Prayers*, and *Summer Crossing* unfold in New York City and its cosmopolitan world of sex and secrets. *In Cold Blood*, Capote's masterwork detailing the aftermath of a multiple murder in Kansas, straddles the border between gothic terror and nonfiction reporting, yet Capote does not employ in it many of the standard tropes of southern gothicism, as he did in *Other Voices, Other Rooms*.[32] Later in life Capote realized that the distance he felt from *Other Voices, Other Rooms* reflected his attempt to escape from his traumatic childhood, which also represented his attempt to escape the South: "The reason that I felt alienated from it for so many years was that I didn't want to face the fact that the book was all about *me* and my problems.... And I realized that the book is a prose poem in which I have taken my own emotional problems and transformed them into psychological symbols."[33] Capote's early years, characterized by a sense of abandonment after his parents' divorce and of estrangement from southern cultural mores, led to feelings of ambivalence about his roots. More than most writers of the Southern Renaissance, Capote chafed against the strictures of such a label, resisting attempts to pigeonhole his literature as artifacts of the decadent South.

The cinematic aspects of Capote's fiction testify to his innovative treatment of many southern story lines, in which visions of Hollywood glamour inspire his southern characters with dreams of escaping their impoverished or otherwise pedestrian surroundings for the glory of cinematic adulation, only then to disappoint them with the emptiness of their desires. Capote plays with such themes in several of the stories collected with *The Grass Harp*, such as "Children on Their Birthdays," which features the young and irrepressible Miss Bobbit, who continually dreams of movie-star celebrity and riches. After spearheading efforts to track down the con artist responsible for fleecing the townspeople, she cajoles them into underwriting her ambitions: "The proposition was that they should pool their money and finance her trip to Hollywood; in return, they would get ten percent of her life's earnings which, after she was a star, and that would not be very long, would make them all rich men" (*GH* 134). This lofty aspiration is cut short when Miss Bobbit is run over by the six-o'clock bus that was to carry her to her destination. In "Jug of Silver," a tale of country children striving to escape their straitened circumstances by winning the prize money offered in a local contest, Capote depicts the young girl Middy "clutching a copy of *Screen Secrets*." Her brother Appleseed fervently believes Hollywood success will end their penury: "Middy's gonna be a big lady in the picture shows. They make lotsa money, the ladies in the picture shows do, and then we ain't gonna never eat another collard green as long as we live" (*GH* 155–56). Capote's comic masterpiece "My Side of the Matter" depicts the narrator's wife Marge regretting that she will not be able to attend the movies ("Oh-h-h, but it's Judy Garland," she sobs), as the narrator then disparages his nemesis (and Marge's aunt) Olivia-Ann for her susceptibility to Hollywood romance: "Olivia-Ann's never seen not even one picture show in her entire fifty-two years . . . but she subscribes to eight movie books. . . . She has this positively morbid crush on Gary Cooper" (*GH* 199–200). Trapped in the South with movie-star dreams in her heart, even the austere spinster Olivia-Ann turns to Hollywood for the fantasies necessary to escape her doldrums.

Capote's collection *Breakfast at Tiffany's, and Three Stories* similarly relies on themes of Hollywood, celebrity, and desire to contrast his protagonists' aspirations with their realities. In the volume's opening novella, Holly Golightly is a pseudostarlet whose career never took flight, despite her agent O. J. Berman's efforts to win her an audition for Cecil B. DeMille's *The Story of Dr. Wassell* (1944), a film starring Gary Cooper; Holly nonetheless lives the red-carpet lifestyle, attending with her admirer Rusty Trawler the premiere of *One Touch of Venus* (1948, dir. William Seiter, starring Ava Gardner).[34] Holly's glamorous lifestyle is undercut by her bouts with the "mean reds," a sure sign that her dreams are unfulfilled by her status as a quasi starlet now dependent on her male friends' financial generosity. In

"A Diamond Guitar," the handsome young inmate Tico Feo exaggerates his background with stories of Hollywood celebrities, particularly "one involving hundreds of dollars and a meeting with Bing Crosby," to win the esteem of his fellow prisoners (*BT* 147). In these moments and in others throughout Capote's corpus, Hollywood glamour serves as the clichéd fantasy of the poor, the desperate, and the self-promotional: movie stars and movie stardom illuminate these characters' dreams, pushing them forward for the brass ring that none succeeds in reaching.

Beyond these brief fantasies of Hollywood fame, films take on a metaphysical meaning in "The Headless Hawk." One of Capote's most psychologically rich narratives, it details the protagonist Vincent Waters's struggles to overcome his history of failed love affairs and wasted potential. The mysterious young artist D. J. moves in with him, and the movies consume their lives:

The movies. Again. In the last month he'd seen so many films, snatches of Hollywood dialogue rumbled in his dreams. . . . And each morning before leaving for work he left on the mantel fifty cents—rain or shine, she went to a picture show. But Vincent was sensitive enough to see why: there had been in his own life a certain time of limbo when he'd gone to movies every day, often sitting through several repeats of the same film; it was in its way like religion, for there, watching the shifting patterns of black and white, he knew a release of conscience similar to the kind a man must find confessing to his father. (*GH* 188)

In this metaphor of film as religion, the cinema erases not merely transgressions but consciousness, allowing the penitent to find freedom from the ravages of his mind. Films become so entrenched in Vincent's life that as he falls asleep, he does so in cinematic terms. At the moment when one's waking thoughts should fade into dreams, he submerges into a stream-of-consciousness fantasy of Hollywood melodrama: "Close-up. Oh, but John, it isn't for my sake after all we've the children to consider a divorce would ruin their lives! Fadeout. The screen trembles: rattle of drums, flourish of trumpets, R.K.O. presents . . ." The ensuing nightmare vision, in which "Vincent recognizes Vincent" in "an old man rocking in a rocking chair, an old man with yellow-dyed hair, powdered cheeks, kewpie-doll lips" (*GH* 189), bears many of the hallmarks of surrealism, as he then endures a grotesque cavalcade of his former lovers. In the story's enigmatic ending, the clichéd image of two lovers standing in the rain is, in Capote's hands, romantic yet terrifying: "Presently, with slow scraping steps, she came below the lamp to stand beside him, and it was as if the sky were a thunder-cracked mirror, for the rain fell between them like a curtain of splintered glass" (*GH* 195). Through her immersion in the cinematic realm, D. J. leads Vincent to the painful rebirth enabling him to escape his solipsism, if only through the violent image of glass piercing him into new life.

Cinema offered Capote more than themes for his fiction, for films influenced how he perceived literature's foundations, structures, and possibilities. In a 1957 interview he acknowledged his debt to film: "I think most of the younger writers have learned and borrowed from the visual, structural side of movie technique. I have."[35] It would be surprising if Capote saw no overlap in technique between his fiction and cinema since he had penned two film scripts—*Beat the Devil* and *Indiscretion of an American Wife*—by the time of this interview. Capote's *Handcarved Coffins* is arguably his most cinematic work, and in the preface to *Music for Chameleons*, in which this novella appears, Capote describes his craft as previously hindered by his reluctance to mix techniques from different genres and media but now benefiting from their melding: "by restricting myself to the techniques of whatever form I was working in, I was not using everything I knew about writing—all I'd learned from film scripts, plays, reportage, poetry, the short story, novellas, the novel. A writer ought to have all his colors, all his abilities available on the same palette for mingling" (*MC* xviii). Mixing together his luminous prose with screenplay dialogue, stage directions, and cinematic tropes, *Handcarved Coffins* represents a strikingly sustained effort in this regard, such as in Capote's use of montage to capture the disequilibrium of the narrator's dream, in which he envisions a serial killer's multiple and gruesome murders: "I entered some sphere between sleep and wakefulness, my mind like a crystal lozenge, a suspended instrument that caught the reflections of spiraling images: a man's head among leaves, the windows of a car streaked with venom, the eyes of serpents sliding through heat-mist, fire flowing from the earth, scorched fists pounding at a cellar door, taut wire gleaming in the twilight, a torso on a roadway, a head among leaves, fire, fire, fire flowing like a river, river, river. Then a telephone rings" (*MC* 84). The hypnotic, alliterative repetition of "fire, fire, fire flowing like a river, river, river" lulls the reader into a somnolent state, until the phone's jarring and onomatopoeic *ring* startles the narrator back to consciousness, in a scene compelling readers to experience its emotional register both visually and empathetically. Furthermore, Capote's parenthetical asides in *Handcarved*

Coffins expand the notations of screenplays and play scripts into brief character portraits, such as in the moment when the detective Jake Pepper admits that he has never questioned his prime suspect for the murders:

> JAKE: Strictly speaking, I've never *questioned* him at all.
> (His quirky cynical smile bent his mouth; he tinkled the ice in his whiskey, drank some, and chuckled—a deep rough chuckle, like a man trying to bring up phlegm.) (*MC* 100)

These few lines compress the lengthy character descriptions typical of novels into film's necessary focus on action, resulting in a hybrid text that reads with the immediacy of a screenplay and the depth of prose. Norman Mailer famously complimented Truman Capote as "the most perfect writer of my generation, he writes the best sentences word for word, rhythm upon rhythm,"[36] and *Handcarved Coffins* exemplifies both Capote's finely attuned ear for prose and his detailed attention to plotting and pace.

But as much as Capote learned from cinematic techniques and employed them in his fictions, he often expressed an unvarnished distaste for Hollywood itself. In his essays and personal letters, he denigrated the town as culturally empty and intellectually vapid. He recounts in "Hollywood," another essay from *Local Color*, anecdotes of aesthetic ignorance—a producer's wife who fails to recognize a Klee lithograph (*LC* 39)—and emotional emptiness: "that sad, jittery lady who once, after the departure of her third husband, threw an Oscar into the ocean" (*LC* 40). He sneers that Los Angeles is a "city of suntanned Uriah Heeps" (*MC* 246), and pronounces with tongue only slightly in cheek: "it's a scientific fact that if you stay in California you lose one point of your IQ every year."[37] In a letter to his friend Leo Lerman, he urges him to avoid Hollywood at all costs: "My darlings, I am *mad* with horror: when I get back, if, indeed, I ever do, then I am taking all of you by your dear little paws and make you swear to me that you will never, never set foot in Los Angeles County. Quel hole!"[38] Such pronouncements vilifying Hollywood span Capote's professional life. Given his distaste for Southern California and its entertainment industry, it is ironic that he died, on August 25, 1984, in his friend Joanne Carson's home in Los Angeles. Capote may have criticized Hollywood and the film industry mercilessly, yet he continued to work in it throughout his career, seduced by its financial inducements and the potential to help him reach ever-widening audiences.

The subsequent chapters of *Truman Capote: A Literary Life at the Movies* explore various aspects of Capote's relationship to the cinematic world, paying particular attention to the ways in which these excursions intersect with themes of homosexuality and southernness. Chapter 2, "Capote in the Queer House of Fame: Stars and Celebrity Personas," addresses Capote's fame and his personal and professional relationships with various Hollywood stars. Capote, more than any other writer of the twentieth century, was recognized as much for his queer performance of fame as for his writing. Long a member of the jet set, Capote ensured his lasting celebrity with his Black and White Ball of 1966, which marked the completion of *In Cold Blood*. Throughout the 1960s and 1970s, his television appearances, particularly on Johnny Carson's *Tonight Show*, kept him in the public eye for reasons other than his literary accomplishments. Capote's deployment of his celebrity persona is strikingly evident in his cameo role in the 1976 film *Murder by Death*, written by Neil Simon and directed by Robert Moore, in which he plays the eccentric millionaire Lionel Twain. Many of Capote's literary and journalistic endeavors, including *Observations* (his photography and prose collaboration with Richard Avedon), "The Duke in His Domain" (his controversial and revealing exposé of Marlon Brando), and "A Beautiful Child" (his homage to Marilyn Monroe), reveal his candid thoughts on celebrities and stardom, deflating the pretensions of some while esteeming the achievements of others. In sum, Capote's performance of celebrity ensured his fame while endangering his reputation as a writer, a dynamic that continues to haunt the reception of his literature.

The third chapter, "Scriptwriter for the Stars," focuses on his produced films: *Beat the Devil, Indiscretion of an American Wife*, and *The Innocents*. These films do not explicitly address homosexual themes, yet Capote embeds such elements as camp humor and transgressive desire in them, imbuing otherwise "straight" films with queer subtexts. *Beat the Devil*, directed by John Huston, features Humphrey Bogart, Jennifer Jones, Gina Lollobrigida, and Peter Lorre in the amusing misadventures of international crooks pursuing uranium-rich African territory, as well as the repercussions of their encounter with an apparently proper British couple. Vittorio De Sica's *Indiscretion of an American Wife* features Montgomery Clift and Jennifer Jones as adulterous lovers, in a much-troubled film cut to the bone before its release. For *The Innocents*, directed by Jack Clayton and starring Deborah Kerr, Capote adapted Henry James's classic tale of horror, *The Turn of the Screw.* Of particular interest in *Indiscretion of an American Wife* and *The Innocents* is Capote's treatment of young boys' sexuality, in that he casts them as potential lovers of adult women. These films allow Capote to continue his thematic treatment of childhood and queer sexuality, as evident in *Other Voices, Other Rooms,* and to dramatize onscreen the desires latent in childhood.

Capote expressed his contempt for the cinematic adaptation of *Breakfast at Tiffany's,* the film that serves as the focus of this study's fourth chapter. Directed by Blake Edwards and starring Audrey Hepburn, George Peppard, and Patricia Neal, it is today celebrated as a beloved classic of American cinema, but the film metamorphoses Capote's melancholy novella into a standard Hollywood romantic comedy. The film of *Breakfast at Tiffany's* removes the novella's homosexual subtext, primarily by recasting its gay narrator as Holly's love interest. Beyond these narrative changes to his vision, Capote felt strongly that Hepburn should not play his heroine Holly Golightly, instead preferring Marilyn Monroe for the part. Capote exerted behind-the-scenes influence to alter the film, but his failures in this regard allowed the film to succeed on its own merits, particularly as an iconic film in Hepburn's career. As Holly Golightly's story shifts from Capote's novella to Edwards's film, its queer story line veers from its foundations yet nonetheless imbues a classic film of heterosexual passion with a rich subtext of countercultural desire.

The fifth chapter, "Capote, Crime, and Capital Punishment," addresses *In Cold Blood,* Capote's nonfiction account of the murder of the Clutters, a Kansas family picked virtually at random for slaughter by two thieves, as well as the artistic repercussions of this book and its film adaptations on his subsequent career. Capote's relationship with the killers Perry Smith and Dick Hickock, which grew during the countless hours he spent interviewing them while writing the novel, influenced his perception of Richard Brooks's 1967 film and its development. This chapter also explores how his experience writing *In Cold Blood* affected the film's creation, particularly concerning its emphasis on realism. The film of *In Cold Blood* succeeds in translating the brutal story of the murder of the Clutter family into a sober and haunting reflection on crime and punishment in America, with its conclusion meditating on the justice of capital punishment in modern society. This chapter focuses primarily on Brooks's 1967 treatment of *In Cold Blood,* but it concludes with analyses of Capote's metamorphosis into a crime expert on

1960s and 1970s television programs and of Jonathan Kaplan's 1996 television miniseries of the same title, starring Anthony Edwards, Eric Roberts, and Sam Neill.

Not content merely to write fiction and screenplays, Capote also wanted to turn his close friend Princess Lee Bouvier Radziwill, the younger sister of Jacqueline Kennedy Onassis, into an acclaimed actress. The following chapter, "Turning a Princess into a Star: Capote, Lee Bouvier Radziwill, and *Laura*," explores this intriguing episode in Capote's cinematic career. After persuading David Susskind to produce a film starring Radziwill, Capote cast her in a television remake of Otto Preminger's 1944 noir thriller *Laura*. Capote's *Laura* evinces numerous continuities with Preminger's film, such that the remake is more a retread than a reimagining of its source. Nonetheless, the alterations evident in Capote's *Laura* reflect queer themes prevalent in his literature, particularly in its treatment of the Pygmalion myth as representative of a gay artistic sensibility. The production was critically panned upon its airing, and Capote's relationship with Radziwill ended abruptly in the 1970s when she refused to testify on Capote's behalf in Gore Vidal's lawsuit against him for defamation.

The chapter "Capote for the Holidays" examines adaptations of Capote's autobiographical holiday fiction. The short stories "A Christmas Memory," "The Thanksgiving Visitor," and "One Christmas" mark a sentimental subgenre of his oeuvre that modulates his public persona from an acid-tongued aesthete into a purveyor of wholesome values of family, friendship, community, and love. In the late 1960s, four of Capote's short stories—"A Christmas Memory," "Miriam," "Among the Paths to Eden," and "The Thanksgiving Visitor"—were filmed as television movies, garnering much critical acclaim: Geraldine Page won Emmy Awards for Outstanding Performance by an Actress in a Leading Role in a Drama for both *A Christmas Memory* (1967) and *The Thanksgiving Visitor* (1969), and Maureen Stapleton won in the same category for *Among the Paths to Eden* (1968). Three of these films— *A Christmas Memory*, *Miriam*, and *Among the Paths to Eden*—were later grouped under the title *Trilogy* and released theatrically. These holiday adaptations, reflecting universal themes of love overcoming alienation, also celebrate a romanticized vision of the South as a land of rural simplicity and moral clarity. This chapter concludes with readings of the 1994 television film *One Christmas*, starring Katherine Hepburn, Henry Winkler, and Swoosie Kurtz, and of the 1997 television remake of *A Christmas Memory*, starring Patty Duke and Piper Laurie. With their tender depictions of southern life, these holiday films cement Capote's popular image as a southern writer, despite his resistance to such a label, as they also, through the character of Buddy, depict Capote as a queer child alienated from southern culture's norms of masculinity.

The eighth chapter, "Capote's Southern Childhoods," tackles the cinematic versions of *Other Voices, Other Rooms*, *The Grass Harp*, and "Children on Their Birthdays" to explore how they tame Capote's conflicted depictions of adolescence. These films portray childhood as a time of innocence and wonder, in stark contrast to Capote's treatment of children in his literature. Capote's *Other Voices, Other Rooms*, a queer bildungsroman, addresses Joel Knox's maturation into homosexuality, and *The Grass Harp* and "Children on Their Birthdays" portray childhood nostalgically while addressing as well the end of young boys' sexual innocence and their emergence into adolescence. For the most part, the film versions of these texts—David Rocksavage's *Other Voices, Other Rooms* (1995), Charles Matthau's *The Grass Harp* (1995), and Mark Medoff's *Children on Their Birthdays* (2002)—filter out Capote's treatment of childhood as a troubling and sexually confusing period and adapt his melancholic tales into narratives of love overcoming isolation. These films reflect the sociocultural milieu of the end of the twentieth and the beginning of the twenty-first century, in which impressive victories were achieved for gay rights while at the same an ambivalence reigned over the question of children's exposure to homosexuality.

Not all of Capote's cinematic endeavors came to fruition, and chapter 9, "Capote's Unfinished Business: Abandoned and Unproduced Projects," discusses these rejected and unfinished screenplays, including an early teleplay of his unfinished novel *Answered Prayers*, the marital farce *Straight Face*, the suspense thrillers *Tyranny* and *Dead Loss*, the reform drama *Uncle Sam's Hard Luck Hotel*, and an adaptation of F. Scott Fitzgerald's *The Great Gatsby*, which director Jack Clayton rejected in favor of Francis Ford Coppola's screenplay for his 1974 film starring Robert Redford and Mia Farrow. These film scripts illuminate Capote's career in unexpected ways, for they represent surprising departures from his literary fare, as they also highlight various stages in his development as a writer. The early version of *Answered Prayers* showcases Tennessee Williams's influence on Capote, and his adaptation of *The Great Gatsby* shares some surprising affinities with *Breakfast at Tiffany's*. Also, Capote's screenplays regarding crime and punishment, including *Dead Loss*, *Tyranny*, and *Uncle Sam's Hard Luck Hotel*, illustrate his continuing interest in the criminal underworld following the publication of *In Cold Blood*.

The final chapter, "Playing Capote: *Tru, Capote, Infamous*, and Other Parodic and Iconic Portrayals," examines various television and cinematic depictions of Capote. Throughout his literary life and beyond, Capote has been aped and performed by others: when he achieved fame in the late 1940s and 1950s, comedians such as Ernie Kovacs and Mike Nichols performed as Capote in their comic skits, and he continued to serve as the butt of satiric performances for impersonators David Frye and Rich Little in the 1970s and 1980s. Increasingly, the story of his life has become fodder for more dramatic fare: Jay Presson Allen's *Tru* (1989) was originally produced theatrically, with Robert Morse winning a Tony Award for his performance, and it was also filmed for the *American Playhouse* series. Bennett Miller's *Capote* (2005), which retells the story of Capote's investigation of the Clutter murders for *In Cold Blood*, features Philip Seymour Hoffman in the Academy Award–winning title role. Douglas McGrath's *Infamous* (2006), starring Toby Jones, Daniel Craig, and Sandra Bullock, likewise addresses Capote's time in Kansas. Capote also appears as a minor character in various films, including *54* (dir. Mark Christopher, 1998), the homage to Steve Rubell's 1970s disco paradise, and *Isn't She Great* (dir. Andrew Bergman, 2000), a biopic of Capote's publicity-hungry rival Jacqueline Susann. Capote coined the term "nonfiction novel" to describe *In Cold Blood*, and as he increasingly becomes a character from the nonfiction novel that was his life, the various cinematic and stage adaptations featuring him suggest that he has metamorphosed into an avatar of adaptation, iconically symbolizing the transition from life to page, and from page to screen.

As a whole, *Truman Capote: A Literary Life at the Movies* examines the contours of Capote's life and fiction and their translations to film, paying particular attention to his homosexuality and his southern roots: how he lived openly as a gay celebrity during homophobic times; how his screenplays bring a camp and queer sensibility to 1950s and 1960s cinema; how film adaptations of his work, particularly *Breakfast at Tiffany's* and *In Cold Blood* but also *Other Voices, Other Rooms*, *The Grass Harp*, and *Children on Their Birthdays*, camouflage their source narratives' queer subtexts; and how cinematic portrayals of his life grapple with his sexuality in telling the story of his life. Capote's place in a queer history of cinema does not allow for a linear assessment of a homosexual artist creating films with explicitly gay themes and story lines; rather, as Alexander Doty posits, "the queerness of mass culture" emerges in three predominant modes, each of which is relevant for assessing the queerness of Capote's cinematic corpus: "influences during the production of texts; historically specific cultural readings and uses of texts by self-identified gays, lesbians, bisexuals, and queers; and adopting reception positions that can be considered 'queer' in some way, regardless of a person's declared sexual and gender allegiances."[39] Doty's perceptive theory of cinematic and pop-culture queerness resonates in much of Capote's film corpus, for the queerness of these movies need not reflect his homosexuality, or indeed any authorial intention on his part, given the collaborative nature of cinematic endeavors. Rather, the queerness of cinema Capoteana arises from converging sources: his life, his fiction, and others' re-creations of them and their themes, whether to enhance or to obfuscate their queer plots. In this respect, the term *queer* expands beyond denotations of homosexuality to include a wide range of characters resistant to or denigrated by cultural expectations of gender and sexual normativity, as will be clear throughout the following chapters.

As appropriate, *Truman Capote: A Literary Life at the Movies* also considers the fundamental nature of southern cinema, a subgenre of American film that defies easy categorization. Warren French suggests that, as the western is one of the defining modes of American cinema, so too should the "southern" takes its place in this pantheon, as he also outlines the economic reasons why the "southern" never achieved commensurate status with the western (primarily because of higher production costs for more elaborate sets).[40] In addition to the inferior position of the "southern" as a Hollywood genre, Capote's cinematic corpus exemplifies the frequent difficulty in identifying southern films. Although the adaptations of Capote's holiday tales (*A Christmas Memory, The Thanksgiving Visitor,* and *One Christmas*) and childhood narratives (*Other Voices, Other Rooms, The Grass Harp,* and *Children on Their Birthdays*) fit comfortably within its parameters by virtue of their geographic setting, *Breakfast at Tiffany's* encapsulates the difficulty of defining the "southern": should this film be considered a "southern," despite its setting in New York City, because its author (but not its screenwriter George Axelrod) and its protagonist grew up in the South, before both moved north to enjoy greater sexual freedoms? It surely contorts the traditional parameters of a genre to consider *Breakfast at Tiffany's* a "southern," yet, at the same time, the film cannot wholly escape its southern roots. The goal of this study is not to argue that all films arising from Capote's body of work must be interpreted through the prism of southern literature and cinema but to show their points of connection with the South that further illuminate their cultural meaning.

In assessing Capote's relationship to Hollywood and cinema, it is important to remember that he was a man of contrasts, contradictions, and sometimes outright falsehoods. As his partner Jack Dunphy explained, "Truman had a way of telling half-truths and whole lies," and Tennessee Williams, while searching for a "polite way of saying he does fabricate," insightfully labeled Capote, not a liar, but a "mythologist."[41] Capote himself confessed his penchant for "remember[ing] things the way they should have been."[42] For instance, in one of Capote's favorite anecdotes, a woman at a bar asks for his autograph—"I want you to write your name on my tummy," she brazenly demands—but her drunken husband, infuriated by her fawning over this celebrity, drops his pants and asks instead that Capote autograph his penis: "Since you're on an autographing spree, would you mind autographing this?" At this point Capote's story diverges, and either he or Tennessee Williams utters the devastating rejoinder: "Well, listen, maybe I can't *autograph* it, but perhaps I could *initial* it."[43] Whether Capote or Williams was the wit behind the punch line depends on the circumstances of the tale's retelling, on whether Capote is winning laughter for his own or for his friend's rapier wit. Such contradictions run throughout Capote's writings and public statements, and they are especially pertinent to his relationship to film. Despite Capote's clear contributions and debts to twentieth-century cinema, which he professed openly and in detail in several interviews, he also denied the relevance of film to his writing. Late in life, in response to the question "How much influence has film had on your writing?" he responded tersely, "Per se, none."[44] It is a surprising statement, for it erases an artistically symbiotic relationship that defines his career: writing fiction adapted for the movies, writing screenplays for the movies, even appearing in the movies in *Murder by Death*, Capote immersed himself and his fiction in a cinematic world where art, narrative, image, celebrity, and money are the currency of the trade, and where he acquitted himself quite well, no matter how much he might deny it.

Capote in the Queer House of Fame
▶ Stars and Celebrity Personas

In *Music for Chameleons* Capote famously declared: "I'm an alcoholic. I'm a drug addict. I'm homosexual. I'm a genius" (*MC* 261). This statement from the twilight of his career reflects his determination to live his life openly, as it also reveals his canny understanding of how to employ his celebrity to maintain his presence in the public eye. These apparently shocking "confessions" were well known to anyone paying him the slightest attention, and so Capote's pronouncement of his troubled genius serves less as an expression of self-realization than as yet another illustration of his extraordinary ability to generate media coverage for himself. Surely, more than any other author of the twentieth century, Capote was recognized, if not lionized, as a celebrity, famous for being famous as much as he was revered as a remarkably talented writer. Moreover, he performed his celebrity queerly, living openly as a homosexual man in nonchalant defiance of American mores. In many ways, Capote enjoyed the role of the gay clown who minces to amuse his various audiences: "I'm this funny, sawed-off fellow with a high voice, and it's hard for people to accept me. But if I come in and say, 'I don't want to sit with the boys, I want to sit with the girls,' everybody giggles and everybody's more comfortable. I do that on purpose to make it easier for people to be around me because then *I'm* easier and the whole thing works better."[1] As a homosexual man employing a stereotypical persona, Capote benefited from his astute recognition that *acting* gay would allow him more comfortably to *be* gay.

Capote was a celebrity, not a Hollywood star, but it is nonetheless helpful to view his fame as analogous to that of stars. As Richard Dyer explains of Hollywood stardom: "The star phenomenon consists of everything that is publicly available about stars. A film star's image is not just his or her films, but the promotion of those films and of the star through pin-ups, public appearances, studio hand-outs and so on, as well as interviews, biographies and coverage in the press of the star's doings and 'private' life. Further, a star's image is also what people say or write about him or her. . . . Star images are always extensive, multimedia, intertextual."[2] Although authors of literary fiction are rarely celebrities in the same manner as film actors, one could replace "film star" with "author" and "film" with "novel" in Dyer's analysis and approximate Capote's marketing of himself and his fictions. Furthermore, exposure and publicity often lead to larger sales and profits, whether of a Hollywood film or a bestselling novel. Celebrities who attend to their public personas carefully, protecting or exaggerating their images while maintaining their presence in the public eye, are often rewarded with financial success due to the echo effect of their celebrity, a dynamic that Capote exploited throughout his career.

Capote clearly understood the demands and payoffs of Hollywood's star system. In discussing the careers of Clark Gable, Spencer Tracy, Bette Davis, and Joan Crawford, he observed, "They were real stars created by the studios for a very specific purpose who were continuously promoted."[3] Indeed, his definition of a movie star parallels (and predates) Dyer's: "Defined practically, a movie star is any performer who can account for a box-office profit regardless of the quality of the enterprise in which he appears" (*DB* 319). In this blunt assessment of the economics underlying Hollywood stardom, in which he distills celebrity as irrelevant to a film's aesthetic success but crucial to its financial prospects, Capote also summarizes the conundrum of celebrity for his own career, for his celebrity often eclipsed his writing.

▶ Capote and the Stars

As a result of his fame and literary achievements, Capote circulated in the same social networks as many movie stars, and his nonfiction writings frequently address his personal reactions to them, commenting on the tension between their star personas and their personalities as he perceived them firsthand. During his childhood Capote revered Hollywood actors, particularly the young celebrities of his generation. In a 1967 interview with Gloria Steinem, he recalled his juvenile fantasy of joining the ranks of child stars of the 1930s, a fantasy that he divulged at the time to his beloved cousin Sookie: "'Sookie,' I used to say to her, 'someday you and I are going to Hollywood, and I'll be a tapdancer in the movies.' . . . I was extremely jealous of all children whose names or pictures were in the paper—Shirley Temple, Bobby Breen, Jackie Cooper, Jackie Coogan; everybody."[4] These childhood sentiments are echoed in his short story "The Thanksgiving Visitor," when the narrator Buddy daydreams about running away from home for a glamorous life in Hollywood: "One thing I knew: I was going to quit that house, that town, that night. Hit the road. Hop a freight train and head for California. Make my living shining shoes in Hollywood. Fred Astaire's shoes. Clark Gable's. Or—maybe I just might become a movie star myself. Look at Jackie Cooper. Oh, they'd be sorry then. When I was rich and famous and refused to answer their letters and even telegrams, probably" (CS 263). Like Miss Bobbit in "Children on Their Birthdays" and Middy and Appleseed in "Jug of Silver," both Capote as a child and his alter ego Buddy in "The Thanksgiving Visitor" find inspiration from dreams of stardom and the life of financial ease that accompanies it. Capote, unlike his fictional counterparts, succeeded in his aspiration of becoming a celebrity and, as a corollary, befriending many Hollywood stars (while antagonizing others).

Katherine Anne Porter, with whom Capote enjoyed a friendly relationship and whose work he greatly admired, observed that he was often "on the prowl for celebrities,"[5] and this desire to mingle with the Hollywood elite reflected his striving both to enhance his personal celebrity and to puncture the personas of those he deemed pretenders. Capote enthusiastically dished dirt about stars, particularly enjoying a pastime known as International Daisy Chain, in which celebrities are linked to one another through their sexual liaisons. (Capote's favorite round of International Daisy Chain links Cab Calloway to Adolf Hitler: "Cab Calloway to Marquesa Casamaury to Carol Reed to Unity Mitford to Hitler.")[6] Although it borders on the titillating, it should not be overlooked that Capote was sexually involved with at least three famous film stars. Recalling his fling with Errol Flynn, Capote confessed its disappointments—"We were both drunk . . . and it took him the longest time to have an orgasm. I never did"[7]—and commenting as well, "Frankly, if it hadn't been Errol Flynn, I don't think I would have remembered it" (*MC* 236).[8] John Malcolm Brinnin recounts Capote's affair with John Garfield, who starred in a string of hits in the 1940s including *The Postman Always Rings Twice* (1946), *Gentleman's Agreement* (1947), and *Force of Evil* (1948), about whose homosexuality Capote declared, "I'm as surprised as you are. After all, he's still Mister Tough Guy to most of the American population. . . . He's sweet . . . and sort of teddy bear cuddly."[9] In a letter to Andrew Lyndon, at the time when *Indiscretion of an American Wife* was filmed, Capote mentioned a fling with its star Montgomery Clift.[10]

Hollywood stars are recurrent subjects of Capote's essays, including the portraits of John Huston, Marilyn Monroe, Humphrey Bogart, Jean Cocteau, and Mae West in *Observations*, a collection that also features luminaries from noncinematic fields, including Jacques Cousteau, Maya Plisetskaya, Ezra Pound, Robert Oppenheimer, and Louis Armstrong. Capote also wrote extended essays on Marlon Brando, Marilyn Monroe, and Elizabeth Taylor, viewing his 1956 Brando essay, "The Duke in His Domain," as an early effort in developing the nonfiction novel. He brought this literary innovation to its fullest achievement in *In Cold Blood*, but his interview with Brando allowed him an early opportunity to hone his journalistic skills, as he sensed the artistic challenges that the trite genre of celebrity interviewing might provide: "I thought, 'What is the most banal thing in journalism?' After a time I realized that it would be an interview with a film star, the sort of thing you would see in *Photoplay* magazine."[11] In treating the celebrity interview as an art form, Capote succeeded in shifting the adulatory tenor of most such ventures into a revealing exposé of an actor's soul.

To enhance his celebrity interviews, Capote believed that he needed to make himself virtually invisible: "Because the ideal portrait is something in which the interviewer is totally removed and you set the whole thing up so that if it's good, the person that it's about comes across with no distortions on the part of the interviewer—well, of course if he's any good he's an artist, and any artist distorts what he touches. But it's not artificial; it's just a form of art."[12] Elaborating further on this journalistic strategy, Capote outlined his ploy for winning Brando's confidences: "The secret to the art of interviewing is to make the other person think he's interviewing you. You tell him about yourself, and slowly you spin your web so that he tells you everything. That's how I trapped Marlon."[13] "The Duke in His Domain" remains one of the most notorious interviews of Hollywood history, a devastating exposé of Brando's intellectual pretensions and troubled family history. Joshua Logan, Brando's director for *Sayonara* (1957), sensed the impending publicity disaster and warned Brando not to grant the interview: "When I heard [of Capote's interest] I almost stripped gears. *The Muses Are Heard* was vicious and personally humiliating to everyone, especially Ira Gershwin and Leonard Lyons. It treated human beings like bugs to be squashed underfoot. And Truman would have even juicier fodder to chew on with us. . . . I knew from his conversation at many parties that he had it in for Brando and wanted to shatter his powerful image."[14] More succinctly, Logan cautioned that Capote would "make idiots of us all."[15] Brando nonetheless spoke with Capote for hours. Capote called the interview "one of the all-time perfect interviews,"[16] and the resulting portrait of Brando—"A deity, yes; but more than that, really, just a young man sitting on a pile of candy" (*DB* 353)—dismisses the star as a pretender, one who confesses that he has lived the "last eight, nine years . . . pretty mixed up, a mess pretty much" (*DB* 315). Capote repeated such derogatory views of Brando in *The Dogs Bark*, dismissing him as "a wounded young man who is a genius, but not markedly intelligent" (*DB* xvii) and summarizing him thus: "No actor of my generation possesses greater natural gifts, but none other has transported intellectual falsity to higher levels of hilarious pretension" (*DB* 414). Inevitably Capote's reporting on Brando became part of the story of the interview, with several voices criticizing him for his treatment of the star. Film critic Pauline Kael defended Brando and riposted that the essay reveals as much about Capote as it does about Brando: "Despite Capote's style and venomous skill, it is he in this interview, not Brando, who equates money and success with real importance and accomplishment. His arrows fit snugly into the holes they have made only if you accept the usual middlebrow standards of marksmanship."[17]

From his interviews and portraits of celebrities, Capote's opinions of various stars emerge, and it is apparent that he appreciated the personalities, foibles, and magnetic beauty of many of Hollywood's elite actresses. As a child, he dreamed of writing a screenplay for Greta Garbo: "When I was twelve, I had a tiresome series of mishaps, and so stayed a good deal in bed, spending most of my time in the writing of a play that was to star the most beautiful woman in the world, which is how I described Miss Garbo in the letter accompanying my script." Later in life, he defended her from aspersions on her intelligence by urging the appreciation of her radiant beauty: "Someone asked, 'Do you suppose she is at all intelligent?', which seems to me an outrageous question; really, who cares whether or not she is intelligent? Surely it is enough that such a face could even exist" (*LC* 14). In *Observations* he painted Marilyn Monroe as "an untidy divinity—in the sense that a banana split or cherry jubilee is untidy but divine" (*O* 85). His deep affection for Monroe shines through such characterizations, and the title of his portrait of her, "A Beautiful Child," limns her winsome innocence. Capote was shocked when she died in 1962, and he eulogized, "She was such a good-hearted girl, so pure really, so much on the side of the angels."[18] Capote drew Elizabeth Taylor as "a sensitive, self-educated lady with a tough but essentially innocent attitude—if you sleep with a guy, gosh, that means you have to marry him!" (*PO* 298). This simple sketch registers his appreciation of her naiveté, despite her lifetime in the limelight due both to her successful film career and to her string of failed marriages. He wrote of Mae West's vulnerability—"Removed from the protecting realm of her hilarious creation, her sexless symbol of uninhibited sexuality, she was without defense"—as he also captured her tart tongue when responding to an ostensible compliment from a fan who recently, at a museum's retrospective showing, had viewed *She Done Him Wrong* (dir. Lowell Sherman, 1933, also known as *Diamond Lil*): "And a dismayed Miss West, seeking shelter in the sassy drawl of her famous fabrication, inquired, 'Just whaddya mean, honey? A *museum?*'" (*O* 90).

In addition to deriding Brando, Capote disparaged numerous other acclaimed stars with acid-tongued quips. Although she is generally recognized as the finest actress of her era, Capote dismissed Meryl Streep as "the Creep . . . she looks like a chicken. . . . She's totally untalented."[19] Of Jane Fonda he sniped, "Jane Fonda is a rather good actress; I think she's very dumb. I've known her since she was seventeen years old; I never thought she had much but fleas in her head," although he conceded, "She was very good in *Klute*, an excellent performance."[20] He also declared that she "has always been, to me, a fake and a bore."[21] In a litany of his dislikes that, in curmudgeonly fashion, includes Santa Claus—"And to hell with Santa Claus, too"—he belittled "Another bête noire: Sammy Davis Jr. Out! Out."[22] Alluding to the star's multiplicity of styles and sounds, Capote proclaimed, "There is no Sammy Davis, Jr."[23] Additional famous men, although not entertainers, who elicited Capote's opprobrium include multimillionaires Paul Getty, Aristotle Onassis, and J. Paul Getty, as he wondered, "What have these three ungenerous superheroes ever done to justify the demands they make upon our attention?"[24] On another occasion while insulting the rich, he labeled Howard Hughes as "the most boring man in the world" and Aristotle Onassis as "very boring."[25]

Capote's short portraits of directors Charlie Chaplin and John Huston, which were published in *Observations*, illuminate his understanding of the travails of the cinematic arts. Filmmaking's collaborative nature bears the potential to destroy a director's vision, but Capote's homage to Chaplin characterizes him as a giant stepping over these pitfalls: "One father to a baby is nature's requirement; the necessity of collaborative seeding is the oddity-making curse of film-art, that blasted heath upon which few giants, and as few middling grown men, stride: those who do, all honor to them" (*O* 18). Of Chaplin's *Limelight* (1952) he exclaimed in a letter to his high school English teacher Catherine Wood, "I loved it."[26] Capote collaborated with John Huston on *Beat the Devil* and labeled him one of the "people I really like."[27] In a portrait that leads to an exploration of the director's preferred themes, Capote celebrated Huston's talent and larger-than-life personality:

> Huston's stylized person—his riverboat-gambler's suavity overlaid with rough-neck buffooning, the hearty mirthless laughter that rises toward but never reaches his warmly crinkled and ungentle eyes . . . all intended as much for his own benefit as that of his audience, to camouflage a refrigerated void of active feeling, for, as is true of every classic seducer, or charmer if you prefer, the success of the seduction depends upon himself never feeling, never becoming emotionally inserted: to do so would mean forfeiting control of the situation, the "picture"; thus, he is a man of obsessions rather than passions, and a romantic cynic who believes that all endeavor, virtuous or evil or simply plodding, receives the same honorarium: a check in the amount of zero. (*O* 10)

Truly, as Capote demonstrates in this portrait, this theme carries across many of Huston's films: the worthless treasure of *The Maltese Falcon* (1941), the lost fortune of *The Treasure of the Sierra Madre* (1948), through to the end of his career with the hollow dénouements of *Prizzi's Honor* (1985) and *The Dead* (1987).

Despite his praise for individual stars, Capote maligned acting and its practitioners as a whole, glibly stating: "all actors are liars, I've never met one that wasn't" (*DB* 153). In addition to questioning their honesty, he insulted the collective intelligence of actors, selecting John Gielgud as the epitome of the profession's vacuity: "But the trouble with most actors (*and* actresses) is that they are dumb. And, in many instances, the dumbest are the most

gifted. Sir John Gielgud, the kindest man alive, an incomparable techni-
cian, brilliant voice; but, alas, all his brains are in his voice" (*DB* 414). Holly
Golightly expresses a similar sentiment in *Breakfast at Tiffany's*, explaining
why she rejects the siren song of a Hollywood career: "I knew damn well I'd
never be a movie star. It's too hard; and if you're intelligent, it's too embarrassing" (*BT* 38). Insulting actors became part of Capote's shtick for his
many television appearances, notably when conversing about the stupidity
of stars with Johnny Carson on *The Tonight Show*, with his parallel assertion
that intelligent actors were poor at their craft. Capote repeated his taunts
of Brando: "He's so dumb it makes your skin crawl." Carson attempted to
defend the collective intelligence of actors, asserting that Jill St. John reportedly had a genius-level IQ, but Truman simply agreed with him: "Yes, she's
a rotten actress." (At this point Carson jovially conceded the argument: "No
one explained it to me like that before.")[28]

In contrast to his essays and gossip about Hollywood celebrities, Capote's
literary fiction focuses more on his characters' Hollywood aspirations than on
actual celebrities, save for the extensive name dropping of *Answered Prayers*,
where on a single page (15) Capote mentions Marilyn Monroe, Lena Horne,
Marlon Brando, Elvis Presley, James Dean, Montgomery Clift, and a score of
others, in a cavalcade of celebrities that does little to advance the plot. The
primary exception to this pattern is his portrait of Montgomery Clift, also
in *Answered Prayers*. The protagonist P. B. Jones first introduces Clift to the
reader because he has viewed *Red River*, the "cowboy love story . . . that made
[Clift] a 'star'" (*AP* 102). Many years after his sexual liaison with Clift during
the filming of *Indiscretion of an American Wife*, Capote conjured a scene in
which the actor joins Tallulah Bankhead, Dorothy Parker, and others at a dinner party but is so intoxicated (or otherwise incapacitated) that he withdraws
into a catatonic state:

> Clift dropped a cigarette into his untouched bowl of Senegalese soup, and
> stared inertly into space, as if he were enacting a shell-shocked soldier. His
> companions pretended not to notice, and Miss Bankhead continued a mean-
> dering anecdote. . . . While she talked, Miss Parker did something so curious it
> attracted everyone's attention; it even silenced Miss Bankhead. With tears in
> her eyes, Miss Parker was touching Clift's hypnotized face, her stubby fingers
> tenderly brushing his brow, his cheekbones, his lips, chin.
>   Miss Bankhead said: "Damn it, Dottie. Who do you think you are? Helen
> Keller?"

"He's so beautiful," murmured Miss Parker. "Sensitive. So finely made. The most beautiful young man I've ever seen. What a pity he's a cocksucker." Then, sweetly, wide-eyed with little girl naïveté, she said, "Oh. Oh dear. Have I said something *wrong*? I mean, he is a cocksucker, isn't he, Tallulah?"

Miss Bankhead said: "Well, d-d-darlin, I r-r-really wouldn't know. He's never sucked my cock." (*AP* 108–9)

Bankhead's rejoinder ends the scene with humor, but it is nonetheless a devastating portrait of Clift—and, according to Donald Windham, a heavily fictionalized account as well.[29] The actor died in 1966 and so was spared Capote's outing of his sexuality and his addictions, but this scene, coupled with the thinly veiled accounts of high society's misdeeds throughout the novel's surviving chapters, illustrates Capote's determination to expose the secrets of friends and lovers past and present. As Amy Lawrence suggests, in outing Clift as a gay addict, Capote paradoxically erases Clift from this episode: "Capote's story isn't really about Clift at all. Even Clift's sexuality can hardly be said to belong to him. A topic of conversation, subject of speculation, 'his' homosexuality is presented as an obstacle for others."[30] The scene can also be read as Capote's indictment of screen personas, which, in Clift's case, masked his homosexuality so that he could be cast as a sex symbol and leading man. Capote's celebrity persona as an author and socialite allowed him relative candor concerning his homosexuality, whereas the homophobia of Hollywood stardom prohibited Clift from enjoying such freedoms.

As these literary portraits and gossipy snippets about Hollywood stars attest, Capote's candor about the rich and famous played a key part in his identity as a writer and as a celebrity in his own right. In penning belles lettres on figures ranging from Brando to Monroe, he elevated the quality of Hollywood journalism, and as a gadabout celebrity, he increased publicity for himself through his acid assessments of the intelligence and craft of various actors. With appraisals ranging from devastating to fawning, Capote's treatment of stars reveals his seriousness as a writer and his insouciance as a cultural commentator. He exploited both of these roles to maintain his own queer celebrity, as the following section explores.

▶ Capote's Queer Celebrity

Capote attended to his celebrity persona throughout his literary and extraliterary career. After his short story "Miriam" won the 1945 O. Henry Award and Herschel Brickell dubbed him the "most remarkable new talent of the year,"[31] Capote was seen as an up-and-coming writer of his generation in the late 1940s. Acclaim was followed by notoriety due to the dust-jacket photograph of *Other Voices, Other Rooms.* In it Capote reclines languorously with pouty lips and come-hither eyes. Combined with the homosexual themes of the novel, the photograph shocked readers of the time, for the author seemed quietly yet defiantly to be inviting them to join him in decadent pleasures. In a subsequent interview Capote described the photograph as "perfectly innocent," claiming elsewhere, "It was part of my complete naiveté. . . . There was nothing calculated about it at all."[32] He dismissed the public outcry: "When people read the book . . . and realized what the theme was, and coupled that with the picture, the whole thing took on a kind of *outré* peculiar quality that it was never meant to have had."[33] Even when proclaiming his guileless intentions, however, Capote puckishly revealed that he understood how the picture would be received: "I suppose some tiresome people thought I looked depraved—ready for man, woman, or fire hydrant."[34] Quite simply, such protestations appear to be part of Capote's performance of innocence, for he also acknowledged that the scandalous photograph successfully marketed the book. John Malcolm Brinnin remembered Capote's defense of the picture—"It's sold a lot of copies, hasn't it? Been printed in every paper from here to Salt Lake City, hasn't it?"[35]—and it is likewise evident in the various professional and candid photographs taken of him throughout his life that he knew how to pose. In Richard Avedon's assessment, Capote "always thought of photography in the same way he thought of the press, as something to be used for the purposes of public relations. He was very inventive; he always had an idea for every session."[36]

Gossipy accounts quickly made Capote's life the stuff of legend, albeit a legend gilded with artifice, exaggeration, and posturing. Writing of the New Bohemians—his term for the early 1950s writers and gadabouts striking their way into the public eye—Charles Rolo summarized and questioned Capote's insouciant celebrity:

> It has been reported that on one of his trips across the Atlantic, Mr. Capote hired the bridal suite on the *Queen Mary*; that in Italy he was taken for the President's son and, stepping into the role of good-will ambassador, did a power of damage to the Communist party; that after traveling through Spain, he landed in North Africa partially accoutered as a bullfighter (and so on in this vein). The legend contains one ounce of fact to every pound of fancy. And it must be

said—without disrespect to Mr. Capote's talents as a myth maker—that not all of the fancy is pure Capote.[37]

Such coverage kept Capote a topic of gossip even when he was not publicizing his fiction, but, above all other concerns, the financial benefits of hype for selling books sparked Capote's fervent efforts at exposure. For his 1959 collaboration with Richard Avedon, *Observations*, a coffee table book combining Avedon's photographs of Hollywood stars with Capote's prose portraits of them, Capote explicitly advised Avedon on publicity for their venture, briefly observing that "Jack Paar sells books" and concluding sternly, after a litany of detailed instructions, "I know I don't have to emphasize how important these matters are, so buckle down."[38] On another occasion he explained the logistics and benefits of a marketing blitz: "My theory about publishing a book . . . is that everything—the reviews, the interviews, and everything else—has to happen within two weeks of publication. If it's scattered, it's not going to work. But if it all comes together simultaneously, you'll spin right up the list."[39] At the same time, Capote realized that serious artists should not be seen as hucksters of their craft, and he deplored publicity hounds in general ("The most pretentious thing is a person who hires a press agent to get his name in the papers") and Gore Vidal in particular ("Because Gore's books are number one or two on the best-seller list doesn't mean anything. That's because he spends half his life on TV") for seeking the limelight.[40] In a 1963 letter to his friends Alvin and Marie Dewey, he criticized Harper Lee for promoting the film version of her novel *To Kill a Mockingbird*: "our friend Nelle . . . is *so* involved in the publicity for her film (she owns a percentage, that's why; even so, I think it *very undignified* for any serious artist to allow themselves to be exploited in this fashion)."[41] Capote's hypocrisy is virtually palpable in these lines: the master publicist and self-promoter condemns his lifelong friend for engaging in the activities he himself pursues, and which he insists his collaborators likewise undertake.

Several of Capote's literary peers disdained his penchant for celebrity, attempting to discredit his authorial achievements by attacking his hucksterism. Brendan Gill, in his memoir of life at the *New Yorker*, recalled Capote avowing, "A boy must hustle his book," and concluded: "Capote promotes himself as other people promote lipstick or baby powder, with an endearing and profitable assiduity."[42] In a *Paris Review* interview in 1974, Gore Vidal scorned Capote for his attention to fame: "Every writer ought to have at least one thing that he does well and I'll take Truman's word that a gift for publicity is the most glittering star in his diadem."[43] To Vidal, Capote's literary achievements were merely "a public relations campaign masquerading as a career."[44] Mary McCarthy similarly sneered that Capote's "greatest contribution to literary innovation was to publicize the author first, the book second."[45] (Capote avenged himself on McCarthy in *Answered Prayers*, when his narrator P. B. Jones snipes, "Creative females are not often presentable. Look at Mary McCarthy!" [*AP* 15].) Even Capote's allies deplored his need for celebrity. His close friend Slim Keith declared in her autobiography, "Celebrity slowed him down and distracted him from his calling."[46] John Malcolm Brinnin sketched Capote's need for fame as almost an obsession—"More hungry for attention than anyone else, he's learned to bestow what he craves. For recipients, enchantment; for himself, a restless longing for a bigger audience"—and once asked Capote, "How are you going to hide yourself in fame long enough to remind yourself who you are? As far as I can see, you've achieved a reputation at the cost of a career."[47] Capote responded to such charges with an appeal to the pecuniary advantages of his celebrity: "When the chips are down, what was it but my reputation that could parlay five figures into six?"[48] Tennessee Williams was one of few who appreciated Capote's talent in seeking publicity, complimenting him as "a great self-publicist" due to his "theatrical personality."[49]

Undoubtedly the greatest social achievement of his life, as well as an opportunity for him to unite the worlds of literary arts and Hollywood, Capote's famed Black and White Ball at the Plaza Hotel in New York on November 28, 1966, commemorated the successful publication of *In Cold Blood*. "Katherine Graham, head of the family that owned *The Washington Post* and *Newsweek*, was to be the guest of honor," David Grafton wrote. "Truman's selection of the publishing magnate . . . was just one more example of his genius for publicity."[50] Truly, Capote orchestrated the media coverage of *In Cold Blood* and the Black and White Ball masterfully. His sedulous attention to publicity led writers at the *New York Times* to marvel at and to lament his marketing chutzpah: William D. Smith referred to *In Cold Blood* as "one of the greatest promotional successes in publishing history," and Eliot Fremont-Smith railed against the "vast, self-generating promotional mill in which everyone—author, publisher, magazine editor, critic, bookseller and reader—is trapped."[51] As with his literary efforts, the cross-pollination between art and hyping art demanded Capote's detailed attention to his creation's public reception, and Leo Lerman described the event as equivalent in its aesthetic pitch to Capote's literature: "The ball was one of his major works. As much a major work as some of his short stories."[52]

In choosing the theme of the Black and White Ball, Capote paid homage to his friend Cecil Beaton's designs for *My Fair Lady* (dir. George Cukor, 1964), as Katharine Graham recalled: "He told me that he'd always loved the black-and-white scene at the racetrack in *My Fair Lady*."[53] With its thematic allusion to the world of cinema, Capote infused his literary celebration with a Hollywood panache also evident in his guest list, which included such stars as Audrey Hepburn, Lauren Bacall, Frank Sinatra, Shirley MacLaine, Henry Fonda, Vivien Leigh, and Claudette Colbert.[54] Capote increased the publicity surrounding the ball to a fever pitch by openly mulling his guest list. As Deborah Davis avers, "Columnists were on the lookout for the big story of the 1966 social season, and Truman's ball had all the right ingredients: mystery (who would be invited?), glamour (the masquerade theme), drama (the frenzied preparations), and, finally, spectacle (the evening itself)."[55] After the ball, Capote denied that it reflected any desire for media attention, claiming artlessly, "It was just what it set out to be. . . . I just wanted to give a party for my friends."[56] The subsequent release of the guest list to the press, which humiliated numerous celebrities and socialites who claimed to have been invited but were not, led many to doubt his protestations of innocence, as this final bit of scandal produced yet more publicity weeks after the party. Indeed, the Black and White Ball metamorphosed into such a cultural watershed that, one year later, a cover story in the December 1967 *Esquire* headlined "We wouldn't have come even if you *had* invited us, Truman Capote!" featured Jim Brown, Kim Novak, Tony Curtis, Pat Brown, Ed Sullivan, Pierre Salinger, Lynn Redgrave, and Casey Stengel publicly consuming their sour grapes over Capote's snubbing.

Beyond his high-profile lifestyle as an author, Capote kept himself in the public eye through numerous appearances on television talk and variety shows. The hosts of such programs appreciated Capote's appearances, as they often created publicity for the shows themselves with Capote's brash performance of his queer celebrity, which mixed quick wit with trash talk about various stars. During an appearance on David Susskind's *Open End* in 1959 when he shared the stage with Dorothy Parker and Norman Mailer, Capote uttered his devastating assessment of Jack Kerouac's and other Beat writers' fiction: "What they do . . . isn't writing at all—*it's typing*."[57] Despite her reputation as an acerbic wit, Parker was rather silent during the program, with Capote and Mailer exchanging assessments of various authors. After Capote complimented E. M. Forster as the greatest living writer, Mailer interjected, "I must say, I find Mr. Capote here *far* the more exciting writer. He excites me far more," to which Capote, in reply, put his face in his hands and laughed.[58] Mailer, after viewing this program, commented on Capote's performance: "Capote did not look small on the show, but large! His face, in fact, was extraordinary, that young-old face, still pretty and with such promise of oncoming ugliness; that voice, so full of snide rustlings and unforgiving nasalities; it was a voice to knock New York on its ear. The voice had survived; it spoke of horrors seen and passed over; it told of judgments that would be merciless."[59] As Janet Winn wrote in her review of the program, "Mr. Capote's weird good looks are well enough known to readers of his book jackets; his voice and inflections are, similarly, a little terrifying. . . . Mr. Capote may *look* effete, but he is not: his mind is vigorous and extremely able."[60]

As much as interviews allowed Capote to embrace the limelight, he could not fully control the ensuing discussions, as when Groucho Marx upstaged him in a 1971 episode of *The Dick Cavett Show*, to the extent that Cavett ironically queried, "Do you feel that Truman is dominating the conversation?"[61] In a moment of clarity, Capote proclaimed that writers should avoid alcohol to preserve their craft—"I don't think anyone can write when they're drinking"—but the conversation took a queer turn when Marx encouraged Capote to marry for the accompanying tax benefits: "Truman, have you ever thought of getting married and splitting the tax?" Capote, obviously nonplussed by Marx's apparent ignorance of his homosexuality, countered, "Well, you find someone for me to marry, and I'll consider it, okay?" Marx gamely replied, "I would marry you in a minute, if you would write another hit book like you did about Kansas. Will you consider this an engagement?" Marx's rhetorical ploy was brilliant, for in appearing to overlook Capote's homosexuality, he prepared the audience for a final titillating line: "I can't give you what you're entitled to . . . ," a euphemistic but clear reference to sex, from which Cavett pivoted to a commercial break.

Johnny Carson, famed host of *The Tonight Show*, invited Capote to appear on his program many times, for Carson knew that Capote would be amusing, if at times rather cruel. Capote's feud with Jacqueline Susann, the sensationalist author of *Valley of the Dolls* (1966) and *The Love Machine* (1969), began on Carson's program when he said she looked like a "truck driver in drag."[62] She threatened to sue, but Capote responded acerbically, "She was told she had better drop that lawsuit because all they had to do is bring ten truck drivers into court and put them on the witness stand and you've lost your case."[63] On the episode of *The Tonight Show* airing November 27, 1973, when he shared the stage with Carl Reiner, the Lennon Sisters, and Jerry van Dyke, Carson introduced Capote as a "writer and conversationalist of the first quality." When Capote entered the stage yo-yoing, Carson deadpanned: "Here I say one of the finest, distinguished writers, and you come out with a yo-yo." Their conversation, in which Reiner joined, ranged over a variety of topics, with Capote weighing in on censorship—"You cannot define pornography, and therefore you cannot censor it"—discussing his uncomfortable travels on the Orient Express, and detailing his recent appearance on the *Sonny and Cher Comedy Hour*. He also commented on several celebrities, again deriding the intelligence of John Gielgud (and of Laurence Olivier as well) and offering a scathing assessment of Marlon Brando: "you cannot get dumber than Marlon Brando . . . he's got great sensibility and no sense." From his yo-yoing entrance to his insulting of various celebrities, Capote played his role of the queer gadabout to perfection—eccentric, candid to the point of rudeness, but always amusing.

The tables were turned on Capote—the taunter became the taunted—when he appeared as the guest of honor on a *Dean Martin Celebrity Roast* in 1974. For this program Martin featured a Man or Woman of the Week whom the various guest stars mocked good-naturedly, and the celebrities roasting Capote included Ted Knight, Audrey Meadows, Donald O'Connor, Rich Little, Joseph Wambaugh, Rocky Graziano, Jean Simmons, and Foster Brooks. Many of the jokes centered on Capote's sexuality. Knight painted an ironic portrait of Capote as a heterosexual lothario, intoning, "Truman Capote is the biggest stud in Hollywood," and then suggesting with lascivious eyes, "Yes, as every leading lady in Hollywood knows, Truman Capote is not only a literary giant . . . ," trailing off to leave the audience surmising the size of Capote's genitals. In contrast, Audrey Meadows, channeling the persona of an editor of the *Saturday Review of Literature*, teased Capote about his gender identity: "He is living proof that in America, you can grow up to be anything that you want. And as a boy, Truman wanted to be Bette Davis." Joseph Wambaugh likewise needled Capote about his effeminacy: "I haven't heard such tributes to a man's background since I left the vice squad . . . . . I respect Truman Capote. In my opinion, he's the greatest male literary

FIG. 1 *Dean Martin Celebrity Roast*: Host Dean Martin with Capote. During the program Capote suffered numerous good-natured barbs from such stars as Ted Knight, Audrey Meadows, Donald O'Connor, and Rich Little, until he turned his appearance to good advantage to sell his book.

figure since Jacqueline Susann." Ever the salesman, Capote accepted the ribbing in good spirits, and his final words to the audience, "If you people had any sense at all, you'd have turned your sets off long ago and started reading my new book, *The Dogs Bark*," revealed the pecuniary motives of appearing on the program.[64]

Capote's more ridiculous television appearances include his performance as Captain Bligh on *The Sonny and Cher Comedy Hour*. He also appeared in the pilot episode of *The Sonny Comedy Revue* in 1974, in a skit in which he played Herb Parns, a daredevil in a yellow jumpsuit and red plastic helmet in an obvious parody of Evel Knievel. Throughout the skit Capote hams up his southern roots to comic effect. "You know how it is with us ole southern boys," he drawls, as Bono, in the role of the interviewer Teddy, asks Parns why he undertakes his daredevil act of getting into a box packed with dynamite. Capote/Parns replies, "Aw shucks, Teddy, it's just that I—" as he then twitches and jerks in imitation of a crude redneck speech impediment, "I'm trying to commit suicide." The skit is not particularly funny, but it showcases Capote's "playing southern" to garner media attention, mocking his southern roots to signify his dismissal of the region.

In another moment of lowbrow humor, Capote appeared as a celebrity panelist along with Jill St. John on *The Cheap Show* (1978), a game show hosted by Dick Martin of *Rowan and Martin's Laugh-In* fame. The show's format involved posing obscure and outrageous questions to the celebrity panelists, who would offer opposing witty answers, only one of which was correct; the contestants opted for the celebrity's answer they found most convincing.

The Cheap Show focused less on trivia and prizes than on celebrity banter, as when Capote flirted with a contestant who was a vice squad officer: "I have a funny feeling I've seen this guy before, vice squad or not." The closing credits of the program caution, "The celebrities have been furnished with questions; answers are provided which may or may not be used," which underscores its reliance on celebrities and humor over knowledge and competition.[65] Chris Bearde, the producer of *The Cheap Show*, recalled Capote's time on the set, for which Capote brought an ample supply of vodka and orange juice and slept—or passed out—for large amounts of time: "He's Truman. What can you do? Do you think he'll be brilliantly funny if I wake him up? He'll probably tell us to all go and fuck ourselves."[66]

Television appearances such as these bestowed upon Capote the publicity he craved, but they came at a cost to his literary reputation. Capote's friend Peter Beard asserted that Capote's huckstering of himself detracted from his vision of himself as an artist: "He'd had a lot of very successful Johnny Carson shows, and he realized that the audience responded to him because it was the Johnny Carson show, not because of his writing."[67] For the author hoping to increase his readership, such moments revealed the paradox of his queer celebrity: fame kept him in the public eye, but often for reasons other than his literary talents. A homosexual playing the bitchy queen and insulting other celebrities may have been amusing, but such performances did little to enhance the critical reception of Capote's literature; on the contrary, they contributed to the perception of him as fundamentally trivial.

Given his infamous appearances on various television programs, Capote considered undertaking a talk show of his own throughout his career, again demonstrating his continued attention to exploiting his celebrity persona. He approached his friend John Malcolm Brinnin with a concept for a television program, albeit one that never reached the airwaves: "What would you say to the idea that you and I work up a television series?—poets reading and talking about themselves. . . . I'm thinking of something with a special angle, visually. Remember that old Carl Dreyer movie about Joan of Arc? The one where what's-her-name [Maria Falconetti] carries the whole thing in close-ups? The camera stays on her face like a microscope and you get this feeling that just one lifted eyebrow's as full of action as a battle scene."[68] If Capote was serious about this plan, it is not surprising that it failed to come to fruition. Dreyer's riveting close-ups of Falconetti in *The Passion of Joan of Arc* (1928) bring a sense of searing emotion to his film, but sustaining this level of heightened feeling in weekly interviews with poets would be exhausting for hosts, poets, and viewers alike. Toward the end of his life in the early 1980s, Capote was involved in discussions to host a talk show on cable television with Joanne Carson, Johnny's second wife who divorced him in 1972, but these efforts never gained traction.[69]

Thanks to his fame and queerly witty persona, Capote was cast in Neil Simon's murder-mystery farce *Murder by Death* (dir. Robert Moore, 1976), which featured a truly all-star cast. Capote played the mysterious Lionel Twain, a fan of detective fiction who summons parodic versions of famous sleuths to his estate to punish them for their outlandish plots and too-clever-by-far solutions. In Simon's hands, Agatha Christie's Hercule Poirot becomes Milo Perrier (James Coco); Jane Marple transforms into Jessica Marbles (Elsa Lanchester), accompanied by her nurse (Estelle Winwood); Dashiell Hammett's Nick and Nora Charles metamorphose into Dick and Dora Charleston (David Niven and Maggie Smith); Hammett's Sam Spade becomes Sam Diamond (Peter Falk), who is accompanied by Tess Skeffington (Eileen Brennan); and Earl Derr Biggers's Charlie Chan is reimagined as Sidney Wang (Peter Sellers), who travels with his son Willie (Richard Narita). Capote's participation in a Simon vehicle reveals a dash of hypocrisy, for he denigrated Simon's talents in a 1973 interview with Andy Warhol: "Neil Simon can write 500 million plays that'll be successes forever and forever, but he will never write a work of art . . . because there is no mystery there. It's simply a formula. That he manipulates and maneuvers around one way or another until there's no mystery to it."[70] Still, Capote also expressed appreciation for some of Simon's plays: Charles McAtee recalled Capote describing *The Odd Couple* as "wonderful," and Capote himself affirmed it was "*very* funny."[71] Also, in a 1975 interview, he described *Murder by Death* as "a great comedy script."[72]

Although Capote claimed that "Neil Simon wrote [the role of Lionel Twain] for me," Simon refuted this assertion, insisting that the film's producer selected Capote because of the author's status as a celebrity: "Truman was the last person I would have thought of for the part of the mystery aficionado. On the other hand, Ray Stark, the producer, was always looking for publicity, perfectly willing to sacrifice the part and hire someone like Truman. . . . He was a great raconteur; we all know how funny he could be on his own, but he got stuck when he had lines to say."[73] Capote's catty commentary on talk shows did not translate well into portraying a character on

FIG. 2 *Murder by Death*: Publicity photo of Capote as criminal mastermind Lionel Twain with, from left to right, Elsa Lanchester (as Jessica Marbles), Estelle Winwood (Nurse Withers), Peter Falk (Sam Diamond), David Niven (Dick Charleston), Maggie Smith (Dora Charleston), and James Coco (Milo Perrier).

film, and his performance is indeed wooden, as he delivers his lines with mechanical venom. As director Robert Moore concluded, "To put Capote at a table with international stars was too much of a test for any literary figure to withstand. It's like saying, 'Wouldn't it be great to get [the President of the United States] to play the President of the United States?' The answer is 'No.'"[74]

Murder by Death exploits Capote's queer celebrity, playing on lisping homosexual stereotypes even in the character's name, Lionel Twain, which puns on the children's toy Lionel Trains. (This joke continues with the street address of the millionaire's remote manor as 22 Twain, which Sidney Wang pronounces, with a stilted Chinese accent, as "too-too twain.") When the detectives first meet Twain, he purrs, "Good evening, ladies and gentlemen. I'm your host, Lionel Twain." The shot captures a hand in an armchair pressing a button, which unleashes a strobing uproar of lighting in various hues, accompanied by music that is disorienting until it resolves into a harsh twang. Jessica Marbles exclaims, "Good God, what an entrance!" and Twain replies, with queer modesty, "Oh, a bit theatrical, Miss Marbles, but I do so love an illusion." When Sam Diamond comments on Twain's youthful appearance despite the character's seventy-six years, Twain rhapsodizes on his narcissism and the requirements for maintaining his youthful glow: "How do I look so young? A complete vegetable diet, twelve hours of sleep a night, and lots and lots of makeup." Twain's queerness is also evident in his distaste for women. When Dora Charleston questions Twain's foretelling of the murder that the detectives have been summoned to solve—"I know it's none of my business, but doesn't that mean you're the murderer, Mr. Twain?"—Capote/Twain responds dismissively and misogynistically, "No wives. I refuse to discuss this with wives," turning aside as if he cannot bear to even look at a woman.

Lionel Twain's queerness corresponds with Capote's homosexuality, and Capote's success as an author likewise aligns him with the character he plays. Twain's desire for revenge stems not from some long-forgotten misdeed of the past, a clichéd trope in many mystery novels, but in his desire for coherent plotting in fiction. When he reveals his identity to the detectives, removing the mask that disguised him as the butler Bensonmum (Alec Guinness), he excoriates his guests for their faulty plotting: "You've all been so clever for so long, you've forgotten to be humble. You've tricked and fooled your readers for years, you've tortured us all with surprise endings that made no sense. You've introduced characters in the last five pages that were never in the book before! You've withheld clues and information that make it impossible for us to guess who did it. . . . When the world learns I've outsmarted you, they'll be selling your dollar-ninety-five books for twelve cents." An appealing poetic justice arises with an esteemed author in real life delivering these lines, even if his acting pales in comparison to the rest of the company. Despite his hammy acting, Capote's sexual and literary convergences with the character make him an apt choice for the role of Lionel Twain.

Praising his performance in *Murder by Death*, Capote professed his acting skills with typical brio, yet with tongue firmly in cheek: "The original intent may have been for me to parody myself, but that's not how it's going to work out. How am I as an actor? Let's just say this, 'What Billie Holiday is to jazz, what Mae West is to tits . . . what Seconal is to sleeping pills, what King Kong is to penises, Truman Capote is to the great god Thespis!'"[75] Such exaggerated posturing could not shield Capote from harsh reviews, such as Vincent Canby's assessment: "Mr. Capote is possibly acting, but it looks more as if he's giving us an over-rehearsed impersonation of himself as people see him on unrehearsed TV talk shows."[76] Capote also self-deprecatingly proclaimed, "If they say I'm a lousy actor, who cares? Whoever said I was a good actor? That isn't the area where my vanity lies."[77] In a more restrained tone during his self-interview in "Nocturnal Turnings," Capote commented that, through his experiences with *Murder by Death*, he came to realize the challenges of acting: "I'm not an actor; I have no desire to be one. I did it as a lark; I thought it would be amusing, and it was fun, more or less, but it was also hard work. . . . the critics gave me a bouquet of garlic. But I expected that; . . . Actually, I was adequate" (*MC* 251). Capote also suggested that financial considerations influenced his decision to participate, claiming that he "did it for the moola—and to satisfy that clown side [of him] that's so exasperating" (*MC* 258).[78] Nonetheless, he was nominated for a 1977 Golden Globe for the male category of Best Acting Debut in a Motion Picture, losing to Arnold Schwarzenegger for *Stay Hungry*. A particular pleasure from the experience arose for Capote in the hope that his archrival Gore Vidal would be jealous: "Gore Vidal must be dying."[79]

In addition to *Murder by Death*, Capote appeared or almost appeared in several other films. In a 1950 letter to Cecil Beaton he mentioned, "Another strange thing: Orson Welles asked me to play a part in a movie he is going to make here. Naturally I declined."[80] He was shot in a street scene for *The Light Touch* (dir. Richard Brooks, 1952), but the producer objected, "Isn't that Truman Capote? You can't use him! Cut him out!"[81] Already famous for being famous in the early 1950s, Capote generated interest from filmmakers, yet his appearances in film, however fleeting, would undermine the suspension of disbelief necessary for viewers to enter the narrative due to the very fact that he was already famous. Capote plays himself in an unbilled cameo role in Woody Allen's *Annie Hall* (1977), in a scene in which Alvy Singer (Woody Allen) and Annie Hall (Diane Keaton) sit on a bench in Central Park and crack jokes about the various passersby. A man wearing a pink jacket is dubbed Mr. Miami Beach, and when two gay men walk by, one wearing white jeans and the other in very short jean shorts, Alvy intones, "that's hilarious . . . they're back from Fire Island." An imposing figure strides past, who they agree must be a member of the Mafia, and then Alvy announces, "There's the winner of the Truman Capote Look-Alike Contest," as Capote himself ambles across their path. Capote wears a cream fedora, gray suit, and red bow tie, and holds a book in his hand. Perhaps what is most surprising about Capote's appearance in the film is that viewers cannot really ascertain that this figure is indeed Capote; shot at medium range, Capote is too distant to identify definitively as himself.

Capote's queer celebrity was in many ways a shield, but when the shield fell, all of his demons emerged for public consumption. As alcoholism and drug abuse took over his life throughout the 1970s and until his death in 1984, he made public appearances when he was physically and mentally incapable of functioning, such as when he was removed from a speaking engagement at Towson State University after drunkenly declaring, "I'm going to read you something I like and if you don't like it, the hell with you."[82] A more widely viewed incident occurred on July 18, 1978, when he appeared on *The Stanley Siegel Show*, a local New York City program. He was obviously incapacitated during the interview, with his head rolling, his mouth open, and his eyes staring off, as he grimaced and opened and closed his eyes, with perspiration visible on his face. "I haven't actually been to bed in forty-eight hours," he declared through slurred words as the interview began. When Siegel asked with concern, "When was the last time you've been to bed?" Capote managed a witty rejoinder: "With whom?" Capote also mused on the challenges of his life, "My life is so strange; it's not like anybody's." Siegel offered to stop the interview, but Capote insisted that they continue, despite his evident discomposure, as they discussed his problems with addiction. When Siegel confronted Capote about his addictions—"You have had a history of alcoholism"—Capote replied, "Alcoholism is the least of it." In a particularly poignant exchange, Siegel asked Capote, "What do you care about?" to which Capote blankly answered, "Well, that's a really good question. I'm beginning to wonder myself." When Siegel asked what would happen to him in the future, Capote candidly mumbled: "The obvious answer is that eventually I'll kill myself, without meaning to." After Siegel ended the interview, he called it "heartbreaking" and "one of the damnedest shows we've seen in a long time."[83] The interview in many ways mirrors Capote's depiction of Montgomery Clift's drug-addled incoherence in *Answered Prayers*. As his editor Joseph Fox lamented, "over and over again at lunch during the last six years of his life . . . he was often almost incoherent because of drugs or alcohol or both" (*AP* xxi). The exposure of Clift's addictions and homosexuality adhered to Capote's narrative goals in *Answered Prayers*, as he revealed many of his friends' sordid secrets in this text, creating a firestorm of publicity but also a backlash in which many of his society friends ostracized him; a bitter irony emerged as he publicly suffered for failings that mirrored Clift's.

In light of Capote's reliance on the media to maintain his celebrity status, it is perhaps surprising that he often professed ambivalence concerning his fame: "It all depends on whether you think fame is an asset or a hindrance in an artistic career. I feel rather indifferent about the whole thing, but then, I've been in public life over twenty years now, and you become neutral about publicity," he proclaimed in a 1968 *Playboy* interview.[84] When *Mademoiselle*'s interviewers posed the question whether his public image was his creation, he denied, in a world-weary tone, that he controlled his celebrity: "Not exactly. There's a certain point where a celebrity image starts to be self-perpetuating. It's like a stone you sink in the sea where the shells and barnacles attach to it until you don't know the truth yourself."[85] His response achieves a surprising poignancy, as he confesses that he has lost himself in the miasma of his celebrity. With more insouciant flair, Capote also professed to David Frost (in a witticism often attributed to Dorothy Parker), "I don't care what anybody says about me as long as it isn't true."[86] Here his words reveal a core truth of celebrity culture: words spoken about a famous person are often more important than truths told, for chatter is more conducive to continued attention than silence. Summarizing his sense of his celebrity, Capote commented on himself in a *Rolling Stone* article by Jann Wenner: "I always attracted a lot of attention, because—well, really— there really isn't anybody else like me,"[87] a striking declaration of his uniqueness both arrogant and modest, yet certainly cognizant of the limelight's benefits to his career. And truly this sword cut both ways, for as much as Capote's fame redounded to his benefit, it also detracted from his identity as an artist.

His queer celebrity and his close associations with Hollywood stars through friendships and filmmaking placed Capote in the public eye throughout his career. In assessing the potentially dire consequences of fame, Capote likened it to poison: "Somebody asked me about a year ago what am I famous for, and I said, 'I'm famous for being famous.' You know? That's one way people can be destroyed. I've always been famous for being famous; but at the same time, I was aware of it. So therefore it didn't affect me, and it wasn't the poisonous thing that it is. It's a subtle kind of poison, and people don't realize when it starts."[88] Capote pronounced himself impervious to fame's poison in this passage, as he also suggested that most people never feel its effects until it is too late to save themselves. It is difficult, when one considers Capote's downward spiral into drugs and addiction from the 1970s until his death, not to believe that he failed to perceive fame's subtle poison coursing through his veins. Capote's theme in *Answered Prayers*, that more tears are shed over answered prayers than unanswered ones, finds a striking echo in plaintive words he attributed to Elizabeth Taylor: "What do you suppose will become of us? I guess, when you find what you've always wanted, that's not where the beginning begins, that's where the end starts."[89] Capote's queer celebrity as a writer, conversationalist, gossip, and publicity hound, pursued so relentlessly throughout his life, brought him wealth, fame, and prestige yet never, it appears, peace.

Scriptwriter for the Stars ▶ Capote's Screen Adaptations of *Indiscretion of an American Wife*, *Beat the Devil*, and *The Innocents*

Long before he penned his first screenplay, Capote rewrote films spontaneously and exuberantly, employing his quick wit and ear for dialogue to amuse his friends when they found themselves bored with a picture playing on the screen. As many dissatisfied filmgoers have discovered, a tedious film can produce ready pleasures if one rewrites and redubs it while viewing it, and Capote enjoyed such pastimes throughout his teen years. His friend Phoebe Pierce Vreeland reminisced about their high school excursions to the cinema: "As we sat there, we would rewrite the movies at the top of our voices, screaming with laughter: 'She should have said . . .' 'He should have said . . .' 'Well, he's hopeless anyway, but if he had only said . . .' It was awful, I mean, from the point of view of the Pickwick [Theater]. 'Out!' We were thrown out of the Pickwick more often than the dust."[1] Such an inauspicious beginning could not foretell the depth of screenwriting's influence on Capote's career, yet even at the beginning of his literary endeavors he aligned himself with the film industry, proclaiming on his application for a fellowship to the artists' colony Yaddo to have "read manuscripts for a motion-picture office."[2] Along with the pseudobiographical tidbits suggesting that he had "written speeches for a third-rate politician, danced on a river boat, [and] made a small fortune painting flowers on glass," the authorial blurb for *Other Voices, Other Rooms* reiterates this claim of script reading to create a Bohemian image of

Capote in which the cinematic world serves as yet another sign of his preco-cious talents and varied interests.[3] Furthermore, as explored in chapter 1, Capote's writing is often cinematic in its vision, which explains why film-makers turned to him at various stages throughout his career.

Despite the cinematic sympathies evident in his writing and the screen-plays he penned throughout his career, Capote on several occasions expressed his dissatisfaction with the screenwriter's art in particular and filmmaking in general. Primarily he rejected the cooperative nature of such endeavors, finding that he lost the "true gratification of writing" throughout the process: "The only obligation any artist can have is to himself. . . . That's why it's so absolutely boring to write a film script. The great sense of self-obligation doesn't enter into it because too many people are involved. . . . I must admit that in a peculiar way I enjoyed [writing film scripts], but the true gratification of writing was completely absent; the obligation was to produc-ers and the actors . . . and not to myself."[4] As Capote and countless other screenwriters have learned, directors often sacrifice writers' artistic visions to their own. Indeed, in *Observations* Capote quotes John Huston as saying, "I became a director because I couldn't watch any longer how my work as a writer was ruined," acknowledging that, to be in control of one's story in the cinematic world, one must sit in the director's chair (*O* 10). Capote, although he did not aspire to directing, voiced a sentiment similar to Huston's in a 1957 interview: "I don't think a writer stands much chance of imposing himself on film unless he works in the warmest rapport with the director or is himself the director."[5] Beyond the ways in which virtually any writer's vision can be overshadowed by the director's, midcentury Hollywood severely restricted films that might evince a queer sensibility, further crimping Capote's style. Harry Benshoff and Sean Griffin explain these circumstances: "queer writers, including Tennessee Williams, William Inge, and Truman Capote, came to Hollywood to oversee or collaborate on films adapted from their plays and novels, but . . . their input was still hampered by the Production Code and Hollywood's formulaic heterocentrism."[6] Capote, who so daringly portrayed homosexuality in *Other Voices, Other Rooms*, was hampered in his freedom to write film scripts by the corporate and moral concerns of Hollywood and its censors. Queer themes nonetheless emerge in his screenplays, but in a more submerged fashion than in his fiction.

As much as Capote braved the challenges of screenwriting throughout his career, he repeatedly privileged his literary endeavors over his cinematic ones. Quite simply, writing fiction represented an art of the highest calling and the highest challenge for him, whereas he casually dismissed the art of screenwriting, deriding it as a simple process of construction for one sufficiently gifted to write credible dialogue: "The only thing that's easy for me to write is film scripts. There's a reason why. You assume you can write dialogue, take that for granted. The thing that's difficult about screenwriting . . . is it's all construction. Once you have the thing constructed in your mind, scene by scene, how it will open and how it will end, the problem's solved."[7] In sum, Capote found much of screenwriting and filmmaking to be tedious, mechanical, and exhausting; worse, it distracted him from his literary efforts. In mid-1953, the hectic year witnessing the production of *Indiscretion of an American Wife* and *Beat the Devil*, Capote wrote to his friend Mary Louise Aswell of his distaste for screenwriting: "I loathe writing for films—the fact that it is undermining is no mere myth. I think the bit I've done so far has done me a certain kind of good (though neither of the pictures is any good at all—but that isn't what I mean)—but that is as far as it should go."[8]

Capote's dismissal of his 1953 pictures has proved premature: *Indiscretion of an American Wife*, notwithstanding its many production difficulties, unites, improbably yet hauntingly, Italian neorealism with Hollywood stars in a story of adultery, loss, and longing, and *Beat the Devil* enjoys a cult following appreciative of its quirky mix of international intrigue and domestic betrayal, as told in Capote's snappy dialogue. Of Capote's screenplays, his masterpiece is undoubtedly *The Innocents*, a 1961 adaptation of *The Turn of the Screw* that chillingly captures Henry James's unsettling tale of children possessed by the dead. Capote's protean talents illuminate each of these screenplays, which represent distinct cinematic genres and sensibilities. Despite their many differences, they are all recognizably Capotean in their shared concerns with issues of identity, community, sexuality, and love, a mix of themes that Capote imbues with his queer touches.

▶ *Indiscretion of an American Wife*

Vittorio De Sica's *Indiscretion of an American Wife* (1953) tells a simple story: Mary Forbes (Jennifer Jones), a married woman, falls in love with another man, Giovanni Doria (Montgomery Clift), while visiting with relatives in Rome. After anguish and indecision, she realizes she must leave him and return to her family in Philadelphia, but Giovanni finds her at the train station and desperately tries to persuade her to abandon her family for him. Mary's nephew Paul (fourteen-year-old Richard "Dick" Beymer), who brings her luggage to the station, reminds her of her love for her family through his obvious devotion to her. Having presumably departed, Paul loiters around the station so that when Mary wavers in her decision and almost absconds with Giovanni, Paul is there to tacitly remind her of her familial responsibilities. After the lovers share heart-wrenching conversations, a torrid farewell in an empty train car, and a humiliating ordeal when they are caught in flagrante delicto, Mary leaves Giovanni to reunite with her family. Such a minimalist plotline was conceived as a cinematic landmark, one that, producer David O. Selznick believed, would unite Italian neorealist cinema with Hollywood stars and glamour in a prestige production destined for critical acclaim.

Italian neorealism, as Millicent Marcus explains of the genre, favors "a filmmaking approach free of artifice, unhampered by fixed screenplays, inspired by real-life subjects, and resolved to tell the unvarnished truth."[9] Marcia Landy, while cautioning against the formulaic nature of defining a diverse corpus, observes neorealism's investment in such features as "location shooting, the use of nonprofessional actors, the focus on contemporary events and not on the historical past, the loose construction of narration, the intermingling of fiction and nonfiction, and the privileging of marginalized and subaltern groups."[10] Whereas Italian neorealism garnered much critical acclaim for its aesthetic achievements despite austere production values, as well as for its progressive (if sentimental) intervention into social issues of post–World War II Europe, Hollywood productions were carefully scripted, relied on star power, and were always conceived with an interest in their financial viability. These two sensibilities share little common ground aesthetically or commercially, yet in its conception *Indiscretion of an American Wife* was to harmonize them into one film.

Among the many midcentury Italian neorealist masterpieces, including Luchino Visconti's *Ossessione* (1943), Federico Fellini's *The Nights of Cabiria* (1957), and Roberto Rossellini's *Rome, Open City* (1945), Vittorio De Sica's films stand out as esteemed works, particularly *Shoeshine* (1946), *The Bicycle Thief* (1948), *Miracle in Milan* (1951), and *Umberto D* (1952). Bert Cardullo praises the director's achievements: "De Sica . . . aspired to, and frequently achieved, the highest cinematic standards, challenging the audience to respond to his unflinching social insights and psychological portraiture."[11] In the early 1950s these artistic triumphs and his status as a preeminent auteur earned De Sica the attention of Hollywood and particularly of Howard Hughes. At Merle Oberon's house De Sica screened *Umberto D* for such Hollywood heavyweights as Charlie Chaplin and Samuel Goldwyn, but as Chaplin cautioned, De Sica's films were not likely to please an American audience accustomed to Hollywood fare: "De Sica, it's great, a great film. . . . But it won't please the Americans, or very few of them."[12] Nonetheless, in 1952 Selznick expressed interest in joining De Sica to film the story "Stazione Termini," the seed from which *Indiscretion of an American Wife* grew. De Sica realized that compromises would inevitably result from working under Hollywood financing, but his vision of neorealism was sufficiently supple, or so he believed, to accommodate American production styles. De Sica affirmed that neorealism transcends reality in its creation of poetry: "Because neorealism is not shooting films in authentic locales, it is not reality. It is reality filtered through poetry, reality transfigured."[13] This aesthetic creed guided his efforts to create cinematic poetry, albeit in this instance under the aegis of a Hollywood production. For as much as De Sica advocated neorealist principles, he also realized that, to a large extent, all cinematic styles create a necessary world of narrative illusion. From this perspective, he expressed surprise that some viewers of *Indiscretion of an American Wife* expected unvarnished reality, apparently believing the shooting of the film to be a simple exercise in allowing the camera to roll and thereby capturing "real life": "Work on it was very complicated. For some extraordinary reason, many people think that all the scenes shot of the station life were authentic, 'stolen from reality.'"[14]

The screenplay of *Indiscretion of an American Wife* was adapted from the story "Stazione Termini" by Cesare Zavattini, who collaborated with De Sica on numerous projects, including many of his finest. Indeed, Capote declared that Zavattini was "in good measure responsible for the successes of De Sica" (*O* 8) and, on another occasion, pronounced, "Eighty percent of the good Italian movies were made from Zavattini scripts . . . all of the De Sica pictures, for instance. De Sica is a charming man, a gifted and deeply sophisticated person; nevertheless, he's mostly a megaphone for Zavattini, his pictures are absolutely Zavattini's creations."[15] As production of *Terminal Station* continued under Selznick's control and De Sica's direction, an English-speaking screenwriter was needed. Before Capote was hired for the job, several famous authors, including Carson McCullers (*The*

Heart Is a Lonely Hunter, The Member of the Wedding), Paul Gallico (*The Snow Goose, Lou Gehrig, Pride of the Yankees*), and Alberto Moravia (*Time of Indifference, The Conformist*), were enlisted to pen the screenplay.[16] The project frustrated the talents of these esteemed writers, and Selznick then hired Capote, paying him a thousand dollars per week, for "entire redialoguing to our satisfaction in fast time."[17] Selznick wrote to John Huston, with whom Capote would collaborate on *Beat the Devil* later in 1953, and credited the young author with salvaging the project at a time of artistic jeopardy: "I think *Terminal Station* has a chance of being quite an extraordinary picture, despite the difficulties that were imposed upon us by the dates, but the picture, however good, will not be so good as it could have been and should have been had we had just a few weeks longer, because we didn't get into our own stride on the script until we finally got Truman Capote."[18] Capote positively assessed his first screenplay in a letter to his former lover Newton Arvin: "I rewrote the scenario for the new De Sica picture . . . and it had to be finished in 3 weeks, as the picture was already in production. Anyway, the whole experience had its amusing moments, and I think I did a pretty good job, all things considered."[19]

While Capote resolved the difficulties with the script, professional and personal conflicts plagued the filming of *Indiscretion of an American Wife*. Primarily, De Sica and Selznick clashed over their respective visions of the film as an exemplar of Italian neorealism or of Hollywood romance. De Sica complained that Selznick attempted to manage every detail of the production, and so he simply ignored Selznick's advice: "Every day he sent me forty- or fifty-page letters, detailing everything. . . . I stopped reading them and began throwing them away as soon as they arrived. I would agree with everything he said and do things my own way."[20] As Montgomery Clift's biographer Patricia Bosworth tells it, "Selznick wanted the movie to look like a slick little love story, complete with a happy ending. Monty sided with De Sica, who thought the picture should depict a ruined romance." She also records that Clift lambasted Selznick as "an interfering fuckface" for his meddling.[21] With the producer and director arguing over key elements of the film, artistic decisions concerning photography mushroomed into major sparring points. Primarily, De Sica's cinematographer Aldo Graziati preferred long shots of the station and the people bustling about in it, in keeping with the neorealist emphasis on everyday faces, lives, and environments. Selznick, however, brought in his preferred photographer Oswald

Morris to counterbalance Graziati's compositions, instructing him to film Jones and Clift in lush and glamorous close-ups, the better to accentuate both their passion for each other and their sheer beauty. Jones's biographer Paul Green wrote that Graziati's "neo-realistic approach was at odds with Oswald Morris who was hired to shoot close-ups of Jones and Clift with the task of making them appear more glamorous in a style in keeping with Hollywood sensibilities."[22] Morris recalled in his autobiography: "By the time I arrived in Italy, [Selznick] had come to a totally crazy arrangement with De Sica whereby I would photograph anything closer than a full-length figure on the two principals, but [Graziati] would shoot the rest."[23]

Personal altercations and egotistical tantrums also disrupted the film's production. Jennifer Jones, Selznick's protégée and wife, was often upset on the set. Since shooting had to be done in the late evening after the train station closed each day, the filming schedule was grueling. Capote believed that Jones's outbursts were sparked by her attraction to Clift: "Jennifer's got some sort of crush on Monty, and believe it or not she didn't realize that Monty really liked fellows. When she found out she got so upset, she went into the portable dressing room and stuffed a mink jacket down the portable toilet."[24] While not stating the motivation for Jones's behavior, De Sica likewise reported that "she threw her hat in the toilet, so that we had to fish it out because we had only one which she used in every scene in the film."[25] Tensions also flared between Capote and Clift, as the film's line producer Wolfgang Reinhardt observed: "there was some kind of competition going on between Monty and Truman. It was the one personal problem that I knew Monty was having."[26] In a letter to Andrew Lyndon, Capote mentioned his initial dislike of Clift, but then the agreeable resolution to their dispute: "I got started on a great feud with Clift—for six weeks we really loathed each other—but then (this is for your eyes alone!) we suddenly started a sort of mild flirtation, which snowballed along until it reached very tropic climates indeed."[27]

For a film so focused on the heterosexual passion of an adulterous affair, *Indiscretion of an American Wife* contains numerous queer undertones, particularly in its treatment of children, children's sexuality, and maternal desire. The film stages a stark contrast in its depiction of children and sexuality: Mary's daughter Kathy, always offscreen but keenly present in Mary's memories, symbolizes the innocent child for whom Mary must sacrifice her sexual desires, whereas her nephew Paul represents children's curiosity and nascent interest in sexuality. His implied competition with Giovanni to win Mary's affections undermines the cultural fantasy of children's sexual innocence, for his insistent courtship of his aunt carries with it erotic undertones. The film thus vacillates in its treatment of children: Kathy, who is frequently represented by a blank and lifeless mannequin in a souvenir store, regulates her mother's sexuality, and Paul, while he determinedly pursues Mary, also monitors her sexuality by stymying her desire for Giovanni. In a final erotic contradiction, this adolescent boy seeks the type of sexual transgression that he denies her with Giovanni. Children desire Mary as mother and as potential lover, yet her desires for adult passion must be sacrificed to protect these ostensibly innocent children.

Foremost, Mary is torn between her desires as an adulteress and as a mother, and Capote stages numerous scenes dramatizing this plight. Her connection to Kathy is evident in the film's opening sequence when she buys a Sicilian peasant dress for her daughter. When she sits down in the train to commence her journey home, she strokes it gently while Italian children play roughly around her. This compartment scene stages in miniature the conflict between familial and sexual desires that plagues Mary's consciousness throughout the film. Furthermore, it is obvious that the man with whom she shares the compartment is sexually attracted to her: he did not offer the seat next to him to the man who preceded Mary onto the train, and he gazes furtively yet hungrily at her. When Mary leaves the train, a buxom woman walks down the aisle and evokes much vocal male admiration, but, more important, she models for Mary the ways in which a wholesome love for one's family preserves a woman from objectification, as this woman calls out "Mamma" as she enters a compartment and thereby escapes the wolf whistles. Within the refuge of the compartment she shares with her mother, this unnamed female character is preserved from the sexual aggressors surrounding her. This brief scene foreshadows the extended sequence in which Mary tends to a pregnant woman who falls ill in the train station. Toward the close of this plotline, the woman's husband intones, "Always her family. Never her," and this lesson in self-abnegation—a woman must deny herself and her needs to preserve the sanctity of her family—is realized at the film's conclusion when Mary leaves Giovanni for the final time.

For Giovanni to win Mary from her family, a task he ultimately fails to accomplish, he must overcome her love for her daughter and the innocence encoded in her. When he finds Mary at the train station, he urges her to remain in Rome with him, but thoughts of her child compel her to return to America. "Then I thought of Kathy. Her hair. Her sweet little neck. Most of all, her eyes. But it was all in separate pieces, like a puzzle I couldn't put together," she cries, as she concludes, "She's a child—my own—and I can't give her up." In reply, Giovanni stresses his willingness to accommodate the child in their relationship: "Have I ever suggested you should give up Kathy? You know I want her to be with us. You know I want us to be together." Mary then explains that her husband is also a child, one who needs her as much as her daughter does: "He sounded so vulnerable, so—so lost. So like a small boy in the dark, calling over and over, 'Where are you? Where are you? When are you coming home?'" Mary's husband, infantilized yet adult in her description of him, encodes both the innocence of the child, one lost without a maternal figure to protect him, and the sexuality of adulthood, a man who presumably desires his wife's return to enjoy sexual pleasures with her—pleasures that she, in his absence, has pursued with another man.

Upon seeing Giovanni, Mary's determination to return home to her daughter and childlike husband yields to the allure of unrestrained carnality. When the 7:30 p.m. train that was to take her away pulls out of the station, her eyes glimmer with desire and anticipation. Departing with Giovanni for his apartment, Mary gazes upon a Sicilian dress similar to the one that she bought for Kathy in the souvenir store, realizes that she has forgotten it on the train (and that she has thus lost this metaphoric representation of her daughter), and then espies her nephew Paul, who has not yet left the terminal. Giovanni and Paul compete for Mary's affections in a homosocial struggle waged in numerous distrustful glances and suspicious posturings. Adolescent sexuality serves as a pervasive theme in Capote's fiction, particularly in *Other Voices, Other Rooms, The Grass Harp*, and *Breakfast at Tiffany's* (in the novella's backstory of Holly's marriage to Doc Golightly when she was barely fourteen). Complementary to Capote's thematic interest in adolescent sexuality, Selznick sketches the dramatic potential in Paul's erotic attraction to his aunt: "Paul should already have entered puberty . . . and be conscious of and deeply interested in and curious about sex, which won't be dwelled on in the picture but which should be obvious from his age, interests, and reactions."[28] To heighten this sexual competition between man and boy, Clift and Beymer are costumed similarly, with each wearing an overcoat that appears slightly too big for him. Moreover, despite his advantage in years, Clift stands only a few inches taller than Beymer, and

FIG. 3 *Indiscretion of an American Wife*: An intergenerational love triangle,
with Mary Forbes (played by Jennifer Jones) forced to choose between
familial love, represented by her nephew (Richard Beymer), and erotic love,
represented by her adulterous lover (Montgomery Clift). Clift's and Beymer's
similar costuming marks the difficulty of the decision Mary faces.

shots of the two thus visually posit them as equals. Mary latches onto Paul
as a reason to leave Giovanni and return to her family—"I wouldn't have
thought there was a chance of our running into Paul. Yet there he was"—and
Giovanni impulsively slaps her when she tells him goodbye. Paul is horrified
by Giovanni's violence—"I saw it! He hit you, Aunt Mary! He hit you!"—
which allows him to tend to his attractive aunt during a moment of emotional vulnerability.

Paul may appear to be a more sympathetic companion for Mary, but he
cannot compete with Giovanni for her love, for she seeks sexual passion
beyond the chaste affections available to her from her family. Later, after
Mary nurtures the Italian woman who falls ill, she again finds Paul, who is
now eating an apple, biting freely of the fruit so suggestive of human sexuality and illicit knowledge. Mary dismisses her nephew—"I'd like you to go
home now," she says—but she also invites him to visit for Christmas. She
then kisses Paul on the forehead and gently slaps him on the cheek, affectionately reenacting Giovanni's assault on her. As Giovanni physically pun-
ished Mary for choosing her family over her sexuality, she replays this scene
to free herself of the child denying her access to adult sexual pleasures.

After dismissing Paul, and after Giovanni proves his devotion by jumping across the tracks to reach her despite an oncoming train, Mary is again ready to be seduced by Giovanni, and they steal into a deserted train car for a passionate rendezvous. The tryst is staged as a masterpiece of midcentury sexual obfuscation: Jones and Clift are filmed in full dress, but viewers know the characters have consummated their reconciliation because, when their lovemaking is interrupted, Jones whispers in anguished horror, "Giovanni!" and casts down her eyes in shame, while Clift straightens his tie. A necktie in need of realignment was a certain sign of erotic consummation in 1950s cinema; as Leonard Leff trenchantly notes, "straightening one's tie in 1953 was like pulling on one's shorts in 2003."[29] Deepening her sexual humiliation, one of the security guards mugs at Mary childishly through the window in the compartment door, enacting a symbolic revenge for the children whom she has momentarily forgotten in her passion for Giovanni. The two lovers are paraded through the station to the magistrate, and an old man tells a tourist, "They caught them making love," another cinematic euphemism suggesting the obvious while not clearly stating it. As Mary grows worried about the possibility of arrest and ensuing scandal, and as Giovanni grows more aggressive with the officers who apprehended them, the commissioner asks her, "Are you separated from your husband?" to which she replies, "No," while again casting her eyes down in shame. The commissioner then inquires, "Any children?" Mary denies Kathy's existence before confessing the truth in a monosyllabic trajectory from denial to acceptance: "No. Yes. One." As she corrects her falsehood and prepares herself to return to her family, she casts her eyes down yet again. Accepting the necessity of returning to her role as an American housewife in Philadelphia, Mary renounces sexual passion, leaves Giovanni behind, and privileges the needs of others over her own.

The queerness of *Indiscretion of an American Wife* emerges in its depiction of a woman disciplined into sexual submission through the intercession of children, as these avatars of ostensible innocence regulate her desires in service to their own, yet it also arises in Clift's performance, which received mixed reviews from critics. Bosworth feels that Clift "plays the cliché situation (the breakup of two lovers) with drama and urgency and a sense of style. Passion clings to his every move, every gesture, every look,"[30] but the performance is also at times stilted and not entirely convincing, for the role of an Italian professor does not suit him well. Selznick starkly pronounced

FIG. 4 *Indiscretion of an American Wife*: Caught in flagrante delicto, Giovanni Doria (Montgomery Clift) straightens his tie, while Mary Forbes (Jennifer Jones) cowers in embarrassment, with the lighting and shadows indicative of sin, shame, and transgression.

that "the thought of Clift being a professor is funny,"[31] acknowledging the disjunction between the star's American roots and his role. Although his homosexuality was not widely known during his acting career, Clift's film persona plays on the strength of his stunningly good looks while also fashioning a subtler form of Hollywood masculinity. His performances relied less on physical stature and more on brooding introspection, contrasting sharply with the more virile masculinities of such contemporary stars as Humphrey Bogart, John Wayne, and Burt Lancaster. This contrast in masculinity shines through in several of Clift's films, such as *Red River* (1948), in which he costars with Wayne, and *From Here to Eternity* (1953), in which he costars with Lancaster. Furthermore, as Kylo-Patrick Hart posits, "Clift's gay male spectators . . . have been able to use their awareness of the actor's physical appeal, sexual appeal, and personal history to engage in an active search for the gay subtexts and alternative readings offered by the actor's films."[32] Such a quest may be simpler in such films as *The Search* (1948), *Red River*, and *From Here to Eternity*, in which Clift plays characters living in homosocial environments where men support one another despite their conflicts: for example, the mortal combat between Clift's and Wayne's characters that concludes *Red River* peters out when Clift's girlfriend, in desperate exasperation, points out to them that "anyone with half a mind would know you love each other."[33]

In contrast, the torrid heterosexual affair of *Indiscretion of an American Wife* may appear an unlikely site to locate another of Clift's queer performances, yet it should be noted that his character exits the narration emotionally unscathed. After he leaps from Mary's departing train and tumbles roughly on the platform, a passerby inquires if he is hurt, with the question taking on the subtextual meaning of whether he has been hurt emotionally by the loss of his lover, but he simply dusts himself off and intones, "No." Some critics derided Clift's performance because of the actor's homosexuality. In an interview between De Sica and Charles Thomas Samuels, Samuels declared, "Another problem with the film is that Clift doesn't seem too masculine and some of the dialogue, by Capote, doesn't give the right impression either," to which De Sica replied, "Yes, they were both pederasts."[34] The movie's creation relied on the talents of these gay men, yet they serve as convenient scapegoats for its perceived failings.

In the end, two separate movies were made: *Terminal Station*, reflecting De Sica's neorealist vision, and *Indiscretion of an American Wife*, reflecting Selznick's Hollywood sensibility. For the American release of the film, Selznick cut De Sica's version to the bone, and it runs only slightly over an hour, which necessitated that he add an introductory short of pop star Patti Page singing two songs, "Autumn in Rome" and "Indiscretion." These melodies are thematically consistent with the film, even if the short does not organically cohere with it. Selznick told De Sica, "If a comment is made to you that my version is short, you have only to ask the unimaginative people who ask you this, [would they] rather have it better in sixty-four minutes or worse in eighty minutes."[35] In reply to Selznick's aggressive editing of his film, De Sica gamely stated, "I cannot pass judgment. . . . Perhaps Selznick cut a little too much. But one kiss more or less shouldn't make such a difference."[36] In the popular press, reviews were mixed at best. *Time* praised the cinematography—"The camera finds in the terminal . . . a certain metal delight"—yet pilloried the film: "but in almost every other respect *Indiscretion* is, for the gifted men who made it, an indiscretion indeed."[37] Such a mocking turn of phrase appeared so regularly in reviews that Moira Walsh, writing in *America*, confessed its clichéd allure: "As has undoubtedly been remarked elsewhere, this is the indiscretion of a distinguished American producer (David O. Selznick) and a distinguished Italian director (Vittorio De Sica)."[38] Arthur Knight, writing for the *Saturday Review*, derided Jones's and Clift's characters and performances: "We can't feel deeply for people we scarcely know, and well before the film is over Clift and Miss Jones have become simply a singularly ill-matched and uninteresting couple."[39] The reviewer for *Catholic World* likewise lambasted Jones's performance, decrying her "phony dramatics" and her acting "as if there were a bad smell on the set."[40] On the other hand, the reviewer for *Newsweek* praised Clift and Jones—"Two fine performances"—but panned the film's plotline as "flagrantly sentimental [and] melodramatic."[41] With grim equanimity, Philip Hartung, the reviewer for *Commonweal*, deemed that the film "labors hard with only so-so results," suggesting that it "isn't really bad; it's just that we expect so much more from De Sica."[42]

Despite the initial optimism he expressed to Newton Arvin, Capote called the film "lousy" and "a stinker."[43] De Sica, on the other hand, came to believe that his film survived its production difficulties with its allure and aesthetic accomplishments intact: "I must say that I like the film: it is full of faults but it convinces me, even moves me. I would not make it again as I would all my other films."[44] The film remains an extraordinary example of Hollywood cross-pollination with international cinematic sensibilities, and viewing the two resulting versions of the same story—*Indiscretion of an American Wife* and *Terminal Station*—illustrates the ways in which a talented director and a determined producer can compose the same raw footage into films strikingly distinct in tone, atmosphere, and emotion. If, in the end, *Indiscretion of an American Wife* could not suture Italian neorealism and Hollywood glamour into an organic whole, it succeeds in telling its simple story of a woman's conflicting desires for sexual passion and for her family. The contrasting camera styles of Aldo Graziati and Oswald Morris highlight the disparities in aesthetic sensibilities as they also reveal the artistic potential of this ill-fated plan: the stark realism of the terminal station, as populated by two of the most beautiful actors in the world speaking Capote's queer words of desire and regret.

▶ *Beat the Devil*

In a send-up of Humphrey Bogart's hard-boiled fare, such as *The Maltese Falcon* (dir. John Huston, 1941) and *The Big Sleep* (dir. Howard Hawks, 1946), *Beat the Devil* lampoons the dark intrigues of film noir with its breezy style and comic sensibility. The film features four international crooks—Peterson (Robert Morley), O'Hara (Peter Lorre), Ross (Ivor Barnard), and Ravello (Marco Tulli)—who have employed Billy Dannreuther (Humphrey Bogart) to act as their agent in a scheme to steal mineral rights in Africa. This basic premise is coupled with a romantic farce as Gwendolen Chelm (Jennifer Jones) woos Dannreuther, with the high-minded adulteress dreaming of abandoning her husband Harry (Edward Underdown) for her new lover, despite Dannreuther's lack of interest in leaving his wife Maria (Gina Lollobrigida) for her. As Gwendolen and Dannreuther's relationship percolates, Maria in turn increasingly succumbs to Harry's physical allure. These various story lines converge, first in Italy and then in Africa, as Gwendolen's exaggerated claims about her husband spark suspicion and intrigue, with the criminals fearing Harry will reveal their plot to the authorities. The film concludes with the ne'er-do-wells arrested and the marriages restored, with Capote's screenplay rewriting its queer transgressions of normative sexual mores into a tidy conclusion, albeit one that refuses to fully undo the topsy-turviness preceding it.

Prior to Capote's screenplay, John Huston's production of Claud Cockburn's novel *Beat the Devil*, written under the pseudonym James Helvick, encountered numerous problems. Cockburn himself wrote an initial draft of the screenplay and, in a letter to Huston, explained his fidelity to the novel and his primary divergence from it: "The screenplay follows the book closely except for one more divagation, which is that in the screenplay they *actually get to Africa*. . . . It seemed to me, after writing it twice the other way, that this is the best way to get an up-beating climax instead of the diminuendo of the book: deliberate in the book but, I felt, nothing much to look at."[45] This concession to an "up-beating climax," to which Capote's screenplay adheres, gives the screenplay a sense of direction and motion, yet Cockburn's script failed to translate his engaging caper tale into an organic whole. Tony Veiller and Peter Viertel were then enlisted to pen the screenplay, but their draft was likewise deemed unacceptable, despite their prior successes, Veiller with such films as *The Killers* (1946) and *Moulin Rouge* (1952), and Viertel with Alfred Hitchcock's classic *Saboteur* (1942).

The various screenplays lacked a sense of cohesion, touching upon Cockburn's various plotlines but with little sense of an overarching genre. In a letter to Huston, Bogart raised concerns about the meandering plotline and registered his ambivalence about the project: "I am not what you'd call disappointed with it, but, on the other hand, I am not delighted. . . . At this moment, it is hard to tell whether it's a drama, a comedy, or an action picture."[46] A week later Bogart expressed similar reservations: "The script seemed to me to lack the comic flavor that the book had, if you know what I mean. It didn't seem to know what it wanted to be, a comedy, a melodrama, or just a yarn."[47] In correspondence with Huston, Bogart, and Capote, David

O. Selznick tersely pinpointed several flaws in the script: "Difficult even [to] determine whether intention drama melodrama comedy farce satire or even in third act slapstick akin [to] Abbott and Costello in Africa."[48] He particularly criticized its inability to focus the audience's sympathy: "Since no audience sympathy single character or relationship, plus no emotion plus no rooting interest, burden is on entertainment values, which at best in minor characters, and on adventure, inherent lacks in which make superb writing of characterizations and relationships more necessary for compensation."[49] (Selznick did not produce *Beat the Devil*. Huston wryly noted, "Selznick had no connection with the picture except that his wife, Jennifer Jones, was in it. It didn't matter: when she signed a contract, David started his memorandums."[50])

To compound Huston's, Bogart's, and Selznick's concerns over early drafts of the screenplay, Joseph Breen of the Motion Picture Academy of America informed Jess Morgan of Santana Pictures, Bogart's production company, that the proposed film failed to comply with the Hays Code and warranted substantial editing if the resulting picture were to be released theatrically. "Throughout the story," his report read, "there appears to us to be an excessive amount of physical contact—kissing and fondling—between Dannreuther and Gwendolen. In view of the fact that these are both married people, this should be eliminated whenever possible." Since the affair between Dannreuther and Gwendolen is central to the narrative, the demand to whitewash it would result in a film fundamentally removed from its satiric treatment of marriage and romance. Some criticisms of the screenplay—"Please eliminate the belch"—were minor, yet they attest to an overriding hostility to the production.[51] The following year after various drafts, Breen reiterated his condemnation of the screenplay's treatment of adultery—"We believe a story of this type, involving characters of this kind, cannot handle an adulterous relationship in a manner acceptable under the Code"—while also rejecting its sly treatment of homosexuality: "There appears to be a slight suggestion of a homosexual attraction between Conquest and Wagwood, which of course should be deleted."[52] Indeed, Conquest and Wagwood, minor characters in Cockburn's novel, were excised altogether from Huston's film.

Given these mounting script troubles, Selznick urged Huston to hire Capote for a major rewrite. In a detailed memo, he praised Huston's artistic genius as a director and writer, while encouraging him to hire Capote to assist with the production's screenplay:

> Once again, if you feel you are at all stale, I do urge you to consider calling in Capote, even if it is only for two or three weeks. . . . He is, in my opinion, one of the freshest and *most original* and most exciting writing talents of our time—and what he would say through these characters, and how he would have them say it, would be so completely different from anything that has been heard from a motion picture theatre's sound box as to also give you something completely fresh—or so at least I think. Moreover, I know you very well, and I know of very few writers other than Capote whose work is of the sort that I *know* would appeal to you. He can also be quite fast, but *only* if he is whipped every day. In this case, he can turn out *at least* one solid scene a day, and more if necessary, and certainly more in collaboration with you. Also, he is easy to work with, needing only to be stepped on good naturedly, like the wonderful but bad little boy he is, when he starts to whine.
>
> I would not presume to suggest that you get someone in under other circum-stances, because I can honestly say to you, without flattery . . . what I had said to many others—that you are perhaps the most gifted screenwriter in the world, apart from your directorial talents. But I qualify this by saying that you are good *only* (a) when you are not preoccupied with problems of getting a picture into work in fast time, as you are now; (b) when you are in the mood; (c) when you catch fire. But in this case I know that you are preoccupied; I sense that you are not in the mood; and I fear that you have not caught fire. I think therefore that you need the stimulus of a talent of sufficient size to merit your collaboration and respect; and as you are presently playing in luck to a degree that for the first time matches your talent, I think that this good fortune has also made Capote available at this present moment—for there is no-one, *no-one* in Hollywood, or Paris or New York whom I feel could give you what Capote can give you . . . and here he is in Rome, ready, eager and willing to go to work with you.[53]

The memo's rhetorical flourishes, with its sense of urgency coupled with disarming, almost fulsome, praise of Huston's genius, showcase Selznick's persuasive talents—and, indeed, Huston followed the advice offered. Selznick's characterization of Capote as a "bad little boy" prone to whin-ing infantilizes him, yet the words about his writing abilities proved true, as Capote's screenplay, often written moments before shooting, kept the project progressing when it otherwise might have floundered. Furthermore, Capote envisioned how the basic premise of Cockburn's novel could be used to parody Bogart's prior films—"I thought that instead of a straight melo-drama, it should be a sort of satire or takeoff on all those movies Bogart and Sidney Greenstreet used to make"[54]—and this satiric touch unifies the otherwise disparate elements of the story.

Capote and Huston share screen credit for writing *Beat the Devil*, yet controversy remains over who penned it. According to Jeanie Sims, Huston's personal assistant, Capote and Huston wrote the lion's share of the script together: "The balance of the final script, i.e., those portions not underlined, are the work of Mr. Huston and Truman Capote jointly. My own estimate, based on the comparison of the two scripts, is that 23% only of the final script can be attributed to Mr. Veiller and Mr. Viertel *jointly*."[55] Veiller and Viertel agreed with Sims's assessment, and in correspondence with Huston, they relinquished any claim to the film: "We have both read the final script on *Beat the Devil* and we waive any claim to screen credit thereon."[56] Capote and Huston, however, disagreed over their respective contributions, with Capote claiming full responsibility. He insisted that, while Huston was "also credited with me for *Beat the Devil*, . . . he never wrote a word."[57] Huston, for his part, asserted, "We wrote together."[58] In his autobiography he recalled their professional collaboration as well as their pastimes: "When Truman and I weren't working on the script, we were sitting in on the poker game."[59] He suggested as well that, despite the chaos of the shoot, they pursued their work with diligence: "Truman Capote and I rewrote . . . on the spot, but it wasn't done frivolously, as has been described. We worked very hard and tried to keep ahead of the picture."[60] Additionally, Patrick Cockburn, Claud Cockburn's son, insisted that his father's screenplay remained the film's foun-dation and that Capote stole credit for its subsequent success: "For admirers like [Capote's biographer Gerald] Clarke, Capote provided 'words that were completely fresh.' In reality, his contribution was limited to a few concluding scenes which had to be altered at the last moment. . . . In subsequent years, as the film acquired a cult following, Capote did nothing to contradict exag-gerated accounts of his own connection with the movie."[61] With screenplays upon which multiple hands toil, it becomes virtually impossible to disentan-gle precisely who wrote which line, but the resulting screenplay of *Beat the Devil* bears Capote's mark in its camp and queer sensibility. Thus the film is in many ways consistent with Capote's corpus, even if such consistency cannot be traced exclusively to him.

These various preproduction difficulties surrounding the screenplay resulted in a rushed shooting schedule, with Capote often writing the dialogue immediately before it was handed to the actors. As Capote recounted, "I worked on [*Beat the Devil*] with John Huston while the picture was actually being made on location in Italy. Sometimes scenes that were just about to be shot were written right on the set. The cast was completely bewildered."[62] He explained in an interview with Gloria Steinem that "there was no script at all. I was writing it day by day, literally. I worked all night, and the parts would be handed out in the morning; the whole thing was quite mad."[63] Amid such pandemonium, the actors found themselves at a loss about their roles and how they should play them. As Robert Morley's biographer (and daughter-in-law) Margaret Morley writes, "The film continued in fits and starts as the script got rewritten every evening. Robert wasn't quite sure who the character he was playing was supposed to be."[64] Jennifer Jones delivered a relaxed performance as the airy and agreeably mendacious Gwendolen, yet she recalled her constant sense of disequilibrium arising from the erratic filming schedule: "I always wanted to know where my character was going . . . whether she was going to drop dead or jump in the ocean or be knocked over the head. The beginning, the middle, and the end was the way I was structured, so it sometimes threw me a little bit not to know from day to day what she was going to do or not do."[65] Beyond the frenetic pace of the filming, a bacchanalian spirit sparked endless opportunities for mirth and merrymaking, if not dissolution and depravity. Capote narrated in a letter to his friend Andrew Lyndon, "The last few weeks have been filled with peculiar adventures, all involving John Huston and Humphrey Bogart, who've nearly killed me with their dissipations . . . half drunk all day and dead-drunk all night."[66] Huston memorialized the improbable vision of Bogart and Capote wrestling: "One night there was arm wrestling. Bogie and Truman were engaged, and it almost became a fight. It did, in fact, turn into a wrestling match. And Truman took Bogie! He pinned Bogie's shoulders to the floor and held him there. Truman's epicene comportment was downright deceptive: he was remarkably strong and had pit bulldog in him."[67]

With Capote's queer script, *Beat the Devil* has been celebrated as a camp classic, although with some disagreement concerning the applicability of the term. Certainly Capote viewed it in this light, calling it "a mad camp" and "the camp of all time."[68] Robert Ebert observes that it "went straight from box office flop to cult classic and has been called the first camp movie."[69] Susan Sontag, in her groundbreaking essay "Notes on 'Camp,'" considers camp to be "a vision of the world in terms of style. It is a love of the exaggerated, the 'off,' of things-being-what-they-are-not," and succinctly summarizing a camp vision, she theorizes, "Camp sees everything in quotation marks. It's not a lamp, but a 'lamp'; not a woman, but a 'woman.'"[70] Sontag includes *Beat the Devil* in her discussion of camp, although she argues that the film fails in this regard: "Probably, intending to be campy is always harmful. The perfection of *Trouble in Paradise* and *The Maltese Falcon*, among the greatest Camp movies ever made, comes from the effortless smooth way in which tone is maintained. This is not so with such famous would-be Camp films of the fifties as *All About Eve* and *Beat the Devil*. These more recent movies have their fine moments, but the first is so slick and the second so hysterical; they want so badly to be campy that they're continually losing the beat."[71] As Sontag's excursus evinces, defining camp elicits endless taxonomical troubles, and the fifty-eight theses in her essay identify various examples of camp while failing to pinpoint the exact meaning of this quicksilver term. It is nonetheless apparent that Capote believed his film to be campy, and viewing it through such a light illuminates its quirky and queer appeal. Certainly one could posit, apropos of Sontag, that *Beat the Devil* is not a caper film but a "caper film," one that knowingly nods at the tropes of the genres while stripping them of their typical registers.

With its tongue-in-cheek style and insistent insouciance, *Beat the Devil* evinces Capote's queer and campy sensibility in numerous scenes. John Huston laughingly said of the film's characters, "The formula of *Beat the Devil* is that everyone is slightly absurd."[72] Foremost, the four villains—Peterson, O'Hara, Ross, and Ravello—are depicted, not as homosexual, but as sexually ambiguous in their homosocial syndicate. When Gwendolen first espies them, she cautions her husband, "Harry, we must beware of those men. They're desperate characters." Harry is confused by her unexpected declaration and wonders aloud, "What makes you say that?" to which Gwendolen replies with arch naiveté, "Not one of them looked at my legs." Harry raises his eyes in mock surprise, but his wife's words effectively undermine any sense of heterosexual desire among these men, as do their professed trades: they pose as merchants of domestic products such as vacuum cleaners and sewing machines as a front for their nefarious dealings. In a later scene Dannreuther states to Ross, "We're drinking to women,"

FIG. 5 *Beat the Devil*: In the background, from left to right, O'Hara (Peter Lorre), Ross (Ivor Barnard), Peterson (Robert Morley), and Ravello (Marco Tulli) look on in curiosity as Maria Dannreuther (Gina Lollobrigida) flirts with Harry Chelm (Edward Underdown) in an image of heterosexual romance that coincides with the foursome's spirited singing of "Blow the Man Down."

but Ross replies with strident misogyny, "Take the drink, but I won't join you in the toast. . . . Women! Hitler had the right idea—keep them in their place." Believing that Peterson and Dannreuther have died in a car accident, Ravello offers Harry a stake in their operation, and as he does so, he leans in closely to him, uncomfortably invading his personal space. Furthermore, when the foursome boards the SS *Nyanga*, the ship that carries them to Africa, they repeatedly sing "Blow the Man Down" for approximately thirty seconds of screen time. The song is, of course, a well-known sea shanty, but its title is also queerly suggestive. (Indeed, if Capote did not intend anything queer in this peculiar moment of homosocial camaraderie and song, viewers attuned to a queer sensibility could nevertheless see in it an allusion to homosexuality. For example, novelist Don Holliday, author of such 1950s and 1960s pulpy queer fiction as *The Sin Travelers*, *AC-DC Lover*, and *So Sweet, So Soft, So Queer*, took advantage of the double entendre of the phrase "Blow the Man Down" for one of his titles.[73]) Within the homosocial world of Peterson, O'Hara, Ross, and Ravello, desires are so focused on pecuniary gain that no trace of heterosexual, or even heterosocial, desire remains, rendering them a queer troupe indeed.

In particular, Peter Lorre's performance as O'Hara brims with queerness because in a metacinematic joke he modeled his character on Capote. As the film's unit publicist Julie Gibson explained, "Truman had that crazy little hairdo, the bangs, and the blond hair, so Peter came down with his hair bleached and bangs cut exactly like Truman's."[74] The resemblance between Capote, twenty-nine years old at the time, and Lorre, who was then forty-nine, is fairly striking. Impersonating Capote in his physical appearance, Lorre also delivers his lines with an affected innocence, such as when he scampers out of Dannreuther's room while commenting, "To be trustworthy is not more important than to seem to be trustworthy," a line reminiscent of Oscar Wilde's witticisms yet in this instance applied to the Machiavellian machinations of a crook. His trenchant musings on the shifting cultural meaning of time—"The Swiss manufacture it. The Italians squander it. The French hoard it. The Americans worship it. But time is a crook"—also speak to his cosmopolitan sensibility coupled with a cynic's outlook on life and its depredations.

Even Bogart's masculine, tough-guy persona became ripe for queer satire in Huston's and Capote's hands. Stefan Kanfer explains that Huston envisioned Dannreuther as "a very Continental type fellow—an extreme figure in a homburg, shoulders unpadded, French cuffs, regency trousers, fancy waistcoats and a walking stick." To such a startling and effeminizing reimagining of his screen persona, Bogart bluntly replied, "As regards your brilliant conception of my wardrobe, may I say that you're full of shit. . . . As regards the cane, I don't have to tell you what you can do with THAT!"[75] Over their careers Bogart and Huston worked together on six films—*The Maltese Falcon* (1941), *Across the Pacific* (1942), *Key Largo* (1948), *Treasure of the Sierra Madre* (1948), *The African Queen* (1951), and *Beat the Devil*—and as Huston noted of Bogart, "His sort of person fitted into my kind of picture."[76] Notwithstanding their esteemed history of collaboration, Bogart was hesitant to abandon his preferred persona as the taciturn, hard-edged antihero, one straddling the line between the licit and the illicit while traveling through a morally corrupt underworld. In Peter Bogdanovich's memorable description of Bogart's standard persona, "He was a man who tried very hard to be Bad because he knew it was easier to get along in the world that way. He always failed because of an innate goodness which surely nauseated him."[77] Although Bogart prevailed in resisting Huston's wardrobe selections, he played along with the campiness of the film, delivering his lines with a knowing wink, as when he declaims to Gwendolen: "I've got to have money. Doctor's orders are that I have lots of money, otherwise I become dull, listless, and have troubles with my complexion." It is difficult to imagine Sam Spade or Rick Blaine, Bogart's characters in *The Maltese Falcon* and *Casablanca* (dir. Michael Curtiz, 1942), uttering such a line, indicating the character's effete attention to his physical appearance in phrasing lifted from women's cosmetics ads, yet in *Beat the Devil* even Bogart allows a queer chink in the armor of his masculine persona.

A camp sensibility need not be limited to undermining the masculinity of the film's villains and protagonist, and the film's romance between Gwendolen and Dannreuther likewise brims with campy twists. Their conversations sparkle with witticisms, exaggerations, and deceptions that remove these exchanges from the typical fare of caper films. When Gwendolen asks Dannreuther about his childhood, he responds, "I was an orphan until I was twenty, and then a rich and beautiful lady adopted me," ironically revealing his prior career as a gigolo. Gwendolen, who is prone to absurd yet endearing flights of fancy, tells Dannreuther why she believes he is traveling to Africa: "You're going to found a new empire and make yourself master of the riches of the world. But you need a beautiful blonde queen to impress the natives as the incarnation of the Queen of Sheba. That's why you're making a pass at me." Dannreuther parries quizzically, "Am I?" to which Gwendolen declares, "Of course. I don't generally go sightseeing with strange men. You don't believe that, do you?" Gwendolen's insistence on her amatory innocence is merely the latest façade she constructs for Dannreuther to view, and when he gamely if wearily affirms, "I believe anything you say," she replies in turn, "Do you? Well, you shouldn't, you know. You really shouldn't." Throughout this exchange, Bogart looks as if he is going to break character and burst out laughing. Thus the scene undermines the film's convincingness while imbuing it with the charm of its failings. Such failures adorn the film with its camp appeal, for these artistic and aesthetic lapses cascade out into unrestrained pleasures.

Jones's performance as Gwendolen has been lambasted by various critics. In *Sight and Sound* Lindsay Anderson suggested that Jones was "plainly less happy in comedy than in strong emotional drama," and Oswald Davis, the film's cameraman, saw her struggling with the role: "I do not believe that

FIG. 6 *Beat the Devil*: Humphrey Bogart as Dannreuther and Jennifer Jones as Gwendolen, in a flirtatious scene in which both appear to be on the verge of breaking character.

Jennifer ever thought she was playing for comedy. She played it straight all the way through with that terrible, phony English accent and Huston felt it best to leave her alone and let things slide."[78] Yet from a camp perspective Jones plays the part with an appealing sense of the game afoot, no matter how confused she might have been by the antics on the set. Gwendolen's determined pursuit of Dannreuther marks her as the sexual aggressor, and she also stands up to the criminals determined to remove any obstacles, including her husband, obstructing their path. When confronting Peterson, she preaches Harry's virtues without believing a word she speaks: "Since the war, my husband has been almost exclusively concerned with spiritual values. He feels that, if he can get away there, in the heart of Africa, he will come face to face with essentials. He wants to work out the problem of sin." Peterson confusedly replies, "Sin?" to which she affirms, "Why, yes, of course. Isn't that what we're all most concerned with? Sin?" A knowing arch creases her left brow, and a gleam in her eye informs the viewer of her willful deception. In Jones's performance, Gwendolen appears as an artless yet cagy reimagination of film noir's femme fatale, one who pursues her desires always with a comic edge to her performance and yet as single-mindedly—although not as ruthlessly—as such legendary antiheroines as Barbara Stanwyck's Phyllis Dietrichson in *Double Indemnity* (1944) and Lana Turner's Cora Smith in *The Postman Always Rings Twice* (1946).

The film's conclusion escalates and completes its camp antics, as it also bring the story back to its opening shots: the four villains are paraded across the town square chained together in pairs, Peterson and Ross, O'Hara and Ravello, literally bound together in homosocial union. In the film's opening, Bogart pronounces in a voice-over of gentle sarcasm, "These are four brilliant criminals at the climax of their most magnificent effort." At the film's conclusion, however, they are outwitted, if accidentally so, by the apparently innocuous Harry, who reports in a telegram to Gwendolen his triumph over the conspirators: "Have myself acquired land Peterson planned to steal. Will be uranium king if survive shocking chill on liver. Am willing overlook your extraordinary behavior providing you join me at once with hot water bottle." Harry, a narcissist who preens in front of a mirror while remaining oblivious to Maria's erotic interest in him, and whose sexual interests seem transposed to the comforts of a hot water bottle, stands triumphant in absentia as the film makes a "hero" of its least heroic and, indeed, least interesting character. As the film closes and Dannreuther intones, "Oh, this is the end . . . the end," one can hear in the words an arch and exaggerated valence appreciative of its subversion of the caper genre. The metacinematic valediction of "this is the end . . . the end" concedes that the film has been excessive in its play, as it winds down with Bogart proclaiming both its completion and its camp.

Upon its release, *Beat the Devil* was panned by critics. While B. G. Marple complimented it as "the amiably maniac product of a decidedly outré combination: John Huston and Truman Capote," these slight words of praise were drowned out by voices such as Lindsay Anderson, who denigrated the film as a private joke unmeant for public viewing: "*Beat the Devil* has the air of an expensive house-party joke, a charade which enormously entertained its participants at the time of playing, but which is too private and insufficiently brilliant to justify public performance."[79] The *New York Times* labeled it "singularly unorthodox," complaining that "the fun wears mighty thin" and that "'Beat the Devil' ends up beating itself."[80] In a review of Huston's career, Peter Barnes laments the film's "witless inanities" and launches particular opprobrium at Capote's screenplay: "Actors of the caliber of Bogart, Morley, and Lorre can do nothing with dialogue (Truman Capote) which lacks wit and meaning."[81]

After the discombobulating filming of *Beat the Devil* and its anemic box-office receipts, many of the various talents were surprised by its cult success when it was rereleased in the 1960s. In 1966 a brief essay in *Film Society Review* praised the film as pioneering—"Ten years or more ahead of its time"—and suggested that "John Huston's satire of his own best early work, and *The Maltese Falcon* in particular, turns out to be his most enjoyable film."[82] Jennifer Jones wryly lamented, "They don't remember me for *The Song of Bernadette*," for which she won the Academy Award for Best Actress in 1944, "but for *Beat the Devil*."[83] Upon Robert Morley's return to London, he had cabled producer John Woolf and wittily warned him of the film's likely failure: "We have now returned to our capital and we hope that yours will return to you. But we doubt it."[84] Yet Jack Clayton, the associate producer of *Beat the Devil*, with whom Capote later collaborated on *The Innocents* and *The Great Gatsby*, declared the film "a masterpiece," while also cautioning against its excesses: "I view it with enjoyment, but only the enjoyment that such a thing could happen. It's a film that shouldn't have been made."[85] Lorre believed that the film's failure at the time of its release resulted from the advertising blitz accompanying it: "It was a deliciously sardonic comedy, meant for art houses; and they opened it with a blood-and-thunder campaign. The people just didn't get it."[86] Huston called it "an amusing, good picture," suggesting as well that it was "ahead of its time" and concluding, "Its off-the-wall humor left viewers bewildered and confused."[87] He also confessed to the joys of self-satire: "It was a bit of a travesty—we were making fun of ourselves."[88] Capote too seemed surprised by the subsequent success of *Beat the Devil*, as he wrote to Selznick: "I've met a lot of people who, for one reason or another, seem to have seen *Beat the Devil*—apparently it is rather good."[89] Gerald Pratley argues in his assessment of Huston's corpus that, with *Beat the Devil*, Huston and his crew were "years before the times," since such a "fragmented, erratic incidental type of black comedy . . . was entirely unexpected when this film was first shown."[90] Likewise, Pauline Kael speaks affectionately of the film, aware of its limitations yet appreciative of its madcap and campy style: "*Beat the Devil* is a mess, but it's probably the funniest mess—the screwball classic—of all time. It kidded itself, yet it succeeded in some original (and perhaps dangerously marginal) way by finding a style of its own."[91] At a time when Hollywood employed gay talent yet resisted portraying homosexuality on the screen, Capote imbued a caper film with a queer sensibility through homosocial villains, subversions of heterosexual romance, and an overarching campiness. Audiences of the 1950s found *Beat the Devil* off-putting due to its outré stylings, but later generations have come to appreciate it for its refusal to take itself seriously and for its queer subversion of Bogart's and Huston's standard fare.

> ▶ *The Innocents*

Among the railleries of shooting *Beat the Devil*, Capote and Huston encoded an inside joke in the film by naming a minor character, the inspector played by Bernard Lee, in homage to Jack Clayton, the film's associate producer. Clayton assumed the director's chair to critical acclaim with *Room at the Top* (1959). On the basis of their friendship and past collaboration, Capote agreed to write the screenplay for *The Innocents*, Clayton's production of Henry James's 1898 novella *The Turn of the Screw* as mediated through William Archibald's 1950 theatrical adaptation, also titled *The Innocents*. Clayton had originally hired Archibald for the film adaptation, but the resulting screenplay adhered too closely to his stage script. In Clayton's words, "while I am a great admirer of the play and I feel that certain elements of it should be incorporated, I think the script follows the play too closely."[92] More bluntly, he also described himself as "saddled with Archibald because he had a contract with Fox stating he must be given the first shot at writing the script."[93] John Mortimer, best known as the creator of the *Rumpole of the Bailey* mysteries, was brought in to doctor the screenplay, but as Clayton remarked, "we only had him for three weeks because he had other commitments."[94] Capote was then summoned for a major rewrite. He declared that his admiration for Clayton influenced his decision to collaborate on *The Innocents*—"I was paid very little for it, and only did it because I've always thought it would make an excellent film and (mainly) because the director is a great friend and someone I admire"—as he likewise reminisced about his distaste for the filming process: "I had to be on the set . . . all the time because of the way the director worked. I really thought being around movie sets, and going to the thing day after day, intolerably boring."[95]

Capote shares joint billing with Archibald for the screenplay in the film's opening credits, with Mortimer credited for additional scenes and dialogue, but Clayton asserted that Capote wrote it in its entirety: "Although he only got half credit, he wrote the whole script, really. . . . It was a very difficult script to do, because you had to keep the Victoriana and at the same time bring the dialogue up to date. It was brilliant."[96] On another occasion, blaming the Writers Guild for the necessity of crediting Archibald for Capote's efforts, Clayton affirmed: "The result on the screen is Truman's version, totally, with a few changes, which I always do on the set. . . . The reason why Archibald is coupled with Truman Capote on the credits is because the

Writers Guild in America have a silly rule that the first writer automatically shares the credit if it is based on a book. Very unfair, I think."[97] Although Clayton proclaimed Capote's complete responsibility for the screenplay, this assertion is incorrect: his screenplay differs markedly from Archibald's theatrical script, but several scenes are directly inspired by Archibald's staging of them.

Upon reviewing *The Turn of the Screw*, Capote discovered that an adaptation would present difficulties due to the subtle style of James's fictions, which so richly plumb the psychologies of his characters: "I thought it would be a snap because I loved *The Turn of the Screw* so much. But when I got into it, I saw how artful James had been. He did everything by allusion and indirection."[98] *The Turn of the Screw* challenges its readers to undertake a quest for an answer—are the children Flora and Miles possessed by the ghosts of Miss Jessel and Quint, or are these phantoms merely the figments of their governess's depraved imagination?—yet it does so by balancing these possibilities against each other, imbuing every scene with mystery and innuendo that unsettles these opposing interpretations. The governess wonders in the novella's climax, as she ponders the possibility that Miles was guiltless, "if he *were* innocent, what then on earth was *I*?"[99] With these words, she acknowledges the possibility that she misrecognized the source of corruption as a ghost, or even as a child, but never as herself. Edmund Wilson observes in his classic essay on James and the ambiguity of his narration that "nowhere does James unequivocally give the thing away: almost everything from beginning to end can be read equally in either of two senses," and Neil Sinyard documents that Clayton kept a copy of Wilson's essay with the film's First Master Script.[100] Following James's lead, Clayton expressed his desire to maintain the novella's ambiguity: "I don't want, you know, to say absolutely what the picture means. There should be an area of uncertainty; that's what I think James intended. I want the audience to exercise its intelligence."[101]

In accordance with Capote and Clayton's determination to maintain the novella's ambiguities, the cast and crew imbued their performances and other contributions with indeterminacy so that viewers, like James's readers, would grapple with the film's ultimate meaning. Deborah Kerr, playing the lead role of the governess Miss Giddens, stated that in her performance she "tried to tread a very narrow tight-rope between Miss Giddens being an internally and sexually tormented woman, and a completely normal human being who found herself beset by evil powers. I think Jack [Clayton] and I both wanted to leave it to the audience, which resulted in the film's strangely disturbing quality."[102] The film's director of photography, Freddie Francis, a two-time Academy Award winner for cinematography for *Sons and Lovers* (1960) and *Glory* (1989), framed his shots to accentuate the story's mysterious aura: "our audiences probably didn't realize . . . that one of the things that contributed towards the horror of the film is that I had these filters made up so only the center of the screen would be fully illuminated. The edge of the screen would always be a little bit dark so that you didn't know whether there was anything there or not."[103]

Indeed, as Capote similarly realized, James's great achievement in the novella, and the genius behind its magic, is that so little happens in a plot upon which so much mystery hangs: "I let several weeks go by before I reread it and then I got the shock of my life. Because Henry James had pulled a fantastic trick in this book: it doesn't stand up anywhere. It has no plot! He's just pretending this and this and that. . . . I kept building up more plot, more characters, more scenes. In the entire book there were only two scenes performable."[104] In Capote's quest to emulate James's ambiguities on film, he needed to dramatize the fantasies generated in the governess's fervid imagination, but also to depict her interacting with these visions in some manner. Nonetheless, in a movie so focused on sexuality and its ambiguities, a concrete indication that the ghosts were real would undermine its psychological depth.

Given this emphasis on ambiguity, the film's greatest crux for many viewers arises in its depiction of a teardrop: when Miss Giddens sees the ghost of Miss Jessel in the children's schoolroom, Miss Jessel weeps, and a single tear falls onto her desk. Clayton believed that this moment would increase the terror but also the pathos of this supernatural encounter: "And then I thought how it might be if I actually saw a ghost sitting at my desk. What would be the most terrifying thing for me? I might think I was having a hallucination, or that it was some trick of the light. But if I suddenly saw a tear mark on a piece of paper, I think it would really frighten me very much, as well as being very sad."[105] Such a teardrop, however, might prove the physical existence of the ghosts, and from this perspective, Capote regretted Miss Jessel's teardrop as a critical error: "I made only one mistake. At the very end, when the governess sees the ghost of Miss Jessel sitting at her desk, I had a tear fall on to the desktop. Up until then it wasn't clear whether the ghosts were real or in the governess' mind. But the tear was real, and that spoiled everything."[106] In an otherwise favorable review of the film, Pauline Kael echoes Capote's self-recriminations, condemning the teardrop for stripping the film of its complexity: "All else can be more or less compromised within the system of the repressed governess's madness; but not that little wet tear, that little pearl of ambiguity."[107]

Capote's self-criticism and Kael's astute observation notwithstanding, fixating on this single tear to resolve the film's mysteries ultimately fails because its ambiguities encourage viewers to question the reliability of Miss Giddens's perceptions. James Palmer argues of this crux that "even the tear is no absolute proof of the reality of the ghosts. . . . The tear is on the desk, but the viewer is also made to wonder if the governess hasn't hallucinated this Doppelgänger."[108] Indeed, why should one presume this tear is real, even if viewers see it? Clayton's direction continually balances out these opposing interpretations. Another moment that might appear to confirm the ghosts' existence occurs in the film's climax when Miss Giddens forces Miles to confess that he sees the ghost of Quint. The camera appears to assume the spectral Quint's over-the-shoulder perspective as he gazes down at Miss Giddens and Miles, but the subsequent shot from this vantage point replaces Quint's shoulder with that of a statue. Thus the second shot posits either that Miss Giddens imagined the ghost looking down at them in the first shot or that Quint, as ghosts are wont to do, simply disappears. One can never be sure whether the ghosts of Quint and Miss Jessel exist or whether Miss Giddens summons them from her own submerged psychosexual fantasies that she expresses through her relationship with Miles and Flora. Indeed, one can never be sure what is happening in *The Innocents*, for Miss Giddens's perspective guides the viewer, and one can never discount the possibility that she is psychologically unbalanced.

The haunting ambiguity that the film achieves, so true to James's literary vision in its transposition to film, adds an intellectual depth to the standard thrills and chills of the horror genre. Building on this element in its advertising campaign, *The Innocents*' trailer proclaimed its goal of elevating the horror film into a genre appropriate for serious audiences: "There has never been a ghost story created especially for the adult moviegoer until *The Innocents*," its narrator ominously intones.[109] As much as this lofty appraisal is underpinned by the film's pedigree—literary roots in Henry James, dramatic roots in William Archibald, screenplay by Truman Capote, filming by an acclaimed new director—it is ironic that this film "for the adult

FIG. 7 *The Innocents*: This shot might reflect the perspective of Quint's ghost or of Miss Giddens's feverish imagination. By counterbalancing such readings, director Jack Clayton ensures that ambiguity clouds the viewer's ability to determine whether Miss Giddens is protecting or preying on the children.

moviegoer" features children as the catalysts of its horror. *The Innocents* appears to be a horror story of ghosts possessing the bodies of innocent children, yet it is also a stunning case study of one woman's psychosexual obsession with children's innocence and her inability to conceive of childhood sexuality other than as corruptive. As James Kincaid pithily declares in his groundbreaking study of depictions of children's sexuality, "We all know that there is a difference between a healthy and normal love of children and a love which is sick and freakish,"[110] but the narrative pleasure both of *The Turn of the Screw* and of *The Innocents* arises in the ambiguity of the governess's love as outwardly protective yet, at least potentially, inwardly perverse. In this manner *The Innocents*, in its treatment of the sexuality of childhood, aligns with Capote's queer themes in his literature, particularly in the ways in which it echoes the gothic treatment of children's sexuality in *Other Voices, Other Rooms*. Capote's novel and *The Innocents* differ markedly in their settings on a decaying southern plantation and a lush English estate, but they unite in their treatment of the queer potential in children's sexuality and its intersection with gothic terrors.

The Innocents begins eerily, with a young girl's voice singing, "We lay, my love and I, beneath the weeping willow, but now alone I lie." In its depiction of lovers lying underneath a willow tree, with the child mourning the loss of her beloved, the film announces its interest in children's understanding and experience of adult sexuality. (The lyricist of this song, "O Willow Waly," was Paul Dehn, a British screenwriter best known for *Goldfinger* [1964] and *Murder on the Orient Express* [1974].) Following the child's voice, which viewers later learn is Flora's, and implying a thematic contrast between children's sexuality and adults' nurturing of children, a woman's voice is heard whispering while her hands are shown clasped in agitated prayer: "All I want to do is save the children, not destroy them. More than anything, I love children. More than anything." The voice, which viewers later recognize as the governess Miss Giddens's when the film concludes circularly with this scene, admits the possibility that she will destroy the children whom she seeks to protect, then subsides into a whimper and adds, "They need affection, love, someone who will belong to them and to whom they will belong." The voice trembles with desperation, betraying that she seeks to sate her need for affection and love through children and that her unfulfilled desires to belong to someone will be projected onto her young charges. These scenes do not appear in Capote's screenplay, which instead begins with a "first-person flashback recalled by Miss Giddens" in which she "is attempting to explain to Miles's outraged uncle and to a spurious Mrs. Grose what had happened at Bly."[111] Clayton's version of the film's opening, by veering from Capote's screenplay, rejects the explanations that Miss Giddens might offer for the tragic events that took place on her watch, thus heightening the ambiguity of the story and the inherent unreliability of her perspective: seeing the mysterious events unfold through her eyes imbues the viewing experience with uncertainty, for the audience is frequently unsure if what the camera captures is what Miss Giddens sees or merely what she thinks she sees.

As the narrative proper begins, it becomes readily apparent that children do need protection, at least from their dissolute guardians. Michael Redgrave plays the role of Flora and Miles's nameless uncle with casual indifference to his wards, explaining as he interviews Miss Giddens for the position of governess at his country estate, Bly: "And as for my London life, well, it amuses me, but it's not the sort of amusement that one could suitably share with children." Such an innocuous statement glides over the uncle's secrets: what precisely are these "amusements" that he cannot share with his orphaned niece and nephew? As the film proceeds, it seems unlikely that his urban pastimes could be more threatening to the children than the ministrations of their new governess who aspires only to nurture them. Reading her application letter aloud, he reminds her of her words—"More than anything, I love children"—as Kerr chimes in with a heartfelt "yes." The uncle disappears from the narrative after this initial scene, forbidding Miss Giddens to trouble him about his wards, but Mrs. Grose (Megs Jenkins), the housekeeper, later states of him: "Many's the time he's worked his magic on me. Even when he was a boy, he could twist you around his finger, and the children are the same way." The uncle thus represents what Flora and Miles may become if Miss Giddens does not intervene in their lives: a practitioner of deceit, secrecy, and a sordid urban lifestyle, pursuing decadent pastimes from which children must be protected, despite the irony that the roots of the uncle's duplicitous adulthood were apparent in his youth.

Because the uncle was played by Michael Redgrave, many viewers assumed that he would return for the film's climax, but his unswerving disregard for the children contrasts sharply with Miss Giddens's unswerving concern for them. Despite the incongruity of casting Deborah Kerr, who was forty years old at the time of the film's shooting, in the role of the young governess Miss Giddens, her performance brilliantly plays on her star persona and her previous box-office hits playing a governess in *The King and I* (1956) and a romantic heroine in *An Affair to Remember* (1957) to subvert the audience's expectations. With such an understanding of her typical roles, viewers might foresee a romance unfolding in the film's climax—with the uncle rushing in to rescue her and the children—but Clayton cagily uses her screen history to hint at a sexual attraction to the uncle, only to then focus on her obsession with the children. When Miss Giddens and Mrs. Grose, walking in a churchyard, discuss the unsettling events at Bly, she fears that the uncle will think her fears are merely "some stupid trick to get him to notice me," a subtle admission of her attraction to him. Also, when the uncle offers her the position of governess at Bly, he employs phrasings—"the person whom I engage," "give me your hand, give me your promise"—evocative of a marriage proposal. By encoding Miss Giddens's attraction to the uncle in the narrative, Capote and Clayton subtly parallel her sexuality—presumably virginal, as evidenced by her propensity in the film's opening sequences for white dresses—with the children's, positing that she too is one of the innocents needing protection to whom the film's title refers, but also hinting at her desire to sully this innocence by engaging in a sexual relationship.

Upon arriving at Bly, Miss Giddens meets Flora (Pamela Franklin), but the first shot of her young charge is the girl's reflection in a pond, a deft employment of the camera to frame the film's mysteries of image and actuality. Following James's themes, Capote depicts Miss Giddens as initially believing that she has arrived in a paradise: James's governess describes the children as "cherubs" and Miles in particular as an "angel,"[112] and in Capote's screenplay Mrs. Grose, discussing the manor with the new governess, asserts a similar viewpoint: "But what I always say is, it's a heaven for children." Miss Giddens further builds this theme of Bly as a celestial paradise for children, saying that Flora "certainly looks angelic." From these initial observations of her new setting as a prelapsarian paradise of eternal innocence, Miss Giddens succumbs to the children's charms. While bathing Flora, Miss Giddens wonders aloud, "And is the other one just as remarkable? Is he too as enchanting?" to which Mrs. Grose responds, "Well, if you like this one, you should be quite carried away by Master Miles." They tickle Flora, snuggled naked in her towels, in a scene that begins to undermine the viewer's belief in children's innocence, for as much as children's nudity, in family photographs of bath-time play and toddlers' guileless exhibitionism, often reflects their innocence, a naked child projected on the screen, no matter the intentions of the director, bears the possibility of being viewed— or, worse, enjoyed—as pornographic. In a letter to Frank McCarthy of Twentieth Century–Fox, censor Geoffrey Shurlock cautioned against Flora's bath for the slightest possibility of a salacious interpretation—"The scene of the little girl running naked from the baths should be handled with proper discretion"—as he also warned against the film's subject matter: "We urge you to recommend that the references to 'obscenities' and 'filth' from a child's mouth be toned down. These words, in connection with a small child, may very well give offense."[113] Shurlock's criticisms, perceptive yet untenable, capture the thematic heart of the film: what precisely is the sexuality of childhood, and can this sexuality be depicted cinematically? Can a young girl's bathing scene remain innocent, if the barest possibility emerges that it might titillate some? Miss Giddens finds Flora's bath time a "remarkable" and "enchanting" experience rather than a pedestrian chore in a governess's day; she is clearly so fascinated with childhood and children's bodies that virtually any activity with them affords a pleasurable frisson. Furthermore, Capote and Clayton appear to have ignored Shurlock's concern about "filth from a child's mouth," for this phrase is used verbatim when Mrs. Grose tells Miss Giddens of Flora's obscenities during the child's hysterical breakdown. Capote and Clayton balance these scenes between innocence and sexuality, but the film demands that viewers consider the possibility that childhood sexual innocence is merely a social façade intended to protect adults from recognizing the predatory nature of their own desires.

With such hints of pedophilic desire circulating around Bly, it becomes apparent that what Mrs. Grose sees as a heaven for children may actually be their purgatory. As Miss Giddens puts Flora to bed after her prayers, the child wonders: "And if I weren't [a good girl], wouldn't the Lord just leave me here to walk around? Isn't that what happens to some people?" From this clue that these children might not be little angels, Miss Giddens perceives that Bly could be a purgatorial realm of eternal stasis. Along these lines, Mrs. Grose tells Miles that "nothing ever changes here," and Miles wishes, "if only everything could go on just as it is now." Along with its registers as purgatory, Bly represents hell itself, as Miss Giddens discloses when she shares her fear with Mrs. Grose in the schoolroom that the children "live and know and share this hell."

Attempting to determine whether Bly is heaven, purgatory, or hell, Miss Giddens becomes increasingly troubled by the unfolding events. Flora's bath-time chant that Miles will return home proves uncannily prescient when Miss Giddens receives a letter indicating that he has been expelled from his boarding school. To enhance the simmering tension, Capote accompanies this revelation with a bit of obvious symbolism as Flora plays with, in her words, "A lovely spider, and it's eating a butterfly." This staging exaggerates Archibald's depiction of Flora's fascination with a dead beetle: "Oh, look—a dead beetle! . . . You'd never know it was dead except that it's on its back and isn't kicking."[114] In both instances the symbolism of the devoured and dead insects unsettles Miss Giddens, but it is as yet unclear to the viewer whether the children or their governess is predator or prey. Miss Giddens learns that Miles has transgressed by being "an injury to the others," a euphemistic phrasing that states not a specific offense but more a state of depraved existence. When discussing this turn of events with Mrs. Grose, who defends the boy, Miss Giddens replies, "You mean you like a boy with spirit. Well, so do I, but not to the degree to contaminate." The camera cuts to a close-up of Miss Giddens as she states "contaminate," registering her dawning fear that this innocent child may infect others with his moral lapses. Mrs. Grose laughs heartily. "Oh, miss, are you afraid he'll corrupt you?" But this is precisely what Miss Giddens fears: that the depravities of this child will bleed not only onto other children but onto herself as well.[115]

Clayton underscores Miles's and Flora's sexual precocity through costuming and framing.[116] At the train station where Flora and Miss Giddens await Miles's return, Flora rushes to kiss him as if she were more his lover than his sister, and their clothes—Miles sports a young man's suit, complete with vest and ascot, while Flora models a beribboned dress with matching hat—presents them as adults reuniting passionately after a long separation. Miles quickly begins his courtship of Miss Giddens, bringing her flowers and lavishing her with compliments—"I think you're far too pretty to be a governess"—to which she smilingly replies, "And I think you're far too young to be such a deceitful flatterer." Miles's flirtations with Miss Giddens undermine a sense of the character as merely a young and sexually innocent boy, for his words distract her from questioning him about his expulsion from school. These questions are never answered conclusively, even in the film's climactic sequence.

The film also suggests the children's sexual experience in contrast to Miss Giddens's sexual innocence in the scene where Miles rides a pony, with Clayton's fast cuts accentuating Miss Giddens's growing uneasiness. As James Palmer argues, "The sexual implications of this dizzying scene are worthy of D. H. Lawrence."[117] Miss Giddens is surprised by the young boy's equestrian skills until Mrs. Grose explains that he learned to ride from the deceased servant Quint, but this revelation frightens her, for his horsemanship thus signifies his eager embrace of Quint's immoral tutelage. When the children and Miss Giddens play a game of hide-and-seek that takes them to the attic and its many secrets, Miss Giddens first sees a picture of Quint. Also in the attic, the children play with a rocking horse while they count to one hundred so that Miss Giddens can hide herself from them. Rocking horses, perpetually in place while energetically in motion, have long symbolized children's sexuality and masturbation, perhaps most famously in D. H. Lawrence's "The Rocking-Horse Winner," and Flora and Miles's play with this toy further hints at their sophisticated knowledge of sexuality while also resisting such an interpretation, for the apparently eroticized symbol is a simple children's toy. Only a depraved mind would see a rocking horse as indicative of children's sexual precocity, yet only a naïve mind would overlook these children's uncanny sophistication. Yet again, Clayton puts the audience in Miss Giddens's position, as viewers waver in interpreting this prop as indicative of children's innocence or of their provocative pleasures.

In contrast to the children's bustling activity, Capote and Clayton often depict Miss Giddens restlessly sleeping, with her moaning indicating both her fears for the children and her submerged sexual desires. In the first such scene, she lies in bed with Quint's image superimposed on her, suggestive of her desire for Quint or of her identification with Quint due to their shared pedophilic interest in children. Then, in a later extended dream sequence, she envisions numerous symbols indicative of her fears of the ghosts and for the children—the music box playing "O Willow Waly," Miles warning Flora about their secret, the vision of Quint on the tower, Miles and Flora holding hands more like lovers than siblings, Flora dancing with Miss Jessel, and Quint guiding Miles with his hand on his back. Clayton describes his use of such montages and dissolves as "faintly original," for he sought to create through them "images which hang there, and have a meaning which applies both to the end of the last scene and the beginning of the next."[118] Miss Giddens's dream montages make apparent the sexual undertones in her concern for the children, and Clayton's dissolves enhance the provocative nature of her fears, as images emerge from one another in her dark fantasies. Throughout the film, Clayton's dissolves compel the viewer to confront this indeterminacy of image and reality. In one striking instance Miss Giddens and Mrs. Grose converse about the children in the estate's solarium while Mrs. Grose waters plants, with the final shot framing her in the right of the screen and a chained and half-naked statue in the left. This scene dissolves to the train station, where Miles comes into focus through the fading statue, a striking allusion to the Pygmalion myth as the young boy appears to come to life from a cold marble statue in response to Miss Giddens's burgeoning desire for him. When Miss Giddens first sees Quint, he too appears to emerge from a statue. Such scenes reinforce the possibility that these visions spring from Miss Giddens's feverish mind, as they also allow the possibility that she animates these artworks through her repressed desires.

As Miss Giddens becomes increasingly fearful for the children's souls, she learns from Mrs. Grose about the mysterious Quint, the uncle's former valet whose ghostly presence seems to contaminate the children: "He was a peculiar man. There were things in his life that could account for violence done him—vicious things. Well, it doesn't do to speak ill of the dead." Despite her hesitations to gossip, this is Mrs. Grose's primary function in the narrative—to give Miss Giddens elliptical clues about the past that further feed her obsessive concern for the children's souls. Mrs. Grose soon tells more, hinting at the improper relationship between Quint and Miles: "You didn't know Quint, miss. Such power he had over people. You can't blame the child. A lonely boy with no father. Quint took advantage, that's all. It made me sick to see Miles trotting after him like a little dog." Again belying her aversion to speaking ill of the dead, Mrs. Grose explains how she caught Quint and the children's former governess, Miss Jessel, together. Archibald's dialogue maintains a sense of Victorian modesty in Mrs. Grose's account of their indecorous liaison—"Using this house, every room—*any* room—I came upon them once in this very room sitting together, laughing together, loudly"[119]—whereas the screenplay indicates that Mrs. Grose caught the lovers in flagrante delicto. In a masterful elision, which Clayton's wife Haya credits to Mortimer rather than Capote, Mrs. Grose says, "Rooms . . . used by daylight as though they were the dark woods."[120] Concentrating on the location of their trysts rather than their activities, Mrs. Grose obfuscates precisely what she saw. Her meaning is nevertheless clear, and Miss Giddens asks in shock: "They didn't care that you saw them?" Mrs. Grose shakes her head, and Miss Giddens's thoughts immediately turn to her wards. "And the children?" Mrs. Grose replies: "I can't say, miss. I—I don't know what the children saw. But they used to follow Quint and Miss Jessel, trailing along behind hand in hand, whispering. There was too much whispering in this house, miss." The ghostly calls that Miss Giddens has heard since entering Bly—the voice calling for Flora that she mistook for Mrs. Grose's, the children's murmuring to each other, the ghosts hissing the suggestive phrases "the children are watching" and "knock before you enter"—hint at secrets kept from Miss Giddens. They also point to the possibility that these secrets are sexual in nature, that the children were privy to the lovemaking of Quint and Miss Jessel and attained an adult knowledge of sexuality that corrupted their innocence.

Miss Giddens's fears reach fever pitch when the children play dress-up on a claustrophobically rainy day, with Miles performing a ballad lamenting the death of his beloved lord. The ballad's speaker is unidentified, but in invoking the lord as a lover and imagining the lord's ghost entering the speaker's chamber, the ballad takes on a homoerotic cast of anticipated otherworldly consummation. The young actor in the role of Miles, Martin Stephens, plays this scene as if channeling Quint's spirit, imbuing his performance with the uncanny implication that the young boy serves as the puppet to a ghostly presence. With Francis's camera framing him and his face lit against a dark backdrop, he stares upward and intones:

What shall I sing to my lord from my window?
What shall I sing, for my lord will not stay?

Here the camera focuses on Miss Giddens, who grows increasingly uncomfortable with the erotic undertones of Miles's ballad. She sits next to an embroidered seat depicting a man wooing a woman, and the mise-en-scène thus contrasts her desires for conventional romance (presumably with the uncle) with Miles's performance of ghostly desires. Casting his eyes down, he continues his eerie poem calling for his lord to come to him. The camera crosscuts between Miss Giddens's mounting horror and tracking shots as he walks to the window.

Concluding his recitation of homosocial desire between lord and liege, Miles whispers, "Welcome, my lord," indicating that his ghostly lover has arrived for him. Capote borrows this scene almost verbatim from Archibald, with the specter of pederasty lurking in both stagings as Miles reaches out to his dead companion.[121] Later when Mrs. Grose defends Miles's relationship with Quint, declaring, "The poor boy needed someone to—," Miss Giddens interrupts: "To corrupt him?" Capote's ambiguous dialogue echoes James's in numerous ways, but particularly in its refusal to state what precisely this corruption might be. Had Miles interrupted Quint and Miss Jessel making love, as Mrs. Grose's words "Rooms . . . used by daylight as though they were the dark woods" suggest, he would have learned of heterosexuality, not homosexuality, yet Miss Giddens fears that their relationship veered into pederasty as well. For Miss Giddens any sexuality, whether heteroerotic or homoerotic, corrupts children equally, because she conceives of sexuality, whether in regard to the children or to herself, only as traumatic—despite the many hints that she keenly desires sexual experience herself.

And indeed, one might well wonder, what do these ghosts desire? Although Miss Giddens perceives pederastic undertones in Quint's relationship with Miles during his performance of the ballad, she also attempts to understand the children's spiritual possession in terms of adult heterosexuality, believing that Quint and Miss Jessel "can only reach each other by entering the souls of the children." From this perspective, Flora and Miles are unwilling vessels of a heterosexual passion transcending the grave, and their preternatural sexuality thus reflects a normative desire that becomes tainted by its corrupting influence on children. Yet both James and Capote imply a latent queerness in the presumed possessions by pairing Miles with Quint and Flora with Miss Jessel. Various scholars have noted the sexual symbolism of the ghosts' appearances—Quint on a phallic tower, Miss Jessel in a vaginal lake, with the children respectively associated with these settings—and thus the queer potential of this haunting multiplies in the ambiguity of the ghosts' motives: to love each other, to love each other through the children, or, like Miss Giddens, to love the children?

The question of Miles's sexual desires, amorphous as they are, drives the film to its climax. When Miss Giddens confronts him about his misbehavior, he affirms his desire to remain appealing to her: "Well, I thought I might be becoming a bore. . . . I mean, good children do get a bit boring, don't they?" He continues, "So I thought, why not go out tonight and wander about in my bare feet? It was a shocking thing to do, wasn't it?" A young child sneaking out of bed and into a garden is perhaps not a shocking act in itself, but Clayton builds the sexual symbolism in the encounter by cutting to a shot of Miles in bed wiggling his bare feet for Miss Giddens. Bare feet are a longstanding symbol of genitalia,[122] and the metaphoric eroticism of the scene is graphically realized when Miles demands, "Kiss me good night, Miss Giddens." Capote's screenplay requires the kiss to be shot "on the mouth, like a man," and the camera records an extreme close-up of their lips pressed together, lasting for a full five seconds.[123] The length of the shot freezes the viewer with the disturbing image of a child amorously embracing an adult, but it is not Miss Giddens who pulls away in disgust, shock, or terror; rather, Miles ends their embrace, as she inhales deeply with the camera focusing on her lips. It is an uncomfortable scene to watch, for Clayton strips away the pretense of children's innocence as Miles pursues his governess sexually. The scene ends with a dissolve matching Miss Giddens with Miles's dead pigeon, which she earlier found hidden beneath his pillow, suggesting the possibility that she too has fallen victim to this cruel child. Subsequently, when discussing Miles with Mrs. Grose, Miss Giddens avers, "Oh yes, he wanted to reveal himself and ask for my help," indicating that she refuses to recognize that he did reveal himself to her—that he could hardly reveal himself more without

FIG. 8   *The Innocents:*
Miles (Martin Stephens)
is about to kiss his
governess Miss Giddens
(Deborah Kerr), in
a close-up that soon
focuses almost exclusively
on their caressing lips.

the film becoming pornographic. Refusing to see that Miles metaphorically stripped himself in front of her and demanded an adult kiss from her, Miss Giddens preserves herself from the necessity of believing these children to be anything other than the innocents that she insists they be, so that she may remain an innocent as well.

Building on this scene of puerile seduction, the film's climactic sequence begins with Miss Giddens confronting Miles about his knowledge of ghosts and, thus, of human sexuality. He enters the drawing room for tea and declares, "How very grand and grown-up," with Miss Giddens agreeing, "Yes, and we can talk together now, like adults." In recognizing Miles as an adult, Miss Giddens admits that he is not the child she believed him to be, yet when Miles reaches for Miss Giddens's hand over the tea table, he then pulls it away after slapping a gelatin mold in an immature and childish gesture. Miles asks her, "Why did you want to be alone with me?" In words that echo Archibald's, Miss Giddens affirms her willingness to hurt those whom she seeks to help: "My father taught me to love people and help them. Help them even if they refuse my help. Even if it hurt them sometimes."[124] As Miss Giddens avowed in the film's opening her desire, "Save the children, not destroy them," it becomes increasingly evident that hurting children is a necessary tactic in her efforts to rescue them.

As this sequence develops, Capote's queer themes emerge when Miles elliptically confesses the reason for his expulsion from school. In James's novella, Miles discloses that his transgressions at school involved other schoolboys—"Those I liked"—which adumbrates a homosocial attraction as the foundation of his troubles.[125] "It must be because I'm different," he states in the film, walking away with his back toward Miss Giddens to hide (yet also to indicate) his shame. She, however, refuses to hear his confession: "But you aren't. You're like any other boy." While Miles does not define the nature of his difference, he admits it, yet Miss Giddens will not recognize any difference that would render the boy anything other than an innocent. Regardless of the exact nature of Miles's difference—whether he is sexually precocious, homosexual, or was raped by Quint—his confession reads as queer, but Miss Giddens will not acknowledge the queerness standing before her. Miles then points out to her that she does, in fact, recognize his queerness, but that she seeks to protect herself from this knowledge: "If you really thought that, we wouldn't be having these conversations. No, my dear, you don't think I'm like any other boy. That's why you're afraid." At this moment, Miles suavely affirms his indeterminate queerness as comfortably as his uncle carries himself in the film's opening when declaring that his decadent pleasures in London take precedence over these children. All the men whom Miss Giddens knows, or thinks she knows—Miles, the uncle, and Quint—are comfortable in their sexuality, and so she can hardly distinguish between Quint and Miles at this point. The screenplay notes, "the two faces, MILES'S and QUINT'S, seem to blur and merge—as though MISS GIDDENS, the observer, were on the point of fainting."[126] Because she is unable to distinguish between a child and an adult, the viewer cannot trust Miss Giddens's perceptions. At the moment of Miles's death, the screenplay reads: "As [MILES] screams, the figure of QUINT is gone, as though it never existed."[127]

After Miles collapses, Miss Giddens declares her triumph over Quint: "He's gone, Miles. You're safe. You're free." Stroking his hair, she avows, "I have you. He's lost you forever," only to discover that her young ward has died from the shock of her ministrations. In the film's final moments, she kisses his dead lips, manifesting her desire for him in an act that replays their earlier kiss. Clayton recorded in his screenplay notes, "she kisses this cold, beautiful dead little face. She kisses it fully, completely on the lips as one would with one's lover."[128] The virginal Miss Giddens finds and kills her first lover, preserving both of them from the degradations of human sexuality, for their love can never be consummated. This provocative finale caused an uproar at the studio: Fox executive Spyros Skouras reportedly sputtered to Clayton, "You can't finish a film like that! Because . . . because . . . it's not *done!*" Clayton reported, "Every two days for two solid weeks, he called, *begging* me to change the ending, which I *would* not and *did* not do."[129] The film ends with the possibility both that the ghosts were real and that Miss Giddens's feverish concern for the children has killed Miles, that what she wished to believe an external menace represented her own denied desires.

In a letter to Alvin and Marie Dewey, Capote expressed his opinion that *The Innocents* was "*very* good" and that they should "be *sure* to see it."[130] For the most part, contemporary reviewers agreed that *The Innocents* succeeds as a masterpiece of psychological horror. Pauline Kael avowed that the film's "beauty is what makes *The Innocents* the best ghost movie I've ever seen: the beauty raises our terror to a higher plane than the simple fears of most ghost stories."[131] Bosley Crowther, reviewing for the *New York Times*, stated that audiences should find themselves "beautifully frightened and even intellectually aroused" by the film, and the magazine *America* celebrates the film for "restor[ing] the . . . lost art of the psychological horror story to its honorable place among screen genres."[132] Kerr received enthusiastic praise in numerous reviews, among them Arthur Knight's paean: "Deborah Kerr deftly touches . . . every aspect of this pivotal character—her unworldliness, her piety, her love for the children, and her deep-seated fears."[133] *McCall's* extolled her "excellent" performance, as well as Jack Clayton's "moody, roving camera" that "catch[es] very mysterious shadows in the mansion and builds up suspense in one long crescendo."[134] The *Newsweek* reviewer likewise commended Kerr for her "perfect" performance and Clayton for his "fine and frightening job."[135] While many reviews overlooked the performances of the child actors Franklin and Stephens, the *Variety* reviewer singled them out for praise: "their performances are extraordinary blends of innocence and sophistry."[136] Ironically, given the determination of both Capote and Clayton to honor the novella's ambiguity, commentators faulting the film accused them of resolving its complexities by leaning too heavily on the psychosexual interpretation rather than on the possibility that the ghosts were real. Stanley Kauffman, reviewing for *New Republic*, noted "the tear-drop that Miss Jessel leaves on the schoolroom desk" as evidence of the film's "contradictions," and the reviewer for *Time* criticized Capote for "pressing hard, much harder than James did, for the psychiatric interpretation."[137] Brendan Gill, writing in the *New Yorker*, dismissed the film as a pale imitation of its illustrious forebear: "With James, the ghosts are always whispering away inside our heads, and no amount of hanky-panky with thunder and lightning and blowing curtains and candles winking out can achieve that interior frightfulness."[138]

Such quibbles aside, *The Innocents* insists that viewers contemplate the queerness of children and the cultural horror of their sexuality, and therein arises its lasting appeal as a story of the indeterminacy and latent terror of sexual desire. As Ellis Hanson brilliantly summarizes, "In *The Innocents* our relation to the sexual child becomes an allegory for queer cinematic spectatorship, cinema as illicit projection, as an inanimate image brought spectrally to life for the seduction of our look."[139] It does so, in the end, by counterbalancing one woman's horror of sexuality with the inherently quotidian nature of eroticism. When Miss Giddens first enters Bly and touches a bouquet of flowers, some dead petals fall; the screenplay records that "at her slight touch the petals seem to shiver off every bloom."[140] The symbolic "deflowering" of this bouquet, with its analogous relationship to the botanically named Flora, indicates that the loss of a flower is a mundane, not an earth-shattering, event. Miss Giddens apologizes profusely, but Mrs. Grose simply replies, "That's all right, miss. It's always happening." And so it is always happening with children, as Capote demonstrates in fiction such as *Other Voices, Other Rooms* and *The Grass Harp* and in films such as *The Innocents* and, to a lesser extent, *Indiscretion of an American Wife*: young children grow into puberty and then adulthood, and in so doing, they develop adult sexual desires, whether heterosexual or homosexual, and the hand that seeks to protect them from sexual knowledge or their own sexual identities can only harm them. Would it be so horrible, Capote asks his viewers, if these children grew up to be like their uncle? Surely only those sharing Miss Giddens's fear of sexuality would shudder at the possibility.

Holly Golightly's Queer World ▶ Blake Edwards's *Breakfast at Tiffany's*

Notwithstanding his screenwriting experiences, Capote criticized cinematic adaptations of fiction. He believed that transforming a written work into a visual one invariably degraded the source: "The transposition of one art form into another seems to me a corrupt, somewhat vulgar enterprise. Nature being what it is, these experimental inbreedings must logically make for Cretin offspring. Why can't a novel be simply a novel, a poem a poem?"[1] He also admitted that his previous involvement with screenwriting cautioned him against writing the adaptation of *Breakfast at Tiffany's*: "From these experiences I learned that it's a fatal mistake to try to adapt my own work into another form. Once you have worked out the characterization and the whole significance of the story for yourself as a short novel, you can't then take that experience and try to work it into a play. . . . You can't alter your original vision to fit another medium. That's the reason I didn't want to do the film version of *Breakfast at Tiffany's*."[2] With these words Capote echoes longstanding criticisms of cinematic adaptations of literature, notably that such films taint their sources: the original text is envisioned as a fountainhead of true art, which its cinematic offspring pollutes. Brian McFarlane observes that "much of the dissatisfaction which accompanies the writing about films adapted from novels tends to spring from perceptions of 'tampering' with the original narrative." It is impossible, however, to translate literature to the screen without altering the source text, for adaptations, by their very nature, must alter their sources in shifting from one medium to another. McFarlane continues, "Such dissatisfactions resonate with a complex set of misapprehensions about the workings of narrative in the two media, about the irreducible differences between the two, and from a failure to distinguish what can from what cannot be transferred."[3] For viewers who concentrate primarily on how an adaptation alters its source text and thus on what is lost in the process, adaptations almost necessarily disappoint. When viewing adaptations as arising from yet not servile to their sources, their unique achievements come into sharper focus.

Certainly Blake Edwards's 1961 film version of Capote's 1958 novella *Breakfast at Tiffany's* succeeds on numerous levels, as it is generally lauded as a cinematic classic. Audrey Hepburn, in her iconic performance as Holly Golightly, enchants audiences with her cool sophistication and elegant costuming, particularly her slim black dress designed by Givenchy. The film features an impressive array of supporting actors, including George Peppard as her love interest Paul Varjak, Patricia Neal as Varjak's lover Mrs. Falenson, and Buddy Ebsen as Holly's abandoned husband Doc. Edwards undertook the project following his commercial smash *Operation Petticoat* (1959). George Axelrod, following his numerous successes in the 1950s with *The Seven Year Itch* (1955), *Bus Stop* (1956), and *Will Success Spoil Rock Hunter?* (1957) and preceding his masterpiece *The Manchurian Candidate* (1962), wrote the screenplay. Axelrod was rewarded for his efforts with an Academy Award nomination for Best Adapted Screenplay, as was Hepburn for her performance as Holly. Beyond the film's strong foundations in its actors, director, and screenwriter, its success is indebted to its music and soundtrack, both for Henry Mancini's film score and for Mancini and Johnny Mercer's haunting music and lyrics for "Moon River," which respectively won the Academy Awards for Best Music, Scoring, and Best Music, Original Song.

The filming and casting of *Breakfast at Tiffany's* sparked numerous controversies—and Capote's vocal displeasure. Capote expressed his distaste for Edwards venomously: "The day I signed the contract they turned around and did exactly the reverse. They got a *lousy* director like Blake Edwards, who I could spit on!"[4] Also, Capote preferred Marilyn Monroe to play Holly Golightly: "Marilyn would have been absolutely marvelous in it. She wanted to play it too, to the extent that she worked up two whole scenes all by herself and did them for me. She was terrifically good, but Paramount doubled-crossed me in every conceivable way and cast Audrey. Audrey is an old friend and one of my favorite people, but she was just wrong for that part."[5] On another occasion he opined of Monroe's suitability for the role: "Holly had to have something touching about her . . . unfinished. Marilyn had that. But Paramount double-crossed me and gave the part to Audrey Hepburn. Audrey was not what I had in mind when I wrote that part, although she did a terrific job."[6] Capote contradicted himself in these, seeing Hepburn both as "wrong for that part" and as doing "a terrific job." His preference for Monroe to play the role of Holly Golightly coincided with his description of her in *Observations*, in which he referred to her as an "expense-account darling," perceptively capturing the mix of naiveté and artifice in Monroe that he saw as Holly's defining features. Monroe, he wrote, seemed, "casually glanced, merely another specimen of the American geisha, the expense-account darling, those cabaret-cuties whose careers progress from tinted hair at twelve to a confiscated husband or three at twenty" (*O* 85).[7]

While Capote believed that studio executives betrayed him in casting Hepburn, producer Martin Jurow countered that he in fact recruited Monroe. According to his recollections, Paula Strasberg, Monroe's dramatic advisor and wife of famed theatrical director Lee Strasberg, refused to consider the role for her client: "There is no way she will play that girl. Marilyn Monroe will not play a call girl, a lady of the evening."[8] Furthermore, Jurow thought that the film would benefit from the surprise of casting Hepburn in the part, in such contrast to her ingénue roles in *Roman Holiday* (1953) and *Sabrina* (1954). In regard to Monroe, he simply stated, "I felt that casting Marilyn as Holly would be too obvious."[9] Other candidates for the role of Holly included Shirley MacLaine, Jane Fonda, and Rosemary Clooney.[10] As Jurow fended off Capote's determination to get Monroe cast in the film, he also needed to convince Hepburn that she should take the role of Holly Golightly. Agreeing with Capote, Hepburn thought she was a poor match for the part: "I read the book and liked it very much. . . . But I was terribly afraid I was not right for the part. I thought I lacked the right sense of comedy. This part called for an extroverted character. I am an introvert. . . . Very often while I was doing the part, I was convinced I was not doing the best job."[11] According to Jurow, Hepburn also expressed reservations about Holly's sexual ethos, and he employed reverse psychology to pique her interest in the part, accusing her of misinterpreting the role: "I cannot believe you don't know the difference between a hooker and a dreamer of dreams, a lopsided romantic. If you think we want to make a movie about a veritable hooker, we don't want you near the script."[12] But despite Jurow's rhetoric, Holly Golightly *is* a "veritable hooker." The sexuality of Holly Golightly's character is whitewashed in Jurow's sketch of her, yet Hepburn's performance is central to the film's success, in that her mixture of sophistication and innocence matches the film's murky depiction of countercultural sexuality as slyly present yet knowingly camouflaged.

Casting decisions are subjective ones, but in this instance both Capote and Hepburn appear to have been rather spectacularly wrong. Certainly the voluptuous Monroe was physically unlike the novella's description of Holly as a "skinny girl" with a "flat little bottom" (*BT* 9); the narrator later comments on her "chic thinness" (*BT* 12). In the novella Holly's age is nineteen, whereas both Monroe (born 1926) and Hepburn (born 1929) were in their early thirties when the film was cast, which makes Capote's statement that "Marilyn was what I wanted—at that age, she was exactly right for the part" objectively untrue.[13] Hepburn's performance as Holly Golightly is an iconic one, for the plaintive need emanating through the character's façade of sexual sophistication, but also for her emblematic costuming. As Donald Spoto declares, "Thanks to the wardrobe designed by her friend Givenchy, the picture made her a fashion icon forevermore. . . . Audrey was henceforth considered a key arbiter, standard and model of elegance and vogue."[14] Givenchy praised Hepburn for her fashion sensibility, realizing that much of his success arose from her status as the ideal model of his fashions: "In film after film, Audrey wore clothes with such talent and flair that she created a style, which in turn had a major impact on fashion. Her chic, her youth, her bearing, and her silhouette grew ever more celebrated, enveloping me in a kind of aura or radiance that I could never have hoped for."[15] Moving from the 1950s to the 1960s, the feminine aesthetic of buxom stars such as Monroe, Jane Russell, Jayne Mansfield, Sophia Loren, Mamie van Doren, and Elizabeth Taylor was supplanted by the svelte look represented by Hepburn (a trend culminating in the rise of fashion model Twiggy in 1966), such that Billy Wilder wryly commented of Hepburn: "This girl, singlehanded, may make bosoms a thing of the past."[16]

Turning to the film's other prominent roles, Jurow recounts an encounter with Capote in which the author declared: "You know, of course, that I want to play the male lead." Because Capote based the narrator of *Breakfast at Tiffany's* on himself, his suggestion to star in the film is not as preposterous as it first sounds, but with the producers recasting Capote's novella as a romantic comedy, it would be incongruous indeed for this short, high-pitched homosexual to play the role of heterosexual gigolo Paul Varjak. Jurow delicately rejected Capote's casting proposition: "Truman, the role isn't good enough for you. All eyes will be on Holly Golightly through every frame of the picture. The male lead is just a pair of shoulders for Holly to lean on. You deserve something more dynamic, more colorful." As Jurow recollects this moment, to his relief Capote agreed: "You're right. I deserve something more dynamic."[17] In casting the role of Paul Varjak, Edwards did not want to hire George Peppard: "I always thought he was a piss-poor actor," he avowed.[18] On another occasion, he pronounced a similar sentiment, albeit in milder terms: "He just didn't have whatever it was that I wanted. He wasn't my cup of tea."[19] The producers, however, saw him as an up-and-coming (and bankable) star, and a Paramount press release described him as "the hottest young actor in Hollywood, a comer with the impact of Jimmy Dean or a young Clark Gable."[20] Producer Richard Shepherd affirmed that Patricia Neal "was always our first choice" as Varjak's lover and patron Mrs. Falenson, also known as 2E, and added, "We wanted somebody who was no-nonsense, someone who could play that kind of strong subterranean sexual role."[21] Of Buddy Ebsen for the role of Holly's abandoned husband Doc, Shepherd stated that "no-one was more suitable to play a hillbilly."[22] As Ebsen recalls, Edwards telephoned to ask him to audition: "Blake Edwards told me he had a part. If I would test for it and get it, he wanted to bet me a case of champagne that I would get an Academy Award nomination."[23] Ebsen did not receive an Oscar nomination, yet his performance imbues the film with an affecting pathos that balances out Holly's excesses.

Capote heaped particular opprobrium on the casting of Mickey Rooney as Mr. Yunioshi, the Japanese-American photographer: "It was the most mis-cast film I've ever seen. It made me want to throw up. Like Mickey Rooney playing this Japanese photographer. Well, indeed I *had* a Japanese photographer in the book, but he certainly wasn't *Mickey Rooney*."[24] Capote's Mr. Yunioshi, although a secondary character mostly incidental to the unfolding plot, is not a caricature. He speaks in unaccented English, with only slight inversions of standard word order indicating that English is not his native tongue, such as when he complains to Holly, "But always you are ringing my bell" (*BT* 12). Likewise, in Axelrod's screenplay, no indication is given that the character's speech should be inflected with such a strong, and supposedly comic, accent. Arthur Marx saw Rooney's performance as evidence of his abilities as "a very fine character actor," although "he was no longer exactly a leading man," and A. H. Weiler, reviewing the film for the *New York Times*, praised Rooney's "bucktoothed and myopic Japanese" as "broadly exotic."[25] Although Rooney's timing for physical comedy was indeed impeccable, the racist caricature of the performance now distorts the film's comic themes. Rooney's biographer Alvin Marill allows that Rooney's clowning results in a "rather funny but archly stereotypical portrayal of 'Mr. Yunioshi,'" and the film's coproducer, Richard Shepherd, condemned the casting altogether: "it was wrong to have Mickey Rooney playing this Japanese character; I felt it was ethnically improper."[26] Edwards, looking back at his film's prized status in Hollywood history, likewise regretted the decision: "I would give anything to be able to recast it."[27] Rooney himself proclaimed, "I was downright ashamed of my role in *Breakfast at Tiffany's*."[28]

Along with the transitions inherent in bring Capote's characters to the screen, the print and screen versions of *Breakfast at Tiffany's* illustrate the shifting narrative and thematic dynamics arising from adaptations. Primarily, Edwards's *Breakfast at Tiffany's* strips Capote's novella of its homosexual subtext, replacing Capote's gay and nameless narrator with Paul Varjak, a heterosexual gigolo who falls in love with Holly. Capote's narrator reflects to some degree Capote himself, as this character declares that he moved to New York City "to become the writer I wanted to be" (*BT* 3). When Holly derides his fiction as focusing excessively on "Negroes and children: who cares?" (*BT* 62), Capote is ironically taunting himself for his own prior works, such as *Other Voices, Other Rooms* and *The Grass Harp*. The film's recasting of Capote's narrator as heterosexual enables its standard romantic comedy ending of love conquering all, one that starkly differs from Capote's melancholy novella in which Holly, as she abandons her cat on the city streets, learns too late that she craves emotional connections only to cast them aside: "But what about me? . . . I'm very scared, Buster. Yes, at last. Because it could go on forever. Not knowing what's yours until you've thrown it away" (*BT* 109). The novella concludes without any sense of romantic resolution, for romance has not been its concern, whereas the film relies on the time-tested cliché of the lovers' embrace overcoming all past and future obstacles to their shared happiness.

The initial screenplay for *Breakfast at Tiffany's* was written by Sumner Locke Elliott, who penned numerous teleplays in the 1950s for *The Goodyear*

Playhouse, Studio One in Hollywood, and *Playhouse 90.* Richard Shepherd registered his displeasure with Elliott's draft, focusing on its botched efforts to rewrite Capote's queer novella into a standard romantic comedy:

> Elliott, to our way of thinking, has seriously failed to capture the warmth, the zest, the humor, the beauty and, more important, the basic heart and honesty that is Holly Golightly. The young man he has written is petty and unattractive in character, borders on the effeminate, which we all detest, and as is the case with Holly and the whole piece, is almost totally devoid of the humor and contemporary flavor that is absolutely vital for this picture.
>
> All of us are convinced that we are correct in assuming that the boy and girl get together at the end of our story, that Holly's problem, which is the principal one, is in some way resolved through the understanding, love and strength of the boy. This requires a completely different kind of male character than has been given to us by Elliott and a far more solid construction of the dramatic elements of the piece.[29]

The "young man" in Elliott's script reflects Capote's presentation of himself in *Breakfast at Tiffany's,* and so it is unsurprising that this character "borders on the effeminate." In demanding a standard romantic comedy plotline, Shepherd excised the homosexual subtext of Capote's novella in favor of an obviously heterosexual male lead, one who would convincingly pursue Holly's affections.

Stripping Capote's source text of its homosexual themes and restructuring it into a romantic comedy, Edwards concomitantly imbued it with queer undertones, as the film flirts with gender play, prostitution, and ostensible sexual deviance in numerous scenes. Radley Metzger, famed as an early distributor and director of erotic films, extolled Edwards's *Breakfast at Tiffany's* as "the most influential movie in the area of breaking down old taboos and letting the age of permissiveness come in."[30] Released in 1961, the film foreshadowed the loosening sexual mores in American culture throughout the ensuing decade, painting a picture of sexually liberated romantics who find true love despite their vocations as quasi prostitutes. In this light, both Capote's and Edwards's versions of *Breakfast at Tiffany's* are queer narratives that undermine conceptions of normative heterosexuality, although the former encodes themes of homosexuality to achieve this effect, whereas the latter concentrates on deviancies from heterosexuality.

Capote first heard the phrase "breakfast at Tiffany's," the queer kernel from which his novella grew, in an amusing story about a one-night stand. A cosmopolitan gay man enjoyed an evening with an attractive rube, as Gerald Clarke recounts:

> Truman had once heard an anecdote and filed it away, waiting for the time he could use it. During World War II a man of middle age entertained a Marine one Saturday night. The man enjoyed himself so much in the Marine's muscular embrace that he felt he should buy him something to show his gratitude; but since it was Sunday when they woke up, and the stores were closed, the best he could offer was breakfast.
>
> "Where would you like to go?" he asked. "Pick the fanciest, most expensive place in town."
>
> The Marine, who was not a native, had heard of only one fancy and expensive place in New York, and he said, "Let's have breakfast at Tiffany's."[31]

The audience of the anecdote knows, of course, that Tiffany's is a jewelry store, not a restaurant, and is invited to laugh at the rube's naiveté. In Capote's novella, Holly expresses her desire for fame and riches—"I want to still be me when I wake up one fine morning and have breakfast at Tiffany's" (*BT* 39)—but the line is presented simply as a wistful dream, not as a mark of her ignorance, and the impossibility of the fantasy is then elided as she evokes the feeling of serenity that Tiffany's grants her: "What I've found does the most good is just to get into a taxi and go to Tiffany's. It calms me down right away, the quietness and the proud look of it; nothing very bad could happen to you there" (*BT* 40). Edwards metamorphoses Capote's fantasy of desire into the film's opening shots, as Holly peers through Tiffany's windows while sipping coffee and eating a pastry. This chimerical vision, so central to the novella's focus on the nexus between financial and amatory desire, is made real in the film, a simple side trip available to Holly whenever she fancies.

The predominant heterosexuality of Holly Golightly's lifestyle in both the novella and the film eclipses Capote's homosexual themes, but to overlook the queer aspects of Holly's world obscures key moments of the text that provide a better understanding of its sexual dynamics and their reimagining in the film. Foremost, Capote codes Holly's two closest friends—the narrator and the bartender Joe Bell—as homosexuals, although he does so with such deft touches of description that some readers fail to recognize that these characters are gay. For instance, both men repeatedly express their love for Holly but always in platonic terms. The narrator realizes his feelings for her—"For I *was* in love with her"—before qualifying this attachment as free from eroticism: "Just as I'd once been in love with my mother's elderly colored cook and a postman who let me follow him on his rounds and a whole family named McKendrick. That category of love generates jealousy, too" (*BT* 76). In a similar vein, Joe Bell protests, "Sure I loved her. But it wasn't that I wanted to touch her," thereby confirming his paternal affection for her rather than his erotic attraction to her (*BT* 9). Such proclamations of asexual affection for Holly reflect American literary mores of the 1940s and 1950s, in which gay writers coded characters as gay rather than forthrightly affirming their sexual identities. As Molly Haskell argues, "The repressiveness of the [1950s] both enabled and forced the homosexual writer to disguise himself,"[32] a necessity that led Capote to downplay or otherwise camouflage the homosexual themes of many of his works.

Within Capote's coded text, a primary clue to the narrator's homosexuality lies in Holly's formulation of how to determine whether a man is gay: "If a man doesn't like baseball, then he must like horses, and if he doesn't like either of them, well, I'm in trouble anyway: he don't like girls" (*BT* 38). These words resonate in the reader's mind when the narrator reports the contents of Holly's bookshelves—"of the books there, more than half were about horses, the rest baseball"—and then feigns interest in horses: "Pretending an interest in *Horseflesh and How to Tell It* gave me sufficiently private opportunity for sizing Holly's friends" (*BT* 35). If this passage were insufficient to convince readers that the narrator holds no interest in horses and, therefore, no sexual interest in women, the episode when Holly takes him horseback riding to disastrous effect also figures him, according to her horses-or-baseball criteria, as a homosexual. Similarly, when Holly tells the narrator that she will not testify against Sally Tomato, the crime boss for whom she delivers coded messages from prison, she calls him a name laden with queer connotations: "Well, I may be rotten to the core, Maude, *but*: testify against a friend I will not" (*BT* 102–3). In homosexual slang, "maude" signifies a male prostitute or a male homosexual, according to Eric Partridge's *Dictionary of Slang and Unconventional English*.[33] Also, Capote's narrator makes a veiled reference to his homosexuality when comparing his rain-soaked journey from Holly's apartment to Joe Bell's bar with another difficult trek he undertook years ago: "Never mind why, but once I walked from New Orleans to Nancy's Landing, Mississippi, just under five hundred miles. It was a light-hearted lark compared to the journey to Joe Bell's bar" (*BT* 105). Nancy's Landing is Capote's creation; it does not exist on any map of Mississippi. Eric Partridge defines the term "nancy" as referring either to the posterior or to "an effeminate man, especially a passive homosexual,"[34] and so Nancy's Landing serves as Capote's code phrase for a gay resort, an imaginary Fire Island or Provincetown on the Mississippi Gulf Coast. The narrator's coy "Never mind why" appears to be a subtle rhetorical move to distract attention from his sexual self-confession—which then draws further attention to it.

Although Holly's friendships with the narrator and Joe Bell are asexual, they allow Capote to voice a liberal sexual agenda through her. Beyond these friendships, Holly espouses forward-thinking views on homosexuality and sexual identity. In words echoing Alfred Kinsey's *Sexual Behavior in the Human Male* (1948), which posits human sexuality as a continuum, Holly avows her potential homosexual inclination: "Of course people couldn't help but think I must be a bit of a dyke myself. And of course I am. Everyone is: a bit" (*BT* 22). She also proclaims the novel's theme about the necessity of honesty in one's affections—"Be anything but a coward, a pretender, an emotional crook, a whore: I'd rather have cancer than a dishonest heart" (*BT* 83)—and her words to the narrator about gay marriage remain topical today: "A person ought to be able to marry men or women . . . No, I'm serious. Love should be allowed" (*BT* 83). Holly's queer world marks her as a participant in the sexual struggle against conformity and conservatism, rather than as merely a charming young woman who inspires protective and paternal love about her. At the novella's end, Capote makes it clear that Holly leaves a queer legacy behind her when Quaintance Smith, who "entertained as many gentleman callers of a noisy nature as Holly ever had," moves into her old apartment (*BT* 110). The name Quaintance alludes to George Quaintance, a painter of the 1940s and 1950s whose art bordered on soft-core gay pornography. In Capote's *Breakfast at Tiffany's*, Holly Golightly's queer world lives on after she flees the constraints of New York City to ensure her freedom.

Beyond her participation in a gay demimonde, Holly herself undermines normative constructions of 1950s heterosexuality. In this light Capote casts her as a queer, if not a homosexual, character, one who subverts traditional erotic paradigms. In the story's frame narrative, Joe Bell updates the narrator about Holly's travels after she departed New York. He reveals that she has broken the taboo of miscegenation when, during her African travels, she "shared the wood-carver's mat," a revelation that makes Joe Bell wince (*BT* 8). Capote also hints that Holly's relationship with her suitor Rusty Trawler involves acting as dominatrix, when she gently yet firmly disciplines him for his rudeness:

> "I want you to behave, Rusty." She spoke softly, but there was a governess threat of punishment in her tone that caused an odd flush of pleasure, of gratitude, to pink his face.
> "You don't love me," he complained, as though they were alone.
> "Nobody loves naughtiness." (*BT* 41)

The traces of sadomasochism in this exchange, as Holly plays the role of the stern governess chastising Rusty for his petulant behavior, imbue their relationship with a queer edge in which, despite Rusty's wealth, Holly rules over him socially and sexually. For Capote, Holly's queerness emerges both in her progressive views on homosexuality and in her flaunting of heteronormativity, as she transgresses racial taboos and indulges in sophisticated sex play.

In Edwards's filming of these queer story lines, Holly shifts from her role as an object of platonic homosexual affection to an object of heterosexual desire, while she simultaneously dismantles heterosexual normativity as understood in the 1950s and early 1960s. Certainly film censors of this period would not allow positive, or even neutral, depictions of homosexuality. In early drafts of the screenplay, Axelrod expanded the small role of Quaintance Smith, who moves into Paul's apartment after Paul moves out. Axelrod's script describes the newly refurbished setting as one of queer excess: "The apartment has been completely redone since Paul left. It is, if possible, even more elaborate."[35] When Varjak climbs through Smith's window to reach Holly's apartment, Smith exclaims preciously: "I have lived in a number of bizarre buildings in my time . . . but this . . . and you may quote me wildly on the subject . . . is far and away the bizarrest of all."[36] Censor Geoffrey Shurlock warned the producers not to depict homosexuality in any light, and in this short scene, he cautioned, "There should be no attempt to give Mr. Smith the mannerisms usually associated with a homosexual."[37] Given Shepherd's determination to film the novella as a romantic comedy with a virile male lead, and given the censors' refusal to permit any depiction of homosexuality, even through such a minor character as Quaintance Smith, Edwards was forced to strip the film of its homosexual story lines and themes. Yet, as *Breakfast at Tiffany's* so tellingly demonstrates, heterosexuality can be queer, too, when one dismisses erotic taboos, as Holly and Paul do through their vocations as romanticized sex workers.

In both the novella and the film, Holly is a prostitute, but only nominally so, as Capote depicts her relative lack of sexual experience despite her reputation: "Not that I've warmed the multitudes some people say: I don't blame the bastards for *saying* it, I've always thrown out such a jazzy line. Really, though, I toted up the other night, and I've only had eleven lovers" (*BT* 82). Adhering to this aspect of her characterization, Edwards shields his audience from conclusively viewing Holly as a prostitute. Although refusing to see Holly as a call girl may necessitate reading naively against the grain, the film repeatedly depicts her circumventing sex with her suitors, a business model that would undermine any prostitute's financial prospects. In the film's opening sequence, Holly returns from her breakfast consumed while gazing wistfully through Tiffany's windows, only to encounter her admirer Sid Arbuck, who has followed her home and demands her attention, reminding her of his earlier generosity: "And when you asked for a little change for the powder room, what do I give you? A fifty-dollar bill. Now doesn't that give me some rights?" In Capote's novella, Holly rejects Arbuck because he has not been so generous, dismissing him for his stinginess in response to her request for powder-room funds: "Oh, Mr. *Ar*buck," she calls. "The next time a girl wants a little powder-room change . . . take my advice, darling: *don't* give her twenty cents!" (*BT* 14). In the film, however, Arbuck disburses the necessary funds, yet is rejected because Holly does not agree with him that fifty dollars grants him any rights to her body. He leaves in a hangdog huff when Mr. Yunioshi threatens Holly, "I going to call the vice squad on you." This scene crystallizes the interpretive crux of Holly's occupation: how can viewers see her as a prostitute, if the film circumvents this conclusion at the same time such scenes virtually demand this conclusion? Capote depicts her rejecting Arbuck because he has not paid to enjoy her company; Edwards depicts the same encounter, yet in this instance Arbuck's money does not grant him entry into Holly's chambers. In both scenarios, Holly's evasion of sex enables one to believe in her essential innocence, no matter how tenuous such a vision might be.

Mr. Yunioshi's threat to call the vice squad would appear to cement the view of Holly as a prostitute, but the scene merely continues to flirt with this possibility rather than to confirm it, as she quiets Mr. Yunioshi by wheedling, "Don't be angry, you dear little man. I won't do it again. If you promise not to be angry, I might let you take those pictures we mentioned," then bids him goodnight with a blown kiss. Is one to assume that Mr. Yunioshi hopes to shoot erotic photographs of Holly? Her promise ends his tirade, but the film never depicts her following through on this enigmatic engagement. Axelrod did little more than transcribe Holly's words to Mr. Yunioshi in this scene from Capote's novella, but if viewers are to take their lead from the book, Mr. Yunioshi appears to be a legitimate magazine photographer, not a pornographer, as Capote writes that Mag Wildwood poses for a series of Mr. Yunioshi's photographs that are to be published in *Bazaar* (*BT* 43). Moreover, if Mr. Yunioshi were a pornographer, he would be unlikely to call the vice squad on Holly, thereby also calling attention to himself. In the novella, Holly's primary nemesis among her neighbors is not Mr. Yunioshi but the coloratura Madame Sapphia Spanella (whose name, with its echo of sapphism, further colors Capote's novella with homosexual allusions). In Holly's interactions with Mr. Yunioshi, the possibility of sex work, whether as a prostitute or as an erotic model, lurks in the background, but Edwards refuses to confirm these suspicions for his viewers, just as Capote refused to do so before him.

Likewise, when Holly outlines her business model for negotiating payment for visiting the convicted felon Sally Tomato in prison, she explains to Paul that she receives money for her companionship rather than for any sexual favors. Hepburn insouciantly delivers the lines "I told him, 'Look, darling, you've got the wrong Holly Golightly. A girl can do as well as that on trips to the powder room. I mean, any gentleman with the slightest chic will give a girl a fifty-dollar bill for the powder room. And I always ask for cab fare, too. That's another fifty dollars.'"[38] Holly's comparison of these business propositions obfuscates the possibility that she prostitutes herself in either scenario: because it is impossible for her to have sex with Sally Tomato during his incarceration, it appears from this financial agreement that Holly's pecuniary success stems from her ability to get men to pay for her company while circumventing the necessity of sleeping with them. Peter Lehman and William Luhr argue of Holly's occupational status, "Although we do see her rejecting the advances of two of these 'rats' in her apartment, the fact that she depends for most of her money upon them . . . would indicate that she is not able to put them all off and that the contract implied with the fifty-dollar 'powder-room' tips is at times fulfilled."[39] Lehman and Luhr are correct if one applies the rules of reality to this romantic comedy fantasy, but the obfuscation of Holly's vocation as a prostitute is key to the film's muddled sexual themes, in which countercultural sexual identities are camouflaged under a thin veneer of normalcy. Sam Wasson, with a particularly apt formulation, summarizes the tensions in Holly's character: "With the help of screenwriter George Axelrod's strategic adaptation, the character became a vision of studio innuendo—as if Mae West birthed her in the Hays Office."[40] That is to say, the film allows one to believe in Holly's innocence even while knowing such innocence is not credible. Edwards similarly observed that many of his viewers simply overlooked the sexual nature of Holly's profession: "I don't think that the majority of the audience in those days really ever thought of Audrey Hepburn as a hooker, as a call girl. . . . when it was over with, they didn't even know."[41] Given her star image as developed in the lighthearted fare of *Roman Holiday* and *Sabrina*, it was difficult for many viewers to see Hepburn in such a sexual role, as Peter Krämer posits: "Audrey Hepburn's celebrated style, respectability, and even nobility finally neutralized Holly's sexual transgressiveness; on or off screen Hepburn was hardly perceived as a sexual being at all."[42]

Whereas Holly's vocation as a prostitute is obscured, the film clearly depicts her eventual romantic interest, Paul Varjak, as a gigolo. Numerous parallels link Holly to Paul: As Holly repeatedly awakens Mr. Yunioshi to let her into their apartment building when she loses her keys, so too does Paul wake her when first finding his new residence. "I'm sorry to bother you, but I couldn't get the downstairs door opened," he apologizes. Holly's cat symbolizes her quest for companionship and a home, and the film links Paul to feline imagery as well, with the title of his book, *Nine Lives*, referring to the folkloric belief in cats' agility and longevity. But the film's refusal to depict Holly in a compromised position, in contrast to its frank depiction of Paul's sexual relationship with his patron Mrs. Falenson, draws a key distinction between Holly and Paul. The scene in which Holly realizes that Paul is a gigolo begins with her being pursued by one of her many suitors, or "rats." She flees to the safety of her bathroom, with the "rat" pounding on the door and calling, "Hey, baby. Where you going? Come on, baby. Open the door. Be a pal. You're breaking up a beautiful party." Holly climbs the fire escape and peers into Paul's bedroom, where she sees that Paul has slept with Mrs. Falenson: he lies in bed, shirtless and presumably naked under the sheets, as Mrs. Falenson emerges fully dressed from his bathroom. Mrs. Falenson leaves some cash on his desk, kisses him goodbye as he sleeps, and departs. Holly then enters Paul's bedroom and implies that she understands the nature of his relationship with his patron: "I must say, she works

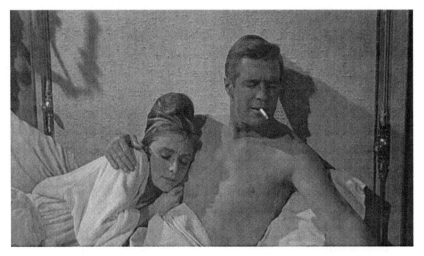

FIG. 9 *Breakfast at Tiffany's*: Holly Golightly (Audrey Hepburn) and Paul Varjak (George Peppard) discuss their love lives in bed. Paul has been undressed to undertake his duties with Mrs. Falenson; Holly, in contrast, undresses herself while escaping her "rat."

late hours for a decorator," she wryly comments, later remarking, "Three hundred dollars? She's very generous. Is it by the week, the hour, or what?" Although Paul takes offense, she soothes his feelings by declaring, "I was just trying to let you know I understand." As filmed, the scene is milder than in Axelrod's screenplay, which depicts Holly entering Paul's bedroom in a bathrobe and declaring, "Look at that . . . tooth marks. Genuine tooth marks,"[43] suggesting that her "rat" literally took a bite out of her. Further, she provocatively expands her soothing words to indicate their shared vocation: "Please don't be angry. I was just trying to let you know I understand. Not only that. I approve. In a way we're really in the same line of business."[44] The censor, however, rejected such frank discussion of the sex trade: "Also, please eliminate Holly's line, 'I was just trying to let you know I understand. Not only that, I approve.'"[45]

Although Holly expresses sympathy to Paul for the degradations of sex work (and solidarity with him in the expunged lines), Edwards's shooting of the scene stresses her sexual escape in contrast to Paul's sexual complaisance. While evading the "rat" in her apartment, she wears her signature black dress by Givenchy, but before slipping through the bathroom window onto the fire escape, she changes into a bathrobe. This costume change is critical to viewers' sympathy for Holly: the fact that she still wears her dress while fleeing the "rat" proves that his sexual advances were success-fully spurned, in contrast to Paul, lying spent and naked in bed following his duties with Mrs. Falenson. Holly comments, "You must be absolutely exhausted. I mean, it is very late, and you were sound asleep and everything." Her words focus on his sleep rather than on the erotic activities preceding it, yet viewers have seen Mrs. Falenson exiting Paul's bathroom and under-stand the reasons for his fatigue. The scene concludes with Holly asking Paul, "Do you mind if I just get in with you for a minute? It's all right. Really, it is. We're friends, that's all," as she cuddles up against his naked body. The scene's juxtaposition of innocence and deviance—the female quasi prosti-tute eluding the clutches of her john, to snuggle against a naked gigolo who has only recently serviced his patron—rewrites the meaning of midcentury American sexual propriety, for viewers are intended to cheer the incipient affection between heroine and hero despite their mercenary circumstances. The necessity of Holly's costume change also becomes apparent, for she must not be dressed in evening wear if she is to join Paul in bed. Her change prior to entering the apartment quells the sexual dynamics between the two sex workers cuddling together, one of them naked.

Another key distinction between Holly and Paul is that Holly desires, or so she proclaims, to be a kept woman, whereas Paul succeeds in his ambition to be a kept man, only to then reject the security of this position. Although Paul appears to have been involved with Mrs. Falenson only sexually, not emotionally, Holly falls in love with her wealthy suitor José, as she confesses to Paul: "Look, I know what you're thinking, and I don't blame you. I've always thrown out such a jazzy line. Really, except for Doc and yourself, José's my first non-rat romance."[46] When José breaks up with her over her complicity in the Sally Tomato scandal, Holly is devastated; in contrast, when Paul ends his liaison with his patron, he is asserting a newly devel-oped sense of agency. Mrs. Falenson accepts the possibility that he has taken a new lover and cavalierly offers him a thousand dollars while joking about the necessity of a male prostitutes' union. She then teases him about his new romance while reminding him of his financial duress: "I do believe love has found Andy Hardy. Let's see . . . a waitress? A salesgirl? No. She'd have to be someone rich, wouldn't she, Paul?" Mrs. Falenson's reference to the Andy Hardy films of the 1930s through the 1950s casts Paul's love for Holly as innocent, naive, and sincere (and ironically reminds viewers that the star of these films, Mickey Rooney, plays a Japanese man in the current picture).

Paul defends himself by casting himself as Holly's protector: "Thing is, I can help her, and it's a nice feeling for a change." Insulted by Mrs. Falenson's jokes, Paul draws pride from his love for Holly and rejects his patron: "When you get yourself a new writer to help, try and find one my size. That way you won't have to even shorten the sleeves," as he exits his walk-in closet, with its many articles of clothing documenting Mrs. Falenson's generosity to him. The deployment of the closet in a film with queer themes, in which Paul dramatically exits from his cosseted life as a gigolo to seek Holly's love, imbues the film's treatment of heterosexuality with an overarching irony: in this instance, the exit from the closet allows the character to be the straight man he has always been and simultaneously to free himself from his queer position as a hired companion to a strong and sexually dominant woman.

To heighten the gendered dynamics of Paul and Mrs. Falenson's relationship, Edwards underscores that his financial dependence on her effeminizes him, which further overturns gendered norms. When she telephones Paul to cancel a rendezvous after her husband's unexpected return, she dubs him "Lucille" to dupe her spouse: "Lucille, darling? . . . I've been trying desperately to reach you. Bill just got back. [a shot of Bill's hand making a drink] A day early, the beast. So I'm afraid I'll have to beg off. You'll explain to the rest of the girls?" In their scenes together, Patricia Neal portrays Mrs. Falenson in a manner to accentuate her power over Paul, emphasizing her character's sexual dominance through her cool patrician mien. Her decisions in this regard infuriated Peppard, as Edwards affirmed: "I do remember a certain tension between [Neal and Peppard], which wasn't bad for their characters—her being a strong woman, and him a kept man. Patricia had suggested in one scene that George sit on her lap. He was horrified. He said he would never do anything like that. To which she replied, 'Maybe you wouldn't, but would Paul?' She really cut him down to size."[47] Reminiscing about the film, Neal summarized her conflicts with Peppard—"And I dominated him a lot more in the script. And he didn't want to be seen in that condition"—suggesting as well that Peppard "seemed to want to be an old-time movie hunk. . . . In the end George played the role as he wanted, and I always felt that had Blake stood his ground, the film would have been stronger. And so would George Peppard."[48] Such disagreements expose the ways in which the queer themes of Breakfast at Tiffany's—in this instance, the dismantling of the starring male's position as sexually dominant—troubled Peppard, who resisted filming scenes that would accentuate his character's weakness.

For example, in scenes not included in the film's release, Axelrod highlights Mrs. Falenson's sexual agency in contrast to Varjak's financial dependence. She speaks of him as if he were an investment, and then, with her intentions clearly expressed, demands immediate dividends. The screenplay sets the scene as Mrs. Falenson "draws him to her and kisses him. When they break she very gently pushes him away from her and toward the bed." She then wheedles, "It's not so bad, is it? Really?" to which Paul gamely replies, "I suppose there are tougher ways of earning a living." One can readily imagine Patricia Neal delivering the following lines with patrician aplomb and sexual anticipation: "You *bet* there are, darling. You just bet there are."[49] The deletion of these scenes builds Varjak's masculinity, lessening his effeminacy and his dependence on Mrs. Falenson, yet the image of the closet remains the defining metaphor for this midcentury American gigolo who must liberate himself from the shackles of heterosexual intercourse when it is coupled to his financial distress.

In Holly's cinematic transition from mercenary to romantic, she must learn from Paul about the meaning of love, and one could well argue that this plotline reinstates traditional gender roles, with Paul freeing himself from Mrs. Falenson's control and then helping Holly to escape from her "rats" as well. When Holly announces her plan to marry Rusty Trawler, the ninth richest man in America under fifty, she does so with financial comfort as her goal: "I need money, and I'll do whatever I have to do to get it. So, this time next month, I'll be the new Mrs. Rusty Trawler." Paul admonishes her, "If I were you, I'd be more careful with my money. Rusty Trawler is too hard a way of earning it." When they reconcile after this fight, they proclaim their mutual desire to marry each other if they were rich, and Holly kisses Paul on the lips. Paul's growing disapproval of Holly's sexual lifestyle reaches its climax when he gives her fifty dollars to go to the powder room at the library, enacting her quasi-prostitutional ritual in a setting that privileges his identity as a writer and that thereby accentuates his newfound freedom from prostitution. This encounter validates Paul's reconceived sense of heterosexual desire as inspired by love rather than penury, and Holly's ultimate acquiescence to his viewpoint superficially cleanses the film of its mercenary treatment of desire.

Beyond the queer dynamics of Holly's and Paul's sexual lifestyles, Edwards's *Breakfast at Tiffany's* paints the early 1960s as a time of recreational excess, particularly in its famed party scene. In Capote's novella, the party is a stag

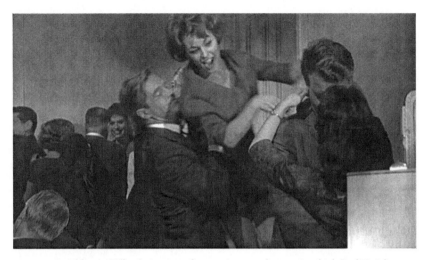

FIG. 10 *Breakfast at Tiffany's*: A scene of suggestive sexual excess in which Paul Varjak (George Peppard) builds a ménage à trois out of miscellaneous party guests.

affair for Holly's admirers—"Within the next quarter-hour, a stag party had taken over the apartment" (*BT* 35)—during which Mag Wildwood intrudes to provide another female body among a sea of men. This party's predominant homosociality is recast in the film as a heterosocial affair of rampant excess and sexual suggestiveness, and Axelrod's script establishes a raucous tone such that the "general effect is rather like the famous Marx Brothers 'state-room scene'" in *A Night at the Opera* (1935).[50] Edwards shot the scene with numerous reversals: a laughing woman stares at herself in a mirror, but a subsequent shot shows her crying as mascara running down her cheeks; a man consults a watch worn on a woman's ankle; a drunken woman talks with another woman, but when the drunken woman looks away, a man stands up beneath her companion, lifting this woman up so that he is now on face level with the drunken woman; a man wearing an eye patch argues with a woman over whether he was supposed to pick her up, and then lifts up the eye patch to reveal his healthy eye; a man sits on Paul, and so he gives him a hotfoot. Also, as Paul escorts José to the fire escape via the bathroom, he plucks a woman away from her male companion and deposits her onto a couple, whose amorous flirtations she appears to join. As Paul and José enter the bathroom, they find O. J. Berman embracing a woman he earlier dubbed Irving, an echo of the novella's interest in homoerotic attractions. The party scene continually flirts with attractions polymorphous and ostensibly perverse, none of which is developed into a coherent story line but all of which contribute to the film's subversion of sexual conformity.

Such depictions of prostitution and sexual excess throughout *Breakfast at Tiffany's* undercut images of Holly as a sexual naïf, despite Hepburn's obdurate good-girl persona, and the film's sexual dynamics further subvert any vision of heteronormativity through the specter of pedophilia haunting both it and Capote's novella. When Holly's abandoned husband Doc finds her in New York, he explains to Paul the circumstances of their marriage: "Now, you might think the average person going on fourteen wouldn't know his own mind. But you take Lula Mae—she was an exceptional person. I'll tell you, son, she just plumb broke our hearts when she run off like she done."[51] In both versions of the narrative, it is clear that Holly had sex with Doc as a young teenager, as she does again in the narrative present. In the novella, she confesses to the narrator that she got no sleep the night of Doc's visit, and then blushes. "Well, I had to. Doc really loves me, you know" (*BT* 73). In the film, Doc carries Holly into her apartment, enacting the traditional iconography of a groom carrying his bride over the threshold. Both versions of the narrative agree that the marriage was illegal, but in Capote's novella Holly simply assumes that the marriage could not be valid—"*Divorce* him? Of course I never divorced him. I was only fourteen, for God's sake. It couldn't have been *legal*" (*BT* 72)—whereas in the film she announces, "It was annulled ages ago, but he just won't accept it," so as to provide viewers with a conclusive resolution to a pedophilic marriage. Indeed, this change in dialogue reflects censors' concerns, as Geoffrey Shurlock insisted that Holly's marriage to Doc be terminated with legal clarity in the film: "You will recall it was agreed that Holly would explain that her marriage to Doc had 'never been a real marriage at all, and that when she left him, the marriage had been annulled."[52] Doc then returns home to Texas, but the specter of his desire for Holly as his child bride permeates the film with a sentimental yet disturbing vision of heterosexuality's pedophilic underbelly.

In alluding to Doc's sexual desire for Holly as a young girl, Edwards develops Capote's narrative interest in the sex lives of children, a theme running throughout much of his fiction and films, particularly *Other Voices, Other Rooms* and *The Innocents*. In this regard, Paul's conversation with Doc takes place as Doc eats a box of Cracker Jack and shares it with Paul. Paul finds the toy prize inside the box—the ring that he and Holly later have engraved at Tiffany's—and offers it to its owner: "It's the prize from the Cracker Jacks.

You want it?" Doc replies that he does not. As the ring symbolizes Holly, she passes first through Doc's hands and then to Paul's, culminating in the climactic scene when he tosses the ring to her—"Here, I've been carrying this thing around for months"—as he exits the taxi transporting her to the airport. The ring, thus transformed from a children's toy into a token of lifelong love, also encodes Holly as a woman whose self and sexuality are traded by men, whether driven by the pedophilic desire of her abandoned husband or the amatory devotion of her suitor. The film concludes with Holly and Paul reuniting, as she also reunites with her discarded cat, and a tidy romance ending writes over, but cannot erase, the queer themes released throughout the film. Love conquers all for these mercenary prostitutes, who really weren't so mercenary after all, and this ending strips viewers' perceptions of their occupations in favor of a romanticized view of heterosexuality, in which love redeems two lost souls through their eternal union. Queerly encoded under a patina of impossible innocence, the love that Holly and Paul share reveals that normative heterosexuality is a chimerical vision, one dependent upon a recalcitrant insistence on presuming the innocence of heterosexuality rather than acknowledging its underbelly of erotic transgressions.

"Too bad about the Tiffany film. I doubt that I will ever go to see it,"[53] Capote wrote in a personal letter to Cecil Beaton in 1961. In a 1963 interview he publicly reiterated, "I thought it was awful. I will never allow another movie version of a novel I've written."[54] He later summarized his dislike for Edwards's film: "The film became a mawkish valentine to New York City and Holly and, as a result, was thin and pretty, whereas it should have been rich and ugly."[55] But as Peter Lehman and William Luhr argue, Edwards's *Breakfast at Tiffany's* is not simply a "mawkish Valentine to New York City" but a complex and contradictory work in itself and in its depiction of the city: "*Breakfast at Tiffany's*, then, expresses an ambiguous, contradictory attitude toward New York City. . . . it is a chic center of cosmopolitan style, energy, exuberance, and attractive nonconformist behavior. . . . On the other hand, this freewheeling lifestyle is superficial and the main characters have to escape it in order to mature and develop a growing relationship that leads them toward true love."[56] In this light, to see Edwards's film as "thin and pretty," as Capote does, is to overlook its sly depiction of the queerness of heterosexuality, in which two quasi prostitutes find love among the vagaries of their occupations and the shifting sexual mores of American culture. Ironically, Edwards's *Breakfast at Tiffany's* may have inspired some of

Capote's subsequent fiction, for the scenes in *Answered Prayers* in which a wealthy and respected female author adopts the narrator/gigolo P. B. Jones as her protégé mirrors Mrs. Falenson's relationship with Paul Varjak. Capote's passionate dislike for *Breakfast at Tiffany's* reflects his disappointment with its lack of fidelity to his vision of the narrative as rich and ugly, yet in their joint queerness, the novella and the film promote a progressive sexual agenda just below the surface of Holly Golightly's "innocent" lifestyle and its intersections with love, romance, and commerce.

Capote, Crime, and Capital Punishment
▶ Richard Brooks's *In Cold Blood*

With *In Cold Blood*, his account of the slaughter of Herb, Bonnie, Nancy, and Kenyon Clutter at the hands of Perry Smith and Dick Hickock, Capote credited himself with inventing the nonfiction novel, one that couples the linearity of a journalistic account with fiction's depth of character, structure, and style.[1] As Capote envisioned, *In Cold Blood* would break down the borders between journalism and fiction through its unflinching realism. In comparing the two genres, he posited that journalism suffers in comparison to fiction because of its inherent linearity: "Journalism, you see, always moves along on a horizontal plane, telling a story, while fiction—good fiction—moves vertically, taking you deeper and deeper into character and events."[2] In another interview Capote admitted the paradox of the term *nonfiction novel* and confessed that he employed it to generate publicity—"About that nonfiction-novel business, I wish I'd never said it. People didn't understand. But one has to do something."[3] He likewise confessed the exaggeration of claiming that he created this genre, acknowledging his creative debt to Lillian Ross: "Some years earlier, Lillian Ross had published *Picture*, her account of the making of a movie, *The Red Badge of Courage*; with its fast cuts, its flash forward and back, it was itself like a movie, and as I read it, I wondered what would happen if the author let go of her hard linear straight-reporting discipline and handled her material as if it were fictional—would the book gain or lose?" (*MC* xiv).

From his analysis of Ross's *Picture*, it appears that Capote intended the nonfiction novel as a literary genre influenced by film, with "fast cuts" and the ability to "flash forward and back." However, in a 1966 interview George Plimpton asked Capote if he employed cinematic techniques in writing *In Cold Blood*, to which Capote replied, "Consciously, not at all. Subconsciously, who knows?"[4] On another occasion he described film's aesthetic influences on *In Cold Blood*: "I wanted to produce a journalistic novel, something on a large scale that would have the credibility of fact, the immediacy of film, the depth and freedom of prose, and the precision of poetry" (*MC* xiv). Despite this typically Capotean mishmash of intentionality—whether he consciously or subconsciously modeled aspects of his nonfiction novel on cinematic structures—it is apparent that *In Cold Blood* is indebted to the narrative strategies of film. Moreover, the book's relationship with motion pictures is symbiotic, in that it has spawned virtually its own film subgenre, beginning with Richard Brooks's 1967 adaptation and continuing with the 1996 television miniseries directed by Jonathan Kaplan. Bennett Miller's *Capote* (2005) and Douglas McGrath's *Infamous* (2006), which are addressed in chapter 10, focus on Capote's journey to Kansas to investigate the Clutter murders and on his subsequent writing of *In Cold Blood*, testifying to the inherent interest in this material and its status as Capote's finest literary achievement.

As the writing of *In Cold Blood* proceeded, many studios expressed keen interest in filming it. Capote recruited a close friend, the socialite Slim Hayward (ex-Hawks), to market the movie rights. She recalls in her memoirs: "I was . . . rather terrified of going into the marketplace to start selling such a property. Fortunately, the offers came right in, and I was soon turning down very substantial sums for 1961: $250,000 from Twentieth-Century Fox, $300,000 from Frank Sinatra. Though the book was still unfinished, I believed in it to such a degree that I was certain if I held out long enough Truman could get a million dollars."[5] Before any deal was inked, Slim married again to become Slim Keith and retired from the project, encouraging Capote to work with the legendary agent Irving "Swifty" Lazar. She notes, "Truman finally agreed, but only under the condition that if Swifty sold the movie rights I would still get a percentage."[6] The bidding war for *In Cold Blood* became contentious, stoking a Hollywood brawl when Lazar and Otto

Preminger scuffled at a nightclub after Preminger accused Lazar of duplicity in their negotiations. Gloria Steinem detailed the altercation in *Glamour*, "A nightclub fight between Irving Lazar, who was the agent in the sale of *In Cold Blood* film rights to Richard Brooks, and producer Otto Preminger, who wanted the rights, has already given headline publicity to that movie yet unmade."[7] Of the melee, in which Lazar's wife slapped Preminger, followed by Lazar hitting him with a water goblet, Preminger punningly piped, "He gave me no warning. . . . Talk about cold blood!"[8] In the end, despite the bruises both physical and professional, Preminger lost, Brooks won, and the film of Capote's work-in-progress seized the limelight long before production commenced.

▶ The Filming of *In Cold Blood* (1967)

In the mid-1960s Brooks's career was at its height. Early successes as a screenwriter, notably for John Huston's *Key Largo* (1948), paved the way for him to assume the director's chair in 1950 with *Crisis*, a dramatic thriller starring Cary Grant. For many of his films, Brooks both wrote the screenplays and directed, including his adaptations of Tennessee Williams's plays *Cat on a Hot Tin Roof* (1958) and *Sweet Bird of Youth* (1962) and other esteemed literary works such as Dostoevsky's *The Brothers Karamazov* (1958), Sinclair Lewis's *Elmer Gantry* (1960), and Joseph Conrad's *Lord Jim* (1965). Throughout his career Brooks earned numerous Academy Award nominations for his directing (*Cat on a Hot Tin Roof; The Professionals*, 1966; *In Cold Blood*, 1967) and for his screenplays, both adapted and original (*Cat on a Hot Tin Roof; Elmer Gantry; Blackboard Jungle*, 1955; *The Professionals; In Cold Blood*). He won the Oscar for his adapted screenplay of *Elmer Gantry*. Measured against this pedigree of literary and cinematic achievement, few directors of the 1960s were as qualified for the process of adapting a major literary work to the screen. Capote, in an undated telegram taped in the copy of *In Cold Blood* that he sent to Brooks, professed, "There is no one I would rather have had it than you. . . . Am very pleased and happy."[9] Capote also declared, "I don't know if any other director would have the strength or the stamina to do this movie right."[10]

Capote explained why, despite his past screenwriting endeavors, he did not undertake the script himself: "Dick did the script because I was too close to it, too involved. But everything was done the way I wanted: a cast of unknowns, black and white, on location in Kansas. I feel I did the right thing. I could have had *any* director, from Antonioni to Jack Clayton."[11] Wisely, Capote also realized that he needed to give Brooks sufficient freedom to make the movie according to his own style: "No director can abide an author staring over his shoulder, and, agreeable as our relationship was, I sensed that Brooks felt my presence made everyone edgy, himself included. He was not unhappy to see me go" (*PO* 272).[12] Certainly Brooks needed license to film *In Cold Blood* according to his personal vision, not in slavish accord with Capote's text, and he therefore refused to show Capote the screenplay: "Truman, I can't work that way. Either you trust me to make it or you don't."[13] Although willing to grant Brooks artistic license in filming *In Cold Blood*, Capote also demanded equal billing with the director, as recorded in the contractual obligations concerning the film's credits: "The Author's name shall be announced on all positive prints, on a separate card, as follows: 'Based on the book By TRUMAN CAPOTE,' the lettering used to announce the Author's name to be the same size as that used to announce the name of the producer-director of the picture."[14] While ceding artistic authority to Brooks, Capote insisted on the credit due him in the film's creation.

On numerous aesthetic points Brooks and Capote agreed. The film would be shot in black and white—color would be "too romantic," said Brooks[15]— and unknown actors would be cast in the lead roles of Smith and Hickock. To generate the story's true horror—that a pair of random strangers might at any moment intrude into a home and murder the entire family there residing—it would not do for the killers to be played by celebrities, who would inevitably bestow an aura of their screen personas on the characters. Looking back at 1960s cinema, with such true-crime classics as *Bonnie and Clyde* (1967) starring Warren Beatty and Faye Dunaway, and *Butch Cassidy and the Sundance Kid* (1969) starring Paul Newman and Robert Redford, it is apparent that Brooks achieved a seedier effect through this decision. It is virtually impossible to scuff all of the Hollywood glamour off top stars, no matter the depth of their portrayal, but unknown actors are free from the pressures of screen personas, quite simply because they have not yet developed them. Some Hollywood executives hoped to cast celebrities such as Paul Newman, Robert Redford, or Steve McQueen in the roles of Smith and Hickock, but Brooks defended his casting decision: "If we used stars, they would change the mood and the style of the piece, bring with them their history, the background of their acting past. . . . If Paul Newman and Steve McQueen came into your living room at night, you wouldn't be frightened."[16] Unrelieved realism stood as Brooks's goal. "Say a Steve McQueen played Dick," he explained. "The audience looks at him and says, 'There's old Steve. He's not a murderer.' We need more realism—an unfamiliar face."[17]

The news that this major production would feature unknown actors ignited a frenzy in Hollywood, and Brooks was besieged by actors imploring him to cast them in any role possible. Even George Hamilton, chafing at the restrictions of such pretty-boy characters as Ryder Smith in *Where the Boys Are* (1960) and Fabrizio Naccarelli in *Light in the Piazza* (1962), charmingly pleaded with Brooks for the role of one of the killers: "I am still terribly interested and will remain so, in your project *In Cold Blood*. . . . I certainly appreciate your idea of using unknowns. There was a time when I would have appreciated it even more, when I was an unknown. In a way the real me is still unknown and I would appreciate the chance to prove this by working with you if it is ever possible."[18] Dashing Hamilton's hopes, Brooks adhered to his plan of casting unknown actors as his leads. A former child star in the *Our Gang* series, Robert Blake had worked in the film industry since 1939, but after the glory days of his youth, he appeared primarily in small and supporting roles. Capote was particularly pleased with Blake's selection to play Perry Smith: "The first time I saw him I thought a ghost had sauntered in out of the sunshine, slippery-haired and sleepy-eyed. I couldn't accept the idea that this was someone pretending to be Perry, he was Perry" (*PO* 269).[19] Blake likewise saw himself in Smith: "I think how different Perry's life might have been if whatever talent he may have had for painting and music had been channeled like mine—and how easily I could have turned out the way he did."[20] Scott Wilson, cast as Dick Hickock, was truly an unknown. He played a small role in *In the Heat of the Night*—the film that won the Academy Award for Best Picture the year of *In Cold Blood*'s eligibility— and Quincy Jones, who was scoring both films, brought him to Brooks's attention. John Forsythe, whose previous cinematic work included Alfred Hitchcock's *The Trouble with Harry* (1955), was cast as the lead Kansas Bureau of Investigation detective, Alvin Dewey, with Paul Stewart taking the role of Jensen, a newspaperman reporting the story. To heighten the authenticity of the casting, some residents of Holcomb, Kansas, including Sadie Truitt and Myrtle Clare, played themselves in the film. Brooks brought in local talent, including Paul Hough and Brenda Currin, drama majors at

Kansas University, to play Kenyon and Nancy Clutter. The film's actors were dedicated to pursuing realism in their performances. Wilson even claimed that Blake and he refused to interact with the Kansas locals: "It's for sure that Dick and Perry never knew the Clutters or anyone else here, so we don't figure we should hang around with them either."[21]

As Capote's *In Cold Blood* employs cinematic techniques in its telling of the crime and its aftermath, Brooks's adaptation adheres to these structural elements. For instance, Capote crosscuts between the Clutters and the killers in the book's opening sequences, and Brooks similarly uses parallel editing to link these story lines. The Clutters proceed through their last day alive unaware of their impending doom, while Smith and Hickock prepare for the robbery and slaughter. The film's opening shot features a bus's headlights barreling down a highway in the dark, cutting to a shot of Smith's boot soles, and this sequence captures some of the film's ensuing motifs: dark travels on the road, and the boot soles that will provide the evidence pinning the murders on Smith and Hickock. Smith, strumming his guitar, is interrupted by a little girl who says, "Excuse me," as his face is spotlighted when he lights a cigarette. In the accompanying scene introducing Hickock, he splutters as he tends to his sick father, "Goddamned outhouse. One of these days soon, I'm changing all that," while Brooks maintains a thematic link to transportation by depicting Hickock stashing a rifle in the backseat of his car. Hickock hears a train whistle in the distance, which soon leads to a shot of a train pulling into Holcomb, Kansas, as the camera then cuts to a series of pastoral shots of the Clutters' home, contrasting the quiet peace of their daily lives with the busy pulse of cars, buses, and trains that are bringing the killers to them. This crosscutting of story lines builds until Smith and Hickock meet their prey, creating a sense of foreboding and ineluctable doom in both the book and the film.

To achieve a higher pitch of realism, Capote and Brooks agreed that the film should be, as much as possible, shot on location. Much cinematic realism is founded upon the precept that the characters should interact with their surrounding environment as a reflection of their identities. Frank Beaver writes of this genre: "the themes of realist films often develop within a 'flow of life' format, where the casualness of common events reveals their content."[22] Another primary aspect of realist cinema, as Julia Hallam observes, is its propensity for "breaking with or departing from the codes and conventions of mainstream, commercial film practice."[23] For Capote, cinematic realism entailed re-creating Smith and Hickock's world, as well as the Clutters', as precisely as possible: "we both wanted the film to duplicate reality, . . . and to have every scene filmed in its real locale: the house of the Clutter family; the same Kansas variety store where Perry and Dick bought the rope and tape used to bind their four victims; and certain courthouses, prisons, filling stations, hotel rooms and highways and city streets. . . . A complicated procedure, but the only possible one by which almost all elements of fantasy could be removed and reality thereby achieve its proper reflection" (*PO* 270). By putting his characters in the actual settings of their real-life counterparts, Brooks imbued his film with a reality both mundane and unbearable. Indeed, Brooks attempted to re-create every scene as authentically as possible, even trying to acquire the gallows upon which Smith and Hickock were executed. Charles McAtee, the Kansas Director of Penal Institutions, remembers that Brooks inquired about purchasing the state's gallows, but the prison would not permit the transaction: "We didn't do that, but we did—and in reflection I don't know why—sell him the latrine facilities that were in Hickock and Smith's cells during their five years plus on death row. . . . I think they were $150 a piece or something like that. I know we got the check from Columbia Pictures."[24]

Capote's and Brooks's pursuit of realism fills the film with an appropriately gritty atmosphere throughout the killers' travels, but the aesthetic achievement of realism also paid dividends for the film's marketing campaign. Quite simply, realism provided a hook designed to entice audiences into the theaters, and the advertisements for *In Cold Blood* trumpeted its successful replication of the events behind it. The film's trailer begins with the rhetorical question "What is the reality behind the appearance?" and then praises Brooks as the artistic talent capable of bringing such a vision to life: "Richard Brooks, a director of great forcefulness, was determined to capture the reality with absolute honesty."[25] At this point, to demonstrate Brooks's single-minded pursuit of realism, the camera zooms in for a close-up of his clenched fist. The voice-over then moves from the director to the setting, tracing Smith and Hickock's travels to the Clutters' home: "Kansas City: the film company moves here because it was from this bus terminal that the real Perry Smith made a crucial telephone call; the real Dick Hickock stopped at this gas station on the way to the fateful meeting with his partner; in this store the killers bought the rope and tape with which they bound and gagged their victims." At each of these destinations, the trailer shows clips from the film to document the veracity of its claims. It then paints a picture of the film crew reliving Smith and Hickock's journeys after the murders: "The relentless pursuit of authenticity leads cast and crew to the actual city streets, the sun-drenched desert highways, the rain-swept country roads, and the garish gambling towns where the real-life drama played out." Blake's and Wilson's physical resemblances to Smith and Hickock are highlighted as well, in a sequence that merges the faces of the killers with those of the men playing them. "So uncanny are the resemblances that they have said, 'Sometimes we get the creepy feeling that we really are those guys,'" the voice-over proclaims, implying that the film's realism bled beyond the screen into the lives of the actors and, by implication, of viewers too.

Brooks's emphasis on unknown actors and true settings succeeds in creating realism aesthetics, although the film's editing tempers his achievements in this regard. Many critics have pointed out that realism requires that directors should, as much as possible, hide their manipulation of the narrative. The film should appear to unfold naturally, as if the camera were simply recording life without external intervention. This trope requires realist films to deny that they are indeed films, positing an illusion of natural life that the camera, by its very presence in capturing a story, must distort to some degree. In this regard Hallam theorizes, "Maintaining a static observational camera, or alternatively following a character as if capturing their actions and interactions as they occur, extends the reality effect by an apparent lack of directorial control over camera and audio-visual input."[26] The construction of *In Cold Blood*, in contrast, registers Brooks's masterful control of his narrative, if at the expense of its realism. The film is edited together with many narrative links uniting the characters and their story lines, such as when Nancy is speaking on the telephone, which cuts to Smith likewise talking on a phone, which cuts to Hickock registering at a hotel with Smith's name, or when Smith throws a cigarette out of their car into a river, which segues to a scene of the investigators dredging a river for the murder weapon. In this manner the editing reveals the artistry of the filmmakers, even if such tidiness in linking elements of the story detracts from the sense that the camera is simply capturing life as it happens. Furthermore, some critics contend the film's muted depictions of violence weaken its claims to realism. Tyler Parker observes in an unfavorable review, "The two murders, therefore, were perpetrated in even colder literary blood, and in a refrigerated Hollywood blood that quite eliminated the actual slaughter."[27] Had

Brooks depicted the violence in its full horror, he would likely be criticized for its gratuitousness, yet for his understated filming of the scene, he could not escape the criticism that it bleached the sequence of its full emotional impact. His decisions in this regard are thus somewhat surprising, for, as Joel Black points out, realist cinema necessitates unfiltered depictions of violence: "Artistic depictions of violence are less likely to seem gratuitous and sensational when, as in the case of *In Cold Blood*, they reenact actual incidents and can be considered a form of psychological or social documentary."[28] Although one can snipe at Brooks's polished editing and restrained filming of the violence as antithetical to a realist ethos, he succeeds in conveying the ineluctable doom that captures the Clutters in its midst, with a verisimilitude that renders the full horror of their meaningless suffering.

Brooks maintains Capote's stark realism in his film, and he also portrays the queer undertones evident in the book's rendering of Smith and Hickock's relationship and their personal lives. If Capote's treatment of queer themes in *In Cold Blood* is subtle, for some viewers, even astute ones, Brooks's handling of the theme is virtually invisible. Vito Russo, the trailblazing critic of queer cinema with *The Celluloid Closet*, argues that the homoeroticism of Smith and Hickock's relationship is erased from the screen: "There is never as much outrage at the sight of heroes who choose violence as there is absolute moral fury when a hero expresses unorthodox sexual feelings. The homoerotic aspects of the buddyhood of Truman Capote's two real-life killers of *In Cold Blood* were absent from the screen version."[29] Russo's perceptive readings of films with queer subtexts opened new avenues of cinematic analysis, yet he is incorrect to state that Brooks removes homoeroticism from his film. On the contrary, Smith and Hickock's queer relationship survives on the screen, and in many ways mirrors Capote's own muted depiction of it. Robert Blake, responding to a query about the film's treatment of sexuality, explains that there "absolutely" was a homosexual subtext despite the clandestine nature of its portrayal: "Richard, for whatever reason, did not put it in the script and didn't talk about it, but we all knew it was there. And I believe his instinct was that it would come out better if we didn't talk about it because, in real life, Perry and Hickock didn't talk about it."[30]

In his book Capote incorporates several queer facets in his characterization of Smith and Hickock, yet he also downplays this material in the narrative, shunting it to the margins of the text; moreover, following the publication of *In Cold Blood*, he denied a gay theme altogether in some interviews.

To George Plimpton's query, "Was there any sexual relationship, or such tendencies, between them?" Capote replied, "No. Not at all."[31] Some reviewers agree, apparently incapable of decoding Capote's veiled references to the criminals' sex lives: James Bannerman, writing for *Maclean's*, criticized Capote's book because Capote "never examines the possibility that they were homosexual."[32] Camouflaged yet not invisible, the killers' sense of their sexualities subtly permeates Capote's depiction of them. According to Ralph Voss, Capote cloaked the narrative's queer subtexts to enhance its financial potential but also to acknowledge the unknowability of these men's sexualities: "Capote wanted to mute the homosexuality for the obvious marketing and cultural reasons, and yet insinuate it more subtly, to make it a definite part of the story in the interest of the truthful reportage he claimed."[33] Indeed, Voss documents that Capote edited out certain homosexual elements from the book's first draft, such as a gender-bending description of Smith—"In profile, he resembles a plump, rather unpleasant, and exceedingly tough lesbian"—and Smith's fascination with a black man's penis: "He had the biggest dick you ever saw. You couldn't help staring at it—you didn't have to be queer or nothing—it was just the biggest dick you ever saw."[34] Although these moments were redacted from the published version of *In Cold Blood*, sufficient such instances remain in the book to encourage readers to see Smith and Hickock, if not as homosexuals, as otherwise estranged from normative heterosexuality.

For example, even when Capote recounts Smith's heterosexual affairs, an overriding queerness subverts any vision of sexual normativity. Smith's father describes his son's dating life—"Yes he had several girl friends, soon as he found a girl to mistreat him or trifle, he would quit her. He never was married as far as I know" (*CB* 128)—with his words suggesting Smith's experience with a range of women but also his dissatisfaction with these affairs. Likewise, the narrator details Smith's past with the nurse Cookie: "Sexual episodes of a strange and stealthy nature had occurred, and love had been mentioned, and marriage, too, but eventually, when his injuries had mended, he'd told her goodbye" (*CB* 98). What could these "sexual episodes of a strange and stealthy nature" be? It can only be conjecture to suggest anal intercourse, but this possibility emerges as a plausible explanation for Capote's obscure phrasing, designed to pique the reader's curiosity but never to sate it. Notwithstanding such ambiguities, it is clear that Smith sees marriage as a duty, not a pleasure: "A wife, children—those were experiences 'a man ought to have,' even if, as with Dick, they didn't 'make him happy or do him any good'" (*CB* 98). For Smith, heterosexuality appears to be a chore to be endured rather than a desire to be fulfilled, and in Capote's depiction of his life, he shares his deepest bonds with men, including his father Tex, the chaplain's clerk Willie-Jay, and Hickock.

Certainly Smith was keenly aware of homosexuality, recounting to Capote experiences in his youth during which he was sexually accosted. Of his time in the merchant marine, Smith declared: "But the queens on ship wouldn't leave me alone. A sixteen-year-old kid, and a small kid. I could handle myself, sure. But a lot of queens aren't effeminate, you know. Hell, I've known queens could toss a pool table out the window" (*CB* 133). Furthermore, during his army stint in Korea, his commanding officer sexually harassed him: "Because the sergeant we had was tough. Because I wouldn't roll over. Jesus, I hate that stuff. I can't stand it. Though—*I* don't know. Some queers I've really liked. As long as they didn't try anything. The most worthwhile friend I ever had, really sensitive and intelligent, he turned out to be queer" (*CB* 134). In this passage Smith appears to be alluding to Willie-Jay, the chaplain's clerk who befriended him in prison, and in many ways Smith's decision to join Hickock on his crime spree results from his failure to reconnect with Willie-Jay. Capote records that "'more than anything in the world,' [Smith] desired a reunion with this man, his 'real and only friend,' the 'brilliant' Willie-Jay," and he describes Willie-Jay as "courting Perry's soul" (*CB* 42–43). Moreover, Capote suggests that Smith's friendship with Hickock emerged from his feelings for Willie-Jay: "his friendship with Dick, whom he had scarcely known until his final few months in Lansing, was an outgrowth of, and counterbalance to, the intensity of his admiration for the chaplain's clerk" (*CB* 44). Prior to reuniting with Hickock, Smith sought homosocial companionship with whichever man would have him: "The journey's aftermath was up to fate; if things didn't 'work out with Willie-Jay,' then he might 'consider Dick's proposition'" (*CB* 45). In these and other such moments of Smith's characterization, Capote portrays his homosocial bonds as the defining emotional ties of his life, which his repeated homophobic statements counterbalance but cannot erase.

While repeatedly professing his aversion to homosexuality, Smith readily admits his attraction to masculinity, albeit not in explicitly sexual language. As Capote's narrator explains, Hickock's appeal to Smith arose from his assured masculinity: "Dick was very literal-minded, *very*—he had no understanding of music, poetry—and yet when you got right down to it, Dick's literalness, his pragmatic approach to every subject, was the primary reason Perry had been attracted to him, for it made Dick seem, compared to himself, so authentically tough, invulnerable, 'totally masculine'" (*CB* 16). Smith's admiration for Hickock latently suggests dissatisfaction with his own masculinity, and Smith also hopes that Hickock will reciprocate the admiration he feels for him: "When he'd told Dick that story [about killing a man], it was because he'd wanted Dick's friendship, wanted Dick to 'respect' him, think him 'hard,' as much 'the masculine type' as he had considered Dick to be" (*CB* 111). Smith's fervent, and likely eroticized, interest in masculinity is also evident in his possessions, which include "photographs clipped from physical-culture magazines (sweaty studies of weight-lifting weight-lifters)" (*CB* 178). Such "physical-culture" magazines in the 1950s, with their endless parade of muscle men posing for the camera, appealed to many homosexual men of the era, especially with their façades of promoting physical health rather than homoerotic lust. Although Capote never records any sexual encounter between Smith and Hickock, Smith compliments Hickock on his physical attractiveness: "Because you have a wonderful smile. One of those smiles that really work" (*CB* 31). On the surface, Smith's stories of rejecting homosexual advances assert his heterosexuality, but his need for homosocial companionship and his fascination with masculinity undermine the image of manhood he seeks to portray.

Such hints of homosexual desire glimmering through Capote's portrait of Smith are less evident in the portrait of Hickock, whose statements are often explicitly homophobic, such as in his dismissive assessment of Willie-Jay: "*He's* the faggot" (*CB* 44). Yet Hickock's sexual history is also troubled, and his incessant proclamations of sexual normativity wear thin through their repetition: "Deal me out, baby. . . . I'm a normal," he claims (*CB* 108, cf. 111). He later avows, "I've always behaved like a one-hundred-percent normal" (*CB* 229). These many claims camouflage Hickock's pedophilic desires:

> He was sorry he felt as he did about her, for his sexual interest in female children was a failing of which he was "sincerely ashamed"—a secret he'd not confessed to anyone and hoped no one suspected (though he was aware that Perry had reason to), because other people might not think it "normal." That, to be sure, was something he was certain he was—"a normal." Seducing pubescent girls, as he had done "eight or nine" times in the last several years, did not disprove it, for if the truth were known, most real men had the same desires he had. (*CB* 201)

Hickock rationalizes that his desires are normal—that "most real men had the same desires he had"—but this justification is empirically untrue.[35] Beyond Hickock's pedophilia, Capote subtly hints that, like Smith, Hickock also feels homoerotic desires, such as when he cryptically states, "I'm a normal. I only dream about blond chicken" (*CB* 93). Capote is likely hinting at homosexual attraction here, for in slang parlance, "chick" more frequently refers to women, whereas "chicken" denotes "a young male prostitute"; "the passive prisoner" in a jailhouse homosexual relationship; or "an adolescent boy regarded as a sexual object for an adult homosexual."[36] Capote certainly knew this last slang usage of "chicken," for the symbolism of Zoo shooting away chicken hawks from Skully's Landing in *Other Voices, Other Rooms* plays upon the image of Joel Knox as the object of Randolph's affections (*OV* 111–16). At the very least, it is intriguing that Capote, who enjoyed more than a casual knowledge of French, would describe this "chicken" as "blond" rather than as "blonde," for it is an elementary linguistics lesson that a French adjective ends in *-e* if it is feminine. In another suggestive scene, Hickock poses for nude drawings by the German tourist Otto during their time in Mexico: "The sketchbook, which Otto gave Perry as a parting gift, contained several drawings of Dick—'nude studies'" (*CB* 119). In this brief and undeveloped passage, Capote hints that Hickock is a gay hustler, for surely posing for "nude studies" for a male German tourist in Mexico does not constitute a standard recreational activity for most heterosexual men.

Within this volatile brew of desires admitted and denied, Hickock exploits the homoerotic possibilities of his relationship with Smith, referring to his friend with such affectionate terms as "honey" and "baby."[37] Indeed, Capote reports that Hickock "proceeded to woo Perry" (*CB* 55). When their plans go awry, Hickock sees Smith as "a wife that must be got rid of" (*CB* 215). When Smith regrets their murderous rampage, he describes Hickock and himself as intrinsically flawed: "When Perry said, 'I think there must be something wrong with us,' he was making an admission he 'hated to make.' After all, it was 'painful' to imagine that one might be 'not just right'—particularly if whatever was wrong was not your own fault but 'maybe a thing you were born with'" (*CB* 110). In these lines psychopathology and homosexuality blur together into a joint sense of the men's moral failings. Smith also believes that all people should restrain their erotic drives, for "he had 'no respect for people who can't control themselves sexually,' especially when the lack of control involved what he called 'pervertiness'—'bothering kids,' 'queer stuff,' rape" (*CB* 202). In one of the climactic moments of the murders when Hickock threatens to rape Nancy—"I'm gonna bust that little girl"— Smith replies, "Uh-huh. But you'll have to kill me first." He then describes Hickock's reaction: "He looked like he didn't believe he'd heard right. He says, 'What do you care? Hell, you can bust her, too.' Now, that's something I despise. Anybody that can't control themselves sexually. Christ, I hate that kind of stuff" (*CB* 243, cf. 286). Smith's stance against unrestrained sexuality creates the greatest paradox in the slaughter of the Clutter family: he preserves Nancy from rape, only to murder her.

Filming Smith and Hickock in a manner to capture their conflicted sexualities presented numerous challenges for Brooks. Peter Bart, reporting on the film's production, observed, "The problem of how to convey Perry's homosexual hang-up eludes Brooks."[38] Nonetheless, Brooks not only took cues from Capote's book in depicting Smith's and Hickock's sexualities but re-created Capote's research into their sexual histories. In one of his research files he notes "THE PAST:—Perry's childhood unhappy. *Crime*— caught in New York. Homosexual experience in Merchant Marine."[39] In a related file he documents such incidents regarding Smith as "Aged 16. First homosexual experience aboard ship. Hated it"; "Dick starts to make love to Inez, while Perry is in the room"; and "Perry's feelings about people who cannot control sexual drives."[40] Drawing together such threads, Brooks envisions the character as haunted by sexual desires he cannot control. In the book Capote includes details from Dr. Mitchell Jones's psychiatric evaluations of Smith and Hickock (*CB* 294–98), in which Jones diagnoses Smith as projecting a "'paranoid' orientation toward the world" and an "emotional detachment and blandness" that provide "evidence of his mental abnormality" (*CB* 297–98). He judges that Hickock's "self-esteem is very low, and he secretly feels inferior to others and sexually inadequate. These feelings seem to be overcompensated for by dreams of being rich and powerful, a tendency to brag about his exploits" (*CB* 295).

Also included in Brooks's research materials are Jones's psychiatric evaluations in full, which contain more detailed analysis of Smith's and Hickock's sexual histories than presented in Capote's novel.[41] Of Smith, Dr. Jones noted: "Conscious scorn for homosexuality with probably underlying trends. Lack of interest in women, but search for motherly type to w[h]om he can have tender feelings." Indeed, effeminacy and homosexuality were recurring topics of analysis during their session, as Jones also observed that

Smith was "very effeminate in his way of moving and gesturing with his hands," as well as detailing Smith's recurring encounters with homosexual men: "He and the friend broke up and moved to separate cells just before the friend's discharge. Perry sa[id] the friend wanted to have homosexual relations [but] Perry had refused." This observation likely refers to Smith's relationship with Willie-Jay. The psychiatrist also noted Smith's homosexual encounters in the services: "Perry said he joined the Army but hadn't liked the regimentation. He said his sergeant was a homosexual who wouldn't raise Perry's rank because he wouldn't 'come across,'" and he succinctly concluded, "He denies homosexual activity." Of Hickock, Dr. Jones reported: "He was propositioned for homosexual activity at times but says he hated anything of that sort." Jones also detailed Hickock's pedophilic tendencies: "He then told me that five or six years ago he had molested some small girls (6–10 years old) but had not been picked up for it. . . . He told of occasional impotency with his wife, saying sometimes he didn't have desire for her. He has masturbated considerably and when he does he thinks of small girls and feeling of their genitals." As much as Brooks researched Smith's and Hickock's sexualities and incorporated his findings into the film, he also did not want to exculpate the murderers because of their troubled backgrounds and repressed sexualities. When Dewey and the newsman Jensen discuss the murders, Jensen summarizes—"They all committed senseless murders. They all felt physically inferior and sexually inadequate"—but Dewey dismisses the relevance of these insights to the case at hand: "So . . . who killed the Clutters?"

In his treatment of the killers' sexualities, Brooks incorporates numerous homoerotic elements to their friendship, such as when Hickock summons Smith to Kansas with a letter that refers to Smith as "honey" and is signed with "love." Arriving at the Kansas City bus station in response to Hickock's call but hoping to find Willie-Jay, Smith encounters frustration after frustration. He wants to make a phone call, but a nun takes the telephone that he was planning to use and apologizes for her mistake, "Young man? Young man, I'm terribly sorry." Soon after, a man in uniform likewise grabs a phone before Smith reaches it. Brooks encodes Smith's troubled history with religious and military institutions in this brief scene, alluding to the cruelty of the nuns who mistreated him in his youth and the sexual harassment he endured in the army, with representatives of these respective institutions hampering him from reconnecting with Willie-Jay. Smith succeeds in reaching Reverend James Post and tells him that he is waiting for Willie-Jay—"I was supposed to meet him right here"—and then adds plaintively, with a tremor in his voice, "Can you tell me where he went?" Smith's words emphasize his loneliness and isolation, as well as his desire to bond with another man. Brooks then includes linked shots of hygiene rituals to connect the killer to his victims: The camera frames Herb Clutter shaving in his bathroom, and as he bends down to wash his face, the camera cuts to Smith raising his face from a sink in the bus terminal bathroom. In contrast to Clutter's modest ablutions, Smith is stripped down to his white underwear, and viewers see a scar on his leg as he washes it in the sink. He then preens narcissistically in the mirror, flexing his muscles and imagining himself in Las Vegas, with "Perry Smith Sings" on a nightclub's marquee. Hickock finds Smith in the bus station restroom and laughs at him. "How come you always go in a trance every time you look in the mirror? Just like you were looking at some gorgeous piece of butt." The accusation of narcissism hints at Smith's homoerotic desires, as does the ambiguous phrasing of "some gorgeous piece of butt," which could be either male or female. From Smith and Hickock's opening reunion and the scenes that precede it, Brooks establishes Smith's alienation from society and his desperation to experience some sort of emotional cathexis with another man, as he crosscuts these scenes with images of the family that will suffer so cruelly for his failure to do so.

Similar to Capote's restrained portrayal of homosocial desires percolating between the two men, Brooks's depiction of Smith and Hickock's friendship balances between homosociality and homoeroticism. When Hickock is driving with Perry by his side, he vows, "I promise you, honey, we'll blast hair all over them walls." Eagerly anticipating their murderous rampage, Hickock's coupling of affectionate terms for Smith with images of horrific violence lessens their amatory timbre. Also, Hickock's heterosexuality is on full display in several key moments of the film, such as when, regretting a past car accident, he tells Smith, "I hate to count how much classy pussy that's cost me." Brooks employs Capote's suggestive phrasing of "blond chicken," but in these instances he does so exclusively to refer to women. Appraising a drive-in restaurant's waitress whom they encounter on their drive to the Clutters, Hickock says, "That waitress. Nice piece of blond chicken," and when they arrive in Las Vegas, Hickock comments, "Never seen so much blond chicken. And all that sweet divorce money," as two buxom women walk

FIGS. 11 AND 12 *In Cold Blood* (1967): In these paired shots, as Herb Clutter (John McLiam) shaves at his home in Holcomb, Kansas, the film's editing cuts to Perry Smith (Robert Blake) performing similar ablutions in a Kansas City bus station, thus linking the converging story lines.

by. In complementary fashion, a scene registering Hickock's homophobia occurs when the two men are hitchhiking and a pair of black men pull over to pick them up. "Come on boys, get in," the driver welcomes, but because one of the men is already sitting in the backseat, Smith and Hickock would each need to sit beside a black man. Hickock snorts, "Not with you," and dismissively waves them away. The scene reads as racist when Hickock rudely gestures that these men should drive on, but it has homophobic undertones as well, particularly because the scene derives from Capote's queer account in which Smith and Hickock encounter "a 'swish' pair of Negro prizefighters driving a 'swish' lavender Cadillac" (*CB* 222).

Brooks tempers such depictions of Hickock's heterosexuality with suggestions of a latent homoeroticism in his relationship with Smith. Most critically, the two men proclaim their mutual commitment in a homosocial enactment of marriage rites. When Hickock says to Smith, after Smith fails to reunite with Willie-Jay, "I'm the only friend you got now. Friend to the end. For better or worse," Smith replies in kind and builds on Hickock's words that are reminiscent of marital vows—"Till death do us part?" Dick's response confirms the bond between the two men: "All we need is a ring, sugar." The two men never physically consummate their relationship, but while they are in Mexico, Hickock brings a woman back to their hotel room. "I'm not bashful, baby," he tells Smith. As Hickock and the woman undress by the bed, Perry drinks in a corner off by himself, and Brooks links the two men in the scene, despite their physical distance, by depicting Smith spit-shining his shoes while Hickock removes his. Smith then ponders over childhood photos that spur memories of his mother, and he hears her cry of "Perry" as if she were in the room. Witnessing Hickock's sexual activity, Smith sees Hickock's prostitute but daydreams of his mother Flo, substituting her face. Viewers realize that this experience with Hickock is not the first time that Smith has witnessed others copulate, for in his flashback he and his siblings watch their mother as she is undressed, with her lover taking off her bra, until her husband Tex storms into the room, tosses the man out, and slaps Flo. The temporalities of the shot mix past and present, with Tex walking past Smith in the present moment as the child version of Smith reacts with tears. Smith then looks across to where Hickock is repeating, "Was it good, baby?" to his lover, who smokes impassively in bed. The scene ends as the camera approaches Smith's eyes. Brooks interweaves varying plotlines of desire in this scene, including Smith's melancholic longing for his mother, as well as his regret over her betrayal of his father; Hickock's heterosexual passion for the prostitute; and the latent desire for Hickock that is hinted at as Smith observes his friend having sex with her.

This brew of friendship, desire, and submerged homoeroticism reaches a climactic pitch in the sequence depicting the Clutter murders in flashback. Smith confesses the crime to Dewey as they drive back to Kansas, explaining that the Clutters were executed as collateral damage to his unsatisfying relationship with Hickock. As the sequence begins, Hickock thinks Smith is insulting his masculinity, and so he replies, "You don't think I got the guts to do it alone. Okay. I'll show you who's wearing the pants. How'd you kill that guy in Vegas anyhow? Love him to death?" This jab at Smith's potential homosexuality asserts Hickock's manhood, but his insistently normal desires are rendered perverse by his plan to rape Nancy. Brooks builds tension as Hickock admits with increasing urgency his desire to molest her, first asking Kenyon about the hope chest in the basement, which the boy says he built for his sister. Hickock leers upward toward the ceiling, as if he could see Nancy through the floors, and his lascivious chuckle of "Oh, yeah" indicates his sadistic intentions. Kenyon corrects him, telling him that the hope chest is a gift, not for Nancy, but for one of his older sisters: "Not her, she's too young." Hickock replies lecherously, "They're never too young, kid." After this unsettling conversation, while Smith is tying up Bonnie, Hickock sneaks up the stairs to Nancy's room. Realizing Hickock's predatory intentions, Bonnie pleads with Smith for her daughter's safety: "Please, don't let him hurt my little girl." Smith hears Nancy's protests— "Don't . . . no, please don't"—when Hickock menaces her with "You ever had a man?" Finding Hickock rubbing her thigh as she whimpers in fear, Smith confronts him about his intentions, and Hickock says, "First I'm going to bust that little girl." Smith tells him no, but Hickock replies, "What do you care? You can bust her, too." The confrontation appears to be escalating to violence between the two men, but it suddenly subsides when Hickock accepts Smith's refusal with a simple "Okay, honey." Smith then pulls the blanket over Nancy, saying, "I despise people who can't control themselves." Hickock's inability to regulate his sexual urges is threatening Smith's affection for him, and it becomes increasingly apparent that the Clutters are tragically incidental to Smith and Hickock's conflicted friendship. Hickock attempts to compel Smith to action by telling him, "It's us against them," but Smith's reply, "This is between us. It's got nothing to do with them," reveals his desire to maintain the homosocial bonds between them by leaving the Clutters in peace.

At the moment of Herb Clutter's murder, Brooks incorporates a flashback to Smith's father Tex, who is holding a shotgun and shouting, "Look at me, boy! Take a good look! I'm the last living thing you're ever gonna see." The various shots are disorienting, thus to mirror Smith's mental confusion, with the camera cutting between Smith's father aiming a shotgun at Smith and Smith slitting Herb's throat. Smith's flashlight shines back on Hickock, and then spotlights Herb. As the flashback of the murders concludes, Smith states in the police car: "It doesn't make sense. I mean what happened. Or why. It had nothing to do with the Clutters. They never hurt me, they just happened to be there. I thought Mr. Clutter was a very nice gentleman. I thought so right up until the time I cut his throat." As Smith earlier fantasized of his father enacting vengeance against Hickock for his sexual activity with the prostitute, he now sees his father as Herb and avenges himself against the man who beat his mother. In both situations his relationship with Hickock becomes embroiled with past familial traumas, and Herb Clutter and his family become a symbol for all the depredations and failed relationships of Smith's life. They are no longer robbery victims but, in Brooks's staging of their deaths, scapegoats sacrificed to these two men's inability to communicate their desires other than through denial, displacement, and violence.

Following the portrayal of the murders, the film's tone and scope shifts from a gritty account of the crimes and the killers' seedy lives to a polemic against the death penalty. While Brooks's film adheres to Capote's parallel structure for much of the narrative, he diverges from his source text with the introduction of the journalist Jensen, who apparently represents Capote himself, although without the distinctive voice, style, and personality. After Smith and Hickock are arrested and tried for the murders, Jensen vocalizes Brooks's critique of the death penalty. When Jensen walks out of the courtroom at the trial's conclusion, a voice-over asks, "How can a perfectly sane man commit an absolutely crazy act?" The voice soon offers an explanation, as the screen depicts Smith and Hickock in their cells: "According to an expert in forensic medicine, neither one of them would have done it alone. But together, they made a third personality. That's the one that did it." Clinical and detached, the commentary injects a tone of objectivity into the film's dénouement, as Brooks concomitantly seeks the audience's sympathy for Smith. In the scene before his execution, the killer requests permission to visit the bathroom. With his face framed by the shoulders of the guards, visually symbolizing his entrapment, Perry pleads, "I gotta go to the toilet." One of the guards refuses his request, advising him, "Try to control yourself." Perry responds, "But that's it. When you hit the end of the rope, your muscles lose control. I'm afraid I'll mess myself." The guard consoles him— "It's nothing to be ashamed of. They all do it"—but Reverend Post interjects, "For God's sake, man!" In a small, meaningful act of compassion, the guards unharness Smith so that he can visit the facilities and thus preserve the shred of dignity left him. The scene's pathos, as a man faces his imminent death while also facing the disgrace of soiling himself, implicitly asks viewers to consider whether they could feel sympathy for a killer.

Complementing the pathos that Brooks elicits for Smith, Hickock criticizes the social-class politics of capital punishment. He declares as they drive to the Clutters, "Ever see a millionaire fry in the electric chair? Hell, no. There's two kind of laws, honey. One for the rich, and one for the poor." He sardonically explains to Jensen his acceptance of his imminent execution: "Hell, hanging's only getting revenge. What's wrong with revenge? I've been revenging myself all my life. Sure. I'm for hanging. Just so long as I'm not the one being hanged." He ends this monologue, with its implicit argument that seeking revenge only incites more violence, with a wink at Jensen, who gives a dry chuckle. Jensen soon voices the futility of capital punishment: "Well, four innocent and two guilty people murdered. Three families broken. Newspapers have sold more papers. Politicians will make more speeches. Police and parole boards will get more blame. More laws will be passed. Everybody will pass the buck. And then, next month, next year . . . the same thing will happen again." Through this cynic's perspective, Brooks condemns the death penalty as an ineffective deterrent against crime, and as the film concludes, he again elicits viewers' sympathy for Smith. Upon climbing the gallows, Smith mistakes the hangman for his father Tex. As the blindfold is pulled over his face and the noose around his neck, he meekly asks, "Is God in this place, too?" The concluding juxtaposition of fathers—the vision of Tex, whose troubled relationship with his son in no small measure contributed to his delinquency, and of God, to whom Smith appeals in his final seconds—highlights his essential loneliness throughout life and at the moment of death.

Brooks's cinematic condemnation of the death penalty sparked spirited rebuttals. Although critics mostly greeted *In Cold Blood* with acclaim, several of the dissenting voices focused their attacks on its argument against execution. Critics such as Edward Murray denigrated the film's "crude concluding protest against capital punishment."[42] Likewise, Dale Adams derided the film's inclusion of "an ever-present reporter" who is "seemingly collecting data for what would become Capote's book" but merely serves as "a one-man Greek chorus, ejaculat[ing] anti-capital punishment bromides."[43] Certainly Brooks was invested in his premise that "the film must somehow say that this tragedy is to some degree the responsibility of all of us. None of us can turn away from one another," and he readily admitted the film's stance against capital punishment: "The crime itself was senseless, the boys' lives before that were senseless, and the end is senseless because it solves nothing. . . . I felt that was an opportunity for me to tell whatever I had to say about capital punishment within the confines of this rather remarkable piece of work."[44] Seeking sympathy for men who commit such depraved acts of violence as Smith and Hickock's, Brooks foresaw the controversy his film was likely to create, yet he stood by his decision to question the morality and justice of the death penalty.

As the film neared completion, Capote voiced his unadulterated praise for Brooks's accomplishments: "I haven't had a thing to do with the movie of *In Cold Blood*, but I watched the first reel . . . and I think it's going to be extremely good."[45] He later proclaimed: "The quality of reality is almost unbearable."[46] In a letter to Tom Shaw of Columbia Studios, Alvin Dewey reported that Capote was quite impressed with the film: "We understand the picture is finished and is really wonderful. We talked to Truman after he saw it in Los Angeles, and he was very pleased."[47] In contrast to these public paeans, Capote diplomatically expressed some reservations about the film, particularly Brooks's narrative emphasis on the killers rather than the Clutters. Still, he realized the impossibility of any film capturing his book in its entirety: "Yes, it's as accurate a rendering of the book as I could have hoped, with the single exception that if it were done the way I would *really* have liked, it would have had to be at least nine hours long."[48] To this criticism, Brooks replied in kind, commenting on the copy of *In Cold Blood* that Capote sent him, with numerous passages underlined, for the director's consideration for inclusion: "There was just no time for them. Using all his passages we'd have about a fourteen-hour movie."[49]

Aside from voices like Murray's and Adam's that took issue with the film for its politics, the critical response to *In Cold Blood* was generally favorable, exemplified by Bosley Crowther's rave review in the *New York Times* extolling it as an "excellent quasidocumentary, which sends shivers down the spine while moving the viewer to ponder."[50] Crowther included the film in his annual list of Ten Best Films.[51] Arthur Knight found that "for all the film's forbidding premise, it unfolds with astonishing warmth and involvement," and ranked it as "one of the finest pictures of the year, and possibly of the decade."[52] Wilfrid Sheed in *Esquire* opined that the film's "result is simple truth, something so rare and strange in the movies as to be aesthetically thrilling."[53] The reviewer for *Time*, while criticizing the film for "unnecessarily belabor[ing] the arguments against capital punishment," praised it mightily, particularly for Blake's and Wilson's acting: "It is their performances that lift the film from documentary competence to near brilliance."[54] Crowning its accomplishments, *In Cold Blood* received several Academy Award nominations, including Brooks for Best Director and Best Adapted Screenplay, Conrad Hall for Best Cinematography, and Quincy Jones for Best Music (Original Music Score). The film itself, however, was not nominated for Best Picture, losing out to *Bonnie and Clyde*, *The Graduate*, *Guess Who's Coming to Dinner*, *Doctor Dolittle*, and the winner, *In the Heat of the Night*. In his analysis of *In Cold Blood*'s competition, Capote commented: "The only three good American films last year were *Bonnie and Clyde*, *The Graduate*, and *In Cold Blood*. *In the Heat of the Night* was a good bad picture. *Guess Who's Coming to Dinner* is a bad movie that got there for sentimental reasons."[55] With its unflinching realism, its provocative insights into the sexual underbelly of the criminals' desires, and its staunch advocacy against the death penalty, Brooks's *In Cold Blood* matches the accomplishments of Capote's book, proving that this story, in separate yet overlapping incarnations, carries an unsettling power while meditating on the unanswerable questions of violence and its repercussions in American culture.

▶ Capote as Criminologist

Following the success of *In Cold Blood*, both in print and on the screen, another facet of Capote's celebrity persona emerged: that of public expert on crime, punishment, and the justice system. With no credentials other than the book he penned, Capote appeared in July 1966 as a witness before the U.S. Senate to discuss the Supreme Court's *Miranda v. Arizona* ruling, which grants criminal suspects the right to a lawyer during police interrogations. Capote opposed the Miranda ruling, arguing that, had it been in effect prior to Smith's and Hickock's arrests and convictions, "any lawyer worth his salt would have advised the boys to say nothing. Had they said nothing, they would not have even been brought to trial, much less convicted."[56] During his testimony, Capote became peeved when he realized that some of the senators had not read *In Cold Blood*, chastising Birch Bayh of Indiana, "Senator, it's all in the book in great detail."[57] In other settings Capote's off-the-cuff pronouncements on crime and punishment, including his claims that a vast conspiracy masterminded the assassinations of John F. Kennedy, Martin Luther King, and Bobby Kennedy, drew sharp criticism. After Capote trotted out such speculation on Johnny Carson's *Tonight Show*, television critic Jack Gould rebuked him, decrying Capote's preference for "his own instant verdicts on TV" as "frightening" and arguing that television networks "have a journalistic obligation to see that cases still pending in the courts are not casually second-guessed outside legal channels."[58] William F. Buckley Jr. criticized Capote as well, particularly for the shoddy logic of his theories of an anti-leftist conspiracy.[59]

To promote *In Cold Blood* and to share his thoughts on crime and punishment in America, Capote also appeared on such television shows as *Good Company*, an interview program hosted by famed attorney F. Lee Bailey.[60] The discussion with Bailey in 1967 was taped at Capote's home in Bridgehampton, Long Island, and Capote's outré personality was strikingly evident, most notably in his clothes—an orange sweater and yellow pants—that matched the yellow armchair in which he sat. He also matched the flowers behind his right shoulder. Capotean braggadocio was on full display: "I personally have never learned one single thing from any critic. Well, maybe once or twice." He also explained that his interviewing style, as practiced while writing *In Cold Blood*, eschewed recording devices to encourage people to speak more freely. He would then transcribe their conversations: "I have the auditory version of a photographic memory." Asked about the screen version, he expressed his approval of Brooks—"I wasn't interested in selling it except to someone who would do it exactly it as I wanted it to be done"—and of the film: "As a movie, it's really extremely good, I think." He also voiced his opinion that the film could not address its subject matter with sufficient complexity and depth within the temporal restrictions of standard feature-length films: "It's a marvelous, remarkable film, but you've got to remember that, for it to really please, it would have had to have been nine hours long." Assuming the role of the public intellectual, Capote expounded his views on the death penalty, arguing plainly against it—"I don't think anyone should be executed"—and then elaborating that if life sentences were effectively enforced, executions would be unnecessary: "I think capital punishment is entirely unnecessary if it is a serious thing of the life sentence." In his most compelling idea about crime and punishment, Capote opined that crimes such as murder should be tried in federal courts to alleviate the possibility of prejudiced juries—"All capital crimes should become federal crimes and should never be tried in state court"—a particularly relevant argument considering that Smith and Hickock were tried in the same community where they committed their crimes. It is difficult to discern, however, any underlying moral or juridical philosophy in Capote's opinions on crime and punishment, for he coupled his argument against the death penalty with cavalier disregard for the unjustly accused: "It sounds very illiberal of me but . . . I would rather one innocent man went to jail than a hundred guilty people went free."

In a similar interview on William F. Buckley Jr.'s *Firing Line* in 1968, Capote argued that the death penalty should be abolished because it is arbitrarily applied and that homicide should be a federal, not a state, crime, to lessen the potential for local citizens to prejudge the case.[61] Such a change of venue would allow cases to be tried on evidence, not emotion. Never shy about making dogmatic statements, Capote also proclaimed, "I think a homicidal mind is incurable," as he and Buckley discussed whether incarceration or treatment would be preferable for certain killers. It appears that Capote, in his new role of crime expert, was attempting to cast off his Bohemian and artistic persona in favor of one of cerebral introspection. When, in introducing Capote, Buckley mentioned the author's supposed past as a riverboat tap dancer, Capote interjected, "No, that's not true," even though such a claim was made publicly and repeatedly, including on the dust jacket of *Other Voices, Other Rooms.*

Also in 1968, Capote hoped to air a documentary, *Death Row, U.S.A.,* but television critic Jack Gould informed his readers: "Informally, it was reported yesterday that A.B.C. had been disappointed with the quality of the show."[62] Studio president Elton Rule declared that the footage was "too grim," to which Capote cheekily replied, "Well, what were you expecting—*Rebecca of Sunnybrook Farm*?"[63] Four years later a similar production, *Truman Capote behind Prison Walls,* aired in December 1972. Because of its controversial subject matter, featuring frank discussions of murder, homosexuality, and the Charles Manson cult, it ran after prime time. For the most part, the program was panned for its lack of a coherent thesis regarding crime and punishment in America. John O'Connor, reviewing for the *New York Times,* dismissed Capote's efforts: "the insights mined by Mr. Capote are banal and ordinary. . . . *Behind Prison Walls* winds up being disturbingly similar to a collection of stories out of the seedy 'true confessions' genre."[64] O'Connor gave a more favorable review to Capote's interviews with policemen in the 1973 airing of *Crimewatch,* for which Capote spoke with law enforcement officers about their personal and professional motivations and ambitions.[65]

Capote's public persona as a criminologist also influenced his subsequent literary and film career, a dynamic most evident in the 1972 television drama *The Glass House*, also titled *Truman Capote's The Glass House*. Capote limited his participation on the project to coauthoring the story with his close friend Wyatt Cooper, the husband of Gloria Vanderbilt and father of Anderson Cooper. Tom Gries directed *The Glass House*, with the screenplay written by Tracy Keenan Wynn, who penned several hit films of the 1970s: *The Longest Yard* (1974), *The Drowning Pool* (1975), *The Deep* (1977). Like *In Cold Blood*, *The Glass House* aims for a searing realism in its portrayal of the criminal underworld, as the opening credits announce: "This motion picture was filmed entirely in a State Prison. Most of the faces and voices are those of actual prisoners. The story and characters are fictitious, but the situations are real." While shooting his film at Utah State Prison, Gries consulted the convicts for technical advice to better achieve a realist pulse. Alan Alda plays the lead role of Jonathon Paige, a professor of political science convicted of manslaughter for accidentally killing the man who hit his wife in a car accident. In his autobiography, Alda details that prisoners offered their counsel on such topics as how to kill another convict, how to make an effective shiv, and how to avoid violent confrontations through the finer points of inmate etiquette.[66] The film couples gritty realism with melodrama in its tale of Paige's attempt to preserve himself from the violence percolating throughout the prison. Rounding out the cast are Victor Morrow as Hugo Slocum, the vicious overlord of a prison gang; Clu Gulager as Brian Courtland, a new and naive guard at the prison; Dean Jagger as the warden; Kristoffer Tabori as Allan Campbell, a fresh-faced young convict mistakenly (or so he claims) arrested during a drug bust; and Billy Dee Williams as Lennox, the leader of the prison's African American population.

In aiming for realism, and also like *In Cold Blood* in this regard, *The Glass House* focuses on the queer potential of the criminal underworld. When Paige, Campbell, and the other new convicts enter the prison, a group of hardened inmates stare at them as they shower. When Paige sits for a haircut, he is the object of lingering leers, and wolf whistles pierce the air as the men walk into the main population of the prison. Paige looks up before entering his cell for the first time, and he sees floors of men staring down at him, with the camera's angle accentuating his puniness against the combined weight of so many convicts. Slocum dismisses Paige—"probably a fag," he sneers—but it soon becomes apparent that Slocum's desire for

Campbell will lead the young man into a fatally compromised position. Campbell naively believes his association with Slocum protects him from the homosexual advances of other inmates, as he tells Paige, "I mean, did you see the faces of those guys when I came in here? I mean, I need someone to protect me around here." He receives a rude awakening when Slocum, preening with a mirror in his hand, gives Campbell a guitar and makes clear his expectation of a sexual relationship: "Pretty soon you're going to find out that there's only a few things Hugo Slocum can't get in this prison. Like, one's a helicopter, and the other one's a woman." The reaction shot of Campbell, as he looks up from the guitar, registers his dawning realization of the submission expected of him. When he wards off Slocum's advances, Slocum warns him, "It's either me, or everybody," a threat proven graphically true when Campbell is gang-raped in the prison's weight room. Paige consoles Campbell—"It doesn't make any difference what happened. You're still a man, you're still the same person you were when you came here"—but Campbell commits suicide soon after, plunging off the third-story guardrail, thus inversely reenacting the earlier shot in which Paige gazed up and realized the predatory dangers of prison desire.

Against this story line of depredations and corruption chime the voices of reform, most notably in the figure of Lennox, who preaches to the inmates about love and tries to convince Paige of his sincerity: "I'm not gaming you, Paige. What I want is for these men to realize their value as individuals and as human beings." In the film's climax, Paige runs away from Slocum and his gang and then shoots Slocum with a makeshift gun that Lennox gave him. In the ensuing confusion, Courtland kills Paige. Discussing the calamitous events, the prison's warden refuses to offer a palliative assessment of the penal system: "I'm not in love with this system. But it's all we got. And it's a lot better than having no system at all." Courtland's aspirations to improve the prison are left unfulfilled, and the film suggests as well how chimerical is the vision of such reforms. The ending is grim, with Paige, Campbell, and Slocum dead and no hope of ameliorating the system that brutalized them. John O'Connor, reviewing for the *New York Times*, proclaimed, "While melodramatic in structure, it is powerfully frank in its details," and other contemporary reviews were similarly positive.[67] The *Hollywood Reporter* avowed, "Without a doubt, this movie will have more effect in bringing about prison reform than any number of riots or demonstrations around the country," and *Daily Variety* judged that the film "succeeded as engrossing [television] fare by underplaying the violence and concentrating sensitively on the pressures and inadequacies of the penal system."[68]

For Capote, crime and its repercussions held an irresistible fascination, and in 1974 he planned to attend the trial of Elmer Wayne Henley, a seventeen-year-old boy complicit in the murder of at least twenty-seven teens. "How could they simply disappear without even the slightest ripple of an uproar?" Capote asked in preparation for his travels.[69] The project was canceled when Capote was hospitalized, as it was reported, for "a pulmonary condition and general exhaustion."[70] Because he failed to follow through on this project, as he also failed to complete his proposed masterpiece *Answered Prayers*, *In Cold Blood* was Capote's last major literary triumph. Subsequent publications such as *The Dogs Bark* and *Music for Chameleons* anthologized short works, many of which had been previously published. In the 1970s he penned several unproduced screenplays, including *Uncle Sam's Hard Luck Hotel*, *Tyranny*, and *Dead Loss*, each of which to some degree addresses crime, punishment, and rehabilitation. (These unproduced screenplays are addressed in chapter 9). Toward the end of his life, Capote mentioned a plan for a future project: "If I live to my old age, I'm going to do a book called *Meditation on Murder*," explaining that this study would focus on "what causes and creates a multiple murderer."[71] In ways too numerous to count, *In Cold Blood* changed the course of Capote's life and literary career, giving him the unqualified success that he sought as well as a new aspect to his celebrity persona. Through the book's chilling account of the randomness and brutality of life, in which chance circumstances and failed connections can somehow spark the murder of an entire family, wholly unaware of their impending doom, Capote touched a primal nerve in himself and in his audiences, with a level of intensity that his subsequent ventures into criminology failed to match.

▶ Jonathan Kaplan's *In Cold Blood* (1996)

Although Capote died in 1984 and Brooks in 1992, popular interest in *In Cold Blood*, the book and the film, remains high, as evident in its many subsequent adaptations and explorations. *In Cold Blood*'s literary legacy includes such works as Gordon Lish's novel *Dear Mr. Capote* (1983), which tells of a serial killer hoping Capote will agree to tell his story; Ande Parks and Chris Samnee's graphic novel *Capote in Kansas* (2005), which reimagines Capote's journey to Kansas to investigate the Clutter murders and his encounters there with Nancy's ghost; and Kim Powers's novel *Capote in Kansas: A Ghost Story* (2007), which explores the repercussions of their time in Kansas for both Capote and his traveling companion Nelle Harper Lee. *In Cold Blood* was filmed again as a 1996 television miniseries, written by Benedict Fitzgerald and directed by Jonathan Kaplan. Kaplan began his career with a series of low-budget sexploitation films such as *Night Call Nurses* (1972) and *The Hustler of Muscle Beach* (1980), but then moved to more dramatic fare, including several films celebrated for strong female leads: *Heart Like a Wheel* (1983), for which Bonnie Bedelia was nominated for a Golden Globe; *The Accused* (1988), for which Jodie Foster won an Academy Award; and *Love Field* (1992), for which Michelle Pfeiffer was nominated for an Academy Award. Fitzgerald adapted Flannery O'Connor's *Wise Blood* for the 1979 cinematic production directed by John Huston— who, Capote declared, "butchered the novel"[72]—as well as penning screenplays of Joseph Conrad's *Heart of Darkness* (1993) for television and the Christian gospels for Mel Gibson's *The Passion of the Christ* (2004). Kaplan and Fitzgerald's miniseries stars Anthony Edwards as Hickock, Eric Roberts as Smith, and Sam Neill as Dewey, as well as featuring Ryan Reynolds in the small supporting role of Bobby Rupp, Nancy Clutter's boyfriend, well before he became a leading man in the following decade. The extended length of Kaplan's miniseries affords ample opportunity to consider episodes not filmed by Brooks, yet the resulting program does not employ this advantage to achieve a deeper aesthetic effect or to reinvigorate analysis of the death penalty in the United States.

Whereas Capote was thunderstruck by Robert Blake's physical resemblance to Smith, the same cannot be said of casting Eric Roberts in this role. Still, some power exudes through the performance, for Roberts portrays Smith as a wounded and unbalanced man, drawn into events beyond his control and ken, and unsure as well of his sexual attractions. Like Brooks, Kaplan builds upon this aspect of Capote's characterization of Smith and includes numerous queer touches in his portrayal of Smith and Hickock's friendship. In a particularly overwrought scene, when they stop at a diner during their travels, Smith rocks back and forth while singing about his avenging angel. As Hickock holds his hand, Smith calms down, but then quickly pulls it away when the waitress comes to ask if they would like dessert. Submerged desire is evident when tears well in Smith's eyes because he assumes that Hickock does not want to travel with him after they rob the Clutters. Hickock replies, "Wrong. Wrong on all counts, honey." He continues consoling Smith, promising him, "And then we're going to Mexico, baby." As they leave the diner, Hickock sees that Smith has urinated on his chair. The scene captures many of the complexities of Smith and Hickock's relationship, yet its emotionality descends into bathos, portraying Smith's incontinence as an overdetermined sign of his inability to control his memories, emotions, or desires.

Adumbrating the homoerotic undertones of their relationship after murdering the Clutters, Smith believes that there must be something wrong with them to commit such a heinous crime, but Hickock replies, as they are driving in Mexico, "You can count me out of that crap, baby. I'm normal." Despite Hickock's protests, the queer dynamics of their relationship are readily apparent in Mexico as they share a boat with the German tourist Otto, who sings "Wunderbar, Wunderbar" while filming Perry in lush black-and-white footage; Hickock, in the background, passionately embraces a woman. Otto's filmmaking casts Smith as an object of desire, with the camera lingering on his buttocks and then on his biceps in side view. Otto disappears from the miniseries after this scene, but the homoerotic undertones remain. When Hickock is having sex with the prostitute Inez in their hotel room, Smith asks for the car keys, then angrily throws the woman out, straddles Hickock on the bed, and confronts him about selling their car. The sublimated sexuality between the two men, however, never

materializes, and their passions are displaced onto other people and other objects, as when Smith compares his guitar to a woman: "You don't know what it's like, Dick—to have a guitar as long as mine and have it stolen. Wax it, shine it, put it to your voice. Treat it like a girl you really had some use for, not like one of those whores you keep promising to marry." Roughly twenty years passed between Brooks's and Kaplan's filming of *In Cold Blood*, yet the potential homosexuality of the killers remains such a taboo subject that it can only be hinted at and then resignified as misplaced heteroerotic desires.

Displacing erotic desires cannot erase them, and Kaplan also shows that for both men, their masculinity must always be proved. It is always tenuous, and thus in need of defense. When Smith excitedly describes the sexual prowess of Japanese women, implying that "you never had a real woman" unless she was Japanese, Hickock responds, while shoving food into his mouth, "Yes, I have," and stares at himself narcissistically in the reflection of a napkin dispenser. Their homosocial sparring reaches its apex when they murder the Clutters, as Kaplan films the sequence to accentuate that they are testing each other. Smith says to Hickock, "You can finish him, tough boy. You'll feel better." When he confesses to Dewey in the police car, Smith claims: "I thought I could make him argue me out of it, make him admit he was a phony, a coward." The murder of the Clutter family, in this depiction, is merely a game of "chicken" taken too far, part of the range of denied desires that led to their murderous rampage. Despite the extended length of Kaplan's miniseries, it leaves a murkier and more confused depiction of the sex lives of Smith and Hickock than Capote's book or Brooks's film, refusing to take advantage of greater social understanding of homosexuality in the 1990s to consider candidly the relevance of sexuality to Smith and Hickock's relationship and the ensuing murders.

Capote criticized Brooks's film for devoting scant attention to the Clutters—"There also wasn't enough on the Clutter family. The book was about six lives, not two, and it ruined it to concentrate so much on Perry and Dick"[73]—and perhaps the greatest difference between Kaplan's miniseries and Brooks's film is that Kaplan dedicates more time to these characters to develop their personalities. In one such scene, Herb teaches Kenyon to drive a truck, but the vehicle lurches under Kenyon's footwork on the clutch. The boy becomes frustrated, but Herb calms him down and Kenyon states, "Nothing scares you," appropriating a similar sentiment expressed in Capote's novel by the family's friend Mrs. Ashida (*CB* 36). Bonnie Clutter, while saying her prayers, speaks to her sense of alienation, intoning tremblingly, "I am a ghost, Lord." Also, Herb's relationship with Nancy is emphasized, particularly his disapproval of her dating Bobby Rupp due to the families' religious differences. (The Clutters were Methodist, the Rupps Catholic.) When Herb sees Nancy kissing Bobby as the young man leaves for the evening, Kaplan cuts to a flashback of a happy family outing when Nancy and Kenyon were young, and Nancy writes in her journal that she loves Bobby despite her father's opposition: "This is forever between me and Bobby." Such depictions humanize the Clutters; they are not merely the victims of homicidal madness, but individuals with their own desires, dreams, and limitations. At the same time, such scenes suffer from a rather maudlin tone and do little to contribute to the dramatic arc of the narrative. By accentuating Herb's disapproval of Nancy's dating life, for instance, Kaplan introduces a melodramatic plotline that does not enhance viewers' understanding of the unfolding events. In the end, the tragedy of the Clutters transcends the daily comings-and-goings of their lives. It matters little whether some typical father-daughter tensions simmered between Herb and Nancy, and it should not be overlooked that they did not live their lives with any thought of their inherent dramatic interest.

Although Kaplan's miniseries strikes many of the same themes as Capote's book and Brooks's film, it is far less invested in criticizing the death penalty. At his execution Smith simply declares, "I think it's a hell of a thing to take a life in this manner. Maybe I had something to contribute." Hickock earlier voices a critique of capitalism and its social divides—"There's two kinds of laws, baby. One for the rich, one for the poor"—as they drive across Kansas to rob and murder the Clutters. Other than these traces of social commentary, Kaplan encodes little analysis of the death penalty and its cultural repercussions in the miniseries, concentrating instead on the violence of the murders. "I didn't want to compromise on the violence, he said. "We made it look exactly like what would happen if you put a shotgun two inches from someone's head and pulled the trigger. But it was all shot in a way that would be acceptable to network television."[74] In sum, Kaplan's miniseries is more concerned with depicting violence than with pondering its roots and consequences, which renders it a flawed re-creation of Capote's vision and of Brook's earlier adaptation. For Capote and Brooks, the Clutter murders sparked deep reflections on the meaning of crime and capital punishment in the United States, as these topics intersect with issues of social class and sexuality, yet the inherent danger of adaptation is that other artists of unlike mind will take the same material and, by accentuating other aspects of the story, blanch it of its brilliance.

Turning a Princess into a Star
▶ Capote, Lee Bouvier Radziwill, and *Laura*

Before Capote remade *Laura* for television in 1968, Otto Preminger's 1944 film was acclaimed as a noir classic for its sexual intrigue, smoky allure, and shocking mystery. Based on Vera Caspary's novel, the film opens with the mysterious murder of beautiful Laura Hunt, or so the situation appears until she stuns the investigating detective, Mark McPherson, by returning to her apartment very much alive. Preminger's film stars Gene Tierney in a memorably cool, mesmerizing performance as the eponymous heroine and Dana Andrews as the laconic and unflappable McPherson. The featured cast includes Clifton Webb as Laura's mentor Waldo Lydecker, Vincent Price as the lothario Shelby Carpenter, and Judith Anderson as Laura's aunt Ann Treadwell. With David Raksin's lush and haunting theme song, also titled "Laura," playing at key points of the narrative, Preminger's film takes on a romantic aura as well, with McPherson, Lydecker, and Carpenter competing for Laura's affections once they learn that the murdered woman is not Laura but Carpenter's former love interest, Diane Redfern. In the film's suspenseful climax, it is revealed that Lydecker mistakenly killed Redfern because, acting in haste and unable to see clearly in the dark, he mistook her for Laura; revealing to Laura his obsessive love for her, he seeks again to murder her for spurning him in favor of Carpenter. McPherson rushes in to rescue Laura and succeeds both in saving her life and in winning her affections. Preminger recorded in his autobiography that "audiences made *Laura* a phenomenal success at the box office. In England alone it grossed more than the production cost," and its success accorded him the financial and artistic freedom to embark on new endeavors of his choosing.[1]

For Capote, remaking *Laura* served as a means not merely to achieve greater acclaim for his literary genius but to create a star. Long intrigued by tales of Sergei Diaghilev, the impresario who directed the career of the Russian dancer Vaslav Nijinsky,[2] Capote envisioned himself in a similar role, transforming his dear friend Princess Lee Bouvier Radziwill, a socialite and the younger sister of Jacqueline Kennedy Onassis, into an acclaimed artiste.[3] (Coincidentally, in the 1970s, Ken Russell hoped to cast Capote as Diaghilev in a film of Nijinsky's life starring Rudolph Nureyev in the lead role, but the project was never filmed.)[4] To achieve this metamorphosis of Bouvier, Capote needed a star vehicle for her. Producer David Susskind recalled Capote approaching him to promote Bouvier's star potential and saying: "Lee Radziwill is going to be an actress, and I think we should all put something together for her. I'm sure she'll be so good that I'll write it for her myself."[5] Capote suggested that they cast her in a remake of John Van Druten's *Voice of the Turtle*, a Broadway smash hit in 1943 that was filmed in 1947 with Eleanor Parker, Ronald Reagan, and Eve Arden, but Susskind, concerned that Bouvier lacked the acting experience for such a demanding lead, in turn proposed a remake of *Laura*.[6] Because the eponymous heroine is off camera for the film's opening sequences when the other characters believe she has been murdered, the artistic fate of the enterprise would not depend solely on Bouvier's performance.[7]

Capote counted Bouvier among his Swans, the flock of beautiful woman of high society who adopted him as their pet, including such figures as Babe Paley, Slim Keith, C. Z. Guest, Gloria Guinness, Marella Agnelli, and Gloria Vanderbilt. Capote wittily defined the Swans: "God gave them good bones; some lesser personage, a father, a husband, blessed them with that best of beauty emollients, a splendid bank account" (*O* 28). Of Bouvier he rhapsodized, "Ah, the Princess! Well, she's easily described. She's a beauty. Inside. Outside."[8] Swayed by Bouvier's charms, Capote embarked on a television enterprise that would bring acclaim to no one. In attempting to fashion Bouvier into an actress, he demonstrated that no Diaghilev can sculpt raw material into success when the raw material does not possess the necessary talent.

Counterbalancing Bouvier's dramatic inexperience, Capote's production features a strong cast of actors, particularly Robert Stack as the straitlaced and taciturn detective McPherson. Stack's performance as Eliot Ness in *The Untouchables* (1959–63) indelibly linked him with law-enforcement roles, and he plays the role of McPherson with cool aloofness masking his growing fascination with the beautiful yet presumably deceased Laura. McPherson radiates calm, control, and discipline; his quirky habit of playing a hand-held child's balancing game, in which one must coax ball bearings into their proper receptacles, encodes the character's steely precision. George Sanders, who won a Best Supporting Actor Academy Award for *All About Eve* (1950), plays Lydecker, and Farley Granger, best known for his roles in Alfred Hitchcock's *Rope* (1948) and *Strangers on a Train* (1951), plays the playboy Carpenter, who woos both Laura and her aunt. Arlene Francis, a well-known television actress who hosted her own program in 1957–58, assumes the role of Treadwell, a woman of advancing years yet with flagrant desire for Carpenter. The character's rapacious sexuality is encoded in her name, for *tread* is an archaic term for copulation.[9] Capote and Thomas W. Phipps were credited for the teleplay, with John Moxey directing; Moxey built his career primarily on television work for such mystery and detective shows as *Mannix*, *Mission: Impossible*, *Matlock*, *Miami Vice*, and *Murder, She Wrote* in the 1960s through the 1980s. *Laura* aired on January 24, 1968, on ABC.

For the most part, Capote's teleplay adheres closely to Preminger's film, with many of its plot points similarly employed to implicate characters as suspects while McPherson unravels the mystery of Laura's murder. The detective initially suspects Carpenter when the playboy claims he attended a concert but cannot correctly identify the music played. Later Carpenter plants a key to Laura's cabin in her apartment, and he is subsequently caught at the cabin, where it appears that he has come to clean, or to dispose of, a shotgun that might be the murder weapon. Once McPherson discovers that she is alive, he suspects Laura of murdering Redfern out of jealousy over Carpenter. Laura learned of Carpenter's affair with Redfern when Lydecker confronted her with a cigarette case that Carpenter had given Redfern, even though it was originally a gift from Laura. McPherson's suspicions increase when it appears that Laura lied about a broken radio at her cabin. The radio plays immediately when McPherson tests it there, but Laura later informs him, when he takes her to the police station for questioning, that she asked a handyman to fix it. Because Laura ignores McPherson's command not to communicate with Carpenter after she has apparently returned from the dead, his suspicions of Laura and Carpenter escalate. Treadwell is suspected as well because of Carpenter's plan to marry Laura. Despite Treadwell's advantage in years over her niece, she enjoys her position as Carpenter's sexual patroness and resists losing control of him. In these various twists and turns that provide the plot's foundation, Capote does not deviate noticeably from Preminger's production.

Also following Preminger's lead, Capote imbues this noir mystery with a queer edge in its depiction of Waldo Lydecker. Notwithstanding his obsessive love for Laura, Lydecker was conceived of as a gay character; ironically, the casting director of Preminger's film objected to Webb playing the role of Lydecker precisely because his performance would accentuate the character's homosexuality. As Preminger recalled: "The head of the casting department, Rufus Lemaire . . . said that he had seen a test Webb made for MGM. He said the man was impossible. 'He doesn't walk, he flies,' implying that he was effeminate."[10] Preminger succeeded in casting Webb in the role, as he also surreptitiously signaled the character's queerness despite ongoing struggles with the Hays Code. As Vito Russo documents, "In the original script for *Laura*, dated April 18, 1944, numerous allusions to the homosexuality of Waldo Lydecker were cut before shooting began. In an opening scene showing Lydecker's apartment, the script says 'the camera pans the room. It is exquisite. Too exquisite for a man.'"[11] Webb portrays Lydecker with a supercilious air of condescension in Preminger's film, and Sanders similarly sniffs dismissively throughout his scenes, playing the part with an effete snobbishness that doubles as queer. In this light, casting Sanders as Lydecker was particularly apt, especially given the many similarities between Lydecker and Addison DeWitt, Sanders's Oscar-winning role in *All About Eve*. Both characters are critics and aesthetes who, despite their outward pursuit of women—Lydecker's obsessive love for Laura, DeWitt's determination to force Eve Harrington (Anne Baxter) to choose him over another man—read as queer. Indeed, the descriptions of DeWitt in *All About Eve* as a "venomous fishwife" and a "Trappist monk" invite suspicions about his sexuality, as does his statement to Eve when he compels her to forgo an adulterous affair in favor of him: "That I should want you at all strikes me as the height of improbability." Lydecker and DeWitt epitomize the quasi-gay characters of 1940s and 1950s cinema, those who could never be labeled as homosexual under the restrictive Hays Code yet who contrast jarringly with the more traditionally masculine characters with whom they share the screen.

Capote maintains these queer edges of Lydecker's character in his adaptation of *Laura*, particularly in an early scene when McPherson arrives to question him about Laura's murder and Lydecker receives his guest while naked in the bathtub. Capote's scene is somewhat preposterous, as is Preminger's before it, for who precisely would receive a detective investigating a murder in the bathtub—or, for that matter, arrange his bathroom as an office, as Lydecker apparently does? The outrageous mise-en-scène of bathroom qua office removes Lydecker from the realm of the normative, and, as he cavalierly dismisses McPherson's questions about the murder, he trumpets his celebrity: "I happen to be the most widely misquoted man in America. When my friends misquote me, I resent it, but from Sergeants McAvity and Schultz I would find it quite intolerable. Would you mind handing me my bathrobe?" As he requests his robe, Lydecker rises from the tub, and although the camera is discreet in its depictions, it is apparent that Lydecker stands naked in close proximity to McPherson. Continuing his interrogation, McPherson asks, "Did you love Laura Hunt?" to which Lydecker replies ambiguously: "Laura considered me the wisest, wittiest, and most worthy man she had ever met. . . . She also thought me her kindest, gentlest, and most sympathetic friend." McPherson pursues this line of questioning as Lydecker takes breakfast at noon—another sign of his decadent lifestyle— repeating, "Did you love Laura Hunt?" Again Lydecker answers elliptically, "You're always asking that . . . Men swarmed around her, but I had my way of dealing with them. Nothing makes a man less appealing to a woman than ridicule, and I've always had a certain gift for it." Never affirming his love for Laura, Lydecker focuses instead on his success in dismissing her suitors. In the homosocial competition for her affections, he seeks not to win Laura for himself but to deny her to other men, those who would likely pursue a sexual, rather than merely an aesthetic, relationship with her.

Additional scenes in Capote's *Laura* accentuate Lydecker's queerness further. In a flashback to a party scene, Treadwell compliments Laura on her costume—"What a divine dress!"—and Laura confesses, "Waldo chose it for me." Treadwell then replies to Lydecker, "I must say, you have wonderful taste, you old wretch." A proven arbiter of women's fashions, Lydecker is also respected as an arts and literature critic, but when Lydecker asks

McPherson if he watches his program, McPherson replies that he does not. Lydecker wonders, "Is it too literate for you?" to which McPherson gruffly answers, "No, too precious," employing a code word signifying that he views Lydecker as queer, unmanly, and effeminate. In subsequent scenes, such sparring between Lydecker and McPherson bolsters McPherson's masculinity at Lydecker's expense. When McPherson uses coarse vocabulary in describing Laura, Lydecker blusters, "How dare you call Laura a dame?" to which McPherson coolly responds: "A lady who gets knocked off generally turns out to be a dame."[12] While McPherson later learns that the beautiful Laura Hunt is most certainly not a dame, this exchange reinforces the audience's sense both of Lydecker's effeminacy in his arch reaction and of McPherson's brusque potency in shocking Lydecker.

Lydecker's queerness emerges in his effete sensibilities, yet his desires are naturalized as outwardly heterosexual. Most obviously, he is a man ostensibly in love with Laura to the point of murdering her in a fit of jealous rage, but also because his interest in Laura is narratively paired with Treadwell's determined courtship of Carpenter. The two older characters, Lydecker and Treadwell, aggressively pursue their attractive young companions, yet it is always apparent, in both Preminger's and Capote's films, that Treadwell enjoys more sexual success with Carpenter than Lydecker enjoys with Laura. Thus, as McPherson proves himself the more virile man by protecting Laura from Lydecker, so too does Treadwell prove herself the more potent lover. When, in Capote's film, Treadwell and Lydecker observe Laura and Carpenter dancing, Treadwell frowns and Lydecker, in a separate shot, groans. Both patrons see the handwriting on the wall in the young couple's obvious attraction, and they struggle to preserve control over their young beloveds. A telling contrast nonetheless emerges in that Treadwell maintains her relationship with Carpenter, as in the scene when these lovers are amorously embracing until Laura and Lydecker interrupt them to return the cigarette case. Furthermore, as Treadwell says to Carpenter while discussing her possible motives for murdering Redfern, "Why would I kill Diane Redfern? Poor girl. You've had twenty Diane Redferns, at least twenty, how many of them did I murder?" A sexual sophisticate well aware that Carpenter's interest in her is pecuniary rather than amatory, Treadwell enjoys Carpenter's tender ministrations, yet she suffers no illusions about her relationship with this gigolo. As she tells Laura, "Shelby and I understand each other. He's no good. I don't mind that. . . . And I'm rich."[13] To

Carpenter himself she says resignedly, "Laura was my niece, Shelby, long before she was your lover," signaling that her familial affections take precedence over her erotic affairs. Still, when Carpenter goes to phone Laura, she tries to regain control: "Shelby! You call Laura, and you walk out of here and you stay out, do you understand? She can't have you. You are mine, and the sooner you understand that the better." Capote must sustain the possibility that Treadwell killed Redfern to prolong the mystery, but once the mystery is resolved, she appears simply as a mature woman in control of her sexuality. Her character's conquests contrast with Lydecker's queerness, both in his effeminacy and in his failure to bed a younger consort—a simple enough task for a wealthy patron, as Treadwell's history with Carpenter illustrates.

Although Capote's script adheres to Preminger's original in many ways, it subtly shifts the film's thematic register from a story of an obsessive lover to one of an obsessive artist, for Capote's Lydecker sees himself as a creator who transformed Laura into his masterpiece. Whereas Preminger's Laura benefits professionally from her friendship with Lydecker, parlaying his endorsement of a fountain pen into a successful career at her advertising firm, in Capote's film Lydecker aligns himself with Pygmalion, the artist who fell in love with the beauty of his sculpture. After Laura admits to Lydecker that she loves Carpenter, he avows, "I feel like Pygmalion, if Galatea had suddenly become a barmaid." His biting words wound her, but as he later explains while preparing to kill her, she allowed him a respite from the very bitterness of himself. If she were to leave him, only his bile would remain. He confesses how he depended on what she provided him with: "The only time in my life I was able to escape from Waldo Lydecker, that tedious iconoclast. I didn't feel the need to defend myself all the time. I could talk to you without making those perpetual caustic comments. How tired I am of all that." Staring at the portrait of Laura over the mantle instead of at the woman herself, with the camera registering his confusion between image and reality, he continues, "She gave me the only happiness I ever knew." As he switches from second-person to third-person pronouns, despite the fact that Laura stands before him, it becomes clear that Lydecker loves her image more than he could ever love the woman who inspired it. Denigrating the idea of physical love, the love Laura would presumably enjoy with Carpenter, he speaks again of the beauty of her image rather than of her: "I understood you better than anyone. You were always drawn to the Shelby Carpenters, those gross physical types. But they were no good for you. They tarnished the image. They weren't for my Laura. I created her out of a quite ordinary girl with commonplace ambitions. I created that rare and lovely being." Again Lydecker gazes at the portrait, seeking comfort and consolation from this empty image before him rather than from the woman whom he seeks to kill.

Along with obsessively focusing on Laura as his creation, Lydecker continues to disparage the erotic physicality of Carpenter's relationship with her: "It was sordid and undignified. Is that what you're going back to?" As Lydecker stalks Laura in her apartment, his prerecorded television program plays in the background, and this plot device explains how he is presumably otherwise occupied while simultaneously pursuing his victim. On the program that plays in the background, Lydecker expostulates about the "disease" of love: "This is exactly what love is. A disease, a poison, a virus. Deadly and consuming. . . . I suffered from this infection for about three years until it became the ruling nightmare of my life. I came to understand how it was that normal rational men and woman are driven by this torment to such desperation that they totally lose control and kill. Not even out of hatred or hysteria, but simply to blot out that one obsessive image from the brain." Lydecker is ostensibly reading from another man's diary in this passage, yet the viewer realizes that the "one obsessive image from the brain" refers to his own obsession, not for Laura, but for his vision of her. As he continues threatening Laura, he accuses her of destroying this perfect image symbolizing his artistic genius: "You killed the one thing I cared for—my one achievement. Did you think that I could let you go now to soil Laura's image in the arms of one filthy lout after another?" The portrait of Laura that hangs in her apartment is superimposed over Bouvier's face as she responds, blurring the boundaries between the woman and her representation. Despite the beauty of both images, it is clear that Lydecker can only see her as sullied by the physicality of human lovemaking. His exaggerated fear—that Laura will love not only Carpenter but "one filthy lout after another"—testifies to the repulsion he feels for the presumably wanton nature of female sexuality. Feverishly imagining Laura indulging her unrestrained passion with an endless stream of men, Lydecker once again proves himself sexually frustrated. Unlike Ann Treadwell, he has manifested no erotic experience, either heterosexual or homosexual, rendering him a crazed virgin driven to psychosis.

As the film concludes, Lydecker dwells on the horror of imagining Laura with Carpenter. In Preminger's version, Lydecker speaks with distaste of Carpenter "kissing you, loving you," whereas Capote's Lydecker states more explicitly, "I could see him making love to you." The primary thematic difference between these closing scenes, however, is the effect of Lydecker's shotgun blast. In Preminger's film, Lydecker smashes his antique grandfather clock in which he hid the shotgun that killed Redfern, and in so doing he metaphorically exposes the secrets of his hidden love and his murderous jealousy. With its concealed compartment, this rococo clock registers as a closet hiding Lydecker's obsessive, unwholesome, and queer desires as well as his rage. In Capote's version, Lydecker's blast destroys the portrait of Laura, maintaining the film's Pygmalion theme as the creator ruins the image of beauty that he sought to preserve, for the perfection of the image could never match the humanity of the woman it was intended to represent.

Through his Pygmalion theme, Capote includes another queer register in the film, for it is Lydecker's creation of Laura that sparks McPherson's love for her. Long before he meets Laura, the detective becomes fascinated by her portrait. As he examines her apartment, the camera closes in on him, following his eyes to Laura's portrait, and it focuses on the portrait again as McPherson leaves her residence, suggesting his lingering desire for her. Stack plays these scenes with a somber detachment that thaws to a sentimental edge, registering McPherson's gradual surrender to a love that could never be. As Lydecker eulogizes Laura on television, McPherson looks through her wardrobe, remaining in her apartment the entire day while stealing many meaningful glances at her image. Because Lydecker created Laura, McPherson's love for her is a testament to Lydecker's aesthetic accomplishments, yet Lydecker himself registers the impossibility of the detective's affections: "I wonder if they've ever had a patient who has fallen in love with a corpse." In these scenes staging McPherson's nascent desire for Laura, including his melancholic love for a corpse, McPherson is responding to the art and aesthetic taste of Lydecker, who sculpted Laura into the image that mesmerizes the detective. McPherson may find Lydecker's television program "precious," but he responds physically and emotionally to Lydecker's artistry. The two men are thus linked through the woman they both love, if only for their homosocial bond to be broken with Lydecker's death.

Capote's *Laura* was not well received critically, and it suffers from numerous aesthetic flaws. Its screenplay is, for the most part, derivative. Bouvier's wooden acting fails to elicit much sympathy for her character, and Moxey's direction is often inelegant and heavy handed. For the most part, the dialogue, prosaic and banal, does not paint the characters' personalities beyond the broadest of strokes, although a sly humor sneaks into the film when Lydecker convulses upon seeing Laura alive: "To think that I wasted that beautiful obituary on a model from Brooklyn." Capote's screenplay reimagines the film's opening sequence to enhance its mystery, beginning with the gunshot blast that kills Redfern and continuing to a scene at the morgue where Treadwell mistakenly identifies the body as Laura's, but here the camera work is awkward: when Stack walks toward the camera, his tie virtually bounces against it.[14] In another moment of clumsy direction, Moxey features close-ups of Lydecker, Treadwell, Laura, and Carpenter after Lydecker asks, "Do you realize, dear friends and enemies, that one of us killed a defenseless girl last Friday?" with the framing of each suspect melodramatically asking the viewer to ponder the painfully obvious supposition that each character is suspected of Redfern's murder. The lion's share of critical opprobrium was reserved for Bouvier, as she was panned for a performance that, indeed, showcases a surprisingly slim range of emotions, despite the various situations—amatory, minatory, revelatory—in which the character finds herself. In addition to critical brickbats for her performance, Bouvier was also criticized, in light of her status as an international celebrity, for her ambition to act. Jack Gould, writing for the *New York Times*, sniffed, "Miss Bouvier . . . is not the first young lady of international society to confuse a smattering of newspaper publicity with the fruits of enrollment in the American Academy of Dramatic Arts."[15] He also took Capote to task for his screenplay, which he describes as a vehicle to feature Bouvier as a "stunning clotheshorse upon whom no discernible thespian demands were made."[16] Capote's aspirations to transform Bouvier into an actress were likewise ridiculed, with Gould referring to him as the "Professor Higgins of the jet set."[17] Behind-the-scenes exposés revealed Bouvier's high-handedness during filming, including her condescending attitude toward the crew, her inexperience with taking direction, and her pampered background, further dimming the project's luster.[18]

According to Capote's screenwriting partner, Thomas Phipps, however, Capote deserves neither credit nor blame for the script: "He hadn't the slightest idea how to do it—to write dialogue or how to construct a television play or anything. He asked me if I would do it with him and I said I would. He went off to Verbier. . . . I sent him the script and he wrote back glowing letters that it was just wonderful. It didn't have one change. So he had nothing to do with it at all. Nothing! Terrible reviews, unfair, because it was perfectly respectable."[19] One must take Phipps's words with a grain of salt: at the very least, Capote knew how to write dialogue and to construct a screenplay. His prior experiences with *Indiscretion of an American Wife, Beat the Devil,* and *The Innocents* testify to his abilities in this regard. It thus appears that Capote was uninterested in the grueling labor of writing a screenplay at this stage of his career and left Phipps to do the lion's share of the work. To a certain degree Phipps is justified in defending his teleplay. Notwithstanding its flaws, one might concede that *Laura* is indeed a "perfectly respectable" film, yet with Capote's name featured in the credits and with the excitement of Bouvier's television debut, expectations were raised to fever pitch, only to be dashed with the production's mediocrity. Also, one can fairly criticize all parties involved in this production for hewing so closely to Preminger's adaptation of Caspary's novel. The performances hit many of the same notes, the screenplay follows much of the original dialogue and plotting, and many of the changes—Lydecker broadcasts his program on television rather than radio, Treadwell and Carpenter's sexual relationship is more openly depicted—reflect changes in technology and sexual mores in the twenty-four years between the two productions, rather than any attempt to recalibrate the story's relationships or mystery.

In a 1979 television interview of Capote, Susskind reminded him of their experiences with *Laura* and ruefully regretted, "It wasn't one of the particular achievements of that year, or of any year . . . the newspapers and the magazines had a field day." He also commented on Bouvier's reception by the critics: "They took this nice girl and crucified her." Claiming to have expected the bad reviews, Capote blamed them on a prejudice against Bouvier rather than on an objective assessment of her performance: "I did foresee that no matter what she did, the press was going to come down on her like hell." Susskind suggested as well that "the young lady today does not cuddle the memory to her bosom. I know that she's bitter about it."[20]

In a sad irony, Capote's friendship with Bouvier, which was the prime impetus behind *Laura*, ended in a public and highly publicized spat. In a 1975 interview of Capote published in *Playgirl* magazine, Richard Zoerink reported Capote's gossipy allegation that "Bobby [Kennedy] had Gore [Vidal] thrown out of the White House."[21] When Vidal sued Capote for libel, Capote cited Bouvier as his source for this allegation, but she denied his claims: "I do not recall ever discussing with Truman Capote the incident or the evening."[22] Stung by this betrayal of loyalties, Capote declared publicly in the weekly *People*, "She's just a treacherous lady, and that's the truth of it. She's treacherous to absolutely everyone."[23] Two years later he referred to her with similar venom—"That little bitch"—in the same publication.[24] Likewise, Bouvier dismissed both Capote and Vidal as unworthy of her attention: "They are two fags. It is just the most disgusting thing."[25] No Diaghilev can control his Nijinsky forever, and the bitter end of Capote's friendship with Bouvier made them fodder for gossip columnists and public chatter, with little of aesthetic merit to compensate the loss of their friendship or to burnish their artistic reputations.

Capote for the Holidays ▶ *A Christmas Memory* (and *Trilogy*), *The Thanksgiving Visitor,* and *One Christmas*

How does an openly gay writer in the 1960s, whose fame skyrocketed due to his portrayal of a gruesome crime and its aftermath, become simultaneously associated with holiday tales of emotional resonance and southern nostalgia? It is one of the great paradoxes of Capote's career, as well as a testament to his expertise with a range of literary and cinematic genres, that television productions of his holiday-themed short stories in the late 1960s—Frank and Eleanor Perry's *A Christmas Memory* (and *Trilogy*) and *The Thanksgiving Visitor*—softened his public image while allowing him to pay tribute to his southern roots. So successful were these 1960s productions that, in the 1990s, another of Capote's holiday tales, "One Christmas," was filmed for the first time, starring Katharine Hepburn in her final screen role, and "A Christmas Memory" was remade starring Patty Duke and Piper Laurie. In this subgenre of cinema Capoteana, the virtues of love, acceptance, and forgiveness are celebrated in southern settings reflective of simpler times and rural pleasures, as they also subtly address the difficulties of a southern upbringing for queer children such as Capote.

Capote readily admitted the autobiographical elements of these holiday stories, in which the protagonist "Buddy" represents himself as a child. With these films' connection to their author's past, audiences were asked to see another side of Capote's unflappable and acerbic personality, centering on the lonely childhood he endured after his parents left him to be raised by cousins. Capote frequently discussed the feelings of isolation, loneliness, and rejection that he experienced during his southern childhood: "But growing up in some place like Monroeville, as it surely must have been in other rural towns, produces, for some particular individuals, a strange loneliness of alienated existence, of social disorientation. For these individuals . . . this loneliness can add to sensibility, and it seems to increase creativity. I know that in a way I have used up some of my loneliness by writing."[1] From this perspective, Capote's holiday narratives carry traces of the künstlerroman tradition: although they do not portray the artist growing into his vocation, they portray the childhood of an author whom viewers would recognize as one of the premier talents of their time. In this manner, these narratives—both the films and the short stories on which they are based—permit their audiences to consider the ways in which Capote's childhood influenced his development as an artist and as a man. Exploring the social disorientation of a southern upbringing for a precocious child such as Capote, these films depict the networks of compassion and understanding available within communities otherwise unsympathetic to sissies who refuse to adhere to stereotypes of southern masculinity. In doing so, they touch on timeless concerns of self, community, family, and love, proving the universality of human emotions in scenes from the childhood of a gay adult celebrity—albeit with varying degrees of success.

▶ *A Christmas Memory* (1966) and *Trilogy*

Capote's short story "A Christmas Memory" was first published in *Mademoiselle* in 1956. The story, warmly received by the public, was subsequently republished in a hardcover gift edition. Capote soon began considering ways to bring the story to the screen, and in a 1960 letter to David O. Selznick and Jennifer Jones, he mentioned this interest: "Do you remember my story, the one I made a record of, 'A Christmas Memory'? I would like very much to make a film of it. . . . It would be entirely visual, with a boy's voice reading the story and a musical score, by, say, Virgil Thompson [*sic*]. It is something Jose Quintero could do well (I think). It *could* be beautiful, if done *very* simply."[2] Quintero produced the theatrical version of Capote's *The Grass Harp* at New York's Circle in the Square Theatre in 1953, and from this experience he understood Capote's conceptions of his characters and how to stage them. Likewise, Virgil Thomson wrote the incidental music for *The Grass Harp*, winning Capote's approval for matching his literary motifs with musical phrasings. Capote's appeal to Selznick and Jones never bore fruit, but Frank and Eleanor Perry, who enjoyed a critical success with their film *David and Lisa* (1962), persuaded Capote to grant them the rights to his story, and to allow them to dramatize it rather than adhering to his vision of "a boy's voice reading the story and a musical score." Over the years from print to film production, the story remained popular with the public, and it was soon being described as a Christmas classic. In the introduction to their 1966 reprint of "A Christmas Memory," which corresponded with the film's airing on December 21, 1966, as part of ABC's *Stage 67* series, the editors of *Ladies' Home Journal* praised the story as "a classic tale, drawn from a flawless memory, [that] belongs to the tradition of Christmas."[3]

The greatest obstacle in filming *A Christmas Memory*, as director Frank Perry stated, arose in its fundamental lack of a plot. The executives at ABC evaluated "the story [as] 'slight and sentimental,' 'lacking in plot,' with 'no suspense,' and 'perhaps not quite up to the high dramatic standards we're projecting for *Stage 67*'" (*T* 23). And truly, nothing much happens in the film, if one is looking for the standard narrative arc of exposition, conflict, climax, and resolution. On the contrary, the film strings together memories of Capote's cousin Sook Faulk, a mentally challenged older woman who was his inseparable companion during childhood. With Geraldine Page and Donnie Melvin in the lead roles, Sook and Buddy undertake numerous activities, such as baking fruitcakes, mailing the cakes to friends, chopping down a Christmas tree, opening presents on Christmas morning, and flying the kites they give to each other. The film winds down with the foretold death of their dog Queenie foreshadowing Sook's demise, which occurs after Buddy has been sent to military school. These various pastimes do not necessitate a climactic encounter attaining a high emotional pitch, yet with its emphasis on interactions rather than actions, the film achieves a quiet and peaceful tone reflective of memory and nostalgia, one that pays homage to Capote's southern roots as a simple and idyllic time.

The film lacks any sort of character development as well. Buddy and Sook do not mature or achieve some deeper realization due to the events unfolding around them; instead, Capote as narrator recalls the love that bound them together and their happy times enjoying each other's company. The "villains" of the piece—characters whom the script refers to simply as First

Relative and Second Relative—chide Sook for permitting Buddy to drink whiskey after the successful preparation of their fruitcakes, and they later insist on singing "Hark, the Herald Angels Sing" to enforce a spiritual meaning to the family's Christmas festivities. Other than these slight interruptions, First Relative and Second Relative do little to upset the general air of peace and calm that Buddy shares with Sook. Capote's description of his relatives in his story—"though they have power over us . . . we are not, on the whole, too much aware of them" (*T* 199)—testifies to the generally tranquil atmosphere of his childhood home, in which he and Sook were allowed to pursue their pastimes without much interference. The only character who might be considered to develop emotionally is the minor figure of Mr. Haha Jones, from whom they purchase whiskey for their fruitcakes. The camera initially shoots him from a low angle to emphasize his height and Sook and Buddy's fear of his intimidating presence. Haha refuses their money but gives them the needed whiskey anyway. He then kindly requests that they share a fruitcake with him. Here the camera records a shift in his personality by filming him directly, thus equalizing him to his new friends. The camera angles suggest Haha's transformation, but it is more a change in perception than in personality: Sook and Buddy learn to see him as their benefactor, rather than as the forbidding figure they feared him to be.

For a film with little plot and character development, *A Christmas Memory* succeeds by immersing its viewers in a southern landscape of loneliness and love, primarily on the strength of Geraldine Page's performance. Warmth suffuses her every move, yet she couples what could devolve into a maudlin portrait with an honest appraisal of her character's mental limitations, and so an occasional off-kilter gleam in her eyes suggests Sook's difficulties in comprehending the world around her. She is often shy and diffident, yet she assumes a brisk and no-nonsense demeanor while purchasing ingredients from the local grocer. When chastised for the whiskey incident, she becomes confused and must confront the fact that she cannot always trust her judgment: "It's because I *am* too old. Old and funny," she weeps. The vulnerability of Page's performance makes the scene painful to watch, for she seems aware of her handicaps and yet unaware of how to move beyond them. Buddy corrects her gently, "Not funny. *Fun*. More fun than anybody," and his words help her to regain her childlike enthusiasm for their ensuing adventures, such as seeking the perfect Christmas tree. Page's transformation into Sook Faulk is all the more remarkable in that she was forty-two years old when the film was produced, yet she convincingly played a character approximately twenty years her senior. Furthermore, she accomplished this transformation without any makeup other than an unkempt wig. Frank Perry reported that after the first day of shooting she wept in joy—"It's because I'm happy, can't you see? Because I love you and this story and because this is going to be my first good movie!" (*T* 30)—as she surely recognized the power and simplicity in the character she was portraying and the performance she was achieving.

With its warm emotions and simple yet haunting depiction of intergenerational affection, *A Christmas Memory* attests to the depth of human connection, and writer Eleanor Perry, tapping into the power of Capote's tale, suggests, "Both the happiness and the grief that come with such a relationship are universal enough to reach and involve an audience" (*T* 264). At the same time, an attenuated undercurrent of queerness registers in the film, not in terms of homosexuality or erotic attraction, but due simply to Capote's presence as narrator. At the outset of the venture, Capote insisted on narrating the film—"not out of vanity," he stated, "but because it was my story, in every sense, and I wasn't going to allow any 'distinguished baritone' to tell it" (*T* 17). In truth, one could well criticize the film for Capote's contributions, for he is not a voice actor, and he does not recite his lines with much tonality or even warmth. Instead, his narration is surprisingly bland, and as numerous friends and critics registered over the years, his voice— memorably described by Norman Mailer as "a cross between an adenoidal prince and a telephone operator"—could by no means be considered mellifluous.[4] But because the voice is so obviously Capote's, it is impossible to forget that the story is indeed his, and so viewers realize that they are watching a queer boy's childhood. The short story and the film's imagery and symbolism, particularly when Sook and Buddy wheel their groceries and then their Christmas tree in a baby buggy, accentuate their alienation from normative reproduction: neither Sook in her past nor Buddy in his future will produce children, but the gifts that they carry in their baby buggy testify to their inherent warmth and emotional fecundity as they create for others a perfect holiday. Also, the scene in which they awaken together in bed underscores their alienation from normative sexuality, both in Sook's present and Buddy's future. Had Capote allowed a "distinguished baritone" to narrate his tale, its queer edges would have been rendered mostly invisible, but by maintaining his proprietary interest in the venture, the queerness

FIG. 15 *A Christmas Memory* (1966): Sook (Geraldine Page) sleeps while Buddy (Donnie Melvin) lies beside her, with their pairing throughout the film tacitly depicting their alienation from all others.

of *A Christmas Memory* subtly asks its audience to recognize alternate patterns of kinship, reproduction, and love.

A Christmas Memory was crowned with acclaim and awards. Jack Gould, reviewing for the *New York Times*, praised Page's luminous performance, lauding her "haunting mixture of strength and childlike innocence, a blend of eccentric weariness and loneliness fused with flights of convivial mischief," although he tempered his approval by noting the film was "not entirely successful in sustaining the pathos of the friendship between boy and woman." Of Capote's narration, he noted succinctly, "the art of interpretive reading cannot be listed as one of his accomplishments."[5] Geraldine Page won an Emmy Award for Outstanding Performance by an Actress in a Dramatic Leading Role, and Capote and Eleanor Perry were likewise awarded Emmys for their adaptation of the story for television. (The film was nominated for Outstanding Dramatic Program, but lost to David Susskind's production of Arthur Miller's *Death of a Salesman*, featuring Lee J. Cobb as Willy Loman.) Beyond the public recognition that *A Christmas Memory* enjoyed, Capote extolled both Page's performance and the production: "Geraldine Page is just wonderful,"[6] he proclaimed, and she portrayed the Sook Faulk character "with an uncanny beauty and accuracy" (*DB* 414). Capote frequently voiced his disdain for actors in his writings, yet he unreservedly admired Page's talents, if also registering surprise at her personal style: "Miss Page is rather unforgettable, come to consider: a Jekyll and Hyde; Dr. Jekyll on stage, Mr. Hyde off. It is purely a matter of appearance; she has better legs than Dietrich, and as an actress can project an illusion of infinite allure—but in private she insists, Lord knows why, in disguising herself under witchlike wigs and costumes of consummate eccentricity" (*DB* 414). In a December 1967 interview, Capote celebrated the two years that saw double success in publication and filming: "Two things which I've really loved . . . have been *A Christmas Memory* and this," referring to *In Cold Blood*.[7] He enthusiastically endorsed *A Christmas Memory* for capturing his childhood experiences with Sook with quiet eloquence: "I thought that was good and still mine. Almost nothing was changed."[8]

Following the success of *A Christmas Memory* (and during the subsequent filming of *The Thanksgiving Visitor*), Capote and the Perrys collaborated on two more of Capote's short stories, "Among the Paths to Eden" and "Miriam," in order to combine them with *A Christmas Memory* into the feature-length film *Trilogy*. Although *Among the Paths to Eden* and *Miriam* do not portray a holiday setting, their union with *A Christmas Memory* into *Trilogy* creates an overarching story line in which the loneliness depicted in each of their plots finds a thematic antidote in Buddy and Sook's sweet friendship and seasonal sharing.

A moving yet simple story, *Among the Paths to Eden* challenged the Perrys in their adaptation, for the plot contains little dramatic action, only the graveside conversation between Ivor Belli (Martin Balsam) and Mary O'Meaghan (Maureen Stapleton), a widower and a woman in search of a husband. As Eleanor Perry reminisced, "Naturally we worried about coming up with a very talky show" (*T* 175). Mary's efforts to ensnare Ivor depend on keeping their conversation flowing, and in light of their shared losses—a father and a wife respectively—she emphasizes both his greater suffering and his potential to adapt to new circumstances: "Of course, a wife isn't the same as a parent, exactly. I mean, a man can have more than one wife without being at all disloyal." She soon suggestively continues, "They say when a man marries again, it's a real compliment to the first wife." Mary notices that beside Ivor's wife's grave stands an unmarked tombstone that awaits him, and she remarks that "there's a place here for you, too," with the camera catching his reflection in the matching headstone. The setting and Ivor's reflection in the headstone imbue the film with a subdued atmosphere of mortality, against which Ivor attempts to assert his freedom, both from the memory of his wife and from Mary. In close-up he states, "I like my independence," a subtle hint that Mary should not pursue him, but she demurely responds, "I firmly believe that a man should be lord and master in his own house."

As the conversation progresses, it seems that Ivor might indeed be ready to remarry, but if so, the object of his attentions would likely be his secretary Esther. Although he chafed against the restrictions that his wife Rose placed upon him, an affectionate tone enters his voice as he recounts Esther's ministrations: "Well, Esther keeps a tight rein on me; she's a little like Rose in that respect. She made me wear this topcoat. Esther says it's not spring until she says it's spring."[9] In a heartbreaking moment of candor, Mary asks Ivor, "How does a woman find a husband when she's not young and pretty?" to which he slowly inhales and replies, "Well, Esther's not young and pretty." At this point it is clear that Ivor will pursue Esther, not Mary. In the bittersweet ending, the two acquaintances part ways, but Mary, never daunted, espies another widower trekking across the cemetery, whom she quietly follows.

A tale of startling simplicity filmed with due attention to the quiet passions of these two lonely people, *Among the Paths to Eden* received critical adulation for its candid portrayal of loneliness. Jack Gould praised the film for its character portraits: "*Among the Paths to Eden* enjoyed the strength of probing characterization and a subdued ring of truth about troubled individuals in moments of personal crisis," although he criticized the plot at its most basic level, pointing out "the inevitable doubt that a sensitive woman would use the grief of others to try to resolve her personal problem."[10] The reviewer for *Time* likewise valued the film's successful portraiture: "When she approaches one slightly retiring fellow . . . the dialogue casts its mood so well that it seems perfectly reasonable when she perches on his wife's tombstone and does her imitation of Helen Morgan singing a blues song. . . . In TV's 'black week,' *Paths* was the brightest Christmas gift of all."[11] Following the path trailblazed by Geraldine Page, Maureen Stapleton won an Emmy for Outstanding Performance by an Actress in a Dramatic Leading Role for *Among the Paths to Eden* in 1968.

"Miriam," the third short story filmed for *Trilogy*, was Capote's first major literary triumph, winning the 1946 O. Henry Award for Best First-Published Story. It recounts the harrowing tale of Miriam Miller, a woman haunted by a child who may be real or who may represent her own tormented psyche. In his introduction to the volume anthologizing this prizewinning story, Herschel Brickell writes that "it is not possible to overlook so perfect a piece of character creation as is to be found in this story, whose principal figure is a devil-child, never quite explained, but real and terrifying, so that she lingers vividly in the memory like something evil and awful."[12] Much like Henry James's *The Turn of the Screw* (and Capote's *The Innocents*), the power of the tale lies in its ambiguity, as readers enter Mrs. Miller's consciousness yet are unsure of the reality of her perceptions. In their adaptation, the Perrys succeed in transforming Capote's tale to the screen, but Eleanor Perry admits that they "departed from, embroidered on, felt the freest with" this adaptation, more than with their other versions of Capote's works (*T* 120). By the end of the Perrys' film, it is clear that Miriam is a phantom of Miss Miller's imagination, resolving the interpretive crux of Capote's story but still succeeding in painting a portrait of a woman driven mad by loneliness.

Whereas Capote's Mrs. Miller is a widow, she is stripped of her deceased husband and given an occupation in the filmed adaptation: Miss Miller (Mildred Natwick) has recently retired from her position as a nanny; however, without any wards to occupy her time, she finds herself wracked by loneliness. The film's opening sequence is shot at the Alice in Wonderland statue in Central Park which, given Lewis Carroll's perverse predilection for young girls, becomes an eerily appropriate setting for the film's narrative concern with childhood, desire, and latent sexuality. The action commences as Miss Miller picks up a ball that a young girl has lost, singing, "I've got your ball! I've got your ball! Now what are you going to do, honey-bunch? Maybe if you're a very good little girl and give your old nanny a kiss, she'll give the ball back." Bribing kisses from unknown children, Miss Miller appears a grotesque mixture of innocence and deviance, hoping to inveigle herself into the lives of strangers. The girl screams in reply, "You're not my nanny," and runs back to her governess. Miss Miller's desperate isolation becomes more evident when she attempts to strike up a friendship with the governess, but the woman gently yet persistently resists her overtures. Miss Miller then visits her former ward Nina, who is now awaiting the birth of her child. Despite Nina's reluctance to allow Miss Miller into her apartment, Miss Miller barges in—"You can spare five minutes for your old nanny, can't you?"—and endorses herself for the position of the child's caretaker: "One thing you know about your old nanny, she's loyal, loyal and devoted." Miss Miller's incessant nattering erodes the patience of those around her, and when she tells Nina not to smoke out of concern for her unborn child, Nina lights a cigarette in defiance. As Miss Miller's loneliness compels her to seek companionship with strangers and former charges, their resistance to her unwelcome friendship undermines her sanity.

If Miss Miller's request for an unknown child's kiss hints at her desire to connect emotionally with the young, the film further points to her subterranean sexuality when she receives an obscene phone call. She rebuffs the caller's proposed rendezvous, but rather than remaining in the safety of her apartment, she proceeds with her plans to attend a movie. At the theater she meets Miriam (Susan Dunfee), the girl who soon becomes her tormentor. At Miriam's request, Miss Miller buys her a ticket to the show. The connections between the two characters are registered in the name Miriam, which Miss Miller learns they share, and in Miriam's hair. "You may not believe this, but when I was a child, my hair looked exactly the same," Miss Miller tells her, but Miriam stares blankly ahead as Miss Miller gazes at her from the side. Miriam disappears from the theater, but then appears at Miss Miller's doorstep later in the evening. After Miriam enters Miss Miller's apartment, Miss Miller compliments her dress, and Miriam replies, "White is my favorite color. White stands for purity, you know." Implicitly contrasting her innocence with Miss Miller's impurity, Miriam demands authenticity in their interactions, rejecting Miss Miller's polite yet vacuous words. As the scene climaxes, Miriam dashes a vase with imitation flowers to the floor. "I told you, I don't like imitations," she coldly intones, implying that Miss Miller is one such imitation for whom she does not care.

Despite Miriam's antagonism, Miss Miller proceeds in her efforts to win the girl's affections, buying éclairs to entice her to return. The camera focuses on the éclairs as Miss Miller waits for Miriam's visit, but time passes and Miriam does not arrive. "Guess she's not going to come, Tommy," she tells her parakeet, but she then discovers that Miriam is lurking in her bedroom. "I've been waiting for you all evening long," Miriam says, implying that the bedroom is the proper venue for their reunion. She then demands a gift from Miss Miller and chooses a locket from her jewelry box. Miriam's rudeness repulses Miss Miller, and the young girl forces a kiss upon her hostess: "But first I'm going to give you a big kiss in exchange for the locket." Miriam bids her good night and calls her nanny, but Miss Miller weakly replies, "I'm not your nanny." As Miss Miller pursued a young girl's affections in the film's opening scene, she now finds herself the unwelcome recipient of such affection. In their climactic encounter after Miss Miller enlists her neighbors' assistance in ridding her of Miriam, Miss Miller discovers that the young girl still resides in her apartment and plans to live with her forever. After Miriam smashes pictures of Miss Miller's various wards on the floor, Miss Miller pushes Miriam out the window, presumably to her death. She retires to her bedroom, but after a few moments of rest, she turns to see that Miriam has returned to her, and the young girl eerily says hello. The audience now knows that Miriam is a figment of Miss Miller's imagination, one who forces her to see through her own hypocrisies, and the film ends at this moment of her eternal imprisonment in the mental cage she has built for herself. As Eleanor Perry explains of the film's bleak ending, "Unless Miriam can be made to vanish, Miss Miller is aware that there will be nothing left excerpt her total immersion in schizophrenia" (*T* 120).

Like *A Christmas Memory* and *Among the Paths to Eden*, *Miriam* showcases a fine actress's extraordinary talents. Mildred Natwick's performance as Miss Miller imbues the character with a dreadful loneliness and despair. The viewer's sympathy for the character is challenged by her self-important nattering—one would not like Miss Miller if one were to meet her—but one cannot help feeling sorry for her even though she is so unlikable, for the character's core humanity is never overlooked. Capote enthusiastically expressed his admiration for Natwick's and Dunfee's performances: "And just wait until you see Mildred Natwick as Mrs. Miller and Susan Dunfee as the little girl!"[13] When *Miriam* was combined with *A Christmas Memory* and *Among the Paths to Eden* into *Trilogy*, the resulting film was well received. It was accepted for the 1968 Cannes Film Festival, but the student riots throughout France that year resulted in the festival's suspension after two days. In the *New York Times*, Howard Thompson extolled the film's delicate probing of the human condition: "The cold fact is that *Trilogy* is all talk and little action. But it quietly says and conveys more about the human heart and spirit than most of today's free-wheeling blastaways on the screen. Delicately, it towers."[14] With its narrative trajectory from isolation in *Mildred* to a woman's quest for love in a cemetery in *Among the Paths to Eden* to holiday nostalgia in *A Christmas Memory*, *Trilogy* captures the journey of the human spirit in tales of loneliness and lives without love, concluding with a vision of a surprising relationship that comforts otherwise isolated figures.

In the November 1968 issue of *Ladies' Home Journal*, a glossy two-page photograph captures Capote sitting before a dinner table crowded with such traditional Thanksgiving dishes as roast turkey, whipped sweet potatoes, cranberry-orange relish, and pumpkin pie. Captioning this feast, the editors introduced Capote through his culinary and literary talents: "Most readers will recognize Truman Capote presiding over our Thanksgiving feast. What most people won't recognize, however, is that Mr. Capote created this menu—in his poignant short story, 'The Thanksgiving Visitor,' an adaptation of which will be shown this month on television."[15] In this puff piece promoting the upcoming film version, Capote reigns over the dinner table as the gentle sage of holiday love, the fabulist distilling the season's magic into tales of heartfelt affection. *The Thanksgiving Visitor*, much like *A Christmas Memory*, was produced and directed by Frank Perry, with the teleplay written by Eleanor Perry. Geraldine Page and Capote reprised their roles as Sook and the narrator, with Michael Kearney replacing Donnie Melvin as Buddy, and with Hansford Rowe as Buddy's nemesis, the bully Odd Henderson. The film aired on Thursday, November 28, 1968, on ABC.

Set against a backdrop of rural Depression-era poverty in Alabama, *The Thanksgiving Visitor* focuses on the unique friendship between Sook and Buddy, with Capote's retrospection emphasizing his friend's generosity of spirit as well as her mental limitations. Capote's reedy voice-over introduces Sook as she tends the plants on the porch—"As she was a child herself, she understood children, and understood me absolutely"—as he also comments on the surprising nature of their friendship: "Perhaps it was strange for a young boy to have as his best friend an aging spinster, but neither of us had an ordinary outlook or background and so it was inevitable in our separate loneliness we should come to share a friendship apart." The two outsiders unite in their otherness, with Sook's compassion and kindness creating an oasis of love for Buddy.

As Sook's difference from southern society registers in her mental capacities, Buddy's difference registers in his queerness. He is transparently a sissy intimidated by antagonistic figures around him and solaced by his friendship with Sook. In an early scene depicting a schoolyard fight, the tomboy Jumbo jumps Buddy's oppressor Odd Henderson from behind, proving that even girls are capable of holding their own against this bully. But Buddy cannot escape his foe, as Capote's voice-over laments. "Alas, even on week-ends, I was the object of Odd's relentless attentions," he intones, with his emphasis on "alas" heightening the melodrama. Later Odd steals the dime Buddy needs to attend the movies and taunts him, "Crybaby! Crybaby, you ain't got the spunk of a field mouse," then lumbers away. From such encounters, the film appears to be developing into the clichéd story of a wimp who grows in self-confidence and learns to defend himself, but *The Thanksgiving Visitor* rejects such expectations in favor of Capote's recalcitrant queerness: this is not the story of a boy who achieves manhood by thrashing his adversary. As Capote writes in the short story, Odd accuses him of being a sissy, and Capote simply agrees: "He was right, I was a sissy of sorts, and the moment he said it, I realized there was nothing I could do to alter his judgment, other than toughen myself to accept and defend the fact" (*CS* 246). Inuring himself to the insults of others, Buddy nonchalantly accepts his queerness in Capote's story, and the film similarly depicts him refusing to enact the culturally sanctioned version of southern masculinity that others press upon him.

As Odd represents the exterior enemy from whom Buddy seeks solace with Sook, his Uncle B represents an interior antagonist, one with whom he must share his home and from whom there is less hope of escape. Learning of his nephew's troubles with Odd, Uncle B advises Buddy to fight: "You've got to get in there and tangle with him. You've got to bloody his nose and blacken his eyes!" When Buddy follows this misguided advice, the attempted skirmish only annoys Odd, who then tangles cockleburs in Buddy's hair to humiliate him further. Concerned that Sook's ministrations are smothering Buddy's fledgling masculinity, Uncle B attempts to introduce him to men's household responsibilities, determining that, in preparing for the Thanksgiving feast, "Buddy's going to kill the turkeys this year." In Capote's story, Sook simply reports Uncle B's concerns to Buddy, but the Perrys stage this encounter in their film, enhancing the dramatic conflict between the man and boy. Sook laughs at the idea, realizing that Buddy is emotionally unfit for such bloody labor, but Uncle B insists that the boy's masculinity stands in jeopardy: "Housekeeping's women's work. It's about time he learned to do a man's job." He then declares directly to Sook, "He's got to stop hanging off your apron strings." Buddy tries but cannot decapitate the turkey, again proving his inability to achieve southern manhood.

Surprisingly, this story line is then abandoned, with Uncle B failing to reform Buddy's effeminized masculinity, and so *The Thanksgiving Visitor* allows Buddy the freedom to retain his queerness, which reflects the man that the audience knows he will grow up to be. Indeed, in one of the film's funniest moments, Buddy lies sick in bed and passes the hours by cutting out pictures from movie magazines, including those of John Gilbert and Greta Garbo. Visiting her convalescing friend, Sook thinks Buddy has cut out a racy picture of three women in bathing suits, which would seem to indicate his interest in the opposite sex; however, on the other side of the page is Buster Crabbe in *Flash Gordon*, which was the true object of his attention. In complementary contrast, Buddy's aunts apparently contribute to his homosocial fascination with film stars. When he tells them that he is going to see Claudette Colbert in *Cleopatra*, they react in horror: "Well, that most certainly is not a story for a young boy to see." Shocked at the prospect of their nephew seeing such a notoriously sexualized figure on-screen, Buddy's aunts inadvertently encourage his homosocial adulation of male stars like Buster Crabbe.

In his youthful queerness, Buddy does not learn to decapitate turkeys or to thrash Odd, but in an attempt to reconcile the boys, Sook insists that they invite Odd to Thanksgiving dinner. Buddy is mortified but fails to dissuade Sook. With Page exhibiting quiet exasperation in her performance as Sook, she tells Buddy that Odd's mother is "real happy that you've felt enough about Odd to ask him over for Thanksgiving, and she said she's sure he'll be just tickled pink to come," as Buddy pulls the pillow over his head in disbelief. Convincing himself that his enemy would never enter his home, Buddy concentrates on the preparations for Thanksgiving, with Capote's voice-over detailing the various activities: "Our most delicate task on Thanksgiving Eve was preparing the table," he states, as he then details each of the guests and their food contributions. A slight hint of heteroerotic attraction emerges in Buddy's reaction to a female guest: "Suddenly, in one year's time, Annabel Conklin had turned into an entrancing young lady. Her hair was beautiful, and her features—eyebrows, nose, lips, and smile—tilted in such an original fashion." As she walks up the porch stairs and kisses Buddy, Capote's voice-over declares, "She smelled like geraniums after rain. I loved her." As a family member, albeit a distant one, Annabel appears an inappropriate object of Buddy's affections.

The plot reaches its climax when, during the holiday feast, Odd steals Sook's cameo. Buddy, who has been sulking in a closet, witnesses the theft and accuses Odd of the crime at the Thanksgiving dinner table, embarrassing his enemy in front of the other guests. Sook defends Odd by stating that the cameo is not missing, but Odd soon confesses and declares, "You must be a very special lady, Miss Sook, to fib for me like that." Buddy feels betrayed that Sook sided with Odd and runs out of the house to take refuge in a hay shack, and when Sook goes to comfort him, he accuses her of treachery: "You betrayed our friendship." In reply Sook voices the narrative's theme: "I know in my heart that deliberate cruelty is the unpardonable sin. Everything else can be forgiven, but that? Just never." They break a wishbone, and Sook wins. The film concludes as she wishes for Buddy's forgiveness for defending Odd. As the credits roll, they walk back to the house.

The Thanksgiving Visitor, like *A Christmas Memory* before it, was greeted with critical acclaim. The reviewer for *Time* appreciated it as "a rare, lyrical hour for television" and conceded praise to Capote as well: "The narrator is Capote himself—squeaky-voiced, but obviously authentic."[16] Jack Gould's *New York Times* review declared the film to be "a perfect sequel to his earlier television success, *A Christmas Memory*," and summarized the appeal of both productions: "Their virtue has been the avoidance of mawkish ritual and a recognition that holidays mirror the hopes, kindnesses, troubles, and disappointments of genuine people living with their own problems. Mr. Capote's televised remembrances have a tenderness of understanding that lingers after the holiday is over."[17] As she was honored two years earlier, Geraldine Page again won the Emmy for Outstanding Performance by an Actress in a Dramatic Leading Role.

Despite the artistic success of *A Christmas Memory*, *Trilogy*, and *The Thanksgiving Visitor*, Capote's collaborations with the Perrys resulted in some lingering ill will. Capote claimed in an interview that he worked with the Perrys—"They're filming two other short stories, 'Among the Paths to Eden' and 'Miriam,' so the three together will make a regular film, a triptych. But those were something I worked on, a true collaboration"[18]—but Eleanor Perry disputed his assertion. In a letter to the *New York Times Magazine*, she registered her resentment that Capote claimed equal credit for the screenplay of *A Christmas Memory*: "I was amused to see, after all this time, the 1967 photograph of Truman Capote with 'his Emmy' for *A Christmas Memory* (*New York Times Magazine*, July 16th). Truman and I both won

Emmys that year for the teleplay except that I wrote it—he merely put his name on it. First billing too! Isn't that amusing?"[19]

▶ One Christmas

A mere eleven pages long, Capote's "One Christmas" is rather short even by short-story standards, and so adapting it into a ninety-minute television movie (with a running time of two hours with commercials) required director Tony Bill and teleplay scenarist Duane Poole to expand numerous plot points from Capote's tale and to create additional scenes and encounters out of whole cloth. In brief, Capote's narrative concerns a trip undertaken when he was a child to visit his father in New Orleans, his discomfort with his father and his desire to return home, but also his dawning realization of his love for him upon reuniting with Sook in Alabama. Bill's *One Christmas* maintains this structure while interweaving four tales of personal growth: Buddy (T. J. Lowther) learns to accept and love his father; his father (Henry Winkler), referred to in the teleplay simply as Dad, matures from ne'er-do-well to concerned parent; Dad's wealthy girlfriend Emily (Swoosie Kurtz) learns to stand up for herself; and Emily's imperious aunt, Cornelia Beaumont (Katharine Hepburn), lets down her façade of patrician aloofness to teach Buddy a lesson about the true meaning of Christmas. A hodgepodge of sentimental story lines, *One Christmas* drowns under the weight of so many miraculous transformations.

The film's opening shot captures Buddy sitting on a porch, perched with a pad on his lap and a pencil in his hand, thus establishing his future as a writer (if only to ignore this aspect of his character throughout the ensuing narrative). Julie Harris plays Sook, but unlike in *A Christmas Memory* and *The Thanksgiving Visitor*, her part in the story is quite small, limited to these opening scenes in which she helps Buddy prepare for his journey to New Orleans, where, despite his hesitations about the journey and his ignorance of geography, he longs to see snow. Although Capote's "One Christmas" does not address his father's distaste for his effeminacy, Bill's film portrays Buddy/Capote's queerness, which Dad sees as resulting from Sook's influence, as a divisive factor between father and son. While driving with Buddy, Dad steals a glance at the boy and says, "First thing we got to do is get you a haircut. You look like a girl. How do you play ball with all that?" To his father's consternation, Buddy simply replies, "I don't play ball." Dad's concern over his son's masculinity grows when, spying a package beside Buddy and inquiring its contents, he learns that it is a fruitcake that his son helped to prepare. "You cook?" he says in dismay. In a similar scene, when the two are dining at a restaurant, Dad exasperatedly asks, "You like baseball at least? Football?" Buddy shakes his head no, and his father asks: "What life are you living there in Alabama?" Buddy replies, "I help Sook mostly," aligning himself with femininity and domesticity, to which his father dismissively replies, "That's women's work." After Dad exploits Buddy to finagle his way into a party hosted by Cornelia Beaumont and Emily, he reads Ernest Thayer's "Casey at the Bat" to him for bedtime in an unsuccessful attempt to interest the boy in sports. When Buddy questions whether they should have crashed the Beaumonts' celebration, Dad tells him, "If no one gets hurt, it's not a lie. More importantly, you had a new experience. And new experiences grow a boy into a man." From this unethical perspective, masculinity is a boy's primary goal, no matter the path taken to achieve it.

As his intrusion into the Beaumonts' private party demonstrates, Dad is a small-time swindler and lothario, and his story arc involves his maturation into fatherhood and responsibility. When Buddy arrives in New Orleans and first espies Dad, he is throwing craps and drinking from a flask, sure signs of a dissolute life. Later Buddy sees the minor character Dixon Hobbs pummel his father for preying on older women to fund his lavish lifestyle. Dad repeatedly steals newspapers from street vendors, and he "borrows" the money that Sook gave Buddy for his travels, using it to wine and dine Emily as he seeks funds for the plane race that promises to make his fortune. He also plays on her heartstrings by promising that he will use the money to send Buddy to a private school. At this nightclub, Dad wheedles Emily, "You know what that boy needs? A solid family. Father, loving mother." The reaction shot captures Emily's romantic agreement, seeing herself in the role of the mother, as she fails to realize that Dad pays their tab with his son's money.

Emily's character is torn in so many diverging directions that her narrative arc flounders. Viewers first see her as a lonely old maid, desperate for Dad's companionship and willing to overlook his shady dealings if she can find love. Also, her aunt Cornelia, who controls the family purse strings, dominates her. When Dad visits Emily at the family residence, Cornelia sharply requests that he not present himself at her home. Emily is frustrated by her aunt's intervention in her love life, but Cornelia responds imperiously, "It's my house, and I'll do as I damn well please." At some point in her past, however, Emily was not the timid woman seen on-screen, for she tells Dad that she rejected numerous suitors to pursue her education and her love of the arts, a course that, over the years, has not helped her to maintain a sense of independence and identity. As Emily is cocooned by her aunt, Cornelia is likewise isolated from family and affection. Hepburn delivers many of her lines with patrician aplomb, such as when she dismisses Dad—"You may leave, if that is what you were about to suggest"—but the character is so one-dimensional that any story arc indicative of a change of heart undermines the fabric of Hepburn's performance.

The story lines of these four unhappy characters converge when Buddy spies Dad and Emily kissing at Dad's Christmas party. Buddy, distraught because he realizes his parents will never reunite, barrels down the stairs and shouts at her, "Stay away from my daddy! You hear me? You're an old maid, not half as pretty as my mommy. Just stay away from him." In the climactic encounter between father and son, with Dad furious at Buddy for ruining his seduction of Emily, Dad punctures both of their fantasies of a better and magical life: "There is no pot of gold for me. There is no snow for you." He then adds, "And as for your momma . . ." as he picks up a picture of her and smashes it on the floor. Soon after, Dad's maid Evangeline (Tonea Stewart) gently chastises him. Playing the clichéd role of the African American maid with a heart of gold who helps the white characters access the love surrounding them, she states, "Your problem is, you been living life so low, you wouldn't know true love now if you had it." In a gimmicky plot device, Buddy runs away from Dad and is hit by Cornelia's car; she takes him into her home to nurse him back to health. Although she first retains her tart tongue, telling Buddy, "I never had any children of my own. Frankly, I never cared for them," she soon metamorphoses into a fount of saccharine wisdom. When Buddy regrets that he has not seen snow, she teaches him the true magic of Christmas and Santa Claus: "Of course there's a Santa Claus! . . . Everyone is Santa Claus. I am. You are. Your father is." Sook speaks these words in Capote's short story, but here they are transferred to the voice of the character whom viewers would see as unlikely to believe them, and so Cornelia's forced transformation is not earned.

Following Cornelia's sermon on the universality of Santa Claus, each character embodies the bounty and the magic of the holiday season. Dad learns that, because he bought a substandard engine for the plane he was

FIG. 16 *One Christmas*: The forbidding figure of Aunt Cornelia Beaumont (Katharine Hepburn in her final performance) reveals her heart of gold to Buddy (T. J. Lowther).

financing, the pilot almost died in a crash, and this realization completes his metamorphosis into a devoted family man. "I came this close to killing a man," he says, holding his fingers together. He then embraces Buddy despite the boy's flawed masculinity: "You're not the son I expected, but then again I'm not the father you deserve." The composition of the scene features Emily in the foreground and Dad and Buddy in the background, as Emily has entered their home and overhears the conversation, yet, despite Dad's apparently sincere marriage proposal, she kisses him goodbye and says, "You have to begin to pay your own way in the world." Once again the woman she used to be, she carries herself with confidence in her capabilities. Evangeline's son Toby, appropriating the role in Capote's story of Buddy's skeptical cousin Billy Bob who does not believe in Santa Claus, is converted to a believer because Buddy gives him a radio—which had been a gift from Emily—but leaves a tag saying that it is from Santa Claus.

All that remains is for Buddy to express his love for his father. Dad has earlier asked, "Do you think I could hear the words, 'I love you, Dad'?" Buddy glumly replied, "The bus will be leaving soon," and walked away. As the film concludes at the bus station, Dad proves his redemption by repaying Buddy the six dollars he borrowed, including an additional dollar for interest.

When Dad plaintively pleads with Buddy, "Can I have a hug?" Buddy gives him one willingly. The bus driver, recalling Buddy and his story of playing an angel in a children's theatrical performance, declares, "I got the angel riding with me again." These words cast Buddy as the salvific angel within the film's themes, yet he has done precious little to achieve the metamorphoses of these various characters, whose maturations unfold mostly without his intervention. Nonetheless, Dad now pays for a newspaper after stealing them previously, and, miracle of miracles, it snows in New Orleans, and so Buddy's wishes come true. The snow appears all the more miraculous in that none of the characters so much as shivered previously, and Buddy was often costumed in short pants.

▶ *A Christmas Memory* (1997)

Whereas Frank and Eleanor Perry's adaption of Capote's "A Christmas Memory" allows the narrative to remain a series of biographical episodes held together by gossamer threads of memory, love, and nostalgia, Glenn Jordan's 1997 television film *A Christmas Memory*, with a screenplay by Duane Poole, imposes a stronger plot structure on Capote's tale. Primarily, the Perrys' film mentions in voice-over that Buddy is eventually deported to military school as the cause of his separation from Sook, but in Jordan's film it is treated as a defining trauma, one that rips Buddy (Eric Lloyd) apart from Sook (Patty Duke) but, in dramatic terms, allows her to confront her domineering sister Jennie (Piper Laurie) and defend herself. In fleshing out "A Christmas Memory" into a two-hour television production, Poole's screenplay incorporates numerous moments from Capote's other stories, primarily *The Grass Harp*. The maid Anna, who appears to be African American and is recognized as such by Buddy's family, claims instead, "I'm pure Cherokee," which echoes the protestations of Catherine Creek in *The Grass Harp*. Also, Buddy and Sook give the hypochondriac Seabone a dropsy cure for Christmas, which connects Sook to Dolly Talbo and her folk medicines; likewise, the role of Jennie, with her stern control of her household and her sharp business sense, appears to be inspired by Dolly's sister Verena. Buddy's antagonistic friendship with the tomboy Rachel mirrors Joel's friendship with Idabel in *Other Voices, Other Rooms*, as it also draws upon accounts of Capote's youth with Harper Lee when they were children together in Monroeville, Alabama, particularly in its story line of the two young children learning to write down their shared adventures. In addition to finding inspiration from Capote's other works, Jordan and Poole extend sequences from the original story in charming ways, particularly Buddy's fear of Haha Jones. "They're never going to find our bodies," Buddy moans when Sook drags him into Haha's café so that they can purchase the whiskey for the fruitcakes. When Sook and Buddy mail their packages of fruitcakes to friends known and unknown, they comment on various celebrities. This year they are sending a cake to Jean Harlow because, as Buddy says, "she's so pretty," but this reminds Sook of their gift the preceding year to Joan Crawford: "Would you believe not so much as a thank-you note?"

The First Relative and Second Relative of the Perrys' production register as little more than external annoyances to the joy that Buddy and Sook find together, but in Jordan's treatment Jennie presents a more intimidating demeanor, ordering her siblings about to carry out her vision for the family. A firm businesswoman, she emphasizes fiscal concerns and profit, which distinguishes her from her tenderhearted siblings Callie (Anita Gillette) and Seabone (Jeffrey DeMunn). At her store, when planning to order new merchandise for the holiday season, she avers, "Everyone wants to look fine for the holidays," with her words revealing her focus on the financial, rather than the familial, aspect of Christmas. There is no doubt that she loves Buddy and Sook, but her impatience with them triggers their fear of her. When Jennie, discussing the family with Callie, says, "Sook is an exception," and Callie asks, "To what rule?" Jennie replies, with exasperation simmering in her voice, "To most every rule I can think of. We love her. Well, we have to, because she's family, but she is our child." Her concern for Buddy is registered in her fear that he is effeminate: "The boy has been with us for two years now; he hasn't a single friend his own age. What's more, he needs to learn a man's ways."

Jennie's concern for Buddy's masculinity establishes the queer edges to the boy's character, which are also alluded to in the film's opening scene when he timidly runs away from Haha's café. In a similar vein, Sook and Seabone accentuate Buddy's isolation from his parents, casting him as an orphan in need of maternal care. Sook tells him, "You're lucky you're not living up in New York City with your mama," casting his home with them in Alabama as a refuge from the metropolitan ills of the North. When Seabone drawls, "I swear this boy looks more like his father every day," Jennie sharply retorts, "Long as that's all he gets from that man," indicating her belief that

Buddy's father would only be an unfit influence on the boy. Effeminate and abandoned, Buddy turns to Sook for comfort, only to find that even this relationship triggers Jennie's suspicions of his queerness.

Whereas the Perrys' *The Thanksgiving Visitor* allows Buddy the queer freedom not to stand up to his bully, thereby forgoing a standard plotline of successfully resisting one's oppressor, Jordan's *A Christmas Memory* rehabilitates Buddy from this queer image by concentrating on his developing relationship with the tomboy Rachel (Julia McIlvaine) and their mutual acquiescence to gender normativity. Buddy is initially rude to her, rude enough that Sook tells him, "It wouldn't hurt you to be a little nicer to that girl." The two children tussle when they argue over the failings of their respective parents. When Sook intercedes, Rachel states, "He didn't hurt me. I won," as she storms off triumphantly. Because Sook insists that Buddy give a fruitcake to Rachel and her family, the two slowly make amends, and Rachel kisses him when he gives her a notebook and pencil for Christmas so that she can write down her stories. Rachel denies that the kiss represents any romantic interest in Buddy—"It didn't mean nothing at all. Don't you go talking about this. Wouldn't want to have to beat you up again"—but when Buddy leaves for military school, she tells him that she has written a story about their night at Haha Jones's café when they believed they witnessed a murder, only to see the "victim" stagger into church the following morning, suffering from a hangover but not a fatal blow. "I'm going to miss you, Buddy," she says as they touch hands. Touching lightly on the künstlerroman tradition in its depiction of Buddy as a writer in training, the film plays on Capote's metatextual identity as a successful author, but ironically so, in that here Buddy's interest in writing wins him the heteroerotic affections of a tomboy who, it appears, must also be cleansed of her gender transgressions.

As Buddy is rehabilitated from Capote's queerness, so too does Sook shift as a character in Jordan's treatment of her story. This version of *A Christmas Memory* foregrounds Sook's emotional maturation as she learns to defend herself against Jennie's imperious orders. At Christmas Eve dinner, Jennie announces that she is sending Buddy to military school because this will be best for his future; although unstated, it also appears that she believes military school will assist Buddy in growing into manhood. Sook, devastated at the prospect of losing her closest companion, cries, "How can shipping him off to strangers be what's right? Sending him away from everything he knows, everyone he loves? How could that ever be right . . . for anybody?"

FIG. 17 *A Christmas Memory* (1997): Buddy (Eric Lloyd) and Sook
(Patty Duke) look upward in many frames, with these images capturing
their dreams of transcendence.

and runs from the table. To increase the pathos of the separation, the film
also depicts Jennie forbidding Sook to say goodbye to Buddy: "This is the
way it has to be," she declares, ostensibly to protect Sook from the distress
of the farewell. The conflict is overblown in its emotional registers, for
Jennie, whose sternness has hitherto been interlaced with evident concern
for her family, transforms momentarily into cruelty so that Sook's resistance
becomes all the more heroic. "No. I won't have it," Sook declares, and then
adds, "Buddy is my friend, and I'm taking him to the bus. And that's just how
it's going to be."

Triumphant in her skirmish with Jennie, Sook states as she and Buddy lie
on the ground flying kites, "Whenever you come back, I'll be waiting. You'll
always find me here for you." This image, linking the film to its beginning
when Buddy was flying a kite alone, demonstrates the community and love
he shares with Sook. When Jennie says goodbye to Buddy, she encourages
him in his maturation, as she also acknowledges the depth of her sister's love
for him. "You can't be a child forever. Your special friend has a way about her
I guess I never really appreciated 'til now. Her love for you shines like those
Baptist windows she's always been so fond of." Buddy hugs her, and a voice-
over concludes the film with Buddy as an adult describing Sook determining,

as she does every year, that the weather tells her it is time once again to commence her holiday ritual of baking fruitcakes. Avoiding the melancholy ending of Queenie's and Sook's deaths that are depicted in Capote's story and the Perrys' film, Jordan's *A Christmas Memory* overwrites Capote's memories in creating a nostalgic tale inappropriate to the queer author behind it, substituting a vision of Buddy as reformed into masculinity and of Sook as a source of love and inspiration from whom Capote will never be separated.

Capote once disparaged television in general, declaring, "This thing has no future whatever."[20] But with the Perrys' films of *A Christmas Memory* and its sequel *A Thanksgiving Visitor*, television proved particularly suited to Capote's holiday short stories, allowing an intimate medium that broadcast directly into viewers' homes to capture narratives short on action but ample in emotion. Juxtaposed with the 1990s adaptations, which rewrite Capote's source texts into standard narrative formats of conflict and climax, these films strikingly illustrate the difficulties of adaptation, in which filmmakers must liberate themselves from a text that inspires them, yet somehow distill its essence into a new medium. In this regard the Perrys' *A Christmas Memory* and *The Thanksgiving Visitor* provide a master class, from which the 1990s productions would have benefited.

Capote's Southern Childhoods ▶ *Other Voices, Other Rooms, The Grass Harp,* and *Children on Their Birthdays*

A dangerous child: such is the image that some readers formed of Capote from the louche dust jacket of *Other Voices, Other Rooms.* As Cecil Beaton and Kenneth Tynan recall, the author delighted in his decadent persona of defiled youth: "Capote tells a story of how he saw two Philadelphia matrons staring fixedly at a display pyramid of his book in the window of a Fifth Avenue book-store. Crowning the pile was a picture of Truman *couchant.* After a while the elder woman adjusted her spectacles, motioned towards the picture, and said beadily: 'Daisy—if that's a child—*he's dangerous!*'"[1]

This photograph, notorious for its relaxed yet defiant sexuality, can also serve as a representation of many of Capote's child characters, who appear on the surface as avatars of innocence and introspection, but whose subterranean desires surface to reveal their queer investments in adult eroticism. Whereas in his holiday tales Capote portrays himself as a queer yet presexual child through the character of Buddy, in *Other Voices, Other Rooms, The Grass Harp,* and "Children on Their Birthdays," Joel Harrison Knox, Collin Fenwick, and Billy Bob similarly confront the sexual pressures of adolescence on their journeys to self-recognition. For Capote, the myth of childhood sexual innocence serves as a cultural façade designed to protect adults, not children, from sexual knowledge, for children need such knowledge if they are to understand their very selves.

Early reviewers of Capote's literature noted his thematic interest in children, with many applauding his efforts in this regard. Popular press reviews of *A Tree of Night, and Other Stories* mostly agreed that Capote's tales featuring children, as the *Time* reviewer stated, "are written with full sympathy for their juveniles."[2] In a review in the *New York Herald Tribune*, Iris Barry posited that Capote's artistic talents surface in his stories of the young: "It is in presenting children—as Mr. Capote does in several of these stories—that he seems to be at once most effective and most perfectly master of his craft."[3] Leslie Fiedler succinctly observed, "Children are Capote's greatest successes," but he also acknowledged the queer underbelly of Capote's treatments of children that "project the invert's exclusion from the family, his sense of heterosexual passion as a threat and an offense."[4] Building on this interpretation, Fiedler believed that Capote's child characters reflect a desire to escape from adult sexuality: "Once the child has been remade by homosexual sensibility into the image of an ambiguous object of desire, the lust for the child is revealed as a flight from woman, the family, maturity itself."[5] Such a skewed interpretation of children's sexuality in Capote's fiction exposes the ways in which stereotypes against homosexuality undermine otherwise insightful analyses of Capote's texts. Nonetheless, whether in explicating or in filming Capote's treatment of children, one must engage with the meaning of sexuality within these narratives, for sexuality is at the heart of these southern bildungsromans of adolescent boys. In transforming Capote's narratives of queer childhood into films, David Rocksavage's *Other Voices, Other Rooms* (1995), Charles Matthau's *The Grass Harp* (1995), and Mark Medoff's *Children on Their Birthdays* (2002) must tackle the complexities of childhood sexuality, as they cinematically depict how Capote's young male protagonists mature into adult sexuality, whether in terms of homo- or heteroerotic attractions.

▶ *Other Voices, Other Rooms*

When published in 1948, *Other Voices, Other Rooms* achieved a striking literary success, bringing fame and significant sales to Capote. Given its homosexual story line, the novel presented numerous obstacles to any filmmaker interested in adapting it to the screen. In Hollywood under the Hays Code, homosexuality was a forbidden topic, and producers would be compelled to strip the novel of its foundations if they were to film it. In 1957 Curtis Harrington, the director of such mysteries as *Games* (1967, starring Simone Signoret and James Caan), *What's the Matter with Helen?* (1971, starring Debbie Reynolds and Shelley Winters), and *Whoever Slew Auntie*

Roo? (1972, starring Shelley Winters), wrote a treatment of Capote's novel for Jerry Wald's production company. Although the treatment remained undeveloped, it is an intriguing document, for it illuminates the many (and florid) changes necessary to bring the story to the screen. In Harrington's conception, Capote's queer bildungsroman would be sacrificed in favor of the story's gothic elements: "As I see the film version treated, the terror-suspense elements of the story would be strengthened and considerably developed. This would entirely remove the homosexual theme that Capote put into the novel, and still not harm it."[6] Conceding the unlikeliness of the undertaking—"Although I realize this is a (very) long shot, I wanted you to see how this story might be approached to make it filmable"—Harrington reimagines the novel's trip to the Cloud Hotel as a climactic encounter of gothic horror: "Then, just as Joel is about to be pushed off the balcony by the terrifying and macabre figure [a living skeleton], somebody comes running out of the corridor and pushes the figure over the balcony. The mask falls away, and Joel sees that it is Randolph, who falls screaming to his death." Joel's savior is the tomboy Idabel, who tells Joel that she witnessed Randolph changing into his costume. When Amy learns of Randolph's death, she explains that he wanted to steal Joel's inheritance so that he could search the globe for his lost love Dolores (not Pepe, as is the case in Capote's novel). Harrington's treatment of *Other Voices, Other Rooms* demonstrates his detailed understanding of Capote's literature and its themes—even the "macabre figure" of the "living skeleton" alludes to Collin Fenwick's Halloween costume in *The Grass Harp*—yet such a radical reimagining of Capote's plotline, particularly in its erasure of homosexual themes, would result in a film thematically and stylistically divorced from its source novel.

Whereas Harrington's treatment of *Other Voices, Other Rooms* emphasizes its gothic qualities to make the novel more filmable in the 1950s, David Rocksavage's 1995 film alludes to Joel and Randolph's homosexuality, but ultimately in a conflicted manner. Starring David Speck as Joel and Lothaire Bluteau as Randolph, the film begins with Joel's voice-over explaining how he came to live at Skully's Landing, the decaying plantation where his father resides. Mimicking Capote's wavering southern intonations, Robert Kingdom's narration as Joel connects the film to the novel's author. "One day, in the spring of 1938, a letter arrived," Joel recalls, a letter he describes as "formal in tone" and "written in a fine italic hand." While he details the letter's contents in voice-over, viewers see the hand writing it with a quill pen, with this hand emerging from a kimono sleeve and featuring a ringed pinky finger. From Joel's queerly inflected voice and from the extravagant mise-en-scène of the letter's penning, the film announces its interest in the encounter between these two queer figures.

Despite Joel's youth—he is just entering adolescence—the film's opening scenes hint at his homosexuality, primarily through other characters' reactions to him. When he overhears his aunt and uncle discussing his future, his uncle impugns his masculinity: "That momma's boy gives me the creeps. His wandering around here with that long face, like he's looking for a tit to suck." Joel's voice-over introduces the minor character of his friend Roger with words stressing their mutual estrangement from other children and their need to escape the drudgery of their everyday lives: "Roger was my only friend in New Orleans. We lived in a world of make-believe and tall tales," he declares, as Roger turns a cartwheel and waves up to Joel from the yard where he is playing. (Although a young boy turning a cartwheel is not a certain signifier of homosexuality, it is a less iconographically masculine activity than, for example, tossing a football or baseball.) Arriving in Noon City to reunite with his long-lost father, Joel wears a light blue shirt and white pants, clothing prissily inappropriate for the town's dustiness, and he attempts to assert his manhood. "I'd like a beer," he says, but the café's owner laughs at this request. When Joel turns away, she adds, "Aw, don't go off in a huff." These early encounters stress Joel's alienation from normative society in New Orleans and Noon City, setting the stage for his acknowledgment of his queer desires.

As Capote's novel focuses on Joel's acceptance of his homosexuality, the film initially adheres to this story line in its depictions of Joel's interactions with Randolph following his arrival at Skully's Landing. Reading Joel's palm, Randolph tells him, "You may find love when you least expect it," with the camera focusing on their entwining hands to accentuate Randolph's seduction of Joel. Randolph also compliments Joel on his attractiveness when planning to paint his portrait: "You have a fine complexion—touches of vermilion." And as Randolph languidly leaves the room, in language brimming with sexual symbolism, he declares: "A flower is blooming inside you, and soon, when all the tight petals unfold, when the bloom of youth burns brightest, you will turn and look, as others have, at the opening of another door." Falling to the allure of Randolph's ministrations, Joel embraces his homosexuality, which is measured in his costume change, as he is now

FIG. 18   *Other Voices, Other Rooms*: Joel (David Speck) models his new
sailor suit as Randolph (Lothaire Bluteau) looks on admiringly, with the
mirror marking the narcissistic tropes often associated with cinematic
depictions of homosexuality.

frequently clothed in an iconographic uniform of queer desire: the sailor
suit.[7] Indeed, in a shot of Joel dressing in a sailor suit, he stares at himself
in the mirror, thus playing on tropes conflating homosexuality with narcissism. Randolph looks on in the background, and Joel's voice-over proclaims,
"Randolph spoke a language only he seemed to be able to understand. He
said that his life was just a joke which he played on himself." Modeling himself as an object of Randolph's desire, Joel becomes attuned to his attractiveness to Randolph, particularly in scenes in which Randolph favors him over
his sister Amy (Anna Levine), who plays her part with kewpie-doll jealousy
darting from her eyes.

Realizing their virtual entrapment at Skully's Landing, both Joel and the
African American maid Zoo (April Turner) attempt to escape, but their
hopes are dashed. Their story lines are told in parallel editing. On her
journey north (where she longs to see snow, like Buddy in "A Christmas
Memory") Zoo walks along fields and dusty roads until she is brutally raped
and thus forced to return to the Landing. In the paired scenes, Joel and
Idabel slog through a swamp, with Joel's clothes—hitherto so pristine—
now mucked with grime to indicate his murky understanding of sexuality,

until a rattlesnake bites him and Idabel carries him back to the Landing. Rocksavage uses Zoo's rape to give the character a new sense of personal integrity, as she describes to Amy the peace that washed over her during the attack. "Zoo, you ain't gotta be a nigger if you don't wanna be. You can be a fine Negro woman," she realizes, and then tells Amy to pour her own coffee. While it is in some measure satisfying to watch Zoo stand up for herself, her new sense of inner strength as catalyzed by rape problematically conflates female empowerment with violence and sexual degradation. Whereas Capote's fictions mostly overlook the discrimination faced by his African American characters, many films adapted from his works expand these story lines to argue for the moral rightness of civil rights and integration. Unlike Zoo, who remains trapped at the Landing at the film's conclusion, Joel eventually escapes, but at this point in the plot his attachment to Randolph deepens. When Randolph attempts to win the affections of the convalescent Joel, declaring "I have a gift for you," he gives him a tiara. Such precious and exaggerated symbolism marks Randolph's desire to remake Joel in his own queer image, as suggested by the elaborate gown in which Randolph dresses himself while reliving his past with his beloved Pepe.

As in the novel, Randolph hides Joel in the ruined Cloud Hotel when his Aunt Ellen comes to visit, an act of deception that reveals his predatory intentions toward Joel. For their journey to the hotel, they wear matching white linen clothes while riding a mule, with these costumes accentuating Joel's mirroring of his mentor. Unlike in Capote's novel (*OV* 225–26), the mule survives the trip to the Cloud Hotel, and as Randolph and Joel return to Skully's Landing, Joel's voice-over declares the perfect kinship between them: "I felt all through me a kind of balance, as though I understood Randolph absolutely." What should be the emotional climax of the film, however, is oddly coupled with animal slapstick. Registering Joel's growing realization of Randolph's flaws, the voice-over continues, "I saw how helpless he was," and so Joel leads the mule and further realizes "how like a child, how terribly alone," as Randolph falls off the mule and drunkenly cries, "We're losing the mule." The emotional connection between them is severed when Joel perceives the limitations of Randolph's worldview. Randolph proclaims, "Imagination is the key to life," but Joel responds, "What good is imagination if you don't have the guts to live it?" Back at Skully's Landing, Joel finds his magnifying glass—a childhood toy indicative of his keen perception—and realizes that Aunt Ellen has come for him while they visited the Cloud Hotel. Outside the mansion, standing on its stairs, he rejects Randolph: "You're a liar, Randolph. I hate you." Then, in shots symbolizing his emotional maturation, he dumps his childhood toys in the river, hugs his catatonic father farewell, and leaves Skully's Landing and Randolph forever.

Capote's ending to *Other Voices, Other Rooms*, with its pederastic overtones, would present a challenge to any filmmaker, and so Rocksavage rewrites the conclusion to erase these allusions to Joel's homoerotic maturation. In the novel, Joel sees Randolph in drag and enters Skully's Landing, with Capote's narration implying a sexual relationship will develop between them: "She beckoned to him, shining and silver, and he knew he must go: unafraid, not hesitating, he paused only at the garden's edge where, as though he'd forgotten something, he stopped and looked at the bloomless, descending blue, at the boy he had left behind" (*OV* 231). In contrast, the film depicts Joel walking away down a dark road as the voice-over proclaims starkly, "I never did come back." These lines register Joel's rejection of Randolph and possibly of his own homosexuality as well, although Rocksavage stages these final scenes with sufficient ambiguity that Joel's sense of queerness might remain. Joel also acknowledges the influence of his experiences with Randolph: "But part of me did stay at the landing. And wherever I go, whatever I do, that voice never leaves me." Separating Joel from Randolph, Rocksavage's film cleanses Capote's queer bildungsroman of its specter of pederasty, but in doing so it blanches Joel's maturation into homosexuality as well.

▶ The Grass Harp

Capote's *The Grass Harp* is in many ways a comic version of *Other Voices, Other Rooms*. Both narratives focus on an adolescent boy who loses his immediate family, moves in with eccentric relatives, and matures into adult sexuality, but whereas *Other Voices, Other Rooms* unfolds in a nightmare vision of the South, *The Grass Harp* inhabits a gentler setting, one where its queer characters seek communion with one another to escape the stifling conformity of their small-minded town. Furthermore, while *Other Voices, Other Rooms* can be seen as a queer bildungsroman, the story of Joel's maturation into homosexuality, Collin's queerness in *The Grass Harp* is muted, as he accedes to heterosexuality in the novella's conclusion.

Before *The Grass Harp* was filmed, Capote adapted his novella for the Broadway stage. Under Robert Lewis's direction, and with Saint Subber producing and Cecil Beaton designing sets and costumes, the play opened on March 27, 1952, at the Martin Beck Theatre. It closed one month later. The play featured Mildred Natwick in the lead role of Dolly Talbo, Ruth Nelson as her sister Verena, Johnny Stewart as Collin Talbo, Georgia Burke as Catherine Creek, and Russell Collins as Judge Charlie Cool.[8] Of this theatrical version of *The Grass Harp*, Capote stated, "I thought Lillian and Dorothy Gish had just the right quality for the two sisters and I did *The Grass Harp* with them in mind. But Bobby Lewis, the director, didn't want them; he was used to a different kind, an Actors' Studio kind of acting."[9] Capote's theatrical script strips his novella of some story lines, particularly that of Collin's friend Riley Henderson, and he replaces Sister Ida, the mother of the child preacher Little Homer Honey, with the traveling cosmetics saleswoman Miss Baby Love Dallas. Also, the play ends with Dolly and Verena reconciling, as the proud Verena humbly requests her sister's companionship—"May I . . . may I come with you, too? I would like to help . . . if you will let me"—in stark contrast to the novella's melancholy resolution after Dolly dies.[10]

In 1960 National Telefilm Associates filmed Capote's theatrical version of *The Grass Harp* in a black-and-white television production for the *Play of the Week* series. While it did not feature both Gish sisters as Capote wished, Lillian Gish stars as Dolly Talbo, with Carmen Mathews as Verena and Nick Hyams as Collin Talbo. Georgia Burke and Russell Collins reprise their roles from the Broadway production as Catherine Creek and Judge Charlie Cool, and Ed Asner, in one of his earliest parts, plays the sheriff. Word Baker and Hal Gerson directed the production, with David Susskind, with whom Capote later collaborated on *Laura*, producing. The teleplay adheres to Capote's Broadway script, with its staging fortifying Capote's themes of inclusivity to endorse the advances of the civil rights movement. Foremost, the relationship between Collin and the family's African American maid Catherine Creek is performed with much affection and familial joviality, arguing for her equality to the white characters. When Judge Cool describes an interracial relationship, he regrets that the law would compel him to punish love: "Still, if he had succeeded in marrying her, it'd have been the sheriff's duty to arrest and my duty to sentence him." Also, when he compliments

Dolly on her free spirit, telling her, "Spirits are accepters of life; they grant its differences, and consequently are usually on the right side," he validates countercultural voices rebelling against the racial prejudices paralyzing the United States. Following the advances of the civil rights movement in the 1950s—the U.S. Supreme Court's *Brown v. Board of Education of Topeka* decision of 1954, Rosa Parks and the Montgomery bus boycott in 1955, and the integration of Central High School by the Little Rock Nine in 1957—Baker and Gerson's telefilm expands on Capote's themes to argue for the moral rightness of African American equality. Amid a favorable review, Jack Gould affirmed that the film "capture[s] beautifully and poetically the essence of the free human spirit that has enough sense to dream."[11]

Thirty-five years later, when Charles Matthau directed a cinematic adaptation of *The Grass Harp*, he proclaimed that Capote's story "made me laugh a lot and touched me in a way that was very uplifting. It is a beautiful, poignant story with great characters."[12] Matthau's production boasts an impressive array of actors in its ensemble cast, including Piper Laurie and Sissy Spacek as sisters Dolly and Verena Talbo, Walter Matthau as Judge Charlie Cool, Edward Furlong as Collin Fenwick, Nell Carter as Catherine Creek, Jack Lemmon as Morris Ritz, Mary Steenburgen as Sister Ida, and Sean Patrick Flannery as Riley Henderson, with Roddy McDowall and Charles Durning playing the minor roles of the barber Amos Legrand and Reverend Buster. In one of cinema's most horrific depictions of familial dysfunction, Laurie and Spacek teamed previously for *Carrie* (1976), playing a fanatical mother and her telekinetic daughter, and so Laurie expressed particular pleasure with the casting of *The Grass Harp*: "This time I would be the good, sweet one, and Sissy would be the horror. It was a deeply spiritual day for me, one of disbelief and thanksgiving."[13] The film also reunited the enduring partnership of Lemmon and Matthau, who costarred in numerous films over their careers. Several of the film's actors were connected to Capote and/or his literature either personally or professionally. His longtime friend Carol Matthau née Marcus, a Swan whom he described as one of the "people I really like," was the director Charles Matthau's mother and Walter Matthau's wife (although Charles Matthau recalls that his grandmother "thought [Truman] was a freak").[14] Doris Roberts, famous for her role as Marie Barone in the television show *Everybody Loves Raymond* (1996–2005), portrays the postmistress Mrs. Richards; in correspondence from 1975, Capote complimented her acting skills: "By the way I think you are a *very* fine actress."[15]

Scott Wilson, who undertook the role of Dick Hickock in Richard Brooks's *In Cold Blood*, plays the small role of Collin's father Eugene. The screenplay was written by Stirling Silliphant, most famous for his Oscar-winning adaptation of *In the Heat of the Night*—which beat Richard Brooks's screenplay of *In Cold Blood*—and for penning successful disaster flicks in the 1970s including *The Poseidon Adventure* (1972), *The Towering Inferno* (1974), and *The Swarm* (1978).

Matthau's *The Grass Harp* faithfully adapts its source text in many ways. Its opening line asks in a voice-over dripping with southern drawl, "When was it I first heard of the grass harp?" thus alerting viewers that the film, like Capote's novella, is told in flashback (cf. *GH* 9). As Capote's narrations in Frank and Eleanor Perry's *A Christmas Memory* and *The Thanksgiving Visitor* mark these films as stories of his own queer past, Boyd Gaines's voice-over similarly emphasizes queer aspects of Collin's character. When Collin (played as a young boy by Grayson Fricke) moves in with the Talbos, Gaines's narration reminisces about his affection for Dolly: "It was a long time before I calmed down enough to notice Dolly Talbo. And when I did, I fell in love," he declares as she is shown baking, costumed in pink sleeves and framed by pink curtains to accentuate her tenderheartedness. The voice also declares, "Classmates said that I was strange, that living in the Talbo house had turned me into an old man, but nothing was ever as much fun as the adventures I shared with Dolly. I dreamed up stories about us, and late at night wrote them down." Alluding to Capote's identity as a writer, the narration marks the story as Capote's, embedding within the film the queer story line of a boy struggling to negotiate his nascent sense of sexuality.

Adhering to the novella's thematic concern with nonnormative sexualities, Matthau's film includes several scenes highlighting Collin's discomfort with heterosexuality and his virtual imprisonment in his aunt Verena's world of conformity. When Verena shepherds Collin into her home, escorting him as if she were his jailer rather than his aunt, Dolly whispers to her, "It isn't right raising a boy in a house full of women." The prison imagery is heightened when, during their engagement scene, Judge Cool tells Dolly that Verena would return her to their prison. Commenting on his camera strategies for portraying the incarceral nature of Verena's home, in contrast to the liberty the characters enjoy when freed from the restraints of civilization, Charles Matthau emphasizes the importance of this theme: "In the Talbo house, I frequently kept the camera static, used long lenses and staged

FIG. 19 *The Grass Harp* (1996): Positioned before pink curtains and clothed in pink as well, Dolly Talbo (Piper Laurie) models a childlike femininity that enamors the boy Collin Fenwick (Grayson Fricke); to the right, Catherine Creek (Nell Carter) observes.

the scene with a minimum of movement. In the riverwoods, I did the opposite to convey the sense of freedom our characters experience."[16] With this contrast between civilization and nature, Matthau limns the ways in which the various characters' desires are stifled when under the scrutiny of others.

Part of the inhibiting control of civilization springs from its tendency to regulate sexuality, and several characters inform Collin of his failed masculinity. When he walks home from the movie theater with his classmates, Maude Riordan unfavorably compares him to another boy, unnamed but presumably Riley Henderson: "He's romantic. He knows how to treat a lady. Not like you. All this time we've known each other, and not once have you invited me or Elizabeth over for a visit. What are you afraid of?" Elizabeth chimes in, "He's worried about Dolly Talbo. . . . The whole world knows Dolly Talbo's gone, and you're gone, too." Collin cries, "Shut up," and, flouting the protocols of southern chivalry, pushes her to the ground. The young boy accompanying them, who is a head shorter than Collin, punches him in the jaw so that he too falls to the ground (cf. *GH* 14). In another scene, Verena's business partner Morris Ritz attempts a man-to-man conversation with Collin: "Well, you're sixteen, huh. Yeah. And throwing it around a little, I bet, huh?" With these words broaching Ritz's interest in Collin's sex life, Collin looks down uncomfortably, but Ritz, in Lemmon's jauntily leering performance, continues: "Next time Verena goes to Chicago, make her bring you, because there's a lot to throw it at there" (cf. *GH* 20). Even Amos the Barber, no model of normative masculinity himself in McDowell's prissy performance, chides Collin for his effeminacy. With Collin shot from behind in the barber's chair, Amos jokes, "About time you got this hair cut, honey. I was about to buy you a package of bobby pins." Amos then wheels him around so that the audience can see that although Collin has aged from eleven to sixteen and is now played by Furlong rather than Fricke, his masculinity is still unfledged. Amos continues speculating about Collin's romantic life—"A boy your age has to be careful about his appearance, especially when he has a rendezvous with Miss Maude Riordan tomorrow night"— before acknowledging Collin's competition in achieving manhood in his home: "Grown up, courting, the man of the house. Well, if you don't count Verena." Gaines's voice-over also acknowledges Collin's veritable crush on Riley Henderson—"I longed to be his friend"—but when Riley requests Collin's assistance in purchasing condoms, or "weasel wrappers," Collin's sexual ignorance is revealed: he understands neither the term nor its role in his friend's sexual conquests. Even when Collin considers dating girls, Gaines's narration implies that he is only deceiving himself—"It didn't take a genius to see Maude was heart-set on Riley. Still, I imagined for a while that I was in love with her"—but when he moves to kiss her, she interrupts, "I don't think that's necessary, Collin, although it was cute of you to take me out." In these scenes and others like them, Collin's inability to assert his masculinity elicits concern or condemnation from other characters, and his trajectory from queerness to normative sexuality structures the ensuing narrative.

The film's treatment of Dolly likewise depicts her as a queer figure, one alienated from romance and courtship throughout her life. Like Collin, she too, despite her advanced years, registers as a child. Enhancing the character's immaturity, Laurie imbued her vocal performance with a childlike register, casting her pitch to mimic a child's: "I had deliberately pitched my voice in a higher register for the childlike Dolly, but because of my cold I had to speak even *higher* in order to get out any sound."[17] Dolly thus represents a child's innocence, and she tells Judge Cool, "Well, no, I've never loved a gentleman. You might say, I never had the opportunity," revealing her virginity and estrangement from romance. Indeed, Riley sees Dolly as in need of protection from the sexual immorality of others, taking offense at the prospect of Sister Ida joining their company and telling Collin: "A loose woman like that is no one to associate with Miss Dolly." When Dolly naively asks Sister Ida, "What is it like, the love of a man?" Ida replies, "Why, honey, it's anything you choose to make it. For me, there is nothing like the touch of a man's hand." Underscoring her ignorance of sex and reproduction, and in contrast to Ida's fecundity, Dolly muses, "I suppose Collin is a close as I've come to having a baby." As much as Dolly appears to mature into sexuality throughout the film, acknowledging and encouraging Judge Cool's court-ship, she rejects his marriage proposal when Verena pleads: "Let me live with you. I'm feeling old. I want my sister." Dolly apologizes to Judge Cool, "Forgive me," and embraces Verena, declaring, "I want my sister, too." The voice-over summarizes, "The judge could not reach her—not with his arms, not with his heart. The sister's bond was too final," as the judge turns around so that viewers see only his back, with the rain falling outside suggestive of his tears.

Within the events unfolding on-screen, Judge Cool seeks to win Dolly's affections, yet his backstory offers a darker view of his sexual past because in his quest for emotional connection, he indulges in actions bordering on the pedophilic. He shares with his friends the story of his correspondence with an adolescent girl: "It's a letter to a girl not much younger than you, Collin. Her name is Heather Fall. . . . Came across [her] in one of those children's magazines that Amos keeps in the barbershop. On the back cover they have the addresses of children who want to correspond with other children." Dolly, overlooking the discrepancy in the correspondents' ages, commends the judge's actions—"That's very noble of you, keeping company with her"—and Judge Cool continues his tale by explaining how he repre-sented himself as a teenager in their exchanges: "Well, I wrote her back as though I was still that fifteen-year-old boy." He continues, "It was fun for an old man sitting alone, listening to the noise of a clock to be growing up again with a sweetheart in Alaska" (cf. *GH* 42). Judge Cool also reports that his son does not approve of his actions, but this hint of censure is the narrative's only acknowledgement that Judge Cool's actions carry a pedo-philic taint. The film portrays his desires as a sincere effort to alleviate his and Heather Fall's mutual loneliness, yet Capote forthrightly limns the pedophilic potential of such a liaison in his short story "Hello, Stranger." In this quasi-biographical dialogue, Capote lunches with former acquain-tance, during which this friend confesses to encounters with young girls that resonate with pedophilic depravity, despite his denials to his wife and to Capote. It is a curious and unsettling thematic linkage in Capote's canon, connecting stories with vastly different settings from different stages in his career, yet alike in depicting older men camouflaging their identities to flirt with adolescent girls. The staging of this scene in Matthau's film, in which Judge Cool tells his story to his friends around the campfire with Dolly as his primary interlocutor, suggests that his courtship of the child Heather Fall parallels his courtship of the childlike Dolly Talbo. He then explains love to Riley: "First you got to learn to love a leaf. Then the rain. Then some day, if you're lucky, the right person." He looks to Dolly, who smiles gently and then shyly glances away. Judge Cool proposes to Dolly as they walk through the woods, asking her "to be the one person in the world" for him, as he lifts her veil, kisses her, and strokes her cheek. In wooing Dolly, Judge Cool finds an age-appropriate mate who cleanses him of the pedophilic specter of courting Heather Fall. Although Dolly rejects him in favor of Verena, he then moves into Miss Burch's boardinghouse, where five women rush out to greet him, and so it appears that his erotic prospects brighten. Like Collin, Judge Cool needs to mature into adult sexuality and cleanse himself of the queer aspects of his character, which he presumably accomplishes in the film's afterlife with one of these many women so anxious to dote on him.

Beyond Collin's, Dolly's, and Judge Cool's difficulties with normative sexuality, many of Capote's other characters express queer desires, whether privately hidden or publicly evident, but Matthau's film overwrites these aspects of their personalities. In particular, Verena Talbo's lesbianism is alluded to throughout the novella. Collin's father Eugene asserts that she is a "morphodyte" (*GH* 10), and Collin observes, "Men were afraid of her, and she herself seemed to be afraid of women" (*GH* 12). Collin also reports that Verena "had been greatly attached to a blonde jolly girl called Maudie Laura Murphy" (*GH* 12) many years ago and would cry while looking over photographs of her lost friend and that "she was too like a lone man in a house full of women and children" (*GH* 15). In the film, however, Verena's meanness results from her disappointment in a teen romance, as Gaines's narration reveals: "No one had seen a man on Verena's arm since she had danced as a debutante with Maiself Talsap, but he took up with Verena's best friend. Verena never recovered." She also confesses her love for Morris Ritz to Dolly when they discuss their prospects in the kitchen: "I loved him, I did. Oh, I admit it, we were kindred spirits." More recognizable as a lesbian in Capote's novella, Verena transforms in Matthau's film into a woman haunted by heterosexual disappointments, with Spacek's performance accentuating the pinched nature of this woman's life and her many unfulfilled desires.

Capote's novella closes as Collin leaves town to become a lawyer, thus aligning himself occupationally with Judge Cool, a queer character marked by his pedophilic desires and unsuccessful pursuit of romance. In the film, however, Collin's heterosexuality is more clearly limned, as he reports in voice-over that "Riley and Maude were married the following fall," and as the screen depicts the newlyweds exiting the church, he realizes that his future must unfold away from the town of his upbringing: "What weakened me was the wait before I knew where to jump. If ever I was going to make the leap, that was the time." In depicting Collin's emotional maturation, the film builds on Riley's recuperation into normative masculinity through marriage. While sitting around the campfire, he earlier confessed to his new friends, "Well, I ain't no good with women"—a surprising statement, given that he purchased condoms to facilitate a sexual encounter with an apparently willing companion in his car—to which Collin added morosely, "Yeah, well, me neither." Now, as the film concludes, Collin and Riley's sister Elizabeth serve as best man and maid of honor in Riley and Maude's wedding, and after Elizabeth kisses him farewell, Judge Cool admonishes him, "You write to Elizabeth. She's a good girl." Counterbalancing these nods to heterosexuality, the film also links Collin back to Capote. Mrs. Richards remarks on his vocational ambitions, "A writer is what you're going to be, eh?" thereby reminding viewers of the queer source of the film they are watching. Gaines's elegiac voice-over reinforces the connection between Collin and Capote: "So little, once it has changed, changes back. Their memory fades with each passing year. Yet the precious moments we shared, that unforgettable autumn of my youth, forever shaped my life as a storyteller." This shift in Collin's vocation underscores the autobiographical elements in Capote's story, inviting the audience to see Collin's story as the story of Capote's maturation into authorship but also, and conversely, to see Capote as heterosexual.

Despite its impressive roster of actors, *The Grass Harp* sinks into tendentiousness and maudlin musings, and the film was poorly received by critics such as Adrian Martin, who lamented that "every key point of the story is laboriously spelt out and reiterated."[18] The film's hokey depictions of southern life also sparked negative reactions. George Meyer complained that "Hollywood can't seem to convey the South without adding cornpone," and Jami Bernard agreed that the film is "a dishwasher-safe movie full of wacky Southern characters."[19] These criticisms are warranted, as witnessed to by the folksy depiction of the town's sheriff constantly accompanied by his pet rooster Ralph. Still, some critics praised Matthau's film for its relaxed pace and the genial unfolding of its story. Peter Stack appreciated the film's tempo—"Sometimes good things come in slow packages"—and Lawrence Van Gelder applauded it as "a sweet, wise, funny, poignant film that rides on a first-rate cast."[20] A faithful yet sterile adaptation, Matthau's *The Grass Harp* sentimentalizes Capote's vision of childhood as depicted in the story of Collin's formative years with Dolly Talbo and other queer and comic figures alienated from southern views of social and sexual propriety.

▶ *Children on Their Birthdays*

In the late 1970s Capote considered filming his short story "Children on Their Birthdays," hoping to cast Tatum O'Neal in the role of Lily Jane Bobbit.[21] He collaborated on this project with his lover John O'Shea, but the antagonistic dissolution of their affair effectively ended its development, despite O'Shea's attempts to persuade Capote to proceed: "I welcome a joint-venture with you in the matter of 'Children on Their Birthdays.' I see no reason that joint-venture could not eventuate in money and credits for both of us."[22] Capote later collaborated on a television script for "Children on Their Birthdays" with Robert MacBride in which his transgressive heroine Miss Bobbit survives the six o'clock bus that kills her in the story, with the narrator Jim affirming in voice-over: "Like I said. Nobody in this town will ever forget her. She arrived with a lot of dreams, and some she took with her, and some she left for us."[23] The story remained unfilmed until Mark Medoff's 2002 production, which stars Tania Raymonde as Miss Bobbit, Joe Pichler as Billy Bob Murphy, Sheryl Lee as Billy Bob's mother El, Christopher McDonald as El's suitor Speedy, and Tom Arnold as the con man Lionel Quince.

Capote's short story "Children on Their Birthdays" is not a parable, yet it becomes one in Medoff's film. Crusader Entertainment, a Christian production company, developed the film, and Howard Baldwin, the film's executive producer, avows, "We feel movies can be extremely commercial but at the same time very family friendly."[24] The film was successful in this regard, winning the Worldfest-Houston Platinum Award for Family and Children's

Films. Capote's story has children as its main characters, yet it is difficult to see why it was deemed suitable for adaptation into a "family friendly" film. The tale's first-person narrator begins by recalling the premature demise of his town's most fascinating citizen, Miss Lily Jane Bobbit—"Yesterday afternoon the six-o'clock bus ran over Miss Bobbit. I'm not sure what there is to be said about it; after all, she was only ten years old" (*GH* 119). The tale unfolds in flashback, with the narrator describing this amoral heroine and her exploits in his small and dusty hometown, concluding at the moment of her death: "Miss Bobbit, running toward those moons of roses, did not seem to hear. That is when the six o'clock bus ran over her" (*GH* 135). Notwithstanding that it is bookended by the misfortune of a child's untimely demise, Capote's "Children on Their Birthdays" is a lighthearted comic narrative. It proffers no readily discernible moral, other than the cautionary note of a child's Hollywood fantasy life ending tragically, and does not moralize on her transgressions or other shortcomings.

Miss Bobbit herself, like the story in which she appears, provides unlikely fodder for a Christian family film. In Capote's story, she proclaims that the "odors of a church are so offensive" and rhapsodizes over her relationship with the devil: "But the way to tame the Devil is not to go down there to church and listen to what a sinful mean fool he is. No, love the Devil like you do Jesus: because he is a powerful man, and will do you a good turn if he knows you trust him. . . . I always called in the Devil to help me get the biggest part in our annual show. That is common sense: you see, I knew Jesus wouldn't have any truck with dancing" (*GH* 127). Later Miss Bobbit wins the town's sham talent show, arranged by a con man, by singing, "If you don't like my peaches, stay away from my can, o-ho, o-ho!" and concluding her act "with a bump [that] upended her skirt to display blue-lace underwear" (*GH* 132). In the film, however, Miss Bobbit sings a torch song, "I Have to Dream" (which plays again during the closing credits, as sung by Celine Dion with her trademark emotionality), with long close-ups accentuating the heartfelt devotion behind her words. Whereas in the short story Miss Bobbit demands that the townspeople bankroll her dreams of Hollywood glory as a reward for bringing the grifter to justice, in the film Billy Bob and Preacher, her two adolescent admirers, anonymously throw the necessary funds into her room with a note attached: "Dear Lily Jane, We give this note in hopes it will help you achieve your dream of making it to Hollywood. We ask for nothing in return but to remain your devoted and anonymous admirers."

Miss Bobbit's cinematic ambitions carry over between the story's two incarnations, as in her declaration in the film: "Of course, my final destination has always been, and will remain, Hollywood, California. You see, my plan is to appear someday in motion pictures." The short story ends abruptly, with her dreams and her life literally crushed by a bus, but in a brazen rewriting of its source narrative, the film concludes with Miss Bobbit safely boarding the vehicle that will carry her to California.

In the film's translation of Capote's short story into a cinematic parable, these shifts in Miss Bobbit's character and Capote's story line are coupled with an increased interest in religious themes. As Miss Bobbit readies herself for the bus ride that results in her death in the story's closing scene, Capote has her looking "as though she were going to Communion, dressed in white and with a white parasol" (*GH* 135). Yet Miss Bobbit is primarily an amoral creature, self-aggrandizing in her Hollywood dreams that she conscripts others to support. Capote's slight gesture toward Christian symbolism in Miss Bobbit's religiously identified attire is magnified in the film to the point that she becomes the town's savior. In this regard the film imposes upon Capote's comic story a religious theme concerning the necessity of atoning for one's transgressions. After Billy Bob and Preacher cut down some roses for their town's bewitching newcomer, Miss Bobbit explains to Billy Bob that he must atone for his sin: "You must make moral restitution, Billy Bob. . . . You have to do something right to cancel out the wrong." The innocent recipient of these unsought roses, Miss Bobbit seeks to compensate El, the roses' owner and Billy Bob's mother, for their loss, and so she and her mother, a talented but mute seamstress, sew the roses back onto the bushes. In lines laden with Christological import, Miss Bobbit declares: "It's moral restitution. A symbol . . . to cancel out the wrong. It is the view of my late lamented father that, whenever possible, we must balance what we ought not to do with what we ought." With her deceased father symbolizing her spiritual Father, her example proves morally infectious. As the film concludes, Billy Bob asks Preacher, "So why'd you send that whole ominous [a childish mispronunciation of *anonymous*] note thing, anyway?" and Preacher replies, "Well, I didn't figure that I could do that whole moral restitution deal alone." The boys move to pinky shake in a gesture symbolizing their renewed friendship, but they handshake instead, in a sign of their maturation.

In addition to this lesson on moral restitution, *Children on Their Birthdays* also tackles a story line of racial integration in the pre-civil-rights South.

In his short story, Capote portrays Miss Bobbit's friendship with Rosalba Cat, an African American girl, to the initial surprise of the townspeople: "Miss Bobbit told everyone that Rosalba was her sister, which caused a good many jokes; but like most of her ideas, it gradually seemed natural, and when we would overhear them calling each other Sister Rosalba and Sister Bobbit, none us of cracked a smile" (*GH* 126). The film elevates this subplot, which tacitly argues for racial integration, into a major plotline in which Miss Bobbit desegregates the community. When Preacher cruelly mistreats Rosalba, Miss Bobbit shames him: "Don't you know that gentlemen are put on the face of this Earth for the protection of ladies?" El, in righteous anger, likewise castigates Billy Bob, not realizing that he attempted to stop Preacher from harassing Rosalba: "Lord knows this town has been witness to every kind of yours and Preacher's mischief. But cruelty is another thing entirely. I am so afraid you'll grow up to be someone I will not care to know." The appearance of this theme in the film is somewhat surprising, for it is never expressed in Capote's "Children on Their Birthdays." It nonetheless appears in other of Capote's fictions, notably "The Thanksgiving Visitor," as voiced by his cousin Miss Sook (cf. *CS* 264–65). The film transposes Capote's moral from one story to another, without paying attention to the stark difference in tone evident between the comic excess of starstruck Miss Bobbit and Capote's nostalgic view of his beloved Miss Sook.

The film's Miss Bobbit is not content merely to chastise two boys for their rudeness to Rosalba; she improves on this by integrating the community's church when she brings Rosalba to a service. While the rest of the African American townspeople sit sequestered in the choir loft—an image that in itself blanches the severity of racial segregation in the South—Rosalba joins the white members of the congregation in the pews. Several shots register the surprise and discomfort of the parishioners, and Pastor Williams then addresses his congregation: "Perhaps many of you are wondering whether God or Satan moves among us this morning; whether that clever deceiver Lucifer is leading us toward the darkness." With these ambiguous words, it is as yet unclear whether the pastor supports Miss Bobbit's efforts to integrate his congregation, and Miss Bobbit interrupts him before his position is clearly defined: "Pastor Williams, I'm sorry to interrupt, but like Jesus, I've been sorely tempted of the devil and can perhaps add some insight to your sermon." A congregant angrily departs, and Pastor Williams sternly commands, "If anybody else wants to go, please do so now," thereby proving his full commitment to racial justice, if only after witnessing the example of a young girl. Miss Bobbit continues her sermon: "First of all, sir, it's easy to sit here on a Sunday morning and talk about being righteous, yet let the devil whisper his meanness in your ear. And it is another thing entirely to resist the devil and be truly compassionate. If merely one person invites him around, the devil can whisper through a whole town. And suddenly everyone's lost their sense of decency." The film's Christian themes blossom further as the local sheriff and mechanic Speedy, who is in love with El, adds: "Jesus also tells us to love the outcast among us. That we may become the true children of our father." Speedy's reference to serving as the "true children of our father" builds upon Capote's title to resignify children's birthdays as a Christian rebirth, and the film's rewriting of Capote's narrative into a Christian parable casts all of the characters, both adults and children, as innocents on the path to salvation.

As Miss Bobbit catalyzes the moral growth of the town, she also catalyzes the preteen Billy Bob into manhood and thereby erases from the film the short story's queer depiction of adolescence. In this coming-of-age love story, Billy Bob must free himself from his Oedipal attachment to his mother El, as evident in a scene in which he spies her dancing alone while reminiscing about the husband she lost in World War II. She then teaches her son to dance and admonishes him to enjoy his youth and to eschew his nascent erotic interest in girls: "There'll be plenty of time for proper courting when you're older. You're too young to be going so crazy over one little girl." His head rests on her shoulder, and this physical cue emphasizes that he is still a boy, his mother's son, rather than a man. Billy Bob responds angrily, "To hell with it! I'd pick all the roses in China for that girl. And there's nothing you can say that'll change my mind," with his words underscoring his determination to free himself from his youth. Beyond Billy Bob's Oedipal complex that complicates his pursuit of Miss Bobbit, his best friend Preacher also falls in love with her, and their shared affections for her test their friendship. Preacher prudently warns Billy Bob, "It's plain to see we both can't court Miss Bobbit. I know you've been thinking about it, just like I have." The two boys therefore decide that, in their position as Miss Bobbit's magazine subscription agents, "Whoever sells the most, the other guy backs off." Preacher realizes that their crushes on Miss Bobbit threaten their friendship—"She's a hard one, Billy Bob. She don't want nothing but to make trouble between friends"—but Billy Bob cannot free himself from his

FIG. 20 *Children on Their Birthdays*: Miss Bobbit (Tania Raymonde) boards the bus that will take her to Hollywood, and thus escapes the untimely demise visited on her in Capote's short story of "Children on Their Birthdays."

love for her. In the short story (and initially in the film), Miss Bobbit rejects the boys' amorous overtures. Preacher pleads with Miss Bobbit, "You've got to decide who's your real, true sweetheart," but she imperiously replies: "Sweetheart? I should have known better than to get involved with a lot of country bumpkins" (cf. *GH* 129).

Later in the film it is clear that Billy Bob does win her favor: she dances with him in one of the closing scenes, replacing his mother as a suitable romantic partner, and she places her hand on his in a tender gesture. The short story's narrator explains, however, that Billy Bob's love for Miss Bobbit paradoxically sparks his sense of queerness and alienation from traditional masculinity: "It has not been easy for him, Miss Bobbit's going. Because she'd meant more than that. Than what? Than being thirteen years old and crazy in love. She was the queer things in him, like the pecan tree and liking books and caring enough about people to let them hurt him. She was the things he was afraid to show anyone else" (*GH* 134). In a masterful subversion of sexual normativity, Capote limns the emergence of heterosexual desire within a queer subtext of estrangement from the self and from prevailing cultural mores. In the film, however, Miss Bobbit enables both racial integration and heterosexual maturation. The closing shots assure viewers that Billy Bob and Preacher value their newfound friendship with Rosalba, and the boys are respectively paired off with Cora Mae and Janice, the girls whom they earlier tormented with their childish pranks. In this manner, Billy Bob and Preacher mature from teen lasciviousness into an adult recognition of the emotional cathexis available through love. In one of the film's opening sequences, Billy Bob witnessed a man caressing a woman's cheek in the general store, while Preacher showed him a magazine featuring scantily clad women. Billy Bob asked Preacher, "You really don't care what God sees when he looks down on you, do you?" but by the film's close, and within its Christian themes, it is evident that God would be proud of the young Christian hero who has metamorphosed from Capote's queer boy into a Christian film's heterosexual man.

Capote's depictions of children ask readers to ponder the sexuality of childhood, to probe the challenges of asserting one's sexual identity in small towns inhospitable to otherness. Whether growing into homosexuality like Joel in *Other Voices, Other Rooms* or into heterosexuality like Collin in *The Grass Harp* and Billy Bob in "Children on Their Birthdays," the discombobulating experience of adolescence challenges these young boys to develop a sense of identity by determining the nature of their sexual attractions. For Capote, then, the experience of adolescence involves jarring dislocations between self and society, yet in these cinematic adaptations, to various degrees, the vagaries of adolescent sexual attraction are whitewashed. Joel removes himself from Randolph's amorous attentions in Rocksavage's *Other Voices, Other Rooms*, Collin merges the queerness of a Capotean voice-over with heterosexual attraction to Elizabeth (with whom he shares precious little screen time) in Matthau's *The Grass Harp*, and Billy Bob ascends to normative erotic desires and Christian manhood by courting a young girl likewise stripped of her transgressive spirit in Medoff's *Children on Their Birthdays*. Writing these narratives in the late 1940s and early 1950s, Capote tackled the subject of adolescent sexuality with more honesty and complexity than these filmmakers some fifty years later.

Capote's Unfinished Business ▶ Abandoned and Unproduced Projects

Despite his prodigious talents as a writer, Capote drafted numerous screenplays and teleplays that were never produced. New York Public Library's Truman Capote Archive holds much of this fascinating collection of material, including an early teleplay of his unfinished novel *Answered Prayers*, the marital farce *Straight Face*, the suspense thriller *Tyranny*, an adaptation of F. Scott Fitzgerald's *The Great Gatsby*, the reform drama *Uncle Sam's Hard Luck Hotel*, and the noir *Dead Loss*. Written at various stages of Capote's career, these scripts showcase both congruencies and surprising departures from his literary fare. It would be too facile to label the projects as failures simply because they were never filmed; they bear Capote's imprint and, if his genius is not always fully on display throughout a given work, his talent shines through in scenes, phrasings, and dialogue. These projects also allow insight into various works, both by Capote and by others, that influenced their conception. The chapter concludes with an overview of a planned film of Capote's *Handcarved Coffins*, which never proceeded beyond discussions of appropriate directors and actors (and for which Capote did not pen a screenplay).

In the late 1950s, Capote was developing themes and plotlines for *Answered Prayers*, albeit in a form markedly different from the one his unfinished novel eventually took, with its three chapters "Unspoiled Monsters," "Kate McCloud," and "La Côte Basque" detailing the sordid dealings of high society. In a letter dated November 14, 1957, Thomas Bohen of MCA Artists informed Capote that he had mailed three copies of the treatment of *Answered Prayers* to interested parties. The cover page of the project describes it simply as "An outline of ANSWERED PRAYERS: a play for camera."[1] Instead of a roman à clef of America's social elite and their scandals, this draft of *Answered Prayers* presents the fictional account of a desperate woman, Ammie Grant, struggling against her brutish lover Eddie. Capote characterizes Ammie similarly to Cousin Randolph in *Other Voices, Other Rooms*, in that she is "wanting, with her child-like nature and orphan mentality, only to be held and told the dark is not there," much as Randolph needs to be told that "everything is going to be all right" (*OV* 154). She lives with Eddie, a lothario with "a clever playboy face more than a little running to ruin," who torments her with insults and veiled threats. The dramatic action of Capote's "play for camera" begins suspensefully, with the mysterious Evangeline Arthur Smith threatening Eddie on the telephone: "I shall have to kill you very soon. You *do* hear me? I said: *very* soon."

Speaking with Ammie, Eddie voices the play's theme: "Remember what St. Teresa said about people getting what they want. . . . 'More tears,' said she, 'more tears are shed over answered prayers than unanswered ones.'" From these lines, it is apparent that Ammie's desire for Eddie's love brings her only pain, and Eddie displays his cruelty when he threatens to give her stuffed monkey, a beloved childhood toy, to his bulldog. She beseeches: "Please don't. Please don't hurt my monkey." When Eddie ignores her pleas, she grows violent, "suddenly shouting" and screaming, "I'll kill you if you do." Mrs. Hammer, the building superintendent's wife, interrupts the lovers' quarrel. The stage directions indicate that Ammie seeks sanctuary in this moment of respite: "Mrs. Grant, having rescued the monkey, but embarrassed by Mrs. Hammer's intrusion, runs into the bathroom and closes the door." Later, when Eddie prepares to leave Ammie, she tries to stop him, but "He tells her to behave herself or he'll lock her in the closet." He does so, and when Ammie thinks that he has taken pity on her and will free her, he disabuses her of these hopes. "Not at all. I just remembered that you might like company," he declares, as the stage directions record that he "tosses her the monkey. Then shuts the door and turns the key."

Because Evangeline Arthur Smith has been heard on the telephone but not seen, it appears increasingly plausible that Ammie employs Evangeline as her alter ego, a menacing fury to avenge herself against Eddie's constant torments. Capote builds this possibility throughout the opening scenes of *Answered Prayers*, but viewers then meet Evangeline and she is not Ammie. Rather, Evangeline seeks vengeance against Eddie because he seduced and then abandoned her sister, who committed suicide. Evangeline's brother likewise died, trying to hold their sibling's persecutor to account for his cruelty. Vengeance now motivates Evangeline's existence, as Capote recounts her dawning realization of her destiny: "Gradually it became clear to her that she was an appointee of God in pursuit of the devil." Eddie defends himself against Evangeline's verbal assaults, claiming that he gave hope to the hopeless, but she dismisses his justifications: "No. You only provided an illusion of hope in order to leave them hopeless." She shoots him, but he survives. When Ammie finds him after escaping from the closet, he moans, "I think I can get up if you'll give me a hand," but she instead picks up the gun as if to shoot him, and the scene dissolves inconclusively. Although it remains unclear whether Ammie kills Eddie, Mrs. Hammer gives Eddie's bulldog, which she has adopted, Ammie's monkey in the final scene, symbolically suggesting that, no matter what has become of the pair, Ammie's childhood ideals have been forever destroyed by her relationship with Eddie.

Written in the late 1950s when Capote was still engaging with the tropes of southern gothicism, this treatment of *Answered Prayers* bears a striking resemblance to Tennessee Williams's plays, particularly in the psychosexual tussling between Ammie and Eddie. Their sparring recalls the verbal duels of Blanche Dubois and Stanley Kowalski in *A Streetcar Named Desire* (1948) and of Maggie and Brick in *Cat on a Hot Tin Roof* (1955), with these lovers wounding each other in desperate attempts to break through their sexual despair. Unlike Williams's masterpieces, however, Capote's "play for camera" aims for drama yet attains only melodrama, particularly in the overdetermined symbolism of Ammie's childhood toy, Eddie's mistreatment of it, and her imprisonment in the closet. Furthermore, the dialogue is often strained: it is difficult to imagine Ammie's line, "Give me my monkey," not descending into camp, yet the play, on the whole, does not appear to be a camp exercise. This early version of *Answered Prayers* incorporates Capote's theme that more tears are shed over answered than unanswered prayers into an intriguing, if far-fetched, story line. One can easily discern why the irony of crying over what one has attained would apply so well to Capote's wealthy friends as he returned to this theme, although never conclusively, until his death.

▷ *Straight Face: A Treatment*

A romantic farce of a withering love blossoming anew, of a family fractured and reformed, *Straight Face* begins as Sylvie Frost, a thirty-five-year-old "sensitive, romantic-looking woman," visits a nunnery in Switzerland to see her eighteen-year-old stepdaughter, Lucy.[2] Sylvie informs Lucy that she and her father Sam are divorcing because he is having an affair with a social worker. (The script originally read "female Labor leader," but this has been deleted and replaced with "social worker." The comic possibilities of an adulterous female labor leader nonetheless appear rich.) In return, Lucy confesses in tears to Sylvie, "I'm going to have a b-b-baby," but she refuses to identify the father. Sylvie flees to Italy to seek counsel from her former college roommate, Florence Bell, "a tall, rakishly attractive, uninhibited extrovert who can devastate with a look, a line, or a lifted eyebrow." Florence works as an advice columnist called Auntie Flo, with Capote apparently punning on the tired euphemism of a woman's menstrual cycle. Auntie Flo also appears to be inspired by Patrick Dennis's novel *Auntie Mame* (1955) as well as its subsequent film version starring Rosalind Russell (1958), for she is similarly a larger-than-life figure whose extravagance is matched only by her heart. Appraising the romantic morass into which her friends have fallen, Flo advises Sylvie: "You, my dear girl, are about to divorce a guy you're still stuck on. . . . Lucy—precious, unmarried little Lucy, bless her wee black heart—is going to have a baby. Well, this is what I suggest you both do. Now, Sylvie, you . . ." As Flo continues, her voice fades out, and viewers would realize that madcap shenanigans are sure to ensue.

In brief, Flo's plan is for Sylvie to lure Sam to Italy, sleep with him, and then pretend Lucy's baby is theirs so that he will stay with her to raise the child. Sam, however, arrives with his new paramour, the social worker Miss Harriet Hoffstetter, memorably described as "a blonde to make a Bishop kick in a stained-glass window" in a line that echoes Raymond Chandler's *Farewell, My Lovely*.[3] Known affectionately as Harry, Ms. Hoffstetter attracts the attention of many more men, including Vittorio, a dancing fisherman, and Dr. Mickey, the physician Sam has summoned to tend to Lucy (who he believes needs medical attention, although he remains ignorant of her pregnancy). In a series of bizarre scenes in a crypt, romantic and humorously macabre escapades unfold. First, Harry believes herself to be enjoying the amatory attentions of Dr. Mickey, but in fact she "has mistaken the skeleton for bony little Dr. Mickey—she is embracing it, clinging to it." Soon Sam takes a stand against Dr. Mickey's romantic interest in Harry, declaring, "Doctor, let's get something straight. I asked you here to take care of my daughter. Harry is not my daughter. Now leave this to me." Vittorio then knocks Sam down, and Dr. Mickey beats Vittorio, with Harry escaping to the doctor's arms. Lucy's opinion of Harry, which she shares with Sam— "Frankly, Daddy dear, I think your friend Harry is a slugfunk"—captures Harry's glib sexuality, appealing to many men yet ever fickle.

With Harry's amatory interests elsewhere, Sam and Sylvie tentatively reunite and, by a strange twist of fate, are locked in a dungeon. The scene fades to black, and viewers are led to believe that the two will share this moment of unexpected isolation to reignite their romance. Flo continues masterminding the various characters' interactions, knocking a flowerpot off the balcony to distract Lucy from telling Sam about her troubles. Sensing her meddling, Sam warns Flo, "I'm not one of Auntie Flo's faithful readers. Some idiot brat who's lost her boyfriend. I'm Sam Frost. So don't try interfering with me or my family." Never dissuaded from her outlandish schemes, Flo chooses the annual fancy dress ball to resolve her various friends' problems, for, as she explains, magic transpires at this event: "every year, at the end of the Vesuvius Ball, the old Duke selects the loveliest creature there. And whomever he chooses, he offers them one wish. One wish that he will make come true. And it *does*." Fairy-tale fantasy sparks the characters' desires, as they attend the ball dressed in costumes indicative of their romantic aspirations and core personalities: Sylvie is the elegant Swan Queen, resplendent in her beauty; Sam is Little Lord Fauntleroy, a young boy in the body of a man; Flo is a buccaneer, swashbuckling through the lives and romances of her friends; and Harry is a bearded lady, visibly personifying the character's gender-switching, as also encoded in her nickname. The Duke chooses Sylvie as the loveliest woman attending the ball, and Sylvie's simple wish—"I would like another glass of champagne. And a ride in the moonlight"—is immediately granted, with the Duke ordering Sam to accompany her in the carriage. After liberally imbibing champagne, Sylvie passes out, so she does not know when morning comes whether she and Sam have reignited their sexual relationship and conceivably conceived the child necessary to facilitate Flo's madcap plan of family reconciliation.

Although it is unclear at this moment if Sylvie and Sam have reconciled, Harry gracefully bows out of her romance with Sam, telling him, "You and Sylvie are happy again; you demonstrated that to the whole world last night. Well—we're happy too. In fact, Albert and I are going to be Mr. and Mrs.," as she prepares to leave with Dr. Mickey. In crosscuts to Lucy's boarding school in Switzerland, viewers learn that her former roommate, the African princess Douboo Ashrofi—"A beautiful young Negress, shiny black as a black olive; she wears two diamonds, one glued to her forehead, the other to her nose"—has conspired to steal Ferdl, Lucy's boyfriend and the father of her child. When Princess Douboo inadvertently reveals to Ferdl that Lucy is in Italy, he leaves to reunite with her, despite the fact that he was kissing Princess Douboo in this very scene. All that remains for a happy ending to be effected is for Sylvie and Sam to reunite once again, and for Lucy to reunite with Ferdl.

Sam and Ferdl, however, cannot locate Sylvie and Lucy, who have hidden themselves away to have their babies, and so, in a series of shots, the two men are shown crossing the globe looking for their lost loves. An establishing shot places the action in an African jungle, as Sam summarizes to Ferdl their misadventures: "Four continents, eleven countries, twenty thousand miles—and not one sign! It's no use, Ferdl. . . . I'm giving up." Flo masterminds the necessary reunion to bring the couples together, and the fathers find the mothers in the hospital where Sylvie has given birth. Flo initially presents Sylvie's and Lucy's children as twins so that Sam will remain ignorant of his daughter's pregnancy, but when she sees Ferdl, she takes one of the babies and places it in Lucy's arms, saying, "Well—not twins after all. One child. One grandchild." From offscreen Harry adds, "And one God-child!" The children are born, the family is reunited, and even troublesome Harry is incorporated into the film's conclusion, allowing for a fecund resolution to a film featuring outlandish twists and turns, an extravagant matchmaker, mistaken identities in a crypt, and a fairy-tale ball. The screenplay veers wildly in tone from scene to scene, and it lacks, for example, the cool sophistication of *Breakfast at Tiffany's*, as it also tackles the taboo subjects of Lucy's unintended pregnancy and the interracial attraction between Ferdl and Princess Douboo. Except for episodic moments in various works and the occasional short story, such as "My Side of the Matter," Capote rarely forayed into the realm of humor, and *Straight Face* testifies to the strength of his comedic talents, even if the end result, in this instance, is a somewhat disjointed exercise.

▶ *Tyranny*

In Capote's words, *Tyranny* tells the story of Billy Lee, a man with no sense of self who embarks on a crime spree to free himself of his emptiness: "The point the film makes is this: B.L.L. is a man who commits this assassination really for no basic reason other than to steal another man's identity because he, B.L.L., thinks of himself as a total nobody, a nothing, a zero."[4] The screenplay weaves between Billy Lee's exploits while escaping and the pursuers on his trail, and Capote describes this narrative framework in dynamic terms: "The movement is contrapuntal—from Billy Lee . . . and his Travels, his encounters, his 'frames' and flashbacks, to the pursuers and their labors, their agonies." Traveling with Charlene, an African American prostitute, Billy Lee is fleeing to Montreal, but amid the suspense of the chase, Capote includes diversionary moments, such as their "wistfully amusing experiences—particularly one at a dude ranch where they stay overnight and he tries to teach her to ride a horse." When low on funds, Billy plans to rob a bank, thus sinking deeper into his life of crime. Charlene, hoping to reform him, asks Billy to marry her when they approach Niagara Falls. He replies, "What? You mean you divorced that old guy back in Honey, Texas"—a moment in Charlene's history that echoes Holly Golightly's past in *Breakfast at Tiffany's*—and when he buys her a drink instead of marrying her, he exposes the vicious streak in his character: "Because nice white boys like me don't marry whores. And we don't marry niggers neither. Now excuse me, lady—I'm gonna take a leak." Such moments as this transform Billy Lee from a likeable antihero into a despicable heel, resulting in disequilibrium for the audience, who are left not knowing whether to root for Billy Lee or for his pursuers.

Billy Lee eludes capture in the United States and reaches Montreal, where he rents a room in a boardinghouse "run by a ninety-year-old, a Frenchman and former fur trapper." This new relationship represents a turning point in Billy Lee's life, as Capote states: "It is with this old man that Billy Lee develops the only real and human relationship of his life, and it is to him that he confesses his crime." The old man reports Billy to the police, telling his new boarder the reason behind his apparent betrayal: "I did what you wanted me to. If you want the glory, there is no other way to have it. And you do want it. And so do I." Similar to narratives as varied as the play and musical *Chicago* (1926, 1975) and Arthur Penn's *Bonnie and Clyde* (1967), the connection between fame and crime drives Capote's screenplay. In assessing Penn's film, Capote affirmed, "One of the most interesting things about *Bonnie and Clyde*, which I consider an excellent film, is that it recognized that the simple desire for notoriety is one of the strongest incitements to crime," a statement that reflects his understanding of fame's allure and potentially unhealthy consequences, as he also incorporates this theme into his *Tyranny*.[5] The fragmentary and episodic qualities of the script indicate that Capote did not polish it into a coherent whole, yet its basic story arc—a fugitive fleeing from the law and finding himself on a journey—bears the potential for Capote to consider issues of crime, justice, and possible redemption, themes particularly significant to him following his research for *In Cold Blood*.

▶ *The Great Gatsby*

Having successfully collaborated with Jack Clayton on *The Innocents*, Capote agreed to pen the screenplay for the director's production of F. Scott Fitzgerald's classic novel *The Great Gatsby*. Starring Robert Redford as Jay Gatsby, Mia Farrow as Daisy Buchanan, Bruce Dern as Tom Buchanan, and Sam Waterston as Nick Carraway, the film was released in 1974. Tennessee Williams praised Clayton as a "cinematic master" and lauded the film as "surpass[ing], I think, the novel by Scott Fitzgerald,"[6] but his words clash with the consensus view that the film fails in its artistic aspirations. Reviewing for the *Nation*, Robert Hatch derided it both for its fidelity to and its reimagining of Fitzgerald's novel: "When it sticks close to the original, it adds nothing; when it deviates, it puts a heavy foot into Fitzgerald's magic."[7] Charles Michener lamented in *Newsweek* that "Jack Clayton, the gifted British director, has succeeded in creating an extraordinary white elephant—lovely to look at, but offering neither updated pertinence, continuous diversion nor, in the end, a satisfying film translation of Fitzgerald."[8] Peter Bart, who was vice president of production at Paramount during the film's creation, belittled it as "dull and stilted, an exercise in style over substance, and not such impressive style at that."[9] The film's failures, however, cannot be attributed to Capote's literary talents, for its final screenplay was written by Francis Ford Coppola after Clayton rejected Capote's draft.

Taming Fitzgerald's novel for the screen provided Capote with extraordinary difficulties, and the deeper he delved into the project, the more he realized the challenges of his source text. As he stated, "When I had the parts disassembled, I saw that there were so many things in that book that are so bad. It was like going into the kitchen and finding the garbage strewn all over."[10] Assuming Fitzgerald's narrative problems as his own, Capote found himself increasingly mired in an unwieldy adaptation, and his screenplay of *The Great Gatsby* suffers from numerous problems, including an over-reliance on voice-over, static plotting, and metacinematic staging. Upon reading Capote's screenplay, Clayton wrote a memo detailing his criticisms, along with his concerns about its viability. Foremost, he judged that the narrative suffered from amorphousness in its plotting—"The material lacks shape: a feeling of progression: excitement. It has, as yet, no point of view"— and he summarized with stark candor: "It also lacks tension, mystery and MAGIC."[11] After reading the script, Peter Bart was horrified: "When Capote handed in his script, it turned out to be the most bizarre exercise in screenwriting I'd ever observed. He had essentially retyped the novel, cutting down the prose but reproducing all the dialogue and adding none of his own. Capote's work was not so much an adaptation as a replication. And reading it, I became vividly aware of the fact that Fitzgerald's dialogue did not 'play.' Much of it was downright lame when isolated from the narrative."[12] With the film's director and Paramount's vice president of production lambasting Capote's script, the production faced the immediate need for a major redrafting if the project were to proceed. As Neil Sinyard put it, "Overall . . . the script seems verbose, ungainly in structure, with too much voiceover and exposition," and these glaring faults indicate Capote's cursory treatment of his adaptation.[13]

Capote's screenplay begins with Nick Carraway intoning to the audience, "Well, here I am again, on the 5.15 from Penn Station to West Egg, Long

Island," a commonplace observation that does not need to be stated as much as shown. The voice-over continues as Nick describes Long Island from an aerial view while commenting on other characters: "The great house below belongs to my neighbor, a certain Mister Jay Gatsby, rich and eligible, so I'm told."[14] Nick outlines his relationship to Daisy and Tom Buchanan, explaining to viewers their shared history and the prospect of their incipient reunion. So much of the plot is told rather than shown that the screenplay fails to capture the electric sexual tension running throughout much of Fitzgerald's novel, such as when Carraway meets Buchanan's mistress Myrtle Wilson. Capote communicates the discomfort of this encounter almost entirely through Carraway's voice-over, so that the staging of the scene would have been secondary to his explanatory words: "I thought, well, he must have been drinking before he got on the train and I just hadn't noticed. But the last person I wanted to meet was Tom's mistress. I cared too much about Daisy for that, although I'll admit to a definite curiosity. It was impossible to conceive of how any woman interesting to the American Prince of Wales could be a part of this burning garbage heap, the University of Dr. T. J. Eckleburg." Carraway's words sterilize a scene brimming with visual potential: Buchanan's drunken stance coupled with Carraway's visceral reaction to him, the grimy setting of George Wilson's garage and the subterranean flirtations carried on inside, and Fitzgerald's image of the optician Dr. Eckleburg and his billboard profanely symbolizing a landscape bereft of divinity other than the one fabricated for one man's commercial interests.

Because scenes such as this depend so heavily on voice-over, Clayton judged that the script lacked the tone and style of Fitzgerald's masterpiece. The irony is that Clayton believed that voice-over, or, as he referred to it, the commentary technique, could be effective for communicating nuances of emotion in a film version of *The Great Gatsby* despite his dislike for the device as a whole. In Penelope Houston's words, Clayton regarded "their use as equivalent to an admission of defeat by the film-maker."[15] In a memo sent to Capote, Clayton conceded that he approved of voice-overs for the draft screenplay, but deemed that Capote's overreliance on this technique failed to capture the lyrical magic of Fitzgerald's prose: "For the first draft, it was decided to a) use a commentary technique and b) to eliminate flashbacks. I am normally no lover of commentaries, but think that GATSBY might be an exception. The right commentary could give the film a style and feeling of Fitzgerald. The commentary in this material, quite apart from it be[ing] wordy and rambling, misses the point that Fitzgerald's own words from the book might be best."[16] The "wordy and rambling" nature of Capote's screenplay consistently substitutes Carraway's metacinematic musings for various characters' interactions; rather than selecting several key scenes of which Carraway might ponder the significance, the voice-overs consistently take precedence over staging.

This problem undermines much of the screenplay, with Carraway stating his reactions to various characters and dramatic situations rather than participating in them. Capote's presentation of Gatsby's lavish parties, which should be exuberant affairs of the sort that Blake Edwards captured in *Breakfast at Tiffany's*, albeit on a much grander scale, are similarly stilted. Instead of laying out a visual feast of riotousness, Capote presents virtually a series of still lifes. The screenplay pronounces that the party scene should unfold "like a series of pictures taken from a rotogravure. The CAMERA gives a still-life glimpse of each of the persons as NICK mentions them." And then, in yet another voice-over, Nick recites of the guests: "and some of them were: The Dwarf, Mr Hornbeam, who was said to be the richest dwarf in the world. And Dr Webster Civet, who was drowned last summer up in Maine," as he then continues through to the "Blackbuck sisters, Ismays, Christies, Auerbachs, Edgar Beaver, Benny McClennahan, Faustine O'Brien, Peter Jewett, Perdita Jones, G. Earl Muldoon, Claudia Hip, the young Quinns, Henry L. Palmetto . . ." Rather than allowing these various minor characters to interact with one another in a madcap montage, Capote presents them in a series of static shots that would be unlikely to capture the dynamism of Gatsby's parties. It should be noted that Fitzgerald similarly introduces a variety of guests to his readers, conveying through a novelistic montage the many faces that populate his protagonist's soirees, yet he renders the tensions of the party as well, for instance by introducing the "Ismays and the Chrysties (or rather Hubert Auerbach and Mr. Chrystie's wife),"[17] making a few words elaborate beyond the characters' names to hint at their duplicities. Capote's screenplay cannot convey such complexities as effectively, for the simple reason that, in this and similarly constructed scenes, he stays on the novel's surface.

Capote's ear for dialogue, so finely tuned in his other literary and cinematic works, fails him in key scenes of his *Great Gatsby* screenplay. When Gatsby succeeds in arranging a rendezvous with Daisy at Carraway's house and regrets his actions, leaden dialogue ensues in a scene that should be one of the emotional climaxes of the film:

GATSBY (Miserably whispering to himself): Oh, God! Oh, God, oh, God!
NICK (Really irritated): What's the matter with you?
GATSBY (Shaking his head side to side): This is a terrible mistake! The worse thing I could have done!

These lines, when contrasted with Fitzgerald's, highlight not only Capote's fidelity to his source text but also his mistranslating of its emotional register:

He followed me wildly into the kitchen, closed the door and whispered "Oh, God!" in a miserable way.

"What's the matter?"

"This is a terrible mistake," he said, shaking his head from side to side, "a terrible, terrible mistake."[18]

Fitzgerald's version of the scene captures the anguish of a man wracked by remorse for his attempt to rekindle a love affair with a married woman, but Capote's staging, with the repetitive phrasing "Oh God" and an overreliance on exclamation points to generate an affective response, does not trust the viewer to grasp Gatsby's regrets. It is striking how similar the words on the page are in the two versions of the narrative, yet how disparate their emotional tenors.

The novel's climax, in which George Wilson murders Gatsby, mistakenly thinking him responsible for Myrtle's death, is surprisingly anticlimactic in Capote's treatment, depriving viewers of the emotional impact of this violent encounter. Following Fitzgerald's lead, Capote sets the stage in Gatsby's swimming pool, with "Gatsby . . . slowly swimming it's [sic] length backstroke. He pauses and floats, looking up at the sky." And then, without any dramatic escalation, the eponymous hero dies: "The smack of a bullet suddenly hits the air. It hits Gatsby in the head, spins him over. Now he is floating on his stomach, face down, dead." In his notes to Capote, Clayton suggested rewriting Gatsby's death scene, with Gatsby recalling a tryst with Daisy, fantasizing that she is there with him, only then to see Wilson, who shoots him. (Clayton's film adheres to this vision.) So brief is Capote's description of the scene that no such dramatic escalation kindles the audience's tension for Gatsby as his death inexorably approaches, with only the thoughts of his love affair alleviating the emptiness of his final moments.

Capote's script ends with a valedictory encounter between Carraway and Tom Buchanan. Buchanan asks, "Well, if you were in my shoes, what would you have done?" and Carraway replies, "I don't know, Tom. I don't know." He further intones in voice-over, "Only Dr. Eckleburg could ever answer that." With these words Capote builds circularity into his screenplay, recalling its beginning when Carraway sketched the train route from Manhattan to West Egg: "Funny, but every time the train stops here and I look into the eyes of that joker Doctor Eckleburg, I think 'God sees everything.'" In Carraway's closing words, Capote stresses Fitzgerald's symbolism, with the mythic figure of Dr. Eckleburg looming over human affairs with neither paternal affection nor divine concern but only the emptiness of hollow oversight. Such an ending rethematizes Fitzgerald's novel and its concern with one's past, as recorded in Carraway's final musings, in a justly famed phrasing of humanity's struggle to move beyond histories both public and private: "So we beat on, boats against the current, borne back ceaselessly into the past."[19] For Carraway, Gatsby's attempt to refashion himself into a man of wealth, sophistication, and social prominence was undone by his past history but also by his present love for Daisy, who symbolized for him both an eternal love and a vision of himself from yesteryear. In Capote's screenplay, the thematic weight of history is shifted onto an existential statement of God's neutrality toward humanity, an insight that corresponds with Fitzgerald's symbolism of divinity on a billboard, yet weakens the novel's meditation on one man's efforts to negotiate his life through his past.

As the novel shifts in tone and theme in Capote's screenplay, so too does Gatsby himself. Capote employs the party scene to query Gatsby's sexual orientation, with various guests pondering the libidinous desires of their mysterious host. In so doing, Capote expands his treatment of queer themes to one of Western literature's most perdurably heterosexual protagonists. A female voice wonders aloud, "Who cares who he is or where he came from? Why is everybody talking about him?" but a man responds: "Do you suppose he could be queer? I've never seen him with a woman. Don't you think that's queer?" Capote also resurrects defining aspects of Holly Golightly in Gatsby. Capote's Carraway comments to Jordan Baker, "He's absurd because he's pretending to be something he isn't. But whatever he really is is genuine," a phrasing that echoes O. J. Berman's assessment of Holly Golightly: "She isn't a phony because she's a *real* phony" (*BT* 30). Also, when Gatsby and Daisy shop for jewelry, they echo Holly's opinion that "it's tacky to wear diamonds before you're forty; and even that's risky. They only look right on the really old girls" (*BT* 39), with Gatsby proclaiming, "In my opinion diamonds only look well on very old women," as Daisy laughingly agrees: "That's true. There's nothing more marvelous than a ninety-year-old woman, blazing with diamonds." In Capote's rewriting of Gatsby, the mysterious millionaire playboy haunted by his lost love metamorphoses into a suspected homosexual and a mouthpiece of Holly Golightly's witticisms, losing core aspects of Fitzgerald's character and transforming unmistakably into a male version of Capote's beloved heroine.

After his screenplay was rejected, Capote expressed conflicting opinions about its artistic merit and the reasons for its rejection. At one time he affirmed the quality of his work, saying that the book was "hell to dramatize because it consists almost entirely of long-ago exposition and, as it were, offstage scenes. Personally, I like my adaptation, but the producers, Paramount Pictures, are of a different opinion. My pity to whoever attempts a rewrite" (*DB* 411–12). But he also admitted his adaptation's limitations to Andy Warhol: "Well, I didn't think my script was too wonderful."[20] In regard to the perpetual quandary for cinematic adaptations of whether to adhere to or to veer from their source texts, Capote recalled that his script was rejected for resembling Fitzgerald's novel too closely: "And I did the first screenplay for the last remake of 'The Great Gatsby.' But *they* didn't like it . . . . I tried to get someone to tell me something. And finally, someone did say . . . 'The real trouble with your script, Truman, is it *is* "The Great Gatsby." It *is* the book.' And I said, 'But that's what you gave me. The book.' And he said: 'But we wanted something more.'"[21] This encounter encapsulates the crux of cinematic adaptations of literature: the resulting screenplay must capture the source text, but it must convey "something more," no matter how this "something more" is defined artistically, while the source text is re-created visually into a new medium. As Capote understood from his prior adaptations, translating a book to the screen demands more than blind fidelity to its original author, and his adaptation of *The Great Gatsby* exemplifies the ways in which a dramatization must seek to capture its own spirit through a work rather than adhering too closely to it. Despite his copious and harsh criticisms, Clayton encouraged Capote to continue working on the script— "I'm afraid there [*sic*] not very encouraging, but I do know that this sequence can be made into something marvelous"[22]—until it became apparent that Capote would not complete the necessary edits, and so turned the project over to Coppola.

▶ *Uncle Sam's Hard Luck Hotel*

Capote's teleplay of *Uncle Sam's Hard Luck Hotel* was projected to be the pilot episode of a new television series to air during NBC's 1973–74 season.[23] Sam Wilcox, its eponymous protagonist, operates a halfway house for parolees, and the screenplay begins as he picks up newly released inmate Ron Evans from prison. Ron, anticipating a reunion with his family, finds that they have abandoned him; therefore, he sarcastically agrees to leave with Sam: "Okay, pal, okay. I'll shack with you but I ain't going to have your baby."[24] At the halfway house Ron is introduced to the other residents, such figures as O'Connor, Chang, Delaney, Ortega, and Willy, a motley group of ex-cons representing an array of ethnicities and races, many of whom are interested in staying straight, many of whom are conspiring for the next big score, and all of whom are easy targets for the local police. As Sam ironically comments, "We've got a whole house full of permanent class-A suspects. None of them can make a decent cup of coffee." These opening sequences introduce the screenplay's key themes of redemption and kinship, as the residents must forge familial ties with one another while they put their lives back on track.

Two contrasting yet complementary story lines emerge among the residents of the house, focusing on the desire of some to revert to a life of crime and on the prejudice others confront as they attempt to rehabilitate themselves. Pat Grady, another resident of the hard-luck hotel, lures Ron into a new scheme, a bank robbery, but one in which, rather than robbing the bank of its cash, they steal the bank's computer hard drive. In Grady's words, "Imagine kidnapping the guts of a computer and holding it for a million dollars ransom—ain't science grand!" In the contrasting plotline, the local policeman Martinez comes to arrest Cole, who is innocent of any recent offense and who cries desperately, "I ain't goin' back to no cage. I'd rather be dead!" Soon after Cole's arrest, Sam reports to the residents of the home that Cole has hanged himself in his cell. Whether guilty or innocent, residents of the home are natural suspects, forced to suffer the pall of suspicion due to their unforgotten pasts.

Sam may be the guardian angel of this halfway house, but he too is a deeply flawed man, which becomes apparent when viewers meet his nineteen-year-old daughter. Capote uses Pamela Wilcox to dramatize Sam's conflict with his own inner demons as he seeks to redeem himself by encouraging the residents in his halfway house to do the same. Pamela urges her father, "All you have to do is forgive yourself. All the rest of us have. You're the only holdout." Viewers learn the tragedy hidden in Sam's past when a local judge tells him, "Six and a half years ago you left a party, dead drunk, got into a car, and proceeded to kill your wife . . . my daughter. You served your time, and I served my bitterness. I don't know that either one did any good." Despite Sam's hope to reform himself through his good works for ex-cons, the story lines of Ron Evans and Cole exemplify in tandem the failures of his home to rehabilitate a criminal and the failures of the police to believe that a man could ever be successfully rehabilitated. The drama thematically puts the criminal justice system on trial, as the judge asks Sam, "Will you be prosecuting the parole system or defending the halfway house?" In a judicial hearing about the Hard Luck Hotel's future, Sam professes, "I lost Ron Evans. But *we* lost Cole Jackson." He explains the therapeutic benefits of the home: "You see, what we do is talk each other into the idea that the next time we hold our heads up, nobody will hit us." It is unclear what the fate of the Hard Luck Hotel will be, but the screenplay ends with the residents clinking their spoons on their coffee cups in approval and appreciation of Sam's efforts on their behalf. This affirmative ending, reminiscent of the "I am Spartacus" climax of *Spartacus* (1960), in which a group of underdogs rally around their champion, injects an air of optimism into a mostly bleak story of men on the edge of society and their troubles reentering it.

▶ *Dead Loss*

The typescript of *Dead Loss* credits Capote with the story and Paul Leaf with the screenplay, and the draft is dated to March 1976.[25] *Dead Loss* begins with a funeral in New Orleans, although it is unclear who has died. It then turns back to tell the story of Ben Fowler, a gynecologist with a gambling problem. Ben is married to Myra while having an affair with Beverly. In addition to his marital difficulties, he must find a way to pay his mounting debts to the menacing casino operator Brent. Brent's wife, a femme fatale seeking a tidy solution to a tedious marriage, proposes to Ben that she will forgive his debts if he kills her husband. Ben is thrown by this suggestion—"I don't know who ever said women were emotional," he stammers—to which Mrs. Brent coolly replies, "It's a rumor started by men." Unfortunately for Ben, he botches the murder of Brent and accidentally kills Joe Harris, the chief of a crime syndicate who was meeting with Brent at his lakeside home to discuss mutually lucrative (but illegal) business opportunities. After Harris's death, his lieutenant George takes over the gang while solving the mystery of who murdered his boss. He initially suspects that Brent double-crossed Harris to gain a wider share of the criminal underworld's profits, but after investigating boat rentals around the lake, he begins to suspect Ben.

While *Dead Loss* initially appears to be a steely noir, with the opening scenes capturing an emotional iciness as the various characters scheme for advantage, the plot unexpectedly devolves into humor and farce. When Mrs. Brent chastises Ben, "You can't expect me to pay you for hitting the wrong man," a sly humor enters the story line, and the plot truly degrades when Ben puts on a blackface disguise when attempting to flee New Orleans with Beverly. He also tries to turn the tables on Mrs. Brent by blackmailing her for hiring him to murder her husband, but the noir tensions of this story of betrayal, murder, and revenge become lost in the chaos of chase and pursuit, including a scene at a gay club that is described as "A transvestite place on the shore of Lake Pontchartrain. Everybody is in elaborate drag." Mrs. Brent tries to cut a deal with George and his gang, but they report this information to Mr. Brent. When Ben meets Mrs. Brent to pick up the money he has extorted from her, they are both shot. As the film concludes, viewers learn that Mr. Brent and Myra have also been having an affair, which loops back to the scene when Myra purchased a life insurance policy on Ben. "Crime doesn't pay," Mr. Brent sardonically declares, as Myra coolly adds, "At least not for the criminal." With the revelation that the scheming Ben and Mrs. Brent were outsmarted by their equally conniving spouses, *Dead Loss* takes the commonplace observation that there is no honor among thieves and ironically extends it to no fidelity among husbands and wives. A strikingly disjointed script that employs the codes of noir effectively in its opening sequences, *Dead Loss*'s devolution into car chases and racial humor derails a story that could have worked if it had remained true to its initial premise of lies, love, and gambling debts that must be paid.

▶ *Handcarved Coffins*

Toward the end of his life Capote was negotiating a cinematic production of *Handcarved Coffins*, his nonfiction account of a Midwestern serial killer included in *Music for Chameleons*. Despite the cinematic qualities of the story—it is virtually a screenplay in itself—Capote believed the project required a fresh perspective: "The way it's written, it's already a film script, but it needs a certain new conception from a certain angle, which I'm going to work out with the person who does write the film script."[26] Lester Persky was set to produce the film. Capote indicated that he wanted Roman Polanski to direct, but in 1977 Polanski plead guilty to the charge of unlawful sex with a minor; he then fled the United States to avoid sentencing. As Capote tersely commented, "Roman Polanski would have done it like a shot, but you can't get him into the country."[27] After Polanski, Capote preferred Hal Ashby, whose numerous hits in the 1970s included *Harold and Maude* (1971), *Shampoo* (1975), and *Coming Home* (1978), because "he has certain qualities I think would be very interesting—a man of that kind of mind doing a mysterious Western town with that limited, enclosed, claustrophobic atmosphere."[28] Jonathan Demme and Sidney Lumet were also considered, and in June 1980 Capote declared, "I think a foreign director would be best, Miloš Forman, but he's busy doing that picture by that man."[29] Casting discussions for the film mentioned Robert Duvall for FBI agent Jake Pepper, Ellen Burstyn for his love interest Addie Mason, and Steve McQueen for the murderous Mr. Quinn, although Capote wanted Carroll O'Connor for that part.[30] Despite these initial conversations, production of the film never commenced.

A career as artistically successful as Capote's is not lessened by these unproduced screenplays and projects, and the possibility that he shelved them because he saw their flaws should not be overlooked. Indeed, we have the example of *Summer Crossing* to illustrate Capote's censoring of his fiction while alive. Alan Schwartz, trustee of The Truman Capote Literary Trust, allowed the posthumous publication of this novel, concluding with various readers that the novel "was a sufficiently mature work that could stand on its own merits and that its intimations of the latter style and proficiency that led to *Breakfast at Tiffany's* were too valuable to be ignored" (*SC* 136–37). These screenplays similarly complement a vision of Capote's career and his artistic successes. Through their connections to his more successful works, they reveal Capote pursuing ideas that long haunted his fiction: issues of love and loneliness in the teleplay of *Answered Prayers* corresponding to similar themes in *Other Voices, Other Rooms*; of sexual sophisticates and the quest for love in *Straight Face* corresponding to *Breakfast at Tiffany's*; of crime and punishment in *Tyranny, Uncle Sam's Hard Luck Hotel*, and *Dead Loss* corresponding to *In Cold Blood*; and of literary influence and its discontents in his efforts to tame Fitzgerald's *The Great Gatsby*. Success has a thousand fathers and failure is an orphan, the old adage proclaims, but despite their unfledged status, it would be dismissive to see these works simply as Capote's rejects, for they illuminate the ways in which various themes and plotlines weave throughout his rich and varied career.

Playing Capote ▶ *Tru, Capote, Infamous,* and Other Parodic and Iconic Portrayals

When asked who should play him in a movie of his life, Capote cheekily replied, "Greta Garbo. It'll be her great comeback part."[1] Although Garbo never abandoned retirement to undertake the challenges of portraying Capote, numerous other talents have impersonated him in performances ranging from the ridiculous to the sublime. Given his distinctive appearance and mannerisms— short of stature, wispy-voiced yet acid-tongued, openly gay—playing Capote invites an actor either to parody the author through excessive exaggeration, or to perform him by embodying but not overemphasizing his famed traits, or to mix the boundaries between these two modes. In the parodic performances of such comedians as Ernie Kovacs, Mike Nichols, David Frye, and Rich Little, Capote serves as the butt of jokes due to his homosexuality and otherwise outré personality. In contrast, dramatic productions and films of Capote's life, including *Tru, Capote,* and *Infamous,* depict him as a tragic figure, one who symbolizes the repercussions of pride and untrammeled ambition. In various incidental cinematic portrayals of Capote, he serves merely as an iconic representative of his era, with directors of films such as *54* and *Watchmen* employing him to embody the zeitgeist of the 1960s and 1970s rather than engaging in depth with his literature or life. Through these various portrayals, the author becomes an emblem of the very celebrity he sought to achieve through his literature, yet his literature ironically is always second-ary to the depictions of Capote himself.

> *Parodies*

From early in his career, Capote emerged as an object of satire and parody, such as in Ernie Kovacs's frequent performances as Percy Dovetonsils, Poet Laureate, on his 1950s television programs. Wearing a zebra-striped smoking jacket and an ascot bordering on a scarf, tilting his head to the side and mincing and lisping throughout, Kovacs impersonates and exaggerates Capote in these performances, clearly playing the stereotype of the homosexual literary aesthete. The outrageous effeminacy of Kovacs's performances was in many ways as shocking a disruption to 1950s social mores as Capote himself, especially considering the many broadcast restrictions on candid depictions of sexuality in even its mildest enactments. As Percy Dovetonsils, Kovacs brought a comic yet lascivious version of Capotean homosexuality to the screen, as in the skit "Leslie the Mean Animal Trainer," in which he flirts with the cameraman: "That chap on the camera has the manliest muscles I've ever seen on his legs . . . a little varicose, but nice."[2] This homoerotic fascination with his offscreen support staff serves as a running gag in the series, with Percy Dovetonsils naming the cameraman Norman in such skits as "Ode to a Germ's Eye Viewpoint" and "Ode to Dieting" in evidence of his continuing attraction. In most of his Percy Dovetonsils performances, Kovacs reads a light comic poem, such as his "Ode to Mona Lisa"—"Mona Lisa, you always smile, / Like heather on the heath. / How come you never laugh out loud? / Could be you have bad teeth"—with such doggerel debasing the literary aestheticism that Percy Dovetonsils ostensibly celebrates.

While such literary play is amusing, the skits' humor is sparked more by Kovacs's queer mannerisms than by the poems themselves. The skits also feature Percy Dovetonsils sipping martinis while commenting on their olives and decorative flowers. In the "Ode to Autumn" skit, he is disappointed with his drink and blames its maker—"Perhaps it's that sassy bartender using mascara again"—as he also archly expresses his sympathy for teetotalers: "Oh, I pity the abstainer." John Malcolm Brinnin described Percy Dovetonsils as "a grotesque imitation of T.—limp posturings, fruity lisp, fluttering hands, the whole pansy *shtick*. Strained and unfunny, the performance sags even for the technicians prepared to laugh, fizzles out in silence."[3] Despite Brinnin's umbrage, Kovacs's creation of the character testifies to Capote's literary and celebrity status in the 1950s, to the extent that the comedian could rely on his audience understanding his parodic allusion. In defending Capote, Brinnin overlooked the skits' outrageous and virtually avant-garde humor, in Kovacs's non sequiturs of queer desire and aesthetic bathos that continually undercut any attempt for them to cohere beyond their excesses.

Similarly, during his years in a stand-up comedy duo with Elaine May in the 1950s and early 1960s, before turning his attention to directing such films as *Who's Afraid of Virginia Woolf?* (1966) and *The Graduate* (1967), Mike Nichols parodied Capote with the character of Mr. Alabama Glass, a homosexual literary aesthete similar in concept and performance to Kovacs's Percy Dovetonsils. In one such skit Mr. Alabama Glass prepares his audience for the baroque plot of his latest play: "I'd like to *apologize . . .* Before the action of the play *begins*, Nanette's husband *Raoul* has committed *suicide* on being unjustly accused of not being homosexual."[4] Nichols draws out and drawls various words—*apologize, begins, Raoul, suicide*— to render a pitch-perfect, if greatly exaggerated, voice parody of Capote's southern nasalities. Nichols's satire merges two gay southern authors into the figure of Mr. Alabama Glass, for the reference to Alabama in the character's name implies a connection to Tennessee Williams, as does the homosexual angst structuring the plot that Mr. Alabama Glass describes to his listeners. Nanette's deceased husband Raoul, tortured at the thought of being mistaken for heterosexual, contrasts humorously with Brick, the long-suffering and repressed protagonist of Williams's *Cat on a Hot Tin Roof,* who apparently loves but cannot acknowledge his feelings for his deceased friend Skipper. During the 1950s, while Capote was becoming the more widely known personality, Williams's career was more firmly established, and he was certainly the more widely recognized literary talent due to the success of *The Glass Menagerie* (1944) and *A Streetcar Named Desire* (1947), as well as their cinematic adaptations. Fusing Williams and Capote into one, Nichols multiplies his satiric range by compressing two leading figures of the Southern Renaissance into a simple queer gag.

Impersonator David Frye rose to fame in the 1960s and 1970s, primarily for his satires of such politicians as Lyndon Johnson and Richard Nixon, yet he extended his range to celebrity culture on a 1970 episode of the long-running variety show *Kraft Music Hall* titled *The Kopykats* (1970), in which he aped both sportscaster Howard Cosell and Capote. In this skit "Cosell," interviewing "Capote," begins with a sports question as "Capote," with frilled cuffs on full display, meanders through his celebrity circle: "Well, before I answer that question, I'd like to mention that Jacqueline Kennedy Onassis is a very, very close friend of mine, and I don't like to go through an entire interview without mentioning *that just once*." Frye squeezes out every possible emphasis on *"that just once,"* with "Capote" also mentioning his friendships with Princess Lee Radziwill, the Duchess of Windsor, Gloria Vanderbilt, and Princess Margaret. The tables turn as "Cosell" launches into a litany of the many celebrities he knows, until "Capote" exasperatedly concludes the scene: "Sports fans, we'll talk more about the zone defense some other time when we can get rid of this name-dropper."[5] In suggesting the ultimate interchangeability of these two men—the masculine "Cosell" is as interested in gossip about jet-setting celebrities as the queeny "Capote"; "Capote" is as interested in football arcana as "Cosell"—the real Capote's queerness becomes interchangeable with the real Cosell's masculinity. Capote remains a comic figure in this skit, but the humorous disruptions to masculinity evident in Frye's performance undermine visions of gender, sexuality, and vocation as stable referents of a person's identity.

In his *Rich Little's Christmas Carol* (1978), impersonator Rich Little plays all of the characters in Charles Dickens's seasonal classic, aping such famed stars as W. C. Fields (Scrooge), Johnny Carson (Nephew Fred), Humphrey Bogart (Ghost of Christmas Past), Groucho Marx (Fezziwig), Peter Falk (Ghost of Christmas Present), Jean Stapleton (Mrs. Cratchit), and Peter Sellers (Ghost of Christmas Yet-To-Come). Indeed, Richard Nixon (Jacob Marley) and Truman Capote (Tiny Tim) are the only celebrities selected for this project whose fame did not rest on their acting careers. In choosing Capote for the role of Tiny Tim, and likewise in casting the gay actor Paul Lynde as Bob Cratchit, Little creates a homosexual version of Dickens's traditional family. In his short scene, "Capote" minces Tiny Tim's classic line "God bless us, every one," and at the show's conclusion "Capote," wearing big pink sunglasses and mugging for the camera, calls out, "Thanks for giving me a small part, Rich," as do the various other "celebrities" who express their gratitude to Little for including them in his parody.[6] Ironically, Capote's nemesis Gore Vidal once proclaimed that "every generation gets the Tiny Tim it deserves,"[7] a statement made literally true through Little's impersonation.

For comics such as Kovacs, Nichols, Frye, and Little, Capote proved an irresistible target: with mannerisms so pronounced, and with a persona so exaggerated, the parodists' primary challenge of ensuring that their audience will understand precisely who is the butt of the joke is alleviated. No other American literary figure of the twentieth century—Faulkner, O'Connor, Baldwin, Styron, Mailer, even Hemingway—invited such a panoply of parodies. Following Capote's death in 1984, although his literature lives on for countless readers, his appropriateness as a target of contemporary parody has dissipated simply because his flamboyant antics have ceased. In death, he no longer provides a present-day target for satirists and parodists. Although the parodic portraits of Capote have waned, Capote remains in the public eye, notably in the various biographically inspired depictions of his life on stage and screen. As his antics and outrageous persona provided fodder for parodists and comedians during his lifetime, since his demise he has increasingly served as the subject of quasi-biographical accounts of his descent into alcoholism and drugs following the publication of *In Cold Blood* and the excerpted chapters from *Answered Prayers*.

▶ *Tru*

Jay Presson Allen's play *Tru*, which she wrote and directed, ran at Broadway's Booth Theatre for 297 performances in 1989 and 1990, with Robert Morse winning the 1990 Tony Award for Best Actor in a Play and the Drama Desk Award for Outstanding One Person Show/Solo Performance. While playing under Kirk Browning's direction at the Shubert Theatre in Chicago during November 19–21, 1991, *Tru* was filmed as part of the *American Playhouse* series. The play is set in the week before Christmas 1975 as Capote confronts the repercussions of publishing salacious chapters of *Answered Prayers*, now that his high-society friends have ostracized him for divulging their secrets. Allen incorporates many of Capote's witticisms throughout her play, such as his provocative statement "It's a scientific fact that for every year you stay in California you lose two points off your IQ" (32).[8] Such moments ensure that her words accurately reflect Capote's character, for they are first and foremost his words, although reassembled into a dramatic monologue exposing his character in a story line of regret and confession. On the whole, the play aims for a sympathetic yet frank depiction of Capote, one highlighting his excesses and his essential humanity as he attempts to understand the events that have resulted in his current state of exile.

Against Louis Armstrong's wistful singing of "A Kiss to Build a Dream On," which imbues the production's opening with a melancholy tone, Capote cracks jokes while commenting on the seasonal setting—"Poinsettias are the Bob Goulet of Botany" (8), he tartly opines. He also accentuates his candor: when speaking to his lawyer on the telephone, he gives biographer Gerald Clarke complete access to his files, describing him as "my Boswell" who "isn't exactly plowing virgin soil" (10), words tacitly promising the audience total openness. Allen counterbalances such light moments with ones of impish gravity, such as when, to indicate his worsening addiction to alcohol, Capote pours a full glass of vodka and ostentatiously drops in a single ice cube. Capote speaks much of his monologue into a tape recorder for Gerald Clarke, and in Morse's energetic performance he is almost perpetually in motion: dancing around his apartment, throwing his hands in the air, slapping his hands to his knees, posing with arms akimbo, and erupting with nervous laughter at his own commentary. "The Poet Laureate of the Lavatory Wall" (12), he calls himself as he discusses his decision to let *Esquire* publish excerpts from *Answered Prayers* and this decision's devastating fallout in his personal life.

Building moments of introspection and humor in alternate beats, Allen depicts Capote as haunted by his fame. He laments its trappings—"Now I'm famous for being famous" (14)—even as he arrogantly trumpets his genius.[9] Dismissing his former friends, he sniffs, "If they were smart, they'd confine their patronage to the merely artistic" (16), implying that their mistake was failing to recognize him as a true artist. He refuses to acknowledge that exposing their secrets did, in fact, constitute betrayal. Accentuating these traces of arrogance in his character, Allen's Capote laments the passage of time as registered in the loss of his beauty, informing the audience, "I have always been an object of desire" (18). The statement appears narcissistically incongruous with the portly and balding image Morse presents, but when the audience laughs in surprise, Morse/Capote insists earnestly, "Yes, I was," before admitting with retrospective longing that the passing years have eroded his attractiveness: "When I was in school, I was amusing and I was pretty" (18). Capote also discusses his relationship with Jack Dunphy, confessing that he is upset that Dunphy is not celebrating Christmas with him. As he descends deeper into drunkenness, he sends telegrams to Babe Paley and Nancy Lady Keith, both seeking and offering forgiveness, for he appears unsure who is the offender and who the offended. The first act concludes as he tells his semiautobiographical story "Dazzle," in which he confesses his childhood desire to change his sex. The lights dim, and Morse transforms into little Truman timidly declaring "I want to be a girl" (25) to the mysterious Mrs. Ferguson, whose disembodied laughter peals offstage. A phone rings to end the sequence, and Capote leaves his apartment to attend a party with Ava Gardner and other friends, suggesting the essential parity between his childhood and adult selves.

Act II is set on Christmas Eve, and Morse enters the stage costumed in queer regalia indicative of Capote's larger-than-life persona—a flowing blue and floral kimono to midthigh (covering gray slacks and a button-down white shirt, necessary for a quick costume change later). He wants to lunch with Babe Paley, and he discusses how mutual friends told Paley that her husband Bill was depicted in *Answered Prayers*, until he sarcastically dismisses his detractors: "Well, they can kiss my serene ass on my couch of many colors" (30). Shifting to a nostalgic mood to escape his present pains, Capote reads from "A Christmas Memory," reminiscing about his childhood holidays with Sook. He then segues to his current Christmas in New York and ponders his mother's suicide, telling the audience that she took thirty Seconals and never woke up. "Writing a truthful book . . . or story . . . there's always a touch of murder in it" (37), he admits, with his words reflecting his loss of his mother, his loss of his friends, and, at least potentially, his loss of himself. Returning to his childhood memories, he recalls the controversy over his childhood literary roman à clef "Mrs. Busybody," a story he claims to have written when he was eight years old, which upset the citizens of Monroeville by spilling their secrets.[10] Capote confesses, "After that, people stopped telling me things" (38), yet it is unclear whether he realizes that the lessons from his childhood have taught him little and that he is merely reenacting this scene from his past in the current dustup over *Answer Prayers*. "The main thing that history teaches us is history teaches us nothing" (38), he intones. Here Allen stresses her theme that Capote's life offers a tragic lesson—with numerous comic motifs interspersed—on how people suffer when they remain incapable of learning from their mistakes. Particularly by balancing his stories of and from childhood ("Dazzle," "A Christmas

FIG. 21   *Tru*: Publicity photograph of Robert Morse starring in the *American Playhouse* production of Jay Presson Allen's biographical play.

Memory," "Mrs. Busybody") against the notorious *Answered Prayers,* Allen stages Capote's current challenges as a result of remaining mired in the preoccupations of his past, albeit with an updated cast of characters.

The play reaches its climax when Capote punches a portrait of himself as a young man, indicating through this burst of violence his frustration that he remains trapped in the traumas of his past. His fist goes through the canvas, and looking at it wryly, he laments with bleak humor, "The Way We Were," alluding with ironic regret to Barbra Streisand's anthem of melancholic lost love. Returning to a more comic mood, Capote discusses the Black and White Ball commemorating the publication of *In Cold Blood* and wonders, "When it's time to go, shall we just . . . laugh?" (41). Morse engages in a quick costume change, putting a blazer over the outfit hidden under his kimono and adorning it with a red scarf. With "The Little Drummer

Boy" playing in the background to remind the audience of the play's seasonal setting of optimism and joy, as well as of the essential childishness of the character before them, he turns off the lights and puts on his hat and sunglasses. In this ambiguous ending it is unclear whether Capote learns anything from his recollections, and it would be biographically untrue to suggest that he did, for his descent into alcohol and drugs continued well beyond any night, real or fictional, of 1975. As the audience applauds the play's conclusion, Morse returns to the stage and strips off the prosthetics and wig camouflaging him as Capote to reveal the actor underneath. In Morse's tour-de-force performance, Capote comes to life as a figure of exaggeration and complexity, of raw emotions simmering beneath a veneer of artifice and humor. The play invites its audience to appreciate insights from his life, despite his inability to free himself from his escalating troubles until his premature death in 1984.

▶ *Capote*

Bennett Miller's 2005 biopic *Capote*, based on Dan Futterman's screenplay and starring Philip Seymour Hoffman, covers the period of Capote's life dedicated to *In Cold Blood*: his decision to write about the murder of the Clutter family, his investigations in Kansas with Nelle Harper Lee (Catherine Keener), his growing relationships with the killers Perry Smith (Clifton Collins) and Dick Hickock (Mark Pellegrino), and the emotional aftermath of their executions. In bringing this story to the screen, Futterman recalls how his vision for the film emerged while reading *In Cold Blood*, for he realized that the man behind the novel provided a story line as compelling as the events depicted therein: "The most interesting character in this book isn't in the book. And you feel his hands behind the scenes."[11] He also explains, "I was writing a movie about a man's ambition winning out over the better parts of himself."[12] As Capote's *In Cold Blood* tells the story of two criminals tainted by their dreams of easy money and the tragic consequences of their greed on an innocent family, Futterman's screenplay turns the focus onto Capote himself, examining how, in writing his nonfiction novel, his personal ambitions clash with his growing concern for the killers and the emotional effects such vanity wreaked upon him. Capote thus becomes the tragic protagonist of his own life story, and Futterman describes his project as akin to classical drama: "What Bennett [Miller] wanted us to be clear about was that this was a story of Capote's ambition being awakened; that, in the way that a character from a Greek tragedy has a fatal flaw that he must confront, Capote was destined to confront himself—and his ambition—through Perry, the moment he got on the train to Kansas."[13] From this perspective, Capote's life serves as a tragedy and a cautionary tale, with the film depicting his slow descent into alcoholism as a symbol of the price paid for excessive ambition.

Capote begins in Kansas on November 15, 1959, with the discovery of the Clutters' bodies. Miller opens the film by holding shots of wheat fields and farm settings for several seconds longer than viewers might expect, asking his audience to ponder the majesty and desolation of country life, then contrasts these scenes by introducing Capote at a riotous party. Discussing his views on fiction and biography, Capote tells his coterie of admirers, "I find autobiographical stories at this juncture of my life to be quite boring," an ironic statement given the film's attention to his life and its tribulations. He also proclaims, "I think being true to who you are is important." These statements alert viewers to the themes developing in the film's story line, but Capote's exaggerated persona as a queer bon vivant cloaks their import as he digresses into an anecdote about James Baldwin. He says that Baldwin told him he did not want his fiction to be viewed as a "problem novel," to which Capote responded, "Your novel's about a Negro homosexual who's in love with a Jew. Wouldn't you call that a problem?"[14] His admirers laugh delightedly at his brash humor, as Truman continues playing for their attention and escalating his performance: "Don't come asking some man from the South whether your book about a black man fucking some Jew when they're both of the same sex is an issue! Don't ask me that!" The light narcissism of this scene builds in subsequent ones, as when, boarding the train that will take Lee and him to Kansas, Capote bribes the porter to praise his books in front of her. Later, upon their return to Manhattan, Capote's partner Jack Dunphy (Bruce Greenwood) says to Lee, "This is the start of a great love affair," but she wearily replies, "Yes, Truman in love with Truman." Capote likewise becomes enamored with his project, puffing up his literary endeavors into a revolutionary aesthetic achievement: "To answer your question, I'm following *Breakfast at Tiffany's* by blazing a different path. By inventing an entirely new kind of writing. The nonfiction novel."[15] Talking to Lee on the phone, he appears amazed by his own genius: "When I think how good my book can be, I can hardly breathe." These moments establish Capote's narcissistic tendencies, portraying him as driven by ambition to write his masterpiece while also hinting at the shallow roots behind his endeavors.

As the film accentuates Capote's prideful ambition, it also showcases his essential bravery for living life openly as a gay man during homophobic times. Whereas Capote's homosexuality long provided a target for satirists during his lifetime, it is increasingly viewed as a sign of his countercultural courage. *Capote* treats Capote's homosexuality frankly and pays close attention to his relationship with Dunphy. Miller's Capote also seeks sexual partners outside the bounds of this relationship: while speaking with Dunphy from a phone booth on a cold winter night, he cruises a local Kansan and then follows him into a gay bar. But his homosexuality marks him as an outsider to the straitlaced Kansans with whom he must interact if he is to write his story. When he meets the lead investigator of the murders, Alvin Dewey (Chris Cooper), Capote casually mentions that his scarf is from Bergdorf's, but he does not receive the admiring reply he expects. With Lee's assistance, he eventually charms Dewey and his wife Marie (Amy Ryan), proving himself capable of ingratiating himself with others while remaining true to his queer personality. The film also suggests that Capote's homosexuality, while alienating him from some people, grants him insight into the suffering of others. When interviewing one of Nancy Clutter's classmates with Lee, Capote comforts the teen: "Oh, it's the hardest when someone has a notion about you and it's impossible to convince them otherwise. Ever since I was a child, folks have thought they had me pegged because of the way I . . . the way I am." Presenting Capote as an outsider sexually and socially, Hoffman modulates Capote's outré persona in such scenes, indicating a core of emotional strength due to the fights he has waged throughout his life over his homosexuality.

The heart of the film explores Capote's relationship with Perry Smith and how he coaxes and cajoles, and virtually seduces and blackmails, Smith into divulging the details of the Clutter murders. The initial encounter between the characters, when Smith is brought to the Kansas courthouse for arraignment, shows their acknowledgement of each other, with their eyes momentarily catching. This hint of emotional cathexis between the gay aesthete and the cold-blooded killer escalates from mutual distrust to a deep friendship, yet one that can never be disseevered from Capote's self-interested pursuit of his story. Upon meeting Smith, Capote notes, "They put you in the women's cell," which prepares viewers for Smith's subversion of masculinity as his relationship with Capote matures, but the killer responds menacingly when Capote brings him some aspirin: "I could kill you if you got too close." Capote notices a copy of *Other Voices, Other Rooms* on the floor of Smith's cell, but instead of offering adulation, the convict insults him: "Your picture's undignified. People recall first impressions." As much as the film illustrates Capote's growing feelings for Smith through their prison interviews, an emotional attachment that is depicted as maternal when Capote spoon-feeds baby food to Smith, nursing him back to health after a hunger strike, Bennett and Futterman consistently depict the author's single-minded pursuit of his story and the duplicities to which he resorts to wheedle the truth from his prey. In his analysis of the character, Hoffman delineates the core mysteries of Capote's seductive style: "How he ultimately captivates a person in front of him, is always very elusive to me. . . . He's a very elusive guy, exactly how he goes about almost capturing somebody's intention."[16] In these scenes Capote repeatedly lies to Smith, telling him, "I have no idea," when Smith asks the title of the manuscript, and although viewers know Capote has written at least half of his book, he tells Smith, "I've hardly written anything." When Smith again asks the book's title, having learned that it is *In Cold Blood* from the news coverage of one of Capote's advance readings, Capote again lies: "I don't know what you're talking about." He then explains that the organizers of the lecture chose the title *In Cold Blood*, disingenuously inquiring: "How could I choose a title when we still haven't talked about that night?" To build the contrast between the two characters' story lines, Miller crosscuts scenes of Capote's advance reading, an early indicator of the success he will enjoy with *In Cold Blood*, with those of Smith witnessing a fellow inmate taken to his execution. When Capote encourages Perry to confess the details of the killings, Miller comments, "Look at him . . . he's just a predator." The staging of these prison scenes continually focuses on Capote's manipulation of Smith, heightening their intimacy for the payoff of information.

Adhering to its tragic themes, the film shows Capote's ambition becoming his undoing. Although he recognizes a kinship to Smith, telling Lee while vacationing in Spain, "It's as if Perry and I grew up in the same house, and one day he stood up and went out the back door while I went out the front," he succumbs to the narcissism of success. At Lee's party celebrating the publication of *To Kill a Mockingbird*, she asks him how he is doing, and he replies, "It's torture the way . . . what they're doing to me." As he smokes a cigarette and sips a martini, he repeats, "They're torturing me." The contrast between the gilded excess of the party and Smith and Hickock's incarceration indicts Capote's shallow self-interest, and Miller and Futterman increasingly portray his attempts to escape the emotional pressures of the situation through alcohol. In presenting Capote's descent into addiction, Hoffman did not want to exaggerate his performance, seeking subtle nuances in staging the character: "You don't want to hit anyone over the head that you're actually watching the progression of an alcoholic."[17] In one such scene, Capote mixes liquor into baby food for a snack, which recalls to the viewer the earlier scene in which he nursed Perry back to health with baby food. Miller calls the spiked baby food a "brilliant metaphor" for its combination of the infantile and the anaesthetic, symbolizing Capote's desire to numb his present pains by returning to childhood.[18]

At the film's conclusion, one realizes that Capote's literary success is assured but that this pyrrhic victory costs him too much emotionally. When watching Smith's execution, he first reacts visibly, but then stares blankly ahead, with the camera silently holding the shot of Smith's body suspended over the floor. In the following scene, Capote is shot from behind to accentuate his isolation as he calls Lee from his hotel room and tells her, "It was a horrible experience . . . I will never get over it." When he wonders if he could have done more to save the men from execution, she bluntly tells him, "The fact is, you didn't want to." In the film's final scene, Capote flies back to New York from Kansas and idly pages through Smith's sketchbook, which includes Smith's drawing of Capote. Hoffman is shot in profile, looking out the plane's window, and Miller explains, "He's in first class in a golden cabin, above the clouds with heavenly light shining in, and yet . . . you know his life is over," know that it is the "beginning of the end" of Capote's career.[19] In this account, Capote's life becomes an exemplum, one in which the author's relationship with Smith, his zealous pursuit of the story, and his tribulations with drugs and alcohol are posited as a cause-and-effect sequence, stripping his biography of deeper complexities in favor of a formulaic plotline. As a biopic, the film succeeds in telling, as it were, a variation on a theme of Capote's life, hitting some notes correctly, striking others discordantly. Still, *Capote* was lavished with praise upon its release, particularly for Hoffman's Oscar-winning performance. Hoffman's physical transformation into Capote is all the more impressive when one realizes the actor is almost six feet tall, but he shrinks into the role, with the help of camera angles

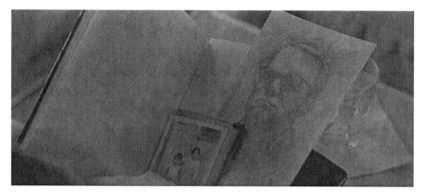

FIG. 22 *Capote*: On his flight back to New York from Kansas, Capote (Philip Seymour Hoffman) reads Perry Smith's private diary. This shot, says director Bennett Miller, suggests that Capote's life is over.

framing him shorter than his true height, such as the over-the-shoulder shots from Dewey's perspective when the two meet. (In other scenes, the illusion does not hold particularly well, and it simply appears that Capote slouches and suffers from bad posture.) Other Academy Award nominations included Miller for Directing, Futterman for Adapted Screenplay, Keener for Supporting Actress, and the film itself for Best Picture.

▶ *Infamous*

Douglas McGrath, the screenwriter and director of *Infamous*, credits George Plimpton's *Truman Capote: In Which Various Friends, Enemies, Acquaintances, and Detractors Recall His Turbulent Career* as the source of his 2006 film, but this acknowledgment is both accurate and misleading. Certainly McGrath borrows the anecdotal nature of Plimpton's oral biography, a form about which Plimpton cautioned his readers, worrying that they "may be put off by the idiosyncrasies of the form—the staccato rhythms of the text, the contradictions in the evidence about a particular episode, and especially the fact that the editors of oral biography do not have the luxury of being guides and interpreters of the subject's life."[20] *Infamous*, however, does not follow Plimpton's lead in telling the story of Capote's life from its beginning to its end. On the contrary, like Miller's *Capote* in this regard, McGrath's film focuses exclusively on Capote's decision to research the Clutter murders and the emotional and professional repercussions of his decision to write *In Cold Blood*, which comprises only a few chapters of Plimpton's oral biography.

As McGrath is uninterested in following his source text in its breadth, he also makes little effort to follow its structure. Plimpton's oral biography moves from person to person, each commenting on a particular aspect of Capote's character or an incident from his life. McGrath sparingly uses this structure, which he refers to as "testimonies," mostly to introduce Capote and his high-society friends to the audience and then to ponder the film's themes at its close.[21] In a string of such testimonies in the film's opening, Capote's Swans sing his praises, with Babe Paley (Sigourney Weaver) pronouncing the virtues of his friendship and the nasality of his voice, "He's so magical . . . you soon forget the most unforgettable sound in the world." Diana Vreeland (Juliet Stevenson) reflects on his countercultural ethos, "Here's a word I loathe: eccentric. Eccentric is a word that boring people use to describe someone I think of as interesting." Slim Keith (Hope Davis) extols his conversational skills: "He's the rarest thing in the world, a good talker who is also a good listener." Through these testimonies, viewers meet Capote and his rarefied world of excess, as represented by the adulation poured upon him by his wealthy friends. Structurally, however, such testimonies mostly serve as opportunities for rhetorical flourishes, and the bulk of the film adheres to standard expositional and narrative strategies.

In contrast to the somber tone of *Capote*, *Infamous* imbues its story with a lighter mood, which becomes increasingly incongruous as it moves from Capote's high-society circles to Smith's and Hickock's arrests and executions. As the film begins, Capote writes on a yellow legal pad. He registers the date, November 16, 1959, and then writes "Answered Prayers"; presently, when words don't come, he draws a squiggly sketch of a face instead. Inspiration strikes when he espies the *New York Times* account of the Clutter murders, and while lunching with Slim Keith, he tells her, "There's a story that's stuck in my teeth like a little piece of pull candy." This small hint of his future obsession builds narratively through light comic moments leading to his journey to Kansas and his exploits there. For example, McGrath depicts Capote as fawning over his friends, as he first calls Paley his "oldest and dearest friend" at an elegant nightclub, and then cuts to his calling Nelle Harper Lee (Sandra Bullock) his "oldest and dearest friend" at a more modest establishment, with these contrasting scenes exposing his penchant for exaggeration and mild duplicity. Describing his efforts to investigate the murders, he recounts his conversation with the district attorney's secretary, who tells him, "The district attorney does not take calls from strange women." With mock naiveté, he reports that his reply was to correct, not his misidentification as a woman, but the aspersion of strangeness: "Who says I'm strange?" Flamboyantly invading Kansas, he joins other reporters in questioning Dewey (Jeff Daniels), but his costuming—an orange scarf and cream winter coat—contrasts with the black suits of the men around him. When one reporter suggests that he writes for the *Ladies' Home Journal*, Capote retorts, "I'm not a reporter; I'm a writer." In this scene Dewey stands at top of stairs, with Truman's short stature accentuated by his placement at the bottom of the flight. Upon meeting Dewey, his precious demeanor is on full display as he promises the investigator that his story for the *New Yorker* will be "as dazzling and unique as a Fabergé egg."

In addition to the humorous incongruities of Capote's travels in Kansas, staged as a fish-out-of-water sequence, Capote's failed attempts to ingratiate himself with the local citizenry elicit pathos as well. He tells Lee at a diner, after attempting unsuccessfully to order J&B scotch, "You of all people know how impossible it is for me to modify myself." Implicitly lauding Capote for his courage to live openly as a gay man, *Infamous* tempers the emotionality of such scenes by contrasting them with others in which the difficulty of his task is played for laughs, such as when he returns to Dewey's office ridiculously attired in cowboy hat, boots, and bolo tie, looking like a child playing a dress-up game of Cowboys and Indians. McGrath stages Capote's initiation to Kansas society at a grocery-store display of Velveeta cheese, as he tells Marie Dewey, who has mistaken Lee for Capote's wife, "If this is the only cheese I find, Mrs. Capote and I might try cyanide." At the Deweys' seasonal celebration, he archly plays the queen, discussing football with Alvin Dewey and confessing, "It always sends shivers up my spine when the men get inside that little huddle and whisper." He succeeds in winning his hosts' affections by dropping various celebrities' names, and he mentions in particular that, during the filming of *Beat the Devil*, he defeated Humphrey Bogart at arm wrestling. When he lets the Deweys' son beat him, lest the boy be embarrassed by losing to a gay man, but then beats Dewey, Capote tells his new friend, "Listen, Foxy. When you're tiny, you've got to be tough. This world isn't kind to little things." The two men shake hands in a sign of friendship and mutual respect, with Capote demonstrating his canny ability to modulate his queer performances to win friends across a spectrum of social milieus.

Also like Miller's *Capote*, *Infamous* focuses primarily on the relationship between Capote and Perry Smith (Daniel Craig). Smith initially rebuffs Capote's overtures and insults his writing, and Capote reports to Lee in a park: "Imagine being told your work lacked kindness by a four-time killer!" The two men nonetheless bond over their mother's suicides, and Smith invites him to read his private materials: "You want to see the ball-busting letter she [his sister] sent me?" Capote often steals glances at Smith, obviously attracted to the killer, but Smith is more focused on using Capote's literary talents to cast a sympathetic light on his case: "Pay attention. This could be good for our book." As much as McGrath paints these scenes with sympathy, they often stretch viewers' credulity and descend into melodrama. When Smith becomes upset and is worried about their lack of privacy in the cell, Capote takes him to a quiet corner and whispers: "This can be our little tree house." Capote hides from Smith the title and contents of the manuscript, promising only that he will allow him to read it when it is completed: "Not until it's perfect. But I promise, it's sympathetic." When Smith learns that the title is *In Cold Blood*, he threatens to rape Capote and partially disrobes him to convince him that the threat is real. McGrath builds the homoerotic aspects of Smith's characterization, such as when the killer recalls murdering Kenyon Clutter and regrets his actions, musing, "Too bad we couldn't be friends." McGrath also uses the flashback of the murders to stage Hickock's aspersions on Smith's sexuality, as he taunts Smith about Kenyon, "Why don't you kiss him?" and "You like boys better?" The homoerotic aspects of Smith's characterization reach their climax when Capote confesses to Smith that their relationship allows him the freedom to be himself—"I don't have to act like a little wind-up toy with you"—and cries, "Perry, I don't want you to die." The two men then kiss. It has been conjectured—but only conjectured—that Capote and Smith engaged in a sexual relationship during the hours they spent together in the course of Capote's investigation of the Clutter murders, but the bathos of this embrace as depicted in *Infamous* turns the searing emotion of a man's imminent execution into a contrived scene of pent-up homoerotic passion.[22]

Infamous stages the ultimate incompatibility of Capote's two worlds, in which the emotional aftermath of his clandestine prison love affair in

FIG. 23 *Infamous*: In Douglas McGrath's staging, interviewer Capote
(Toby Jones) and prisoner Perry Smith (Daniel Craig) approach to embrace
in Smith's cell.

Kansas clashes with the cosmopolitan milieu of New York City and his
high-society friends. Recounting the story of the Clutter murders to Slim
Keith, he quotes Smith—"Right before I cut his throat, I was thinking how
nice he was"—and he repeats this story to Babe Paley at dinner and then to
Vreeland and Marella Agnelli (Isabella Rossellini) in conversation. Through
this repetition it is apparent both that Capote is traumatized by the events
and must narrate them to achieve some sense of catharsis, and that he is
sculpting the story so that it will achieve its full literary effect. Viewers see
that Capote has written on a yellow legal pad various phrasings of Smith's
confessions, until he puts a checkmark by the one reading, "I thought he was
a very nice gentleman. Soft spoken. I thought so right up to the moment I
cut his throat." Ultimately, Capote's ambitions for literary celebrity triumph
over his concern for Smith and Hickock, and while walking with Nelle he
decides: "Death would be better for the book. It would satisfy the readers
more, and it would make the title work, too."

The film concludes by inviting its viewers to ponder the morality of
Capote's actions. At dinner with Paley, Agnelli, and Bennett Cerf (Peter
Bogdanovich), Capote is asked: "Do you think your book is worth a human
life?" After Smith's execution, Capote confesses to Paley, "He said he loved
me . . . and he always had," but he attempts to distill meaning from the experience, telling her as well, "Babeling, life is painful. It's the one experience

that unites rich and poor. I suppose I'm able to endure it because I can alchemize what wounds me into art." Rather tendentiously, so that viewers will understand the disjunction between his words and his life, Paley muses aloud, "Yes, but . . . at what cost?" Returning to the testimonial style, McGrath portrays Cerf explaining: "It made him, and it ruined him." In the film's closing scene, Capote invites Lee to lunch, telling her that he has enjoyed a productive morning of writing *Answered Prayers*. The camera, however, focuses slowly on its final shot of a pen, eyeglasses, and a legal pad with no words other than "Answered Prayers" written on it—evidence that, in finishing *in Cold Blood*, Capote has immolated his muse, and the words will no longer come.

The great irony of *Infamous* is that, in condemning Capote for self-aggrandizement through his fictionalized treatment of the Clutter murders, McGrath follows in his footsteps. When Capote and Lee argue over his developing project, she takes him to task for incorporating fictional elements into a nonfiction story:

CAPOTE: Yes, of course it will be true, but . . .

LEE: But what? Either it is, or it isn't.

CAPOTE: You're not understanding. I'm, I'm going to bring fictional techniques to a nonfiction story.

LEE: What fictional techniques? The ones where you make stuff up?

The argument continues, until Capote angrily asks, "What is your stupid fucking point?" to which Lee replies, "That you shouldn't be doing what you're doing. The truth is enough." Lee speaks with moral clarity in these scenes, and Capote's unwillingness to adhere to this simple ethical code in pursuit of his story indicts his narcissistic ambitions. Rather than learning the lesson that Lee voices in the scene, McGrath aligns his project to a Capotean sensibility. He admits that he originally wanted to title his film "Every Word Is True," and also admits how such a title would be incorrect: "I'm not presenting it as the total truth; it's not a documentary."[23] The film thematically castigates Capote for interweaving fiction into his novel, yet it takes great liberties with the story of Capote's life, embellishing a nonfiction story with dramatic flourishes deemed appropriate for cinematic adaptation.

Capote's appearances as the protagonist of biopics such as *Tru, Capote,* and *Infamous* testify to the inherent interest of his fascinating life story, as it touches on a wide array of themes and issues: the challenges of writing and the writer's life, the debts a writer owes to his sources, the prejudice against homosexuals in pre-Stonewall America, and the gossipy world of the American elite. Beyond these films of his life, Capote also appears in cameo roles in biopics based on the lives of his contemporaries, as well as iconically representing the decadence of the 1960s and 1970s in short scenes in various movies. Andrew Bergman's *Isn't She Great?* (2000), a biopic of novelist Jacqueline Susann, depicts Susann (Bette Midler) becoming enraged while watching Capote (Sam Street) interviewed on television. The journalist, specifically mentioning Susann, asks him about his competition, to which Capote replies: "Jackie Susann, please. That's not writing, that's typing! She's a virtual illiterate." Susann throws her shoe at the television, and Capote continues, "She looks like a truck driver in drag." In re-creating Capote, the filmmakers appropriate his memorable barb about Jack Kerouac's literary talent as typing rather than writing, and then follow it with his cruel assessment of Susann's looks. To capture Capote's studied nattiness, he is costumed in a white hat with black band, complementing his white suit and black scarf, but in this short scene Capote becomes an amalgam of himself, in which various phrases are patched together no matter their origin within the story of his life.

Likewise in *54*, a dramatized account of the nightly decadence at Steve Rubell's notorious nightclub, Capote's cameo appearance grants the filmmakers the opportunity to ground their story in truth, for Capote was indeed a frequent guest at Studio 54. Indeed, he praised it frequently, stating that "never has there been a night club as amusing as Studio 54" and ludicrously calling it "one of the most innocent, beguiling places I've ever seen," although few would label this orgiastic lair a site of innocence.[24] The film tells the fictional (and rather banal) story of Shane O'Shea (Ryan Phillippe), an attractive young man who enjoys the sexual hedonism he discovers there until he realizes the empty allure of this gilded lifestyle. In the scene featuring Capote, Rubell (Mike Myers) silences the many revelers and calls out, "Mirror, mirror, on the wall, who's the fairest of them all? Truman? Truman Capote, where are you?" to which Capote, as played by Louis Negin, replies,

FIG 24 *54*: Truman Capote, played by Louis Negin, enjoys the revelries of Studio 54, with such standards tropes of homosexuality as narcissism (the mirror) and pederasty (the suspended boy) on display.

"Here, sugar." A preteen boy (with hair coifed to match Phillippe's) descends from the ceiling and hands Capote a looking glass. Capote preens in the mirror, and then grabs the boy's foot as he ascends back to the metaphorical heavens. Ironically, as much as this moment relies on Capote's fame so that audiences will recognize that the disco was populated by an endless parade of celebrities, the film depicts O'Shea as ignorant of this important guest, with Phillippe intoning in voice-over: "I mean, all these famous people, and I didn't know who any of them were. And they'd all go, 'Truman. Oh, Truman!' and I'd be thinking, who the fuck is Truman?"

In Zack Snyder's *Watchmen* (2009), a film based on Alan Moore's graphic novel deconstructing the grand myths of the superhero genre, Capote appears as little more than an iconic representation of the mid-to-late twentieth century. *Watchmen*, whether the graphic novel or its cinematic adaptation, has little in common with Capote's fiction; indeed, Capote does not appear at all in Moore's text. As the film's opening credits roll, the accompanying images span from the 1940s to the 1980s, as Bob Dylan's "The Times They Are A-Changin'" plays and newspaper and television headlines record the passage of the decades—"Japan Surrenders," "Russ Have A-Bomb," "Vietnam War Escalates." Brief tableaux depict the Watchmen at various

FIG. 25. *Watchmen*: Greg Travis as Andy Warhol and Greg Armstrong-Morris as Truman Capote in the opening credits of *Watchmen*, a superhero film with little apparent connection to Capote's fiction.

stages of their careers, such as Dr. Manhattan's meeting with John F. Kennedy (with Kennedy's assassination following) and Ozymandias's visit to Studio 54. Ironically, in this montage Capote is not depicted in the shot of this nightclub; rather, he appears in an image of Andy Warhol (Greg Travis) displaying a portrait of the superhero Nite Owl, with Capote (Greg Armstrong-Morris) at his side, as a camera clicks to acknowledge their celebrity. Warhol and Capote do not speak in their few seconds of screen time, yet they, perhaps more than any other artist and writer, communicate the zeitgeist of the late twentieth century. They do not need to act or interact in this scene; they communicate their era simply by their inclusion in the film.

A writer of genius and a celebrity of dubious merit, a queer figure of countercultural unorthodoxy devastated by his expulsion from high society, Truman Capote is a figure of striking paradoxes who has become an icon for his age. With his screenplays, the adaptations of his fiction, and the dramatizations of his life, he attracts continuous attention as an artist of unquestionable talent, as an irrepressible celebrity and social gadabout, and as a cautionary tale against the dangers of narcissism and drug abuse. In the many contradictions at the heart of Capote's life and literature emerges a mixed body of films and other works, both his own and of others, that can be collectively known as Cinema Capoteana, a corpus riddled with conundrums and contradictions, yet equally blessed with talent and vision, much like the author himself.

Notes

CHAPTER 1   Capote and the Cinema

1   Clarke, *Capote*, 413.
2   Burstein, "Tiny Yes, But a Terror?" 16.
3   Grobel, *Conversations with Capote*, 222.
4   Dunphy, *"Dear Genius,"* 27. Dunphy's memoir is highly fictionalized, including the framing device of Capote's drunken encounter with a priest questioning his vows; nonetheless, it accurately reflects key moments in Capote's life, as well as his reactions to various people and places.
5   Clarke, *Too Brief a Treat*, 43, 103.
6   Jones refers to the film as *An American Tragedy*, incorrectly renaming it with the title of Theodore Dreiser's novel from which it is adapted. Capote's lawyer Alan Schwartz declares that *Answered Prayers* "was to be an intricate, exuberant, witty, and mischievous novel, all told through the eyes of a never-to-be-forgotten character who in many ways reminded Truman of Truman himself" (*SC* 130), and his editor Joseph Fox describes Jones as "a sort of dark Doppelgänger of the author himself" (*AP* xiv).
7   Grobel, *Conversations with Capote*, 172; Clarke, *Too Brief a Treat*, 246, 248.
8   Clarke, *Too Brief a Treat*, 249. For Capote's animosity toward Hemingway, of whom he baldly stated, "I hated him," see Brian, "The Importance of Knowing Ernest," 101.
9   Clarke, *Too Brief a Treat*, 275.
10   Warhol, "Sunday with Mister C.," 30.
11   Clarke, *Too Brief a Treat*, 449.
12   Ibid., 43.
13   Ibid., 275.
14   Ibid., 311; Grobel, *Conversations with Capote*, 159–60; Burke, "Sweeter Options," 269; Grobel, *Conversations with Capote*, 168–69.
15   Clarke, *Too Brief a Treat*, 243; Grobel, *Conversations with Capote*, 158.
16   Grobel, *Conversations with Capote*, 159.

17   Brown, "Plate du Jour," 35–36.

18   Folks, "Southern Renascence," 835.

19   Allmendinger, "Female Influence," 53–54.

20   Fowler, introduction, vii.

21   King, "Framework of a Renaissance," 20.

22   King, *A Southern Renaissance*, 3.

23   Ibid., 195.

24   Clarke, *Capote*, 62–63.

25   Brinnin, *Truman Capote*, 6.

26   *Time*, "Spare the Laurels"; Trilling, "Fiction in Review," 133.

27   Robinson, "The Legend of 'Little T,'" 6.

28   Girson, "'48's Nine," 14.

29   Newquist, *Counterpoint*, 80.

30   Lee, "Southern Gothic," 220.

31   Gross, *Redefining the American Gothic*, 59.

32   For a reading of the gothic qualities of *In Cold Blood*, see Savoy, "The Face of the Tenant."

33   Norden, "*Playboy* Interview: Truman Capote," 53.

34   Capote was acquainted with Harry Kurnitz, the screenwriter of *One Touch of Venus*, and compared him to Marilyn Monroe in regard to their awkward sociability: "Marilyn Monroe was very amusing when she felt sufficiently relaxed and had had enough to drink. The same might be said of the lamented screen-scenarist Harry Kurnitz, an exceedingly homely gentleman who conquered men, women, and children of all classes with his verbal flights" (*MC* 253).

35   Hill, "The Art of Fiction XVII: Truman Capote," 45.

36   Mailer, *Advertisements for Myself*, 465.

37   Davis, *Party of the Century*, 251. Capote also uses the memorable phrase "suntanned Uriah Heep" to describe the secretary of the escort service depicted in *Answered Prayers* (52, 125).

38   Clarke, *Too Brief a Treat*, 49.

39   Doty, *Making Things Perfectly Queer*, xi; see also Doty's *Flaming Classics*.

40   French, *The South and Film*, 3–13.

41   Dunphy, "*Dear Genius*," 124; Devlin, *Conversations with Tennessee Williams*, 354.

42   Windham, *Lost Friendships*, 39. For Windham's account of Capote remembering events "the way they should have been," see in particular the account of Capote's friendship with André Gide (48–49).

43   This version of the anecdote is taken from Capote's appearance on Johnny Carson's *Tonight Show*, February 7, 1975. For an additional version of the

narrative in which Capote delivers the punch line, see *MC* 251; for the version in which Tennessee Williams delivers the comic coup de grâce, see *PO* 503; for the version in which Capote's companion John O'Shea is the wit, see Brinnin, *Truman Capote*, 155.

44 Grobel, *Conversations with Capote*, 91.

CHAPTER 2   Capote in the Queer House of Fame

1 S. Keith, *Slim*, 226.
2 Dyer, *Heavenly Bodies*, 2–3.
3 Warhol, "Sunday with Mister C.," 43.
4 Steinem, "Go Right Ahead," 150.
5 Clarke, *Capote*, 149.
6 Clarke, *Too Brief a Treat*, 170.
7 Clarke, *Capote*, 181.
8 Gore Vidal reports that Capote told the story thus: "Errol Flynn followed me up to my room at the Beverly Wilshire, and when I refused to have anything to do with him, he threw all my baggage out the window" (Clarke, "Petronius Americanus," 46).
9 Brinnin, *Truman Capote*, 37.
10 Clarke, *Too Brief a Treat*, 210.
11 Newquist, *Counterpoint*, 78.
12 Brian, *Murderers and Other Friendly People*, 101.
13 Kanfer, *Somebody*, 150.
14 Logan, *Movie Stars, Real People, and Me*, 101.
15 Thomas, *Marlon*, 123.
16 Grobel, *Conversations with Capote*, 102.
17 Kael, *Kiss Kiss Bang Bang*, 192.
18 Clarke, *Too Brief a Treat*, 359.
19 Grobel, *Conversations with Capote*, 172.
20 *The Tonight Show*, 27 Nov. 1972.
21 Grobel, *Conversations with Capote*, 172.
22 Karpel, "We'd Get Along without You Very Well," 114.
23 *The Tonight Show*, 12 Feb. 1973.
24 Karpel, "We'd Get Along without You Very Well," 114.
25 *The Tonight Show*, 12 Feb. 1973.
26 Clarke, *Too Brief a Treat*, 209.
27 Capote, "Holly and Hemlock," 3.
28 *The Tonight Show*, 27 Nov. 1972.
29 Windham, *Lost Friendships*, 118–19.

30 Lawrence, *The Passion of Montgomery Clift*, 151.

31 Brickell, *O. Henry Memorial Award*, xiv.

32 Newquist, *Counterpoint*, 77; Frankel, "The Author," 36.

33 Steinem, "A Visit with Truman Capote," 210.

34 B. Long, "In Cold Comfort," 128.

35 Brinnin, *Truman Capote*, 39.

36 Fleming, "The Private World of Truman Capote," 24.

37 Rolo, "The New Bohemia," 118.

38 Clarke, *Too Brief a Treat*, 269.

39 Kostelanetz, *The End of Intelligent Writing*, 92.

40 Talley, "An Afternoon with Truman Capote."

41 Clarke, *Too Brief a Treat*, 382.

42 Gill, *Here at The New Yorker*, 317.

43 Clarke, "The Art of Fiction L: Gore Vidal," 148. For more of Vidal's barbs on Capote, see Abbott and Mitzel, "Gore Vidal," 4, 7–8.

44 Brinnin, *Truman Capote*, 172.

45 Norden, "*Playboy* Interview: Truman Capote," 51.

46 S. Keith, *Slim*, 230.

47 Brinnin, *Truman Capote*, 8, 121.

48 Ibid., 149.

49 Devlin, *Conversations with Tennessee Williams*, 301.

50 Grafton, *The Sisters*, 223.

51 Smith, "A Success Money Didn't Buy"; Fremont-Smith, "Literature-by-Consensus."

52 Plimpton, *Truman Capote*, 249.

53 Ibid., 248.

54 For the complete guest list, see Davis, *Party of the Century*, 261–66.

55 Ibid., 164.

56 Ibid., 234.

57 Winn, "Capote, Mailer, and Miss Parker," 27.

58 Ibid., 27.

59 Mailer, "Of a Small and Modest Malignancy," 135. For another account of their evening together, see Mailer, "The Capote Perplex."

60 Winn, "Capote, Mailer, and Miss Parker," 28.

61 *The Dick Cavett Show*, 25 Mar. 1971, disc 3, DVD.

62 Clarke, *Too Brief a Treat*, 441.

63 Grobel, *Conversations with Capote*, 143.

64 *The Dean Martin Show*, 24 Jan. 1974, on *The Dean Martin Celebrity Roasts* DVD.

65 *The Cheap Show*, episode 2.

66 Plimpton, *Truman Capote*, 369.

67 Ibid., 412.

68 Brinnin, *Truman Capote*, 133.

69 Grobel, *Conversations with Capote*, 15.

70 Warhol, "Sunday with Mister C.," 37.

71 Plimpton, *Truman Capote*, 225; Clarke, *Too Brief a Treat*, 421.

72 Grunwald, "The Literary Aquarium of Truman Capote," 26.

73 Capote quote in Grobel, *Conversations with Capote*, 174; Simon quote in Plimpton, *Truman Capote*, 367.

74 Clarke, *Capote*, 475.

75 Ibid., 475; cf. Greenfeld, "Truman Capote, the Movie Star?" 17.

76 Canby, "Simon's Breezy 'Murder by Death.'"

77 Greenfeld, "Truman Capote, the Movie Star?" 17.

78 Capote contradicted himself on the issue of his remuneration for appearing in the film; asked whether he received "a lot of money for his acting debut," he responded with a determined "Oh Lord no" (Greenfeld, "Truman Capote, the Movie Star?" 17).

79 Greenfeld, "Truman Capote, the Movie Star?" 17.

80 Clarke, *Too Brief a Treat*, 144.

81 Clarke, *Capote*, 212.

82 Krebs, Notes on People, 34.

83 *The Stanley Siegel Show*, 18 July 1978.

84 Norden, "*Playboy* Interview: Truman Capote," 53.

85 Packer et al., "We Talk to . . . Truman Capote," 367.

86 Frost, "When Does a Writer Become a Star?" 23. P. B. Jones, the narrator of *Answered Prayers*, also voices this sentiment (48).

87 Wenner, "Coda: Another Round with Mr. C," 54.

88 Medwick, "Truman Capote: An Interview," 312.

89 Capote, "Elizabeth Taylor," 151; cf. *PO* 319.

CHAPTER 3   Scriptwriter for the Stars

1 Plimpton, *Truman Capote*, 28.

2 Clarke, *Too Brief a Treat*, 13.

3 The blurb appears on the dust jacket of the original edition of *Other Voices, Other Rooms*; it is reprinted in Robinson, "The Legend of 'Little T,'" 6.

4 Newquist, *Counterpoint*, 80–81.

5 Hill, "The Art of Fiction XVII: Truman Capote," 45.

6 Benshoff and Griffin, *Queer Images*, 99.

7 Grobel, *Conversations with Capote*, 90.

8 Clarke, *Too Brief a Treat*, 222.

9 Marcus, *Italian Film in the Light of Neorealism*, 19.

10 Landy, *Italian Film*, 14.

11 Cardullo, "Actor-Become-Auteur," 174.

12 De Sica, "Hollywood Shocked Me," 12.

13 De Sica, "De Sica on De Sica," 31.

14 De Sica, "Hollywood Shocked Me," 13.

15 Hill, "The Art of Fiction XVII: Truman Capote," 45.

16 Epstein, *Portrait of Jennifer*, 293.

17 Leff, commentary track.

18 Selznick, memo to John Huston, undated.

19 Clarke, *Too Brief a Treat*, 205–6.

20 Samuels, *Encountering Directors*, 155.

21 Bosworth, *Montgomery Clift*, 220.

22 Green, *Jennifer Jones*, 134.

23 Morris, *Huston, We Have a Problem*, 182.

24 Epstein, *Portrait of Jennifer*, 294.

25 Samuels, *Encountering Directors*, 155.

26 Epstein, *Portrait of Jennifer*, 294.

27 Clarke, *Too Brief a Treat*, 210.

28 Leff, commentary track.

29 Ibid.

30 Bosworth, *Montgomery Clift*, 221.

31 Capote, *Indiscretion of an American Wife* screenplay.

32 Hart, "Gay Male Spectatorship and the Films of Montgomery Clift," 75.

33 Joanne Dru as Tess in *Red River*.

34 Samuels, *Encountering Directors*, 155.

35 Leff, commentary track.

36 *Time*, "Cinema: New Picture."

37 Ibid.

38 Walsh, review of *Indiscretion of an American Wife*, 407.

39 Knight, "A Long Wait between Trains," 25.

40 *Catholic World*, review of *Indiscretion of an American Wife*, 143.

41 *Newsweek*, review of *Indiscretion of an American Wife*, 104.

42 Hartung, review of *Indiscretion of an American Wife*, 117.

43 Clarke, *Too Brief a Treat*, 106n1, 220.

44 De Sica, "Hollywood Shocked Me," 13.

45 Cockburn, letter to John Huston, 10 Mar. 1952.

46 Bogart, letter to John Huston, 19 Nov. 1952.

47 Bogart, letter to John Huston, 26 Nov. 1952.

48 Morris, *Huston, We Have a Problem*, 76.
49 Selznick, interoffice communication to John Huston, 23 Feb. 1953.
50 Huston, *An Open Book*, 247.
51 Breen, letter to Jess Morgan, 12 Mar. 1952.
52 Breen, letter to Jess Morgan, 13 Feb. 1953.
53 Selznick, interoffice communication to John Huston, 30 Jan. 1953 (also in Selznick, *Memo from David O. Selznick*, 442–43).
54 D. L. Keith, "An Interview with Truman Capote," 38.
55 Sims, letter to Morgan Maree, 18 Jun. 1953.
56 Veiller and Viertel, letter to John Huston, 4 Jul. 1953.
57 Grobel, *Conversations with Capote*, 161.
58 Ibid., 163.
59 Huston, *An Open Book*, 248.
60 R. E. Long, *John Huston: Interviews*, 130.
61 Green, *Jennifer Jones*, 141.
62 Hill, "The Art of Fiction XVII: Truman Capote," 45.
63 Steinem, "Go Right Ahead," 149.
64 Morley, *Larger Than Life*, 155.
65 Epstein, *Portrait of Jennifer*, 298.
66 Plimpton, *Truman Capote*, 125; cf. Clarke, *Too Brief a Treat*, 213.
67 Huston, *An Open Book*, 247. For Capote's account of this wrestling match, see Bogdanovich, "Bogie in Excelsis," 98–99.
68 Clarke, *Too Brief a Treat*, 215, 217; cf. Brinnin, *Truman Capote*, 83.
69 Ebert, "Beat the Devil."
70 Sontag, "Notes on 'Camp,'" 279, 280.
71 Ibid., 282.
72 Kael, *Kiss Kiss Bang Bang*, 235.
73 For a brief overview of Holliday's queer pulp fiction, see Stryker, *Queer Pulp*, 41.
74 Youngkin, *The Lost One*, 370. Ironically and appositely, Don Lee Keith in "An Interview with Truman Capote" describes Capote as "a kind of cherubic Peter Lorre" (40).
75 Kanfer, *Tough without a Gun*, 174.
76 R. E. Long, *John Huston: Interviews*, 46.
77 Bogdanovich, "Bogie in Excelsis," 94.
78 Anderson, "In Brief: *Beat the Devil*," 148; Morris, *Huston, We Have a Problem*, 80 (cf. Thomson, *Showman*, 586).
79 Marple, review of *Beat the Devil*, 143; Anderson, "In Brief: *Beat the Devil*," 148.
80 H.H.T., "The Screen in Review," 11.

81 Barnes, "The Director on Horseback," 281, 285.

82 *Film Society Review*, review of *Beat the Devil*.

83 Plimpton, *Truman Capote*, 130.

84 Morris, *Huston, We Have a Problem*, 83.

85 Plimpton, *Truman Capote*, 130.

86 Sennett, *Masters of Menace*, 177.

87 R. E. Long, *John Huston: Interviews*, 130; Huston, *An Open Book*, 248.

88 R. E. Long, *John Huston: Interviews*, 79.

89 Clarke, *Too Brief a Treat*, 225.

90 Pratley, *The Cinema of John Huston*, 103.

91 Kael, *Kiss Kiss Bang Bang*, 236.

92 Sinyard, *Jack Clayton*, 84.

93 Rebello, "Jack Clayton's *The Innocents*," 52.

94 Ibid., 52.

95 Clarke, *Too Brief a Treat*, 334; Ruas, *Conversations with American Writers*, 40.

96 Plimpton, *Truman Capote*, 129.

97 Sinyard, *Jack Clayton*, 91.

98 Clarke, *Capote*, 334.

99 James, *The Turn of the Screw*, 132.

100 Wilson, "The Ambiguity of Henry James," 130; Sinyard, *Jack Clayton*, 93.

101 Palmer, "Cinematic Ambiguity," 189.

102 Rebello, "Jack Clayton's *The Innocents*," 53. James's governess is unnamed; Archibald names the character Miss Giddens in his play, and Capote maintains this editorial decision.

103 Mazzella, "'The story . . . held us,'" 12.

104 Grobel, *Conversations with Capote*, 158–59.

105 Gow, "The Way Things Are," 14.

106 Clarke, *Capote*, 334.

107 Kael, *I Lost It at the Movies*, 166.

108 Palmer, "Cinematic Ambiguity," 206.

109 "*The Innocents*: Trailer."

110 Kincaid, *Child-Loving*, 3.

111 Recchia, "An Eye for an I," 30.

112 James, *The Turn of the Screw*, 28–29.

113 Shurlock, letter to Frank McCarthy, undated.

114 Archibald, *The Innocents*, 108.

115 This dialogue, with its focus on contamination and corruption, echoes James's (17).

116 The film's costumes were designed by Motley, the company name of the sisters Margaret Harris, Sophie Harris, and Elizabeth Montgomery Wilmot.

117 Palmer, "Cinematic Ambiguity," 202.

118 Gow, "The Way Things Are," 12.

119 Archibald, *The Innocents*, 101.

120 For Haya Clayton's crediting of this line to Mortimer, see Sinyard, *Jack Clayton*, 91.

121 Archibald, *The Innocents*, 76–77. In his two-act play Archibald uses this scene as the climax of act I.

122 Anthony Stevens declares, "A single foot is phallic, as when fitting into a shoe" (*Ariadne's Clue*, 406). Jean Chevalier and Alain Gheerbrant agree: "Both Jungian and Freudian analysts would see phallic significance in the foot" (*A Dictionary of Symbols*, 399).

123 Archibald and Capote, *The Innocents* screenplay, 98.

124 For Archibald's phrasing, see *The Innocents*, 129.

125 James, *The Turn of the Screw*, 132.

126 Archibald and Capote, *The Innocents* screenplay, 133.

127 Ibid., 136.

128 Sinyard, *Jack Clayton*, 106.

129 Rebello, "Jack Clayton's *The Innocents*," 55.

130 Clarke, *Too Brief a Treat*, 331.

131 Kael, *I Lost It at the Movies*, 167–68.

132 Crowther, "The Innocents"; *America*, review of *The Innocents*, 481.

133 Knight, "Innocents Abroad," 39.

134 *McCall's*, review of *The Innocents*.

135 *Newsweek*, review of *The Innocents*, 53.

136 *Variety*, review of *The Innocents*.

137 Kauffman, "Ghosts, Grime, and Grandeur," 20; *Time*, "Cinema: Evil Emanations."

138 Gill, review of *The Innocents*.

139 Hanson, "Screwing with Children in Henry James," 388.

140 Archibald and Capote, *The Innocents* screenplay, 10.

CHAPTER 4   Holly Golightly's Queer World

1 Clarke, *Capote*, 225.

2 Drutman, "Capote: End of the Affair."

3 McFarlane, *Novel to Film*, 12.

4 Grobel, *Conversations with Capote*, 157–58.

5   Clarke, *Capote*, 269.

6   Zoerink, "Truman Capote Talks," 128.

7   Capote frequently commented on the appropriateness of various actresses for playing Holly Golightly. In a 1966 interview he opined that he "would have liked to see a kid called Tuesday Weld play" the role (Capote, "Capote on Theatre," 13); he also declared that Jodie Foster would be "ideal for the part" if a remake were made (Grobel, *Conversations with Capote*, 158). Of Mary Tyler Moore's performance as Holly in the Broadway production of *Breakfast at Tiffany's*, Capote stated, "When I first watched her play this part in the musical I didn't like her," but he conceded that, after adjusting his expectations for the role, he "began to like Mary Tyler Moore very much and see she has a great quality" (Capote, "Capote on Theatre," 13).

8   Jurow, *Marty Jurow Seein' Stars*, 75. On Strasberg's influence on Monroe, see Summers, *Goddess*, esp. 162–63.

9   Jurow, *Marty Jurow Seein' Stars*, 74.

10 Ibid., 75. Capote said in a 1966 interview that "when Shirley Maclaine was first around, you know 15 years ago, she would have been very good" (Capote, "Capote on Theatre," 13).

11 Spoto, *Enchantment: The Life of Audrey Hepburn*, 204.

12 Jurow, *Marty Jurow Seein' Stars*, 77–78.

13 Zoerink, "Truman Capote Talks," 128.

14 Spoto, *Enchantment*, 203.

15 Mohrt, *The Givenchy Style*, 10.

16 Ibid., 82.

17 Jurow, *Marty Jurow Seein' Stars*, 74.

18 Shearer, *Patricia Neal*, 213.

19 "*Breakfast at Tiffany's*: The Making of a Classic."

20 Gristwood, *Breakfast at Tiffany's*, 72.

21 Shepherd, commentary track; "*Breakfast at Tiffany's*: The Making of a Classic."

22 Gristwood, *Breakfast at Tiffany's*, 126.

23 Ebsen, *The Other Side of Oz*, 191.

24 Grobel, *Conversations with Capote*, 157–58.

25 Marx, *The Nine Lives of Mickey Rooney*, 216; Weiler, "The Screen: 'Breakfast at Tiffany's,'" 28.

26 Marill, *Mickey Rooney*, 46; Shepherd, commentary track.

27 "*Breakfast at Tiffany's*: The Making of a Classic."

28 Rooney, *Life Is Too Short*, 264. Rooney adds that "the whole damn movie was just too too precious."

29 Shepherd, letter to Y. Frank Freeman, 16 Apr. 1959; cf. Gristwood, *Breakfast at Tiffany's*, 34.

30 Corliss, "Radley Metzger, Aristocrat of the Erotic," 23.

31 Clarke, *Capote*, 314. Donald Windham claims the title *Breakfast at Tiffany's* was originally his, for an unfinished book "about sex between servicemen and civilians during the war" (*Lost Friendships*, 57).

32 Haskell, *From Reverence to Rape*, 251.

33 Partridge, *A Dictionary of Slang*, 727. This usage of "maude" is dated to the 1940s.

34 Partridge, *A Dictionary of the Underworld*, 462.

35 In Capote's novella, Smith moves into Holly's apartment, not Paul's, after she leaves New York City.

36 Descriptions of scenes not appearing in the final cut of the film refer to George Axelrod's *Breakfast at Tiffany's*, first draft, 24 Aug. 1959. These lines appear on page 144.

37 Shurlock, letter to Luigi Luraschi, 17 Aug. 1960.

38 These lines from the film mirror Capote's words, at *BT* 26.

39 Lehman and Luhr, *Blake Edwards*, 1:61–62.

40 Wasson, *A Splurch in the Kisser*, 59.

41 "A Golightly Gathering."

42 Krämer, "The Many Faces of Holly Golightly," 63.

43 Axelrod, *Breakfast at Tiffany's*, first draft, 29.

44 Ibid., 30.

45 Shurlock, letter to Luigi Luraschi, 17 Aug. 1960.

46 These lines from the film mirror Capote's words, at *BT* 82.

47 Shearer, *Patricia Neal*, 212.

48 "*Breakfast at Tiffany's*: The Making of a Classic"; Neal, *As I Am*, 213.

49 Axelrod, *Breakfast at Tiffany's*, first draft, 26.

50 Ibid., 47.

51 These lines from the film mirror Capote's words, at *BT* 67.

52 Shurlock, letter to Luigi Luraschi, 17 Aug. 1960; this letter is reproduced in part in Gristwood, *Breakfast at Tiffany's*, 80–81.

53 Clarke, *Too Brief a Treat*, 330.

54 Wilcox, "The Other Truman," 56.

55 Norden, "*Playboy* Interview: Truman Capote," 169.

56 Lehman and Luhr, "I love New York!" 31.

1   Capote's "creation" of the genre of nonfiction novel, as well as the para-doxical term itself, has elicited much critical debate, particularly at the time of *In Cold Blood*'s publication. Phillip Tompkins, discerning numerous factual inaccuracies in *In Cold Blood*, trenchantly wonders, "We might ask of the 'nonfiction novel' that it contain no fiction. And if it does, why does it?" ("In Cold Fact," 125). See also Heyne, "Toward a Theory of Literary Nonfiction," and Hollowell, "Capote's *In Cold Blood*: The Search for Meaningful Design."

2   Steinem, "A Visit with Truman Capote," 240.

3   Alexander, "A Nonfictional Visit with Truman Capote."

4   Plimpton, "The Story behind a Nonfiction Novel," 42.

5   S. Keith, *Slim*, 229.

6   Ibid., 229.

7   Steinem, "A Visit with Truman Capote," 240; cf. Daniel, *Tough as Nails*, 171.

8   *Newsweek*, "Cutting Room."

9   Capote, telegram to Richard Brooks.

10   Clarke, *Capote*, 385.

11   Tallmer, "Truman Capote, Man about Town"; cf. *PO* 270.

12   In another interview Capote stated that because *In Cold Blood* is documentary, Brooks "has to stay with the facts but he's fully entitled to recreate those facts in his imagistic terms" (Drutman, "Capote: End of the Affair").

13   Clarke, *Capote*, 385.

14   Information on credits is in file "IN COLD BLOOD—casting," Margaret Herrick Library Archive 3-f.143.

15   Bart, "Firing Line."

16   Daniel, *Tough as Nails*, 175.

17   Bart, "Firing Line."

18   Hamilton, letter to Richard Brooks, 27 Aug. 1966.

19   Blake credits Capote with enhancing his performance: "He taught me more about acting than anyone. . . . He always called me 'Bobby B.' Just be yourself, Bobby B. Let it come from inside of you" (Grobel, *Conversations with Capote*, opposite p. 86).

20   Howard, "A Nightmare Lived Again," 104B. Given Blake's trial for the 2001 murder of his wife Bonnie Lee Bakley, this frank self-assessment of his murderous impulses from 1967 takes on a chilling air. Blake was acquitted of the murder charge but was found liable for wrongful death in a civil suit filed by Bakley's children.

21 Howard, "A Nightmare Lived Again," 104A–104.

22 Beaver, *Dictionary of Film Terms*, 250–51.

23 Hallam, *Realism and Popular Cinema*, 4.

24 Plimpton, *Truman Capote*, 186.

25 "*In Cold Blood*: Trailer."

26 Hallam, *Realism and Popular Cinema*, 106.

27 Parker, *Screening the Sexes*, 296.

28 Black, *The Reality Effect*, 113.

29 Russo, *The Celluloid Closet*, 135.

30 Daniel, *Tough as Nails*, 178–79.

31 Plimpton, "The Story behind a Nonfiction Novel," 39.

32 Bannerman, "Capote's Unanswered Questions."

33 Voss, *Truman Capote and the Legacy of "In Cold Blood,"* 113.

34 Ibid., 104–5.

35 In her analysis of pedophilia and its perpetrators, Sarah Goode concludes that "somewhere in the region of one in every five men is likely to have some degree of sexual attraction to children" (*Understanding and Addressing*, 20). Goode's findings are sufficiently disturbing, yet it is clear that Hickock's need to see himself as normal only cloaks his sexual abnormality.

36 Dalzell, *The Slang of Sin*, 200, 297; Chapman, *New Dictionary of American Slang*, 68.

37 For "honey," see *CB* 15, 22, 188, 194, 199; for "baby," see 90, 119. These and other terms of affection are used repeatedly throughout the book.

38 Bart, "Firing Line."

39 Brooks, "Breakdown of Novel and Breakdown by Character," 7.

40 Brooks, "Breakdown of Novel," 38 (corresponding to Capote's depiction of the scene, *CB* 133), 42 (corresponding to *CB* 147), 58 (corresponding to *CB* 202).

41 The following material is quoted from Dr. Mitchell Jones's psychiatric evaluations of Perry Smith and Dick Hickock, respectively dated 21 Mar. 1960 and 28 Mar. 1960. The report was attached to Jones's letter to Capote, dated 25 July 1960. Brooks had access to this report. It is included among his papers concerning the production of *In Cold Blood*, and it is available at the Margaret Herrick Library Archives, "*In Cold Blood*—Folder Research 57."

42 Murray, "*In Cold Blood*," 134.

43 Adams, "Twice Convicted, Once Executed," 249.

44 Bart, "Firing Line"; Daniel, *Tough as Nails*, 174.

45 Steinem, "Go Right Ahead and Ask Me Anything," 149.

46 Hoge, "Truman Capote Swings in the Sun."

47 Dewey, letter to Tom Shaw, 14 Oct. 1967.

48 Norden, "*Playboy* Interview: Truman Capote," 169.

49 *Newsweek*, "In Capote Country," 96.

50 Crowther, "Graphic Quadruple Murder," 59.

51 Crowther, "The Ten Best Films of 1967."

52 Knight, "Cold Blood, Calm Reflection."

53 Sheed, review of *In Cold Blood*.

54 *Time*, "Anatomy of a Murder."

55 Jennings, "Truman Capote Talks," 53.

56 Robertson, "Capote Says Curbs on Police Hurt 'The Innocent.'" In a follow-up article in the *New York Times* addressing Capote's testimony, Professor Yale Kamisar of the University of Michigan Law School lambastes Capote's comments as "arrant nonsense" (Zion, "Capote's View on Confessions Scored," 36).

57 *Newsweek*, "Other Voices, Other Rooms," 27.

58 Gould, "Truman Capote Defines His Concept of Justice."

59 Buckley, *The Governor Listeth*, 91.

60 *Good Company*, Nov. 1967.

61 *Firing Line*, 3 Sept. 1968.

62 Gould, "Capote Is at Odds with A.B.C."

63 *Time*, "Truman and TV," 73.

64 O'Connor, "A Diverse Trio."

65 O'Connor, "Capote Studies the Police."

66 Alda, *Never Have Your Dog Stuffed*, 137–38.

67 O'Connor, "C.B.S. Adapts Capote's 'The Glass House.'"

68 Parish, *Gays and Lesbians in Mainstream Cinema*, 159.

69 *Newsweek*, Newsmakers, 38.

70 *Washington Post*, "No Capote Bylines."

71 Ruas, *Conversations with American Writers*, 55.

72 Grobel, *Conversations with Capote*, 160.

73 Daniel, *Tough as Nails*, 174.

74 Appelo, "Partners in Crime."

CHAPTER 6   Turning a Princess into a Star

1 Preminger, *Preminger*, 78.

2 See, for example, Capote, "Blind Items," for his thematic use of the Diaghilev legend in telling contemporary gossip.

3   In *Laura*, Princess Lee Bouvier Radziwill is credited as Lee Bouvier, and so I refer to her by that name in this chapter; however, when quoting commentary referring to her as Radziwill, I do not alter the quotation. Bouvier married Prince Stanisław Albrecht "Stash" Radziwiłł in 1959; they divorced in 1974.

4   Clarke, *Too Brief a Treat*, 448. Although Capote never portrayed Diaghilev on-screen, in *Answered Prayers* he paints him as a "killer fruit . . . a certain kind of queer who has Freon refrigerating his bloodstream" (*AP* 8).

5   Shivas, "'Laura'—In Blue Blood."

6   On the early casting of Bouvier in *Voice of the Turtle*, see Gent, "Lee Bouvier Gets Role in a TV Play."

7   *The David Susskind Show: Truman Capote Tells All.*

8   Clarke, "Bye Society," 124.

9   Specifically, the *Oxford English Dictionary* defines this usage of "tread" as the "action of the male bird in coition" and dates it to the thirteenth century. This coded reference to male sexuality in Treadwell's name further establishes her as more sexually powerful than Lydecker.

10 Preminger, *Preminger*, 73.

11 Russo, *The Celluloid Closet*, 46.

12 The dialogue follows Preminger's film, in which Lydecker asks, "Is this the home of a dame?"

13 Capote's dialogue echoes Preminger's film in this scene.

14 In Preminger's *Laura*, McPherson states that Treadwell identified Redfern's body, but the scene is not depicted on camera.

15 Gould, "Cashing In on Crashing Bores."

16 Ibid.

17 Gould, "Theme Song Is Still the Best Asset of 'Laura,'" 75.

18 For example, see Shivas, "'Laura'—In Blue Blood."

19 Plimpton, *Truman Capote*, 360.

20 *The David Susskind Show: Truman Capote Tells All.*

21 Zoerink, "Truman Capote Talks about His Crowd," 54.

22 Vespa, "Sued by Gore Vidal," 35.

23 Ibid., 35–36.

24 *People*, "Going Home: Truman Capote," 58.

25 Vespa, "Sued by Gore Vidal," 36. For a more detailed account of Capote's feud with Vidal and Radziwill, see "Jackie-O., Gore Vidal, and Joseph-Who?" in Grobel, *Conversations with Capote*, 175–84.

1 D. L. Keith, "An Interview with Truman Capote," 38.
2 Clarke, *Too Brief a Treat*, 282–83.
3 Capote, "A Christmas Memory," *Ladies' Home Journal*, 87.
4 Mailer, "The Capote Perplex."
5 Gould, "Capote's 'A Christmas Memory.'"
6 Tallmer, "Truman Capote, Man about Town."
7 Carmody, "Capote and Friends."
8 Steinem, "Go Right Ahead," 149.
9 In Capote's story, Rose's name is Sarah.
10 Gould, "The Paths to Eden."
11 *Time*, "The Nights before Christmas," 35. In television parlance, "black week" is the period surrounding Christmas, when audience numbers typically sag.
12 Brickell, *O. Henry Memorial Award*, xiv.
13 *Mademoiselle*, "Capote and the Perrys."
14 Thompson, "Carnegie Cinema Has Trilogy by Capote."
15 *Ladies' Home Journal*, "Truman Capote's Thanksgiving," 123.
16 *Time*, "Truman and TV," 73.
17 Gould, "Thanksgiving Story."
18 Steinem, "Go Right Ahead," 148.
19 Eleanor Perry, letter to the editor, *New York Times Magazine*.
20 Plimpton, *Truman Capote*, 55.

CHAPTER 8. Capote's Southern Childhoods

1 Beaton and Tynan, *Persona Grata*, 29.
2 *Time*, "Private Light," 110.
3 Barry, "Short Stories of Truman Capote," 2.
4 Fiedler, "Capote's Tales," 396, and "The Profanation of the Child," 26.
5 Fiedler, *No! in Thunder*, 284.
6 Harrington, memo to Jerry Wald.
7 For the homoerotic elements of sailor culture, see Baker and Stanley, *Hello Sailor!*
8 In Capote's theatrical script, Collin's surname is Talbo, but in Capote's novella and in Charles Matthau's film of *The Grass Harp*, the character's surname is Fenwick.
9 Drutman, "Capote: End of the Affair."
10 Capote, *The Grass Harp: A Play in Two Acts*, 66.

11   Gould, "'Grass Harp': Capote's Work on Free Human Spirit."

12   *The Grass Harp: Production Notes*, 3.

13   Laurie, *Learning to Live Out Loud*, 314.

14   Capote, "Holly and Hemlock," 3; Edelman and Kupferberg, *Matthau*, 88.

15   Clarke, *Too Brief a Treat*, 445.

16   *The Grass Harp: Production Notes*, 4.

17   Laurie, *Learning to Live Out Loud*, 317.

18   Martin, "Fanatic Tale Is as Overwrought as Its Subject."

19   Meyer, "'Grass Harp' Feels Stepped On"; Bernard, "Capote Film Plays on the 'Harp' Strings."

20   Stack, "'Grass Harp' Plays Its Story Sweetly"; Van Gelder, "Misfits and Mischief Makers."

21   O'Shea, letter to Alan Schwartz.

22   O'Shea, letter to Truman Capote. For Capote's disastrous relationship with O'Shea, see Clarke, *Capote*, 443–60, 499–508, 522–32.

23   Capote and McBride, "Children on Their Birthdays" teleplay.

24   "The Making of *Children on Their Birthdays*."

CHAPTER 9   Capote's Unfinished Business

1   Capote, "Answered Prayers," unpublished and unfilmed screenplay.

2   Capote, "Straight Face: A Treatment."

3   Chandler, *Farewell, My Lovely*, 325.

4   Capote, "Tyranny."

5   Norden, "*Playboy* Interview: Truman Capote," 60.

6   Williams, *Memoirs*, 178.

7   Hatch, review of *The Great Gatsby*, 446.

8   Michener, "Cooling the Jazz Age."

9   Bart, "The Beautiful and Damned," 140.

10   Clarke, *Capote*, 437.

11   Clayton, "Comments."

12   Bart, "The Beautiful and Damned," 140.

13   Sinyard, *Jack Clayton*, 172n9.

14   Capote, "The Great Gatsby."

15   Houston, "*The Innocents*," 114.

16   Clayton, "Comments."

17   Fitzgerald, *The Great Gatsby*, 66.

18   Ibid., 92.

19   Ibid., 189.

20 Warhol, "Sunday with Mister C.," 30.

21 Greenfeld, "Truman Capote, the Movie Star?" 17.

22 Clayton, "Comments."

23 Gent, "N.B.C. Arranges Program Exchange with B.B.C."

24 Capote, "Uncle Sam's Hard Luck Hotel."

25 Capote and Leaf, "Dead Loss."

26 Ruas, *Conversations with American Writers*, 41.

27 Ibid., 54.

28 Ibid.

29 Actors considered from Grobel, *Conversations with Capote*, 155; Capote quote in Windham, *Lost Friendships*, 156–57. From the date of this correspondence, Capote's phrase "that picture by that man" appears to refer to Forman's adaptation of E. L. Doctorow's *Ragtime*.

30 Clarke, *Too Brief a Treat*, 461; Grobel, *Conversations with Capote*, 156.

CHAPTER 10   Playing Capote

1 Collins, "Twenty Questions: Truman Capote," 270.

2 Kovacs, Percy Dovetonsils skits: "Leslie the Mean Animal Trainer," "Ode to a Germ's Eye Viewpoint," "Ode to Dieting," "Ode to Mona Lisa," and "Ode to Autumn." For a study of Kovacs's influence on early television comedy, see Horton, *Ernie Kovacs and Early TV Comedy*, esp. 18–32 and, for Percy Dovetonsils, 43–44.

3 Brinnin, *Truman Capote*, 142.

4 *Nichols and May: Take Two.*

5 *Kraft Music Hall: The Kopykats.*

6 *Rich Little's Christmas Carol.*

7 Vespa, "Sued by Gore Vidal," 36.

8 Quotations taken from Jay Presson Allen, *Tru.* Kirk Browning's production of the play, starring Robert Morse, differs slightly. This witticism is discussed in chapter 1, p. XXX.

9 This quotation is discussed in chapter 2, p. XXX.

10 Capote mentions a story written during his childhood titled "Old Mr. Busybody" in his interview with Hill, "The Art of Fiction XVII: Truman Capote," claiming, "I had been noticing the activities of some neighbors who were up to no good, so I wrote a kind of *roman à clef* called 'Old Mr. Busybody' and entered it in the contest. The first installment appeared one Sunday, under my real name of Truman Streckfus Persons. Only somebody suddenly realized that I was serving up a local scandal as fiction, and

the second installment never appeared" (37). The story's publication in the *Mobile Press Register* remains unconfirmed.

11 "The Making of *Capote*."

12 Futterman, *Capote: The Shooting Script*, 113.

13 Ibid., 114.

14 Clarke recounts this anecdote in *Capote*, 204.

15 On Capote's claims about inventing the nonfiction novel, see chapter 5, p. **<xref>**000

16 Hoffman and Miller, commentary track of *Capote*.

17 Ibid.

18 Ibid.

19 Futterman, *Capote: The Shooting Script*, 131; Hoffman and Miller, commentary track of *Capote*.

20 Plimpton, *Truman Capote*, ix.

21 McGrath, commentary track of *Infamous*.

22 For various hypotheses concerning whether Capote and Smith engaged in a sexual relationship, see Voss, *Truman Capote and the Legacy of "In Cold Blood,"* 120. No conclusive evidence corroborates this supposition.

23 McGrath, commentary track of *Infamous*.

24 *The David Susskind Show: Truman Capote Tells All.*

Cinema Capoteana

54. Dir. and screenplay Mark Christopher. Perf. Ryan Phillippe, Salma Hayek, Neve
Campbell, and Mike Myers, with Louis Negin as Truman Capote. Miramax, 1998.

Annie Hall. Dir. and screenplay Woody Allen. Perf. Woody Allen and Diane Keaton,
with an uncredited cameo by Truman Capote. MGM, 1977.

Beat the Devil. Dir. John Huston. Screenplay by Truman Capote and John Huston,
adapted from a novel by Claud Cockburn (as James Helvick). Perf. Humphrey
Bogart, Jennifer Jones, Peter Lorre, and Gina Lollobrigida. Santana Pictures, 1953.

Breakfast at Tiffany's. Dir. Blake Edwards. Screenplay by George Axelrod, based on a
novella by Truman Capote. Perf. Audrey Hepburn, George Peppard, Patricia Neal,
Buddy Ebsen, and Mickey Rooney. Paramount, 1961.

Capote. Dir. Bennett Miller. Screenplay by Dan Futterman. Perf. Philip Seymour
Hoffman as Truman Capote, Catherine Keener, Chris Cooper, Bruce Greenwood,
Clifton Collins, and Mark Pellegrino. Sony Pictures Classics, 2005.

Children on Their Birthdays. Dir. Mark Medoff. Screenplay by Douglas Sloan,
adapted from a story by Truman Capote. Perf. Sheryl Lee, Christopher McDonald,
Joe Pichler, Tania Raymonde, and Tom Arnold. Crusader Entertainment, 2002.

A Christmas Memory. Dir. Frank Perry. Screenplay by Truman Capote and Eleanor
Perry, adapted from a story by Truman Capote. Perf. Geraldine Page and Donnie
Melvin, with narration by Truman Capote. ABC, 1966.

A Christmas Memory. Dir. Glenn Jordan. Teleplay by Duane Poole, adapted from a
story by Truman Capote. Perf. Patty Duke, Piper Laurie, and Eric Lloyd. Hallmark
Entertainment, 1997.

The Glass House. Dir. Tom Gries. Teleplay by Tracy Keenan Wynn, adapted from
a story by Truman Capote and Wyatt Cooper. Perf. Alan Alda, Vic Morrow, and
Billy Dee Williams. Tomorrow Entertainment, 1972.

The Grass Harp. Dir. Word Baker and Hal Gerson. Prod. David Susskind. Play by
Truman Capote. Perf. Lillian Gish, Carmen Mathews, Nick Hyams, Georgia
Burke, Russell Collins, and Ed Asner. Talent Associates, 1960.

The Grass Harp. Dir. Charles Matthau. Screenplay by Stirling Silliphant and Kirk
Ellis, adapted from a novella by Truman Capote. Perf. Edward Furlong, Piper

Laurie, Jack Lemmon, Walter Matthau, Roddy McDowall, Sissy Spacek, and Mary Steenburgen. Fine Line Features, 1996.

In Cold Blood. Dir. Richard Brooks. Screenplay by Richard Brooks, adapted from a novel by Truman Capote. Perf. Robert Blake, Scott Wilson, and John Forsythe. Columbia Pictures, 1967.

In Cold Blood. Dir. Jonathan Kaplan. Teleplay by Benedict Fitzgerald, adapted from a novel by Truman Capote. Perf. Anthony Edwards, Eric Roberts, and Sam Neill. Pacific Motion Pictures, 1996.

Indiscretion of an American Wife. Dir. Vittorio De Sica. Screenplay by Truman Capote, adapted from a story by Cesare Zavattini. Perf. Jennifer Jones, Montgomery Clift, and Richard Beymer. Columbia Pictures, 1953.

Infamous. Dir. Douglas McGrath. Screenplay by Douglas McGrath, adapted from an oral history by George Plimpton. Perf. Toby Jones as Truman Capote, Daniel Craig, Sandra Bullock, Sigourney Weaver, and Jeff Daniels. Warner Independent, 2006.

The Innocents. Dir. Jack Clayton. Screenplay by William Archibald and Truman Capote, adapted from the novella *The Turn of the Screw* by Henry James. Perf. Deborah Kerr, Megs Jenkins, and Michael Redgrave. Twentieth Century Fox, 1961.

Isn't She Great. Dir. Andrew Bergman. Screenplay by Paul Rudnick. Perf. Bette Midler, Nathan Lane, Stockard Channing, and John Cleese, with Sam Street as Truman Capote. BBC, 2000.

Laura. Dir. John Llewellyn Moxey. Prod. David Susskind. Teleplay by Truman Capote and Thomas W. Phipps. Perf. Lee Bouvier, Robert Stack, and Farley Granger. ABC, 1968.

Murder by Death. Dir. Robert Moore. Screenplay by Neil Simon. Perf. Eileen Brennan, Truman Capote, James Coco, Peter Falk, Alec Guinness, Elsa Lanchester, David Niven, Peter Sellers, Maggie Smith, Nancy Walker, and Estelle Winwood. Columbia Pictures, 1976.

One Christmas. Dir. Tony Bill. Teleplay by Duane Poole, adapted from a story by Truman Capote. Perf. Katharine Hepburn, Henry Winkler, Swoosie Kurtz, and T. J. Lowther. Karpf-Davis Entertainment Television, 1994.

Other Voices, Other Rooms. Dir. David Rocksavage. Screenplay by Sara Flanigan and David Rocksavage, adapted from a novel by Truman Capote. Perf. Lothaire Bluteau, David Speck, Anna Levine, and April Turner. Golden Eye Films, 1995.

The Thanksgiving Visitor. Dir. Frank Perry. Teleplay by Eleanor Perry, adapted from a short story by Truman Capote. Perf. Geraldine Page and Michael Kearney, with narration by Truman Capote. ABC, 1968.

Trilogy. Dir. Richard Perry. Screenplay by Eleanor Perry and Truman Capote, adapted from short stories by Truman Capote. Perf. Geraldine Page, Mildred Natwick, Martin Balsam, Maureen Stapleton, and Susan Dunfee. Francis Productions, 1969.

Tru. Dir. Kirk Browning. Script by Jay Presson Allen. Filmed at the Shubert Theatre, Chicago, Nov. 1991. *American Playhouse*, PBS, 1992.

Watchmen. Dir. Zack Snyder. Screenplay by David Hayter and Alex Tse, based on a graphic novel written by Alan Moore and drawn by Dave Gibbons. Perf. Malin Ackerman, Billy Crudup, Matthew Goode, and Jackie Earle Haley, with Greg Armstrong-Morris as Truman Capote. Warner Bros. and Paramount, 2009.

Works Cited

Abbott, Steven, and John Mitzel. "Gore Vidal: The *Fag Rag* Interview." *Fag Rag* 7–8 (Winter–Spring 1974): 1–9.

Adams, Dale. "Twice Convicted, Once Executed: A Literary Naturalist's Interpretation of Richard Brooks's Film *In Cold Blood.*" *Literature/Film Quarterly* 37.4 (2009): 246–61.

Alda, Alan. *Never Have Your Dog Stuffed, and Other Things I've Learned.* New York: Random House, 2005.

Alexander, Shana. "A Nonfictional Visit with Truman Capote." *Life* 18 Feb. 1966: 22.

All About Eve. Dir. Joseph Mankiewicz. Perf. Bette Davis, Anne Baxter, and George Sanders. Twentieth Century Fox, 1950.

Allen, Jay Presson. *Tru: From the Words and Works of Truman Capote.* New York: Samuel French, 2013.

Allmendinger, Blake. "Female Influence in 'My Side of the Matter.'" Bloom 51–62.

America. Review of *The Innocents.* 13 Jan. 1962: 480–81.

Anderson, Lindsay. "In Brief: *Beat the Devil.*" *Sight and Sound* 23 (Jan.–Mar. 1954): 147–48.

Appelo, Tim. "Partners in Crime: Remaking 'In Cold Blood'—Anthony Edwards and Eric Roberts Stretch to Remake Truman Capote's Crime Story." *Entertainment Weekly* 22 Nov. 1996, ew.com.

Archibald, William. *The Innocents.* New York: Coward-McCann, 1950.

Archibald, William, and Truman Capote. *The Innocents* screenplay. 1961. British Film Institute Archives.

Axelrod, George. *Breakfast at Tiffany's.* First draft screenplay, 24 Aug. 1959. Margaret Herrick Library Archive.

Baker, Paul, and Jo Stanley. *Hello Sailor! The Hidden History of Gay Life at Sea.* London: Longman, 2003.

Bannerman, James. "Capote's Unanswered Questions." *Maclean's* 5 Mar. 1966: 42.

Barnes, Peter. "The Director on Horseback." *Quarterly of Film, Radio, and Television* 10.3 (1956): 281–87.

Barry, Iris. "Short Stories of Truman Capote." *New York Herald Tribune Weekly Book Review* 27 Feb. 1949: 2.

Bart, Peter. "The Beautiful and Damned." *GQ* May 2000: 139–43.

——. "'In Cold Blood'—On the Firing Line." *New York Times* 16 Oct. 1966: 123.

Beaton, Cecil, and Kenneth Tynan. *Persona Grata*. London: Wingate, 1953.

Beaver, Frank. *Dictionary of Film Terms*. New York: McGraw-Hill, 1983.

Benshoff, Harry M., and Sean Griffin. *Queer Images: A History of Gay and Lesbian Film in America*. Lanham, Md.: Rowman & Littlefield, 2006.

Bernard, Jami. "Capote Film Plays on the 'Harp' Strings." *New York Daily News* 11 Oct. 1996: 70.

Black, Joel. *The Reality Effect: Film Culture and the Graphic Imperative*. New York: Routledge, 2002.

Bloom, Harold, ed. *Truman Capote*. Philadelphia: Chelsea House, 2003.

Bogart, Humphrey. Letters to John Huston, 19 and 26 Nov. 1952. Margaret Herrick Library Archive 5.f-47.

Bogdanovich, Peter. "Bogie in Excelsis." *Roger Ebert's Book of Film*. Ed. Roger Ebert. New York: Norton, 1997. 92–103.

Bosworth, Patricia. *Montgomery Clift: A Biography*. New York: Harcourt Brace Jovanovich, 1978.

"*Breakfast at Tiffany's*: The Making of a Classic." *Breakfast at Tiffany's*. Dir. Blake Edwards. 1961. Paramount Centennial Collection, 2009. DVD.

Breen, Joseph (Motion Picture Association of America). Letters to Jess Morgan, Santana Pictures, 12 Mar. 1952 and 13 Feb. 1953. Margaret Herrick Library Archive 5.f-48.

Brian, Denis. "The Importance of Knowing Ernest." *Esquire* Feb. 1972: 98–101, 164–70.

——. *Murderers and Other Friendly People: The Public and Private Worlds of Interviewers*. New York: McGraw-Hill, 1972.

Brickell, Herschel, ed. *O. Henry Memorial Award Prize Stories of 1946*. Garden City, N.Y.: Doubleday, 1946.

Brinnin, John Malcolm. *Truman Capote: Dear Heart, Old Buddy*. New York: Delacorte, 1986.

Brooks, Richard. "Breakdown of Novel," ts. Margaret Herrick Library Archive, "*In Cold Blood*—Breakdown of Novel" folder.

——. "Breakdown of Novel and Breakdown by Character / Flow of Action," ts. Margaret Herrick Library Archive, "*In Cold Blood*—Breakdowns #20 folder.

Brown, Cecil. "Plate du Jour: Soul Food: Truman Capote on Black Culture." Waldmeir and Waldmeir 31–36.

Buckley, William F., Jr. *The Governor Listeth: A Book of Inspired Political Revelations*. New York: Putnam, 1970.

Burke, Tom. "The Sweeter Options of John D. MacArthur and Truman Capote." *Esquire* Dec. 1970: 210–14, 255–69.

Burstein, Patricia. "Tiny Yes, But a Terror? Do Not Be Fooled by Truman Capote in Repose." *People* 10 May 1976: 12–17.

Canby, Vincent. "Simon's Breezy 'Murder by Death.'" *New York Times* 24 June 1976: 26.

Capote, Truman. "Answered Prayers." Unpublished and unfilmed screenplay. New York Public Library Capote Archives, box 34, folder 1.

——. *Answered Prayers: The Unfinished Novel.* New York: Random House, 1987.

——. "Blind Items." *Ladies' Home Journal* Jan. 1974: 81+.

——. *Breakfast at Tiffany's, and Three Stories.* 1958. New York: Vintage, 1993.

——. "Capote on Theatre: A Negative View." Interview. *Playbill.* Special Milwaukee edition for the Palace Theatre production of *Fiddler on the Roof* (1966): 3–4, 13.

——. *A Christmas Memory.* New York: Random House, 1956. Reprinted in *Ladies' Home Journal* Dec. 1966: 87+.

——. *The Complete Stories of Truman Capote.* New York: Random House, 2004.

——. *The Dogs Bark: Public People and Private Places.* New York: Random House, 1973.

——. "Elizabeth Taylor." *Ladies' Home Journal* Dec. 1974: 72–78, 151.

——. *The Grass Harp, including A Tree of Night and Other Stories.* 1952. New York: Vintage, 1993.

——. *The Grass Harp: A Play in Two Acts.* New York: Dramatists Play Service, 1954.

——. "The Great Gatsby." Unpublished and unfilmed screenplay, 1971. Margaret Herrick Library Archive 99.f-916.

——. "Holly and Hemlock: Truman Capote Lists the Books He Will Give His Friends for Christmas." *Chicago Tribune Book World* 1 Dec. 1968: 1, 3.

——. *In Cold Blood: A True Account of a Multiple Murder and Its Consequences.* New York: Random House, 1965.

——. *Indiscretion of an American Wife* screenplay. Carbon ts. Truman Capote Papers of the New York Public Library, box 34.

——. *Local Color.* New York: Random House, 1950.

——. *The Muses Are Heard.* New York: Random House, 1956.

——. *Music for Chameleons.* New York: Random House, 1980.

——. *Other Voices, Other Rooms.* New York: Random House, 1948.

——. *Portraits and Observations: The Essays of Truman Capote.* New York: Modern Library, 2008.

——. "Straight Face: A Treatment." Unpublished and unfilmed screenplay. New York Public Library Capote Archives, box 16, folder 1.

——. *Summer Crossing.* Afterword by Allan U. Schwartz. New York: Random House, 2006.

——— . Telegram to Richard Brooks, undated. Margaret Herrick Library Archive, "*In Cold Blood*—Script #1" file.

——— . "Tyranny." Unpublished and unfilmed screenplay. New York Public Library Capote Archives, box 21, folder 2 (screenplay) and box 21, folder 3 (synopsis).

——— . "Uncle Sam's Hard Luck Hotel." Unpublished and unfilmed teleplay. New York Public Library Capote Archives, box 21, folder 4 (8 Nov. 1973), and box 21, folder 5 (revised by Joseph Landon, 24 Jan. 1974).

Capote, Truman, and Richard Avedon. *Observations*. New York: Simon & Schuster, 1959.

Capote, Truman, and Paul Leaf. "Dead Loss." Unpublished and unfilmed screenplay, 3 Mar. 1976. New York Public Library Capote Archives, box 4, folder 1.

Capote, Truman, and Robert McBride. "Children on Their Birthdays." Unpublished and unfilmed teleplay, Sept. 1979. New York Public Library Capote Archives.

Capote, Truman, Eleanor Perry, and Frank Perry. *Trilogy: An Experiment in Multimedia*. New York: Macmillan, 1968.

Cardullo, Bert. "Actor-Become-Auteur: The Neorealist Films of Vittorio De Sica." *Massachusetts Review* 41.2 (2000): 173–92.

Carmody, Deirdre. "Capote and Friends See 'In Cold Blood' at Quiet Screening." *New York Times* 13 Dec. 1967: 53.

Catholic World. Review of *Indiscretion of an American Wife*. May 1954: 143–44.

Chandler, Raymond. *Farewell, My Lovely*. 1940. *The Big Sleep* and *Farewell, My Lovely*. New York: Modern Library, 1995.

Chapman, Robert L., ed. *New Dictionary of American Slang*. New York: Harper & Row, 1986.

The Cheap Show. Hosted by Dick Martin. Episode 2, guests Truman Capote and Jill St. John, 1978. UCLA Film and Television Archive.

Chevalier, Jean, and Alain Gheerbrant. *A Dictionary of Symbols*. Trans. John Buchanan-Brown. Oxford: Blackwell, 1994.

Clarke, Gerald. "The Art of Fiction L: Gore Vidal." *Paris Review* 15 (Fall 1974): 130–65.

——— . "Bye Society." *Vanity Fair* Apr. 1988: 118–29, 168–73.

——— . *Capote: A Biography*. New York: Simon & Schuster, 1988.

——— . "Petronius Americanus: The Ways of Gore Vidal." *Atlantic* Mar. 1972: 44–51.

——— , ed. *Too Brief a Treat: The Letters of Truman Capote*. New York: Random House, 2004.

Clayton, Jack. "Comments on Truman Capote Script (as Shown to Truman)." Typewritten memo, Jan. 1972. Margaret Herrick Library Archive, 99.f.917.

Cockburn, Claud. Letter to John Huston, 10 Mar. 1952. Margaret Herrick Library Archive 5.f-50.

Collins, Nancy. "Twenty Questions: Truman Capote." *Playboy* Dec. 1980: 259, 270.

Corliss, Richard. "Radley Metzger, Aristocrat of the Erotic: An Interview." *Film Comment* 9.1 (1973): 19–29.

Crowther, Bosley. "Graphic Quadruple Murder: Capote's 'In Cold Blood' Opens at Cinema I." *New York Times* 15 Dec. 1967: 59.

————. "'The Innocents': Film from James Tale Is at Two Theatres." *New York Times* 26 Dec. 1961: 15.

————. "The Ten Best Films of 1967." *New York Times* 24 Dec. 1967: 55.

Dalzell, Tom. *The Slang of Sin*. Springfield, Mass.: Merriam-Webster, 1998.

Daniel, Douglass K. *Tough as Nails: The Life and Films of Richard Brooks*. Madison: University of Wisconsin Press, 2011.

The David Susskind Show: Truman Capote Tells All. Dir. Chet Lishawa. Prod. Jean Kennedy. Originally aired Feb. 1979. 1984. VHS.

Davis, Deborah. *Party of the Century: The Fabulous Story of Truman Capote and His Black and White Ball*. Hoboken, N.J.: Wiley, 2006.

The Dean Martin Celebrity Roasts: Man of the Hour, Truman Capote. Prod. Greg Garrison. 1973. Guthy-Renker Entertainment, 2003. DVD.

De Sica, Vittorio. "De Sica on De Sica." *Vittorio De Sica: Contemporary Perspectives*. Ed. Howard Curle and Stephen Snyder. Toronto: University of Toronto Press, 2000. 22–49.

————. "Hollywood Shocked Me." *Films and Filming* 2.5 (Feb. 1946): 12–13.

Devlin, Albert J., ed. *Conversations with Tennessee Williams*. Jackson: University Press of Mississippi, 1986.

Dewey, Alvin. Letter to Tom Shaw, Columbia Studios, 14 Oct. 1967. Margaret Herrick Library Archive, "*In Cold Blood* —Al and Marie Dewey #33" folder.

The Dick Cavett Show: Comic Legends. Perf. Dick Cavett, Groucho Marx, Truman Capote. Prod. Judy Englander. May 25, 1971. Daphne Productions, 2006. DVD.

Doty, Alexander. *Flaming Classics: Queering the Film Canon*. New York: Routledge, 2000.

————. *Making Things Perfectly Queer: Interpreting Mass Culture*. Minneapolis: University of Minnesota Press, 1993.

Drutman, Irving. "Capote: End of the Affair." *New York Times* 20 Nov. 1966: D3.

Dunphy, Jack. *"Dear Genius . . .": A Memoir of My Life with Truman Capote*. New York: McGraw-Hill, 1987.

Dyer, Richard. *Heavenly Bodies: Film Stars and Society*. New York: St. Martin's, 1986.

Ebert, Roger. "Beat the Devil." rogerebert.com. 26 Nov. 2000.

Ebsen, Buddy. *The Other Side of Oz*. Ed. Stephen Cox. Newport Beach, Calif.: Donovan, 1993.

Edelman, Rob, and Audrey Kupferberg. *Matthau: A Life*. Lanham, Md.: Taylor Trade, 2002.

Epstein, Edward Z. *Portrait of Jennifer: A Biography of Jennifer Jones.* New York: Simon & Schuster, 1995.

Fiedler, Leslie A. "Capote's Tales." *Nation* 2 Apr. 1949: 395–96.

——. *No! in Thunder: Essays on Myth and Literature.* Boston: Beacon, 1960.

——. "The Profanation of the Child." *New Leader* 23 June 1958: 26–29.

Film Society Review. Review of *Beat the Devil.* Jan. 1966: 13.

Firing Line. Hosted by William F. Buckley Jr. Interview of Truman Capote, 3 Sept. 1968. Hoover Institution, 2010. DVD.

Fitzgerald, F. Scott. *The Great Gatsby.* 1925. New York: Scribner, 1992.

Fleming, Anne Taylor. "The Private World of Truman Capote." *New York Times Magazine* 9 July 1978: 22–25.

Folks, Jeffrey. "Southern Renascence." *The Companion to Southern Literature.* Ed. Joseph M. Flora and Lucinda H. MacKethan. Baton Rouge: Louisiana State University Press, 2002. 835–40.

Fowler, Doreen. Introduction. Fowler and Abadie vii–xii.

Fowler, Doreen, and Ann J. Abadie, ed. *Faulkner and the Southern Renaissance.* Jackson: University Press of Mississippi, 1981.

Frankel, Haskell. "The Author." *Saturday Review* 22 Jan. 1966: 36–37.

Fremont-Smith, Eliot. "Literature-by-Consensus." *New York Times* 26 Jan. 1966: 28.

French, Warren, ed. *The South and Film.* Jackson: University Press of Mississippi, 1981.

Frost, David. "When Does a Writer Become a Star? Truman Capote." *The Americans.* New York: Stein & Day, 1970. 17–23.

Futterman, Dan. *Capote: The Shooting Script.* Foreword by Gerald Clarke. London: Hern, 2006.

Gent, George. "Lee Bouvier Gets Role in a TV Play." *New York Times* 29 June 1967: 87.

——. "N.B.C. Arranges Program Exchange with B.B.C." *New York Times* 27 June 1973: 111.

Gill, Brendan. *Here at The New Yorker.* New York: Random House, 1975.

——. Review of *The Innocents. New Yorker* 6 Jan. 1962: 72.

Girson, Rochelle. "'48's Nine." *Saturday Review of Literature* 32 (12 Feb. 1949): 12–14.

"A Golightly Gathering." *Breakfast at Tiffany's.* Dir. Blake Edwards. 1961. Paramount Centennial Collection, 2009. DVD.

Good Company. Hosted by F. Lee Bailey. ABC, Nov. 1967.

Goode, Sarah. *Understanding and Addressing Adult Sexual Attraction to Children: A Study of Paedophiles in Contemporary Society.* New York: Routledge, 2010.

Gould, Jack. "Capote Is at Odds with A.B.C." *New York Times* 31 Oct. 1968: 95.

——. "Capote's 'A Christmas Memory.'" *New York Times* 22 Dec. 1966: 50.

——. "Cashing In on Crashing Bores." *New York Times* 4 Feb. 1968: 29.

———. "'Grass Harp': Capote's Work on Free Human Spirit Begins on 'The Play of the Week.'" *New York Times* 29 Mar. 1960: 75.

———. "'The Paths to Eden': Maureen Stapleton and Martin Balsam Star in Sensitive Drama by Capote." *New York Times* 18 Dec. 1967: 95.

———. "Thanksgiving Story: Capote's Vignette of Boyhood Warmly Done— Geraldine Page Repeats Role." *New York Times* 29 Nov. 1968: 91.

———. "Theme Song Is Still the Best Asset of 'Laura.'" *New York Times* 25 Jan. 1968: 75.

———. "Truman Capote Defines His Concept of Justice." *New York Times* 15 June 1968: 71.

Gow, Gordon. "The Way Things Are: Jack Clayton in an Interview." *Films and Filming* Apr. 1974: 10–15.

Grafton, David. *The Sisters: Babe Mortimer Paley, Betsey Roosevelt Whitney, Minnie Astor Fosburgh; The Life and Times of the Fabulous Cushing Sisters.* New York: Villard, 1992.

The Grass Harp: Production Notes. New York: FineLine Features, 1996.

Green, Paul. *Jennifer Jones: The Life and Films.* Jefferson, N.C.: McFarland, 2011.

Greenfeld, Josh. "Truman Capote, the Movie Star?" *New York Times* 28 Dec. 1975, sec. II: 1, 17.

Gristwood, Sarah. *Breakfast at Tiffany's: The Official 50th Anniversary Companion.* London: Pavilion, 2010.

Grobel, Lawrence. *Conversations with Capote.* New York: New American Library, 1985.

Gross, Louis S. *Redefining the American Gothic: From "Wieland" to "Day of the Dead."* Ann Arbor: UMI Research Press, 1989.

Grunwald, Beverly. "The Literary Aquarium of Truman Capote." *W* 14–21 Nov. 1975: 26.

Hallam, Julia. *Realism and Popular Cinema.* With Margaret Marshment. Manchester: Manchester University Press, 2000.

Hamilton, George. Letter to Richard Brooks, 27 Aug. 1966. Margaret Herrick Library Archive, "*In Cold Blood*—Casting Correspondence #2C."

Hanson, Ellis. "Screwing with Children in Henry James." *GLQ* 9.3 (2003): 367–91.

Harrington, Curtis. Memo to Jerry Wald, 5 Aug. 1957. Margaret Herrick Library Archive, Curtis Harrington Papers, Jerry Wald Production, f. 636.

Hart, Kylo-Patrick. "Gay Male Spectatorship and the Films of Montgomery Clift." *Popular Culture Review* 10.1 (1999): 69–82.

Hartung, Philip. Review of *Indiscretion of an American Wife. Commonweal* 7 May 1954: 117–18.

Haskell, Molly. *From Reverence to Rape: The Treatment of Women in the Movies.* 2nd ed. Chicago: University of Chicago Press, 1987.

Hatch, Robert. Review of *The Great Gatsby*. *Nation* 6 Apr. 1974: 446.

Helvick, James [Claud Cockburn]. *Beat the Devil*. Philadelphia: Lippincott, 1951.

Heyne, Eric. "Toward a Theory of Literary Nonfiction." Bloom 63–76.

H.H.T. "The Screen in Review: 'Beat the Devil.'" *New York Times* 13 Mar. 1954: 11.

Hill, Pati. "The Art of Fiction XVII: Truman Capote." *Paris Review* 16 (Spring–Summer 1957): 34–51.

Hoffman, Philip Seymour, and Bennett Miller. Commentary track for *Capote*. *Capote / In Cold Blood* Double Feature. Columbia Pictures, 2007. DVD.

Hoge, Alice Albright. "Truman Capote Swings in the Sun." *Chicago Daily News* 24 June 1967, Panorama sec.: 4.

Hollowell, John. "Capote's *In Cold Blood*: The Search for Meaningful Design." Bloom 129–47.

Horton, Andrew. *Ernie Kovacs & Early TV Comedy: Nothing in Moderation*. Austin: University of Texas Press, 2010.

Houston, Penelope. "*The Innocents*." *Sight and Sound* 30.3 (1961): 114–15.

Howard, Jane. "A Nightmare Lived Again." *Life* 12 May 1967: 98–104B.

Huston, John. *An Open Book*. New York: Knopf, 1980.

"*In Cold Blood*: Trailer." *Capote / In Cold Blood* Double Feature. Columbia Pictures, 2007. DVD.

Inge, M. Thomas, ed. *Truman Capote: Conversations*. Jackson: University of Mississippi Press, 1987.

"*The Innocents*: Trailer." *The Innocents*. Dir. Jack Clayton. 1961. 20th Century Fox, 2005. DVD.

James, Henry. *The Turn of the Screw*. 1898. New York: Modern Library, 1930.

Jennings, C. Robert. "Truman Capote Talks, Talks, Talks." *New York* 13 May 1968: 53–55.

Jurow, Martin. *Marty Jurow Seein' Stars: A Show Biz Odyssey*. As told to Philip Wuntch. Dallas: Southern Methodist University Press, 2001.

Kael, Pauline. *I Lost It at the Movies*. Boston: Little, Brown, 1965.

———. *Kiss Kiss Bang Bang*. Boston: Little, Brown, 1968.

Kanfer, Stefan. *Somebody: The Reckless Life and Remarkable Career of Marlon Brando*. New York: Knopf, 2008.

———. *Tough without a Gun: The Life and Extraordinary Afterlife of Humphrey Bogart*. New York: Knopf, 2011.

Karpel, Craig. "We'd Get Along without You Very Well." *Esquire* June 1974: 114+.

Kauffman, Stanley. "Ghosts, Grime, and Grandeur." *New Republic* 8 Jan. 1962: 20–21.

Keith, Don Lee. "An Interview with Truman Capote." *Contempora* 1 (Oct.–Nov. 1970): 36–40.

Keith, Slim. *Slim: Memories of a Rich and Imperfect Life.* With Annette Tapert. New York: Simon & Schuster, 1990.

Kincaid, James R. *Child-Loving: The Erotic Child and Victorian Culture.* New York: Routledge, 1992.

King, Richard H. "Framework of a Renaissance." Fowler and Abadie 3–21.

———. *A Southern Renaissance: The Cultural Awakening of the American South, 1930–1955.* New York: Oxford University Press, 1980.

Knight, Arthur. "Cold Blood, Calm Reflection." *Saturday Review* 30 Dec. 1967: 33.

———. "Innocents Abroad." *Saturday Review* 23 Dec. 1961: 38–39.

———. "A Long Wait between Trains." *Saturday Review* 24 Apr. 1954: 25.

Kostelanetz, Richard. *The End of Intelligent Writing: Literary Politics in America.* New York: Sheed & Ward, 1974.

Kovacs, Ernie. Percy Dovetonsils skits: "Leslie the Mean Animal Trainer," "Ode to a Germ's Eye Viewpoint," "Ode to Dieting," "Ode to Mona Lisa," and "Ode to Autumn." Youtube.com.

Kraft Music Hall: The Kopykats. Dir. Dwight Hemion. Perf. Edie Adams, David Frye, Frank Gorshin, George Kirby, Rich Little, and Will Jordan. NBC, 11 Nov. 1970.

Krämer, Peter. "The Many Faces of Holly Golightly: Truman Capote, *Breakfast at Tiffany's,* and Hollywood." *Film Studies* 5 (2004): 58–65.

Krebs, Albin. Notes on People. *New York Times* 15 Nov. 1977: 34.

Ladies' Home Journal. "Truman Capote's Thanksgiving." Nov. 1968: 122+.

Landy, Marcia. *Italian Film.* Cambridge: Cambridge University Press, 2000.

Laurie, Piper. *Learning to Live Out Loud: A Memoir.* New York: Crown Archetype, 2011.

Lawrence, Amy. *The Passion of Montgomery Clift.* Berkeley: University of California Press, 2010.

Lee, Robert. "Southern Gothic." *The Handbook to Gothic Literature.* Ed. Marie Mulvey-Roberts. New York: New York University Press, 1998. 217–20.

Leff, Leonard. Commentary track for *Indiscretion of an American Wife.* Dir. Vittorio De Sica. 1953. Criterion Collection, 2003. DVD.

Lehman, Peter, and William Luhr. *Blake Edwards.* 2 vols. Athens: Ohio University Press, 1981–89.

———. "'I love New York!': *Breakfast at Tiffany's.*" *City That Never Sleeps: New York and the Filmic Imagination.* Ed. Murray Pomerance. New Brunswick: Rutgers University Press, 2007. 23–31.

Lish, Gordon. *Dear Mr. Capote: A Novel.* New York: Holt, Rinehart & Winston, 1983.

Logan, Joshua. *Movie Stars, Real People, and Me.* New York: Delacorte, 1978.

Long, Barbara. "In Cold Comfort." *Esquire* 65 (June 1966): 124+.

Long, Robert Emmet. *Truman Capote: Enfant Terrible.* New York: Continuum, 2008.

——, ed. *John Huston: Interviews.* Jackson: University Press of Mississippi, 2001.

Mademoiselle. "Capote and the Perrys." Oct. 1967: 141.

——. "Truman Capote on Christmas, Places, Memories." Dec. 1971: 122–23, 176.

Mailer, Norman. *Advertisements for Myself.* New York: Putnam, 1959.

——. "The Capote Perplex: An Open Letter from Norman Mailer." *Rolling Stone* 19 July 1973: 8.

——. "Of a Small and Modest Malignancy, Wicked and Bristling with Dots." *Esquire* Nov. 1977: 125–48.

"The Making of *Capote.*" *Capote / In Cold Blood* Double Feature. Columbia Pictures, 2007. DVD.

"The Making of *Children on Their Birthdays.*" *Children on Their Birthdays.* Dir. Mark Medoff. Artisan Entertainment, 2002. DVD.

Marcus, Millicent. *Italian Film in the Light of Neorealism.* Princeton: Princeton University Press, 1986.

Marill, Alvin H. *Mickey Rooney: His Films, Television Appearances, Radio Work, Stage Shows, and Recordings.* Jefferson, N.C.: McFarland, 2005.

Marple, B. G. Review of *Beat the Devil. Films in Review* 5 (Mar. 1953): 143–44.

Martin, Adrian. "Fanatic Tale Is as Overwrought as Its Subject." *The Age* 5 Nov. 1996, Arts sec.: 5.

Marx, Arthur. *The Nine Lives of Mickey Rooney.* 1986. New York: Berkley, 1987.

Mazzella, Anthony. "'The story . . . held us': *The Turn of the Screw* from Henry James to Jack Clayton." *Henry James Goes to the Movies.* Ed. Susan Griffin. Lexington: University Press of Kentucky, 2002. 11–33.

McCall's. Review of *The Innocents.* Jan. 1962: 14.

McFarlane, Brian. *Novel to Film: An Introduction to the Theory of Adaptation.* Oxford: Clarendon, 1996.

McGrath, Douglas. Commentary track for *Infamous.* Dir. Douglas McGrath. Warner, 2006. DVD.

Medwick, Cathleen. "Truman Capote: An Interview." *Vogue* Dec. 1979: 263, 311–12.

Meyer, George. "'Grass Harp' Feels Stepped On." *Sarasota Herald-Tribune* 11 Oct. 1996: 17.

Michener, Charles. "Cooling the Jazz Age." *Newsweek* 1 Apr. 1974: 72.

Mohrt, Françoise. *The Givenchy Style.* Foreword by Hubert de Givenchy. Paris: Assouline, 1998.

Morley, Margaret. *Larger Than Life: The Biography of Robert Morley.* London: Robson, 1979.

Morris, Oswald. *Huston, We Have a Problem: A Kaleidoscope of Filmmaking Memories*. With Geoffrey Bull. Lanham, Md.: Scarecrow, 2006.

Murray, Edward. "*In Cold Blood*: The Filmic Novel and the Problem of Adaptation." *Literature/Film Quarterly* 1 (1973): 132–37.

Neal, Patricia. *As I Am: An Autobiography*. With Richard De Neut. New York: Simon & Schuster, 1988.

Newquist, Roy. *Counterpoint*. Chicago: Rand McNally, 1964.

Newsweek. "Cutting Room." 17 Jan. 1966: 54.

——. "In Capote Country." 24 Apr. 1967: 94, 96.

——. Newsmakers. 14 Jan. 1974: 38–39.

——. "Other Voices, Other Rooms." 1 Aug. 1966: 26–27.

——. Review of *Indiscretion of an American Wife*. 12 Apr. 1954: 104–5.

——. Review of *The Innocents*. 1 Jan. 1962: 52–53.

Nichols and May: Take Two. Dir. Phillip Schopper. Perf. Mike Nichols and Elaine May. Castle Hill Productions, 1996.

Norden, Eric. "*Playboy* Interview: Truman Capote." *Playboy* Mar. 1968: 51–53+.

O'Connor, John J. "Capote Studies the Police on' Crimewatch.'" *New York Times* 8 May 1973: 87.

——. "C.B.S. Adapts Capote's 'The Glass House.'" *New York Times* 4 Feb. 1972: 63.

——. "A Diverse Trio—Ireland, Jail and Rothschilds." *New York Times* 7 Dec. 1972: 107.

O'Shea, John. Letter to Alan Schwartz, 9 Dec. 1975. New York Public Library Capote Archives, box 23A, folder 5, "Correspondence n.d., 1938, 1961–1975."

——. Letter to Truman Capote, 4 Mar. 1980. New York Public Library Capote Archives, box 23A, folder 6, "Correspondence 1976–1984, 1992."

Packer, Barbara, Laurie Deutsch, Barbara Bussmann, Ann Beattie, and Judi Silverman. "We Talk to . . . Truman Capote." *Mademoiselle* Aug. 1968: 366–67.

Palmer, James. "Cinematic Ambiguity: James's *The Turn of the Screw* and Clayton's *The Innocents*." *Literature/Film Quarterly* 5 (1977): 198–215.

Parish, James Robert. *Gays and Lesbians in Mainstream Cinema*. Jefferson, N.C.: McFarland, 1993.

Parker, Tyler. *Screening the Sexes: Homosexuality in the Movies*. New York: Holt, Rinehart & Winston, 1972.

Parks, Ande, and Chris Samnee. *Capote in Kansas: A Drawn Novel*. Portland, Ore.: Oni, 2005.

Partridge, Eric. *A Dictionary of Slang and Unconventional English*. 8th ed. Ed. Paul Beale. London: Routledge, 2002.

——. *A Dictionary of the Underworld*. London: Routledge, 1949.

People. "Going Home: Truman Capote: The Famous Author Makes One of His

Periodic Visits to the City of His Birth, New Orleans, and Finds Sentiment and Southern Comfort." 26 Jan. 1981: 56–58.

Perry, Eleanor. Letter to the editor, *New York Times Magazine*, 17 July 1978. Margaret Herrick Library Archive, Eleanor Perry Collection, folder 48, "*Trilogy*."

Plimpton, George. "The Story behind a Nonfiction Novel." *New York Times Book Review* 16 Jan. 1966: 2–3, 38–43.

——. *Truman Capote: In Which Various Friends, Enemies, Acquaintances, and Detractors Recall His Turbulent Career*. New York: Nan A. Talese, Doubleday, 1997.

Powers, Kim. *Capote in Kansas: A Ghost Story*. New York: Carroll & Graf, 2007.

Pratley, Gerald. *The Cinema of John Huston*. New York: Barnes, 1977.

Preminger, Otto. *Preminger: An Autobiography*. Garden City, N.Y.: Doubleday, 1977.

Rebello, Stephen. "Jack Clayton's *The Innocents*." *Cinefantastique* 13.5 (June–July 1983): 51–55.

Recchia, Edward. "An Eye for an I: Adapting Henry James's *The Turn of the Screw* to the Screen." *Literature/Film Quarterly* 15.1 (1987): 28–35.

Red River. Dir. Howard Hawks. Perf. John Wayne and Montgomery Clift. 1948.

Rich Little's Christmas Carol. Dir. Trevor Evans. Perf. Rich Little. HBO, 1982.

Robertson, Nan. "Capote Says Curbs on Police Hurt 'The Innocent.'" *New York Times* 22 July 1966: 11.

Robinson, Selma. "The Legend of 'Little T.'" *PM Picture News* 8 (14 Mar. 1949): 6–8.

Rolo, Charles. "The New Bohemia." *Flair* Feb. 1950: 27–29, 116–18.

Rooney, Mickey. *Life Is Too Short*. New York: Villard, 1991.

Ross, Lillian. *Picture*. New York: Rinehart, 1952.

Ruas, Charles. *Conversations with American Writers*. New York: Knopf, 1985.

Russo, Vito. *The Celluloid Closet: Homosexuality in the Movies*. Rev. ed. New York: Harper & Row, 1987.

Samuels, Charles Thomas. *Encountering Directors*. New York: Putnam, 1972.

Savoy, Eric. "The Face of the Tenant: A Theory of the American Gothic." *American Gothic: New Interventions in a National Narrative*. Ed. Robert K. Martin and Eric Savoy. Iowa City: University of Iowa Press, 1998. 3–19.

Selznick, David. Interoffice communications to John Huston, 30 Jan. and 23 Feb. 1953. Margaret Herrick Library Archive 6.f-54.

——. *Memo from David O. Selznick*. Ed. Rudy Behlmer. 1972. New York: Modern Library, 2000.

——. Memo to John Huston, undated. Margaret Herrick Library Archive, John Huston Papers, f. 54.

Sennett, Ted. *Masters of Menace: Greenstreet and Lorre*. New York: Dutton, 1979.

Shearer, Stephen Michael. *Patricia Neal: An Unquiet Life*. Lexington: University Press of Kentucky, 2006.

Sheed, Wilfrid. Review of *In Cold Blood*. *Esquire* 69 (Mar. 1968): 52.

Shepherd, Richard. Commentary track for *Breakfast at Tiffany's*. Dir. Blake Edwards. 1961. Paramount Centennial Collection, 2009. DVD.

———. Letter to Y. Frank Freeman, 16 Apr. 1959. Margaret Herrick Library Archive 34.f-3.

Shivas, Mark. "'Laura'—In Blue Blood." *New York Times* 14 Jan. 1968, sec. 2: 17.

Shurlock, Geoffrey. Letter to Luigi Luraschi, Paramount Pictures, 17 Aug. 1960. Margaret Herrick Library Archive, Motion Picture Association of America, Production Code Administration Records.

———. Letter to Frank McCarthy, 20th Century Fox, undated. Margaret Herrick Library Archive, "*The Innocents* (20th Fox, 1961)" file.

Sims, Jeanie. Letter to Morgan Maree, 18 June 1953. Margaret Herrick Library Archive 5.f-51.

Sinyard, Neil. *Jack Clayton*. Manchester: Manchester University Press, 2000.

Smith, William D. "A Success Money Didn't Buy: Capote's New Book Best-Seller Before It Was Written." *New York Times* 20 Feb. 1966: F16.

Sontag, Susan. "Notes on 'Camp.'" *Against Interpretation and Other Essays*. New York: Farrar, Straus & Giroux, 1966. 275–92.

Spoto, Donald. *Enchantment: The Life of Audrey Hepburn*. New York: Harmony, 2006.

Stack, Peter. "'Grass Harp' Plays Its Story Sweetly." *San Francisco Chronicle* 11 Oct. 1996: C3.

The Stanley Siegel Show. Guest Truman Capote. WABC-TV, New York, 18 July 1978. Television. UCLA Film and Television Archive.

Stanton, Robert J. *Truman Capote: A Primary and Secondary Bibliography*. Boston: Hall, 1980.

Steinem, Gloria. "'Go Right Ahead and Ask Me Anything' (And So She Did)." *McCall's* Nov. 1967: 76–77+.

———. "A Visit with Truman Capote." *Glamour* Apr. 1966: 210+.

Stevens, Anthony. *Ariadne's Clue: A Guide to the Symbols of Humankind*. Princeton: Princeton University Press, 1998.

Stryker, Susan. *Queer Pulp: Perverted Passions from the Golden Age of the Paperback*. San Francisco: Chronicle, 2001.

Summers, Anthony. *Goddess: The Secret Lives of Marilyn Monroe*. New York: Macmillan, 1985.

Talley, Andre Leon. "An Afternoon with Truman Capote: Tales Told by the Tiny Terror." *W* 23–30 July 1976: 8.

Tallmer, Jerry. "Truman Capote, Man about Town." *New York Post Weekend Magazine* 16 Dec. 1967: 26.

Thomas, Bob. *Marlon: Portrait of the Rebel as an Artist*. New York: Random House, 1973.

Thompson, Howard. "Carnegie Cinema Has Trilogy by Capote." *New York Times* 7 Nov. 1969: 40.

Thomson, David. *Showman: The Life of David O. Selznick.* New York: Knopf, 1992.

Time. "Anatomy of a Murder." 22 Dec. 1967: 78.

——. "Cinema: Evil Emanations." Review of *The Innocents.* 5 Jan. 1962: 59.

——. "Cinema: New Picture." Review of *Indiscretion of an American Wife.* 26 Apr. 1954: 110.

——. "The Nights before Christmas." 29 Dec. 1967: 34–35.

——. "Private Light." 14 Mar. 1949: 110+.

——. "Spare the Laurels." 14 Mar. 1949: 113.

——. "Truman and TV." 29 Nov. 1968: 73–74.

Tompkins, Phillip. "In Cold Fact." *Esquire* June 1966: 125+.

The Tonight Show. Hosts Johnny Carson and Ed McMahon. Guests Truman Capote, Joe Frazier, Tammy Grimes, and Robert Klein. NBC, 27 Nov. 1972.

——. Guests Truman Capote, McLean Stevenson, David Toma, and Mel Tormé. NBC, 12 Feb. 1973.

——. Guests Senta Berger, Truman Capote, Henry Fonda, and Chita Rivera. NBC, 7 Feb. 1975.

Trilling, Diana. "Fiction in Review." *Nation* 31 Jan. 1949: 133–34.

Van Gelder, Lawrence. "Misfits and Mischief Makers in a Portrait of the Artist." *New York Times* 11 Oct. 1996: C5.

Variety. Review of *The Innocents.* 6 Dec. 1961: 6.

Veiller, Tony, and Peter Viertel. Letter to John Huston, 4 July 1953. Margaret Herrick Library Archive 5.f-51.

Vespa, Mary. "Sued by Gore Vidal and Stung by Lee Radziwill, A Wounded Truman Capote Lashes Back at the Dastardly Duo." *People* 25 June 1979: 34–36.

Voss, Ralph F. *Truman Capote and the Legacy of "In Cold Blood."* Tuscaloosa: University of Alabama Press, 2011.

Waldmeir, Joseph J., and John C. Waldmeir, eds. *The Critical Response to Truman Capote.* Westport, Conn.: Greenwood, 1999.

Walsh, Moira. Review of *Indiscretion of an American Wife. America* 17 July 1954: 407.

Warhol, Andy. "Sunday with Mister C.: An Audio-Documentary by Andy Warhol Starring Truman Capote." *Rolling Stone* Apr. 1973: 28+.

Washington Post. "No Capote Bylines." 19 Jan. 1974: B2.

Wasson, Sam. *A Splurch in the Kisser: The Movies of Blake Edwards.* Middletown, Conn.: Wesleyan University Press, 2009.

Weiler, A. H. "The Screen: 'Breakfast at Tiffany's.'" *New York Times* 6 Oct. 1961: 28.

Wenner, Jann. "Coda: Another Round with Mr. C." *Rolling Stone* Apr. 1973: 50, 52, 54.

Wilcox, Ed. "The Other Truman." *Coronet* Dec. 1963: 53–57.

Williams, Tennessee. *Memoirs*. Garden City, N.Y.: Doubleday, 1975.

Wilson, Edmund. "The Ambiguity of Henry James." *The Triple Thinkers: Ten Essays on Literature*. New York: Harcourt, Brace, 1938. 122–64.

Windham, Donald. *Lost Friendships: A Memoir of Truman Capote, Tennessee Williams, and Others*. New York: Morrow, 1987.

Winn, Janet. "Capote, Mailer, and Miss Parker." *New Republic* 9 Feb. 1959: 27–28.

Youngkin, Stephen D. *The Lost One: A Life of Peter Lorre*. Lexington: University Press of Kentucky, 2005.

Zion, Sidney E. "Capote's View on Confessions Scored." *New York Times* 23 July 1966: 54.

Zoerink, Richard. "Truman Capote Talks about His Crowd: From Marilyn Monroe's 'Little Affair' with Bobby Kennedy, to Lee Radziwill and the International Jet-Set." *Playgirl* Sept. 1975: 50–51+.